Contents

Total Relationship Marketing

Third edition

Evert Gummesson

Marketing strategy moving from the 4Ps – product, price, promotion, place – of traditional marketing management to the 30Rs – the 30 relationships – of a new marketing paradigm incorporating service-dominant logic, B2C, B2B, C2C, CRM, many-to-many marketing, and the value-creating network society

ELSEVIER

AMSTERDAM • BOSTON • HEIDELBERG • LONDON • NEW YORK • OXFORD
PARIS • SAN DIEGO • SAN FRANCISCO • SINGAPORE • SYDNEY • TOKYO
Butterworth-Heinemann is an imprint of Elsevier

Butterworth-Heinemann is an imprint of Elsevier
Linacre House, Jordan Hill, Oxford OX2 8DP, UK
30 Corporate Drive, Suite 400, Burlington, MA 01803, USA

Third edition 2008

British Library Cataloguing-in-Publication Data
A catalogue record for this book is available from the British Library

Library of Congress Cataloging-in-Publication Data
A catalog record for this book is available from the Library of Congress

ISBN 13: 978-0-7506-8633-4

For information on all Butterworth-Heinemann publications
visit our web site at www.elsevierdirect.com

Typeset by Charon Tec Ltd (A Macmillan Company), Chennai, India
www.charontec.com

Printed and bound in Hungary
08 09 10 11 12   10 9 8 7 6 5 4 3 2 1

Working together to grow
libraries in developing countries

www.elsevier.com | www.bookaid.org | www.sabre.org

ELSEVIER   BOOK AID International   Sabre Foundation

Total Relationship Marketing

This book is dedicated to the future of our daughters Charlotte and Madelene.

Figures and tables

Preface and acknowledgements to the third edition

Revising and updating is a wonderful opportunity to test the viability of one's own ideas and to bring them to others. It is an obtrusive reminder that markets, customers, companies, society and technology keep changing. Relationship marketing (RM) and customer relationship management (CRM) have become accepted – and debated – parts of marketing. We still have a long way to go to separate unrealistic theory and research, advocacy, rhetoric and hype from what can lead to hands-on action in a true relationship spirit. As before, my effort to sort this out is expressed by the title of the book: *Total Relationship Marketing*.

What's new in this third edition and what stays put:

- I'm proud to say that the 30 relationships approach, the 30Rs, stays fit after 25 years when the ideas started to brew in my head and after 15 years since the 30Rs became complete. Many liked the Rs from the start, others were puzzled, others joked about them and yet others claimed that the Rs were too many. A commentary in *The Times Higher Education Supplement* advocated that the traditional 4Ps (product, price, promotion, place) are superior as students and executives can keep 4 things in their heads but not 30. This is a gross understatement of their intellectual capacity. I know numerous people – both students and CEOs – who have learnt the alphabet (26 letters) and can handle multiple strategies simultaneously. *Reality is complex – it is not a sound bite or a one-liner – and marketing complexity has to be addressed with an open and daring mind.* I still do not hesitate to say that this is the most complete attempt so far to cover RM/CRM on a strategic level and offer the beginnings of a theory. So the 30Rs stay.
- *Each R* has been scrutinised for revision and updating. For example, information technology (IT) keeps changing our lives and relationships. The general notion of e-relationships (R12) stays but it is demanding to try to discern the big picture because of all new technology and inventive service. Another example is the green relationship (R15), which in its broadened sense includes corporate social responsibility, CSR. It is literally hotter than ever. Specific elements of the relationships need to be adjusted but their core messages remain.
- *Theories, concepts* and *vocabulary* change. Integrating the new ones with the text and dropping the outdated ones turned out to be a challenge, no, a nightmare. I did not

have access to the Holy Grail and its miraculous power to make everything consistent. But I want to be remembered for being one of the first to try, hoping that others can improve it further. With the *service-dominant logic, S-D logic,* certain conceptual dilemmas begin to get sorted out. The meaning of S-D logic will be explained and integrated with RM throughout the text. In the third edition there is even more emphasis on networks and network theory. In marketing, network thinking has almost exclusively been applied in B2B. Through the concept of *many-to-many marketing,* network theory can form the foundation of all types of marketing, B2B as well as B2C. The customer-centric concepts of *lean consumption* and the *customer value network* supplement the production-centric lean production and the conventional supplier-centric value chain. Chain is replaced by network to show that events are not sequential and linear but iterative and non-linear. Further, the customer centric view of marketing is suggested to be broadened to *balanced centricity,* a trade-off between the needs of all stakeholders of a network. As a consequence the former Chapters 8 and 9 have been revised and merged into a new Chapter 8.

■ Marketing deals with the *generation of revenue* and revenue must exceed cost. Don't you ever forget it! Over the past 50 years I have seen numerous efforts to find general models and indicators to get financial control over marketing. The cry for marketing accountability and metrics is currently loud – again. The problem is to design metrics that work in practice and provide genuine guidance. All the same it is essential to keep the assessment of marketing effects, both quantitative and qualitative, on the agenda. Chapter 6 is an updated effort to do so.

■ As in earlier editions, concepts and ideas are constantly accompanied by short *cases* and *examples* to facilitate reading and make it easier to relate them to practice. Cases and examples have been substituted wherever they have gone stale. In a five year period some lose their pitch; they may have danced just one summer. Others change and need updating but there are also those that are robust enough to stand the test of time; they are classics. I have tried to avoid superficial hypes, however appealing they may look at the time. At the end of each chapter a *Questions for Discussion* section has been added to support classroom use.

■ I have been careful to include *references,* update them and give recognition whenever possible. This is the first time I revise a book when Google, Wikipedia and other Internet-based sources are both easily accessible and rich in information. It made updating easier. As anybody can get into Google and find a host of sources on any subject, I have found it practically impossible to give reference to websites or information that is widely spread through the media. I have always checked several sources and tried to assess the credibility of the information.

I'm grateful for this opportunity to prepare a third edition. I'm also grateful to a large number of people who have stimulated my work over the years. We meet around the world at conferences and at each other's universities, and we meet in publications. Many have become good friends. The personal networking facilitates academic work immensely. I especially want to mention a group of people who have offered research, publication or speaking opportunities. I can't add them all to the list but many are also found among the references in the book.

My roots are in Northern Europe. The Nordic School has become a designation for researchers and practitioners in Sweden and Finland who started to take an interest in services in the late 1970s. They focused on service management and marketing where relationships and interaction formed the core. The Nordic School has gradually found that quality, value, RM, CRM, networks and service represent a new foundation for marketing. The Marketing Technology Centre (MTC) in Sweden supported my work on service and later on relationships at a stage when nobody thought much of it. Christian Grönroos, Hanken, Helsinki, and Uolevi Lehtinen, University of Tampere, and their colleagues helped to build a sustainable platform for theory generation in marketing. My affiliation with their schools became a driver of my own thinking. And so did later Bo Edvardsson and his colleagues at the Service Research Center (CTF) Karlstad University, Sweden, not least through the QUIS symposia. My cooperation with these institutions has continued after I took up my position at the Stockholm University School of Business. For a period it became a heartland for innovative and unorthodox research within a theory-creating and qualitative tradition. Its PhD students provided much of the research resources and so did its Marketing Academy. Leif Edvinsson with a foot in both business and academe and a world authority on intellectual capital, has supported the broadening and renewal of marketing. A large number of practitioners have provided encouragement by engaging me in consulting and speaking assignments, and thus kept me in touch with the realities of marketing.

Many from other countries have been instrumental in paving the road for RM. Bernard Taylor, long time Editor of *The Journal of Long Range Planning,* accepted my first effort in the mid 1980s to publish the 30R approach – although there were only 9 relationships at that time. An ongoing dialogue with the international icon of marketing, Philip Kotler, Northwestern University, keeps being a source of inspiration. Much of what The Nordic School and others have stood for over the years has been skilfully conceptualized and expanded into the S-D logic by Steve Vargo and Bob Lusch; I greatly value the cooperation with them. At an early stage David Ballantyne engaged me in the International Colloquia in Relationship Marketing and recently in the Otago Forum on Service-Dominant Logic thus offering extraordinary opportunities to conduct a global dialogue. My recent acquaintance with the IBM project Service Science and its leader Jim Spohrer holds many promises for the future. A very special thanks to Akiko Fujioka, Japan, and Cristina Mele, Italy, who have been instrumental in adapting my book for publication in their home countries. As to methodological issues and research approaches, Barney Glaser, co-creator of grounded theory has become a friend and coach, later with committed support by Andy Lowe. Barney not only thinks grounded theory, he lives it.

During the process of creating this third edition my long time colleague and friend Chris Lovelock, pioneer in service and enthusiastic contributor to marketing renewal, unexpectedly passed away. Chris, I'll miss our dialogue!

Among others who have contributed to my thinking and helped to create a dialogue in their home countries and globally and are: in Australia Adrian Payne, Louise Young and Ian Wilkinson; in Canada Ulrike de Brentani, Michèle Paulin and Ronald Ferguson; in Germany Friedhelm Bliemel, Anton Meyer and Bernd Stauss; in Ireland Stephen Brown, David Carson, Tony Cunningham, Damien McLoughlin and the late Liam Glynn; in Latin America Jaquie Pels and Javier Reynoso; in New Zealand Rod Brodie, Richard Brookes, Nicole Coviello and Brendan Gray; in Poland Kazimierz Rogozinski and Richard Nicholls; in the UK Michael Baker, Keith Blois, Douglas Brownlie, Martin Christopher, Bob Johnston, Michael Saren, Michael Thomas and Nikos Tzokas; and in the US David Bejou, Len Berry, Mary Jo Bitner, Stephen W. Brown, Shelby Hunt, Jay Kandampully, Parsu Parasuraman, Atul Parvatiyar, Roland Rust, Jag Sheth, and Pat and Joan Townsend.

A special thanks to the team at Elsevier who has made this third edition possible.

Evert Gummesson
Stockholm University School of Business,
SE-10691 Stockholm, Sweden
eg@fek.su.se; www.fek.su.se/home/eg/
January 2008

Introduction

The purpose of this book is to contribute to a more realistic approach to marketing management. It addresses the question: 'What do you learn if you look at marketing as relationships, networks and interaction, and what can you do with this knowledge?' This way of approaching marketing is referred to as relationship marketing (RM), and within this concept the topical issues of customer relationship management (CRM) and one-to-one marketing belong.

The book has been written for all those who want to develop their knowledge of marketing: practitioners, students, educators and researchers. As marketing management permeates every activity in today's business – and not only the marketing and sales departments – this book will be of particular interest to top executives and managers of all types of functions.

Chapter 1 is an introduction to RM and its 30 relationships, the 30Rs, prevalent in business. This is by far the broadest and most comprehensive framework of RM that has been designed; hence the reference to total relationship marketing. Each relationship is then covered in more detail in Chapters 2–5. Chapter 6 is about marketing metrics and return on relationships (ROR), that is, the financial effects of RM and the effects on relationship-oriented marketing and business planning. Chapter 7 deals with RM and new organizational formats, captured under the term network organization; the chapter also puts RM and its organization in the context of the market economy. Chapter 8 covers theories and experiences that have formed the foundation of RM, describes how RM and CRM have emerged from these, and forebodes a paradigm shift in marketing.

The structure of the book, particularly the presentation of the 30Rs, is, in a sense, encyclopaedic – a hypertext in modern terminology – which gives readers the option to look up what they are interested in without having to read every page in sequence from cover to cover.

Chapter

1

Relational approaches to marketing

INTRODUCTION

The chapter presents the purpose and outline of the book, and the concepts of relationship marketing (RM), customer relationship management (CRM), one-to-one marketing and many-to-many marketing are defined. The ideas of a new general marketing logic, the service-dominant logic (S-D logic) are discussed together with certain basics of marketing, among them the problem with customer centricity and the need for a broader stakeholder focus, balanced centricity. Although marketing attempts to be scientific, the importance of tacit knowledge emerging from reflection, experience, common sense and intuition is brought to the fore. The reader is urged to see marketing through the 'relationship eye-glasses' and to adjust to a paradigm shift in marketing. To help in this process the general characteristics of relationships and a summary of the 30 specific relationships of RM, the 30Rs, are introduced.

The relational realities of marketing

Two practical experiences from business drew my attention to the importance of relationships in marketing.

I was hired by a market leading northern European management consulting firm which had just been acquired by the large international PA Consulting Group headquartered in London. One of my tasks, besides doing consulting assignments, was to sell the services of a group of consultants. My knowledge of marketing was based on textbooks used in business school education and practical experience as a marketing manager of consumer goods. I was taken by surprise when realizing that (at that time in Northern Europe) the consulting company did little or nothing that the books prescribed. No explicit marketing strategy, no marketing organization, no marketing planning, no marketing research, no specialized sales force, no advertising and no public relations.

Should the fresh consultant tell the CEO the bad news – that they were doing everything wrong – followed by the good news: I'm here to set it right? There was a disturbing fact, though. The company was doing well. It must be doing something right.

Through observation and advice from senior colleagues – one had worked for 14 years as consultant to the same large corporation – I learnt that one thing in particular mattered beside the professional knowledge: the network of relationships that the individual consultants belonged to through past and present professional achievements, birth or membership of social groups. And furthermore, relationships were equally important internally when consultants were selected by their colleagues to staff new assignments.

> Creating and maintaining a network of relationships – outside as
> well as inside the company – constituted the core marketing of the

consulting firm. Credibility and referrals built on performance in the
assignments and the relationships that developed there. Advertising,
public relations, branding, and other marketing activities were
supportive, but they were not the core of their marketing.

Another significant experience occurred during the 1980s while I was working as a
consultant to Ericsson. The then CEO, Björn Svedberg, commissioned one assignment with
the following words: 'Evert, explain to us what we are actually doing in our marketing
and selling!' Ericsson is known for being a leading supplier of telecom equipment and
systems and for its mobile phone operation in alliance with Sony. At that time each sale
was large, complex, high tech and long term. A major marketing strategy – although
it was not officially perceived as such – was the creation and maintenance of long-term
relationships with a few large telecom operating companies, as well as the cultivation of
relationships with research institutions, own suppliers, government agencies, politicians,
banks, investors, the media and others. The relationships concerned many people in
several tiers and functions within the customers' organizations and also within Ericsson's
own organization.

> Ericsson's success over its 130 years of existence has been based on
> a combination of state-of-the-art technology and a well-developed
> network of relationships.

These two experiences taught me a very obvious and common-sense lesson: when
your current real world experience clashes with your previous experience and received
theories, rethink! I found that my textbook knowledge and experience of marketing
management and consumer marketing was not adequate. Simply put:

| INSIGHT | When – after careful scrutiny – you find that the terrain differs from your map, trust the terrain and your own judgement! |

Aren't these experiences just history in the third millennium? No! And are the lessons
applicable to smaller businesses? Yes! Grönroos tells the example of rice merchant Ming
Hua in ancient China, many thousands of years ago.[1] He developed an initially slow rice
business to become the local market leader. What did he do? He did relationship marketing!

---

[1] Grönroos (2007, pp. 29–30).

So did the milkman in sociologist Odis Simmons' study from the 1960s.[2] From this case, Simmons who was not a marketing scholar but had practical experience from work as a milkman, developed a theory of RM based on the core concept of 'cultivated relationship'. The home delivery of milk is a small industry today but it has had its offsprings. Stew Leonard started out as a milkman, then build a dairy product store and now operates 4 huge fresh food stores in Connecticut and New York, known for service excellence and for cultivating relationships.

So relationships are part of human nature. They are timeless. They are independent of culture. They are there in every type and size of business.

Why did it take marketing theory so long to discover what practitioners already felt and acted on? Relational approaches in marketing gradually became the object of research and conceptualization during the past decades and the 1990s marked a breakthrough with skyrocketing interest. Let us look at the state-of-the-art and peek into the future.

RM, CRM, one-to-one, many-to-many: what are they really?

Relationship marketing (RM) is usually defined as an approach to develop long-term loyal customers and thus increasing profitability. My definition is more generic:

> Relationship marketing is interaction in networks of relationships.

Let's now look at the core concepts that constitute RM: relationships, networks and interaction.

Relationships require at least two parties who are in contact with each other. The basic two-party relationship of marketing, the dyad, is that between a supplier and a customer (Figure 1.1).

Figure 1.1 The basic marketing relationship

---

[2] Simmons (1993). His study it is an application of 'grounded theory' which is dicussed further at the end of Chapter 8.

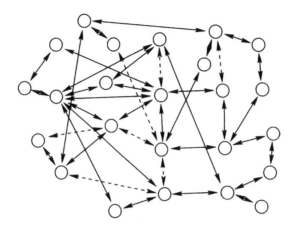

Figure 1.2 A network of relationships

A *network* is a set of multi-party relationships, which can grow into enormously complex patterns. A graphic pattern of a network is shown in Figure 1.2. In the relationships, the simple dyad as well as the complex networks, the parties enter into active contact with each other. This is called *interaction*.

Returning to our initial two cases, and although consultancy and telecom have gone through changes, the significance of relationship, networks and interaction remains. Their application may vary with time as technology and market conditions change, but their essence is timeless. A management consulting company provides service to business-to-business (B2B) clients; it is not business-to-consumer marketing (B2C). Ericsson is a combination of B2B (systems for telecom operators) and B2C (mobile phones). The telephone once changed interaction among customers and the mobile phone has given rise to a second wave of customer-to-customer interaction (C2C).[3] The phone and computers have increased C2C intensity and made it part of marketing. Although the frameworks presented in marketing textbooks have claimed to be universally valid, they dealt with consumer goods marketing: cola drinks, painkillers, cookies and cars. The textbooks did not include services, only marginally B2B and almost entirely left out C2C. There was not a word about relationships, interaction and networks – and there still is very little. The textbooks diverted the mind from substantive and universally significant issues.

In the wake of RM followed one-to-one and CRM (Customer Relationship Management). The last two concepts represent the same basic thinking but today CRM is the most frequently used term.[4] I prefer to see RM as the overriding concept for a new type of marketing and CRM as techniques to handle customer relationships in practice.

---

[3] See further Nicholls (2005).

[4] For an overview of current definitions see Chapter 8. Peppers and Rogers launched one-to-one in 1993. Comprehensive books with somewhat different approaches to RM/CRM include Storbacka and Lehtinen (2001); Christopher, Payne and Ballantyne (2002); Bruhn (2003); Little and Marandi (2003); Egan (2004); Buttle (2006); Payne (2006) and Donaldson and O'Toole (2007).

My definition of CRM follows from the RM definition:

> CRM is the values and strategies of RM – with special emphasis on the relationship between a customer and a supplier – turned into practical application and dependent on both human action and information technology.

Today, RM/CRM provide a framework for such diverse marketing situations as described by the cases of the PA Consulting Group, Ericsson, Chinese rice merchant Ming Hua, and the milkman. These cases offer glimpses of the significance of relationships, networks and interaction in B2C and B2B, in small local businesses and global giants, and in diverse types of businesses, countries and cultures, and again: their existence seems timeless. RM is a general marketing approach and in my view an antecedent to a paradigm shift in marketing.

Many-to-many marketing is an extension of RM/CRM and one-to-one marketing to show the complexity of relationships when we leave the two-party relationship, the dyad, for the multi-party relationship. The world is a network of relationships and many-to-many is my designation for its marketing application. This book is focused on RM but it forebodes the need to broaden marketing to its networks. This has been done, especially in B2B, but the concept of many-to-many encompasses all marketing. My definition is:

Many-to-many marketing describes, analyses and utilizes the network properties of marketing.

The case of Mr. Ray is an illustration of B2B marketing strategy with a many-to-many network perspective.

CASE STUDY | **Mr. Ray and his many-to-many mini-world[5]**

As part of a long-term strategy to strengthen its position in the American market, a European machine manufacturer planned to buy a company in the United States. They had found a candidate and a group from the buyer visited the company during a couple of weeks. The project leader explains:

'I worked together with the CEO of our US subsidiary, his COO and CFO, and our Director of Manufacturing from headquarters in Europe. The owner and founder of the US company was known as Mr. Ray and that was also the brand

---

[5] Taken from Gummesson (2008a); the case is based on Bagelius (2003). Reprinted with permission.

of the company's machines. During a hectic period we analyzed Mr. Ray's company from all possible angles. In the US, Mr. Ray was a well-known brand in its niche. The company was interesting to us considering their products, company size and market share. We found it to be well managed. The accounting seemed correct and we had no feeling that they were withholding information. But we also discovered that the company was somewhat under-financed and that product development had been held back.

'Most of the evenings we spent with Mr. Ray or members of his management team. They took well care of us and showed us the sights of the neighborhood, among others the city art museum, which was sponsored by Mr. Ray. We were invited to Mr. Ray's home and got to know his family.

'One day we were on our way to lunch in Mr. Ray's Cadillac. I insisted on being the host. Mr. Ray had been very generous to us but within decent limits. We stopped at a farm which has been rebuilt to a self-service restaurant. When we carried our loaded trays to the table I noticed that several guests greeted Mr. Ray very politely. Some even stood up and bowed.

'When we came back after lunch, two of us proceeded with the collection and analysis of financial data. The other two concentrated on the relationship between the employees and Mr. Ray, his executives and his family. My suspicion that many of the employees were relatives and friends was corroborated. It also turned out that many of the suppliers, key customers, local media, politicians and city government members had a close personal relationship to Mr. Ray and his family. The company was in fact a large family, a network of friendly relationships with Mr. Ray as its hub.

'Back home we could present a bright picture of Mr. Ray's company, a picture that was largely based on fact. From a financial and marketing aspect the company was definitely a suitable candidate for acquisition. Yet our recommendation was to abstain. The main reason was that the company was dominated by relatives and friends. Traditions and norms in the United States would make it very difficult for a European company to exert leadership. And just imagine what a future conflict could lead to in the form of claims in courts, where Mr. Ray would stand out as the local hero and we as the bad guys from overseas! We had already had one unfortunate experience at home. We bought a company where the former owners two years later – without regard to the agreement – started anew in direct competition with the company we had acquired. They changed the color of their machines to blue, that was all. Despite our efforts to stop them legally, they continued and we became the real losers.'

The book is about these and other relationships. The relationships will be listed, described, analysed, illustrated and discussed. RM is not just another bag of tricks to capture customers; it offers a wide range of conditions for more efficient management and marketing – and opportunities of making money. This will be elaborated on throughout the book.

In the late 1990s, half of the large US corporations ('the *Fortune* 500') had Relationship Managers and the number is probably growing.[6] Key Account Managers (KAMs) who are in charge of large B2B customers, as well as CRM managers to handle the transition to CRM systems, have grown in numbers. These positions, however, can only be supportive; RM/CRM have to permeate the whole organization and its culture to become effective.

A new logic for marketing: S-D logic

Since the 1970s, when services marketing was discovered and up till now the division between goods and services has been taken for granted, even if it has been questionned from different directions. Although services in official statistics constituted more than half of economic activity in developed countries, they were neglected in marketing and management. The goods/service division is peddled in official statistics and political debates and a nation's economic development is commonly referred to the industrial (manufacturing) sector, the service sector and the agricultural sector. This way of looking at our economy is totally production centric; there isn't a customer in sight.

But goods are different from services, aren't they? Yes – and no! The two are a faithful, married couple and they are always holding hands. Therefore there are no clear-cut goods marketing or services marketing situations. Further, in statistical reports goods and services are arbitrarily defined. Even a seemingly simple service category such as 'hotels' includes a large variety of marketing situations that defy 'hotels' as a meaningful categorization for marketing purposes. Each marketing situation is made up of a unique set of features and dependent and so many other variables than just goods and services. Marketing is complex and all efforts to make approximate generalization based on armchair reasoning is likely to lead us astray both is practicing and researching marketing.

The fact that goods and services appear together has disturbed many over the years.[7] This is not new but eventually it is seriously catching the imagination of marketers. Efforts have been made to get *product* accepted as a joint term for goods and services and to use *offering, package* or *solution* as all inclusive concepts for what the customer buys.

---

[6] Whiting (1998).

[7] The first were probably Wyckham, Fitzroy and Mandry (1975).

It has not worked. When you read 'products' in a marketing text it generally means goods, and the other concepts are only used in select cases.

Two articles by Vargo and Lusch (2004a) and Lovelock and Gummesson (2004) independently of each other argued that the conventional criteria used to distinguish goods from services did not do their job. These criteria, for services referred to as the IHIPs (intangibility, heterogeneity, inseparability and perishability), could equally well be turned around and attached to goods. The basic problem of course was that goods and services cannot be separated but an obsolete paradigm has led us to believe so. Goods – things – always appear with services – activities.

It was not until Steve Vargo and Bob Lusch in another article presented a new marketing logic – service-dominant logic, usually referred to as S-D logic – that many of the scattered thoughts from the past began to fall in place.[8]

As S-D logic affects the way RM/CRM is presented in this new edition of my book, a summary of its characteristics is given below and will be referred to throughout the text:

- *Goods/services integrated and replaced by service (in the singular) and value proposition*: As has been discussed above the division of the economy in goods and services has caused constant headache over decades. It has been kept at bay with painkillers which eventually, as is the case with all medication addressing symptoms and not the root cause, has spawned side effects and failed to kill the pain. *Value proposition* is used in S-D logic to stress that the supplier has a proposition, encompassing the *service* that this proposition can render and the price the customer pays. To avoid the wrong associations it is important to note that 'service' as used in S-D logic refers to the service given by whatever we purchase, irrespective of this being goods or services (as these terms are used in official statistics). To avoid a mix-up with conventional thinking I also use *value*.
- *Knowledge*: In S-D logic the application of specialized skills and knowledge through deeds, processes and performances is the fundamental unit of exchange and it defines service. Knowledge is also the fundamental source of competitive advantage. Further, service provision is integration of resources between the parties involved with the supplier and the customer in its core.
- *Operand and operant resources*: Behind the S-D logic is the transfer from a goods-dominant logic (G-D logic) where the resources were land, animal and plant life, minerals and other physical objects. These were *operand* resources, those which you do something to; *operant*

---

[8] The original article by Vargo and Lusch (2004b) together with commentaries by eight marketing scholars appeared in the same issue of the *Journal of Marketing*. For a progress report on S-D logic as well as critique, see an anthology edited by Lusch and Vargo (2006a); a special issue of *Marketing Theory* (2006); and a special issue of the *Journal of the Academy of Marketing Science* (2008). For critical views see Stauss (2005); Achrol and Kotler (2006); and Shembri (2006). For an overview of the value concept, see Korkman (2006).

resources are those who do it. In G-D logic, the No. 1 resource is the operand resource. In S-D logic the operant resource – the skills and knowledge how to do something – is the No. 1 resource. And who does it, who is the operant resource? When we started to hear that 'customers are our most valuable resource', customers were seen as operand resources; you do something *to* them. Companies were the operant resources, those who did it. S-D logic changes these taken-for-granted and long obsolete approaches. The customer has been promoted from a passive operand resource to an active operant resource.

- *Co-creation of value*: For example, buying a car is classified as the outcome of goods marketing, renting a car as the outcome of services marketing. For each customer, however, value is created in his or her interaction with the car. It is driving to a desired destination; driving the car well or badly; taking good care of it, or neglecting its maintenance; praising its convenience, or cursing traffic jams, absence of parking space, and the rising gas price; enjoying music and the privacy, or getting bored by long, lonely hours in the car; and so on. The car remains a value proposition whether it is driver owned, owned by your employer, bought with borrowed money, leased, rented or owned by your parents. *Value actualization* is in the hands of the customer and consequently suppliers and customers *co-create value*.

- *Network extension*: The development of S-D logic has an open source code; anyone can contribute to improvements. Further, the customer as an operant resource and co-creation of value are not only a supplier–customer affair, it can be extended beyond the mere dyad and embrace further stakeholders. This aligns with my RM concept and even more so with the many-to-many concept. It can be applied in complex and adaptive networks in which we are embedded in society such as intermediaries, competitors, friends, government, the media, and not least other customers, C2C.

- *Marketing definition*. Summing up, the marketing definition emerging in S-D logic says that 'marketing is the process in society and organizations that facilitates voluntary exchange through collaborative relationships that create reciprocal value through the application of complementary resources'.[9] You will find later that this definition is well aligned with the message of this book.

In connection with S-D logic I want to draw the attention to a grand ongoing project started by IBM in 2004, Service Science, Management and Engineering (SSME), usually referred to as Service Science. It is a project with high momentum that makes an effort to spread service thinking in the academic world and among practitioners. It is particularly focused to get education at institutes of technology to include service and to make manufacturing companies see their output as service rather than just goods. As this is a gigantic

---

[9] Lusch and Vargo (2006a, pp. xvii–xviii).

undertaking the project still is at an initial stage, but the expectations are high that it will open up new ways of approaching both marketing and management in general.

A general conclusion from S-D logic is that customers are gaining a more significant and active role in marketing. It also means that customers are becoming more powerful as the next case displays.

CASE STUDY	**Consumer power**

The customer's role in marketing is gradually being understood. Even advertising agencies, who traditionally work with mass marketing, are rethinking. As a token of this, consumers were recently recognised to have a more influential role in marketing than the professional marketers. Every year the American journal *Advertising Age* nominates the best advertising agency. In 2006, the award did not go to a traditional agency but to – the consumer! Through the Internet, email, mobile phones and other IT media and C2C interaction through communities, individual customers reach out in the world. Consumers control the brands more than the legal brand owners do. Web-based chat groups, hate sites and fan clubs have been around for some time. Now we also have blogs and the TiVo (which keeps commercials off your TV). In an instant, YouTube, which lets anybody show their videos on the Internet, has become a smashing hit.[10]

---

[10] Based on Creamer (2007). About the customers' increasingly pivotal role in service development, see Edvardsson *et al.* (2006).

As customers become more intimately intertwined with each other, with suppliers and with other network actors, the boundaries between previously taken-for-granted categories and roles become fuzzy and overlapping. Should they be considered parties or are they just one? Engeseth (2006) takes it all the way and advocates the concept of *one*. Like man and wife in the Bible the two become one flesh. It aligns with S-D logic and the co-creation of value and with the customers more eminent role in marketing. But not all suppliers and customers want to go to bed with each other. I conclude we need two perspectives; first, to view the parties separately and stress their differences in roles and goals and, second, to view them as one by stressing their affinity. The boundaries between customers, suppliers, competitors, governments and other have to be recognized for what they really are: fuzzy and overlapping.

We should do the same with the conventional divide between goods and services. When the terms goods and services (services in the plural) are used in this text they represent a certain emphasis or perspective. They are used when either the *things aspect* or the *activities aspect* is in focus for analysis or action. We can also use the term services in a loose sense when we talk about hotel services, maintenance services and so on.[11] The lack of consistency is not a consequence of sloppiness as a mainstream academic might conclude but an expression of respect for a complex and systemic reality.

The numbers of marketing situations are like the stars in the sky. We cannot really count them and allocate them to general categories which consider the necessary details. The situations are composed of similarities and differences, of modules that can be shared in different configurations and customized or mass-customized to take care of situations that closely resemble each other.

How do RM/CRM and the S-D logic harmonize with the most recent definition of marketing proposed by the American Marketing Association (AMA) in 2004? The new definition can have serious consequences. According to AMA's magazine *Marketing News*[12] ... the American Marketing Association is responsible for the official definition of marketing, used in books, by marketing professionals and taught in university lecture halls nationswide'. The definition is:

'Marketing is an organizational function and a set of processes for creating, communicating and delivering value to customers and for managing customer relationships in ways that benefit the organization and its stakeholders.'

I would like to challenge the following issues:

- 'Marketing is an *organizational function*...' Within the Nordic School tradition we have long talked about the marketing function as something that is spread throughout the organization.[13] Marketing is not solely confined to one of a series of compartmentalized silos in an organizational hierarchy. It is also a state of mind, a culture and the collective consciousness of an organization.
- '... for creating, communicating and a delivering value *to* customers ...' This statement exposes the traditional marketing management thinking that the supplier does something to the customer unidirectionally; customers remain operand resources and their capacity as operant resources is not recognized. Research in services marketing and B2B has shown that suppliers do things *with* customers. You communicate with somebody and a message is only accepted on the conditions of the receiver unless

---

[11] See also the discussion about the meaning of service in Grönroos (2007).

[12] Keefe (2004, p. 17).

[13] The Nordic School is a designation for research in service, relationships and networks emanating from Northern Europe; see Gummesson, Lehtinen and Grönroos (1997) and Grönroos (2000, 2006).

brute force, fear or lack of choice is present. RM puts emphasis on an open dialogue and interaction. There is also value for suppliers, why else would they bother? It could equally well be claimed that customers deliver value to suppliers. This is all within the spirit of relational approaches to marketing. Together with the S-D logic it leads me up to questioning the relevance of the B2C expression. In B2B it is not evident who is the seller and who is the buyer, the first or the second B. In B2C it is business-to-customer but it could just as well be the other way around, C2B. It may sound like a word game, but expressions like B2C subconsciously block our perception. Therefore I will henceforth use an extended acronym: *B2C/C2B*.

■ '... for *managing* customer relationships ...' It reminds me of the nasty sergeant in the movie *An Officer and a Gentleman.* With the dictatorial military power vested in him, he shouted, abused and forced the soldiers to do anything he wanted; the relationship was aggressive. Suppliers should not one-sidedly be encouraged to manage customers; relationships are also managed by customers. The attitude is not interactive and most people resent being managed by their bank, supermarket or car supplier. Test it on your family: Who manages the relationships? Is it the husband, the wife or (increasingly) the kids?

■ '... that benefit the organization and its *stakeholders.*' I suspect that in 'stakeholders' the customers and employees are hidden. But I fear that in today's short-term economy with more boardroom attention given to finance and accounting than to marketing, the focus is on shareholder value.

The suggested revisions are shown below:

'Marketing is a <u>culture</u>, an organizational function and a set of processes for creating, communicating, and delivering value ~~to~~ <u>with</u> customers and for ~~managing~~ <u>interacting in networks of</u> ~~customer~~ relationships in ways that benefit the organization, <u>its customers</u> and ~~its~~ <u>other</u> stakeholders.'

My version finally reads:

Marketing is a culture, an organizational function and a set of processes for creating, communicating, and delivering value with customers and for interacting in networks of relationships in ways that benefit the organization, its customers and other stakeholders.

In this version the definition points to essentials both contributed by RM/CRM and S-D logic.

Society is a network of relationships – and so is business!

Relationships are at the core of human behaviour. If we dissolve the social networks of relationships, we dissolve society and the earth is left with a bunch of hermits. In that case no marketing is needed, for two reasons. The short-term reason is that hermits live alone. They breed their own sheep for wool, cheese and meat, they grow their own vegetables, and they tailor their own clothes, if any. They do not need mobile phones because there is no one to call. No market for Nokia or Motorola.

The long-term reason is that the human race will be extinct after one generation. But if it is true that nature has a genetic urge for multiplication, couples and families will spring up and the atomistic world of individuals will turn into a growing network of relationships.

As citizens and family members we are surrounded by relationships in our daily lives. We have relationships at work, with neighbours, with stores and other providers. Driving a car is a complex social interaction with other drivers in a network of roads.

People have girlfriends and boyfriends, go steady, marry, have an affair, divorce. Many have used matrimony as a metaphor for commercial relationships: to enter into marriage with a customer or to divorce a supplier. 'Business dancing' has been suggested as another metaphor.[14] Dancing is a dynamic relationship. You can invite somebody to dance with you. It can be a smooth waltz, but you can also step on your partner's toes. Peters[15] makes it even more dramatic: 'Today's global economic dance is no Strauss waltz. It's break dancing accompanied by street rap. The effective firm is much more like carnival in Rio than a pyramid along the Nile.'

Relationships are central for business people. Craftsmen exchange services with other craftsmen whom they know and trust. The first thing I heard about business was that you need to be well connected, and that it helps to have relatives in high places and to belong to the right clubs. People who knew each other did business and then the seller wined and dined the buyer. As individuals, we voluntarily enter formal relationships through associations. Rotary, for example, brings people together from different trades and professions. The Rotarians get to know each other and business relationships are facilitated by the long-term friendship that develops among them.

Marketing and business are subsets or properties of society. In practice, relationships, networks and interaction have been at the core of business since time immemorial. They have certainly not gone unnoticed by business people.[16] For example, Ericsson has expanded and remodelled its network for 130 years. The sad story is that relationships have too long gone unnoticed in research and education. Does the current interest in RM/CRM imply that marketing theorists are getting closer to marketing reality? Are we beginning to discern the marketing content of Japanese keiretsus, Chinese guanxies, global ethnic networks, the British school tie, trade between friends, loyalty to the local pub and so on?

---

[14] Wilkinson and Young (1994).

[15] Peters (1992, p. 17).

[16] One of the early academic proponents for a network view of the market was Thorelli (1986).

Marketing theory has not invented these phenomena, practice has. Some practitioners have lived them, others have not. A book can draw your attention to relationships by adding them to the map, making them visible.

Relationships between customers and suppliers are the ground for all marketing. Within the conventional marketing management mode of thinking, much of marketing is reduced to impersonal exchange through mass promotion and mass distribution. The manufacturer offers products and services via an intermediary and the consumer offers money. The manufacturer and even the retailer are no more than brand names; they may even be totally anonymous to the consumer, who in turn is just a statistic. This approach to marketing does not comply with the reality of society.

In contrast, the RM/CRM spotlight is on the *individual*, on the *segment of one*. It's one-to-one marketing. But focus is also on groups of like-minded people, *affinity groups*. The group members share a common interest, they want a relationship with the supplier, its products and services, and even with each other. Golfers, environmentalists, computer geeks and Harley-Davidson owners belong here. They form *communities*.

The roots of RM/CRM

During the industrial era, mass manufacturing of standardized goods gave birth to mass marketing and mass distribution. During this brief period of our history, marketing theory and education evolved around consumer goods marketing. Services marketing and B2B – where relationships were also central during the industrial era – remained blank spots in research and education.

Research and practice in marketing during more than 30 years point particularly to the significance of relationships, networks and interaction. Literature on RM/CRM has emerged at an exponential rate in many languages. With certain exceptions, the literature is narrow, characterized by treating single issues in RM such as consumer loyalty, databases for smarter direct marketing, call centres, customer clubs or CRM software systems. These are all valuable bits and pieces, but they lack the coherent framework of an overriding theory.

The more radical theories that have contributed to RM/CRM stem from *services marketing* and *the network approach to B2B*. A first effort to merge these two schools was presented by Gummesson in 1983. Relationships, networks and interaction play a subdued role in traditional *marketing management*, popularly referred to as *marketing mix* or the *4Ps* (product, price, promotion, place). It has hegemony over marketing education throughout the world, but refers first and foremost to the mass marketing of standardized consumer goods. Despite its limitations it is erroneously presented as a general marketing theory.[17] In the area of *sales management* and *negotiations*, relationships are emphasized but often limited to a salesperson's interaction with a buyer or to negotiations between teams. However, for B2B a series of models on *organizational buying behaviour* developed around 1970 that show a more complex, partly network-like type of marketing.

These three approaches – services marketing, B2B as networks and traditional marketing management – are central in the RM/CRM root system. The roots have been extended through S-D logic and many-to-many marketing and may keep doing so with the future aid of the Service Science project.

These were all influences from marketing but there are also influences from adjacent non-marketing areas. One area that has significantly contributed is *quality management*. In its core are customer perceived quality and customer satisfaction. Quality management has inspired the concept of *relationship quality*, that is, the efforts to improve quality of relationships, and not just the quality of goods and services. Relationship quality emerged in the large quality programme of Ericsson in the early 1980s. The purpose was to make explicit the fact that relationships are part of customer perceived quality. This is far from the traditional engineer's production-centric quality concept. Often the human aspect, the h-relationship, 'to be liked', sorts out the winner from the loser.[18] *Lean production* as a quality strategy expanding into *lean consumption* and the *supplier value chain* into the *customer value chain* also belong here. This will be further explained later.[19]

Accounting has often stood out as a nightmare for marketers and salespeople, and been felt as a bureaucratic obstacle to relationship building. Investors, stock market analysts, top management and controllers have, however, gradually begun to question the role of traditional accounting: Do we really measure what matters? Modern accounting goes beyond the mere financial numbers and accountants, who are by training historians, acknowledge the impact of customers, employees, knowledge, IT readiness, environmental effects, corporate social responsibility and innovation as antecedents to future profit. The current efforts to design accounting for today's and tomorrow's business life are found under the concepts of the *balanced scorecard* and *intellectual capital*. They help to give a framework to the measurement of *return on relationships (ROR)*. Chapter 6 is dedicated to marketing metrics and marketing's contribution to the bottom line.

There is also a connection to *organization theory*. RM is also a result of – or possibly a cause of – new organizational structures and processes where the roles of customer and supplier are not as clear-cut as in Figure 1.1. The fuzziness stands out better in Figure 1.2,

---

[17] For critical discussions of marketing management theory, see Brownlie and Saren (1992); Brown (1998); Gummesson (2002); Grönroos (1997); Saren *et al.* (2007).

[18] Gummesson (1987b, 1993); Holmlund (1997).

[19] Lean production and lean consumption combined into lean solutions is treated by Womack and Jones (2005a, b).

where suppliers and customers interact in a network together with competitors, own suppliers, intermediaries and others. RM is not happening in a vacuum, it is mirroring other events in business and society. When organization is discussed in the following chapters, it is treated as a network of relationships and referred to as the *network organization*.

IT is the latest branch of the RM root system. It is easy to get enthralled by the media hype and the trendy praise for all the blessings of technology. What in this daily hullabaloo will exert sustainable influence and what is just a short-lived, albeit colourful, butterfly? We begin to discern some answers, to see IT in a context as part of marketing theory. IT has a lot in common with RM. The Internet, email and mobile telephony form new networks within which we can interact. IT has not fathered RM as is sometimes claimed, only changed it. Even if the ideas of CRM date far back under other names, IT has made it possible to go further and has caused the explosion in CRM software. The IT influence is covered specifically in 'the e-relationship', but is also an integral part of the whole book.

Marketing offers no fully fledged theory, but the word theory will be used here in a broad sense. The most complete theory that has a link to marketing is the neoclassical micro-economic theory, also called price theory. Its severe shortcoming is that in order to reach a self-imposed desire for rigour and theoretical completeness, a series of limiting assumptions have to be made, such as all customers being the same, all suppliers being the same and all products being the same. It disregards differentiated offerings and brands, service, quality and relationships. Thus, micro-economic theory distances itself from the variety and complexity of real life, and the validity of the theory becomes weak, even non-existent.[20]

Furthermore, the borderline between theory and practice is thin. To design theory, researchers interview and observe marketers and customers. Activities and decisions in companies form empirical evidence for theory. Thus, there is no *a priori* conflict between theory and practice; they are two sides of the same coin. There often is, however, animosity between representatives of theory and practice who claim that their side of the coin shines brighter. Such pseudo-conflicts do not contribute to knowledge development and are left aside here.

Basic values of marketing

Management thinker Peter Drucker, who died in 2006 almost 96 years old and until the end listed as the No. 1 management guru in the United States, said somewhere that 'the problem with good ideas is that they quickly degenerate into hard work'. There is invariably

---

[20] Hunt and Morgan (1995).

a gap between ideas and action, between RM philosophy and CRM application. The gap can be caused not only by lack of implementation skills and stamina, but also by difficulties in grasping the essentials. There may be a lack of data, or inability to put data together in a meaningful pattern or map – 'theories' – which facilitate decisions and actions. The difficulties are caused by at least four 'random variables': customers, competitors, the general economy and technology change. None of these and their interdependence can be predicted with accuracy.

The gap is also caused by marketers who have not internalized marketing values. Drucker was an early proponent of customer centricity. In his classic management book from 1954, he says: 'Marketing … is the whole business seen from the point of view of its final result, that is, from the customer's point of view.'[21] As Michael Baker in the United Kingdom points out '… the distinction between success and failure in competitive markets may be reduced to two basic issues, first, an understanding of customer needs, and, second, the ability to deliver added value …'[22] This is the essence of *the marketing concept* and the antecedent to creating customer satisfaction and loyalty. This *marketing-oriented* and *customer-centric approach* is in opposition to *product* and *production orientation*, according to which the customer is obliged to buy what is available or not buy at all. Production orientation is typical of markets with a shortage of goods and services, and markets of centrally planned economies, but also of complacent industries in wealthy market economies such as in Europe and the United States.

Being customer centric has become a widespread slogan. It is understood and implemented to a varying degree. It may just be perceived as a fad which it is timely to confess to, or yet another smart trick to trap the consumer. The customer in focus values have not killed the old values, just pushed them into a corner from which they make recurring and successful efforts to break out. But a basic question is if customer centricity is realistic. Several researchers and consultants have suggested programmes for the implementation of customer centricity.[23] My contention is that *customer centricity as the prime target for business is non-implementable and not fit to form the foundational credo of marketing*. It could be a transient goal – but it has been so for 50 years by now. There are different perceptions of its success, all the way from just being nice rhetoric and not actionable (with some exceptions) to being a commodity that '… no longer gives companies the edge in competitive situation … and every extra dollop of marketing orientation results in ever-diminishing returns'.[24] Satisfied customers are not the only drivers of success. A balance of interests can only be actualized in a context of many stakeholders. After the *one-party focus*

---

[21] Drucker (1954, p. 36). For a discussion on the past and future of marketing, see Baker (1999a, b).
[22] Baker (2006, pp. 197–198)
[23] See Shah *et al.* (2006) for an overview.
[24] Brown (2007, pp. 151–152).

(the customer), RM introduced a *two-party* focus (customer and supplier) and there is an emerging multi-party focus (multiple stakeholders) through many-to-many marketing. I call for *balanced centricity*. It means that in long-term relationships and a well-functioning marketplace all stakeholders have the right to satisfaction of needs and wants.

INSIGHT   I propose that inadequate basic values and their accompanying procedures – the wrong paradigm – is the biggest obstacle to success in marketing. If marketers and top management do not understand and accept relationship values as a natural vantage point, there will be neither positive effect of RM, nor of the installation of computerized CRM systems, eCRM.

The most fundamental values of RM/CRM are well in line with the tenets of S-D logic. They will be presented here in somewhat different terminology:

1 *Marketing management should be broadened into marketing-oriented company management*: Since the early 1970s, I have made a distinction between the marketing and sales *department* and the marketing and sales *function* in order to emphasize that marketing and sales are more than just the activities of specialized departments. They are functions that must permeate every corner of an organization, not least the minds and actions of management. I have introduced the terms *part-time marketer (PTM)* and *full-time marketer (FTM)* to stress that FTMs are people who work in departments designated to marketing and sales tasks (see further R4 in Chapter 3). PTMs are all the rest of the employees and they also include actors in the external environment like customers and the media. PTMs exist in every organizational unit. They influence the relationship with customers through service encounters, face-to-face, ear-to-ear, email-to-email, mobile phone message-to-message and computer-to-website. Marketing management in this sense requires marketing orientation of the whole of the company, that is, marketing-oriented management.

2 *Long-term collaboration and win–win*: The core values of RM are found in its emphasis on *collaboration and the creation of mutual value*. It includes viewing suppliers, customers and others as *partners* who co-create rather than *opposite parties*. Back in 1976, Baker suggested that marketing be defined as 'mutually satisfying exchange relationships'. RM should be more of *win–win* than *win–lose*, more of a *plus sum game* than a *zero sum game*. In a plus sum game, the parties increase value for each other; in a zero sum game, what one gains is the loss of another. A constructive attitude is expected by all those involved and all should find the relationship meaningful. If these conditions are fulfilled, the relationships may become sustaining. For a supplier, it is important to retain existing

customers, a fact which is increasingly being stressed. Extending the *duration* of the relationship becomes a major marketing goal. Too much emphasis has been put on the acquisition of new customers and too little on caring for existing customers. RM/CRM encourage *customer retention* and discourage *customer defection* well aware of the fact that *attraction marketing* – getting new customers – must also be persued. Although collaboration is the core property of RM, my RM concept holds that *both competition and collaboration are essential in a functioning market economy*. Traditional marketing is prejudiced in favour of the benefits of competition. It sees collaboration as inhibiting the forces of the market. The misunderstanding is obvious among those politicians and business leaders who advocate competition as a cure-all for society's problems, a counter-reaction to the socialistic advocacy for central planning and regulations.

3 *All parties should be active and take responsibility*: RM should not be mixed up with traditional selling, which represents the supplier perspective and does not put the customer and an interactive relationship in focus. In relationship selling, the initiative comes from the salesperson and depends on '... how well the relationship is managed by the seller'.[25] In this sense, relationship quality and a long-term relationship become the consumer's trust in the salesperson based on the salesperson's present and past performance.[26] But the initiative to action cannot be left to a supplier or a single party of a network; everyone in a network can, and should, be active. Contrary to the mythology of marketing, the supplier is not necessarily the active party. In B2B, customers initiate innovation and force suppliers to change their products or services. Consumers suggest improvements but have a tough time getting lethargic and complacent suppliers and legislators to listen. Chat groups on the Internet empower customers to reach out at no cost but time; it makes C2C interaction possible. Customers can exert pressure on suppliers and it may even go so far that hate sites are created. At the same time, the supplier has more and better information available to act on. In services marketing consumers are often both producers and 'project leaders', whereas the role of the provider is limited to offering an arena.

4 *Relationship and service values instead of bureaucratic–legal values*: Bureaucratic–legal values are characterized by: rigidity; legal jargon; application of dysfunctional laws and regulations; a focus on internal routines; more interest in rituals than in results; belief in the supplier as the expert and the customer as ignorant; the customer being a cost and a residual of the system; customers as masses and statistical averages; and the importance of winning over the customer in a dispute. These values historically dominate governments and their agencies. Its representatives have previously disclaimed marketing, but the international wave of privatization, deregulation and demand for

---

[25] Levitt (1983, p. 111).
[26] Crosby, Evans and Cowles (1990).

competition, as well as the failure of the command economies, has forced a change. RM is a valid concept for public organizations as well, and an understanding of how marketing could be applied to public bodies to the benefit of the consumer/citizen is growing. Unfortunately, bureaucratic–legal values are also common in private companies. RM requires different values based on relationships and service to the customer. These values establish that all customers are individuals and different in certain respects; that the outcome is the only thing that counts; that customers are the source of revenue and should be in focus; and that the supplier's task is to create value for the customer.[27]

These values were written long before S-D logic managed to distil them and other ideas into a more communicative and consistent message. RM may stand out as a naively idyllic and benign agenda that is purely academic and not paying attention to the harsh realities of marketing practice. It requires more ethical behaviour than traditional marketing. But all business people do not base their activities on RM/CRM values as presented here. We will come back to this on several occasions.

A different set of values: marketing as tricks

RM may sound like everybody is in agreement and no manipulation or persuasion takes place. This is not so. A boy–girl relationship includes many attempts to play tricks to get the other party do as you want. It's the same in marketing. Stephen Brown of University of Ulster, Ireland, has described manipulation vividly though the case of Joseph Duveen.[28]

CASE STUDY **The Duveen legacy**

Joseph Duveen dominated the art market for Old Masters during the first half of the twentieth century. In Brown's terminology Duveen created 'lustomers', customers who were driven crazy by the lust to acquire the right art. He used skilled manipulation, which Brown has conceptualized into the 4Ds:

■ *Dearth*: '… there is nothing like scarcity to stimulate the gotta-get-it urge among lustomers'.

---

[27] See Gummesson (1993, pp. 40–42).
[28] Brown (2007); quotations from pp. 150–151.

■ *Denial*: 'He understood that people appreciate things all the more if they are difficult to obtain ...' and '... disdain what comes easily.'

■ *Distinction*: '... dangling deliciously unobtainable carrots definitely helps drive consumers wild with desire, but unless the product or service itself is distinctive – and confers distinction on its possessors – it is pointless playing the strategic stock shortage game ...'

■ *Discourse*: Duveen '... was a superlative storyteller' and '... convincingly demonstrated that story orientation rather than customer orientation is the *real* secret of marketing success'.

Today's markets surround us with Duveen followers. When Apple's charismatic CEO Steve Jobs launched the iPod, when the countdown started for the release of the last *Harry Potter*, and when hysteria broke out over H&M's limited edition of designer clothes by Stella McCartney and Karl Lagerfeld, backed up by Madonna as fashion model in advertisements, we recognize the Duveen legacy. These are all strong brands to which customers develop a parasocial relationship (see R13 in Chapter 3) but the activities also support C2C interaction in social networks of customers with a shared lifestyle.

Just like J. K. Rowling and Apple and H&M investors, Duveen became wealthy but perhaps more important was the social recognition bestowed on him by the Queen; he first became Sir Joseph Duveen and later Baron Duveen of Millbank.

In international B2B marketing bribes and political pressure are ubiquitous. So is unethical lobbying with spin-doctors that upset democratic procedure; hyped 'promises' and outright lying and lying by omission (the marketing of financial instruments and food products); and deliberately confusing customers by non-comparable propositions (phone operating companies). We encounter this daily.

All this is embarrassing both for practitioners and professors and is silently swept under the carpet. But as it keeps happening in contemporary society just like it has done over the centuries it may be in the human genes. The task of the marketer is not to reform mankind and society but to do business on prevailing conditions. In today's complex markets it is not enough to be street-smart, you must also be book-smart and utilize scientific research. For example, there are market researchers who have specialized in transforming small children into big-time consumers. Part of this is to 'educate' kids to more efficiently nag their parents for more products, fancier brands and seductively 'tasty' sugar-based junk food.

If you want to be cynical – but realistic – the definition of marketing could be:

Marketing is a set of tricks to squeeze maximum, short-term profits out of consumers, citizens, other companies and the government, to the benefit of the management and shareholders of the supplier.

I am sure that many experience marketing just like this and it is often true. But morals and ethics always invite to a balancing act and the supplier is not the sole villain. The customer is often ignorant and unwilling to learn, wants everything cheap and so on. Marketing seems forever doomed to be manipulative to a degree. Why not openly acknowledge it and either accept it or do something about it?

RM versus transaction marketing

RM is often presented as the opposite to *transaction marketing*, the one-shot deal.[29] In transaction marketing, the fact that a customer has bought once does not forecast the probability for repurchase, not even if a series of purchases have been made. A customer may repeatedly use the same supplier because of high switching costs, but without feeling committed to the supplier or wanting to enter a closer relationship. Transactions lack history and memory and they don't get sentimental.

In RM, loyalty – especially customer loyalty – is emphasized. In the 'loyalty ladder',[30] the lowest rung is the contact with a *prospect* who hopefully turns into a *customer* and a first purchase. Recurrent customers are *clients*; those who have come back and a long-term relationship is in the making. In the next stages the client becomes a *supporter* and finally an *advocate* for the supplier.

Transaction marketing has no ambition to climb the loyalty ladder. Still, it is often a realistic and functional option. A purchase can concern standardized goods at lowest price within a specified delivery time and grade of quality. Such deals are made, for example, on metals exchanges. A consumer may only buy a home on a single or a few occasions in a lifetime and rarely has surgery on the appendix more than once. IT offers new alternatives and can facilitate the consumer's search for the lowest price of a branded product, or even bidding on an international auction website such as eBay. Through the deregulation of telecom services, the customer can choose the operator with the lowest rate at a specific hour to a specific destination.

But even a one-shot deal can mean deep interactive relationships. If a company builds a new office, the interaction with the builder and a network of providers may be intense for a year or two. The company may not build another office for the next few decades. If you

---

[29] See Jackson (1985a, b), who treats marketing and RM in the B2B context.
[30] Christopher, Payne and Ballantyne (2002, pp. 47–49).

have surgery and stay in a hospital, the interaction will be intense and painfully intimate, but both parties hope that the relationship will be superfluous as the wound heals.

In order to conceptually incorporate transaction marketing in RM, it can be seen as the zero point of the *RM scale*.[31] The scope of the relationships can then be enhanced until a customer and a supplier are practically the same organization. The *zero relationship* of RM has a *price component* within which the lowest price connects the buyer and the seller. Micro-economic theory advocates that price be the sole determinant of a purchase. This limitation makes the theory a blind guide to marketing management, as it only represents one extreme point on the relationship scale. The zero relationship also has a *convenience component* which implies that the customer often buys where it is simplest and most convenient on a certain occasion. On such occasions price is almost immaterial.

The fact that this book is about RM and advocates relationships as essential in marketing does not imply a religious belief in relationships as a magic panacea. On the contrary, we know that human relationships can be a source of insurmountable hassle as well as of unlimited joy. But we cannot live without them. The larger share of world literature and entertainment deals with relationships between adults, parent and child, police and crook, and not the least between the players in a business venture.

A relationship should not be retained if it works badly. Long-term relationships and customer care are not the same as admitting customers to the geriatric ward of the supplier, attaching them to the bed and keeping them on life support. Relationships should not necessarily be broken just because there is a conflict, however. They can often be restored and improved or they may be the best option for the parties despite a conflict. The beginning of a relationship is often romantic and passionate. It is when the passion phase fades that the real work of building a relationship starts.

Jackson[32] succinctly states a common-sense RM strategy: 'Relationship marketing ... can be extremely successful where it is appropriate – but it can also be costly and ineffective if it is not. Conversely, transaction marketing ... can be profitable and successful where it is appropriate but a serious mistake where it is not.'

The value-creating network society

A host of concepts are trying to capture the spirit of our current and future economies. The post-industrial society tells us what we are running away from but not where we

---

[31] See also Grönroos' 'marketing strategy continuum' (1991, 2007), and an elaboration of this scale in Lehtinen, Hankimaa and Mittilä (1994).

[32] ackson (1985a, p. xi). See also Dwyer, Shurr and Oh (1987); Anderson and Narus (1991); and Paulin, Perrien and Ferguson (1997).

are heading. The service society, the knowledge society and the information age all centre around a resource or a product. The global society, the glocal society (*glo*bal and lo*cal* dimensions are simultaneously growing in importance), and the virtual society highlight the 'place' aspect.

I prefer to talk about society in two complementary dimensions. One is *the value society*, stressing value creation as the desirable outcome of economic activity and consumption. As consumers and citizens, we are not specifically looking for goods, services, knowledge, information or other 'products'. We want something of value. Therefore companies place value propositions on the market and so does the government sector. The customer's role as co-creator of value used to be associated to certain services and B2B situations. As we have seen, the S-D logic treats co-creation of value as general to all marketing and purchasing situations.

The other dimension is *the network society*, stressing the overriding structure of organizations and society. Companies and markets are networks of relationships within which we interact, completely in accordance with the definition of RM. Manuel Castells describes the network society in three thick volumes, which have received global accolade. He speaks about the corporation as 'the network enterprise': 'Networks are the fundamental stuff of which new organizations are and will be made.'[33]

Merging value and networks we get *the value-creating network society*. RM and CRM operate within its spirit. We are dealing with elusive phenomena such as everything goes faster and faster; globalization with ever-growing transnational corporations and alliances; the European Union (EU) expanded to 25 nations and the euro replacing former national Deutschmarks, Finnish marks, guilders, lire, Irish pounds and other currencies; deregulation and privatization and the increasing dominance of a commercial market economy even where it does not function; the ever-increasing importance of intangible values such as knowledge and brands; and the whole of the IT evolution. Networks with blurred boundaries between a company, its market and society display the whole of management and business in a new light.

Reflective researchers and reflective practitioners: merging science with common sense and tacit knowledge

Running a company revolves around two eternal themes: make sure you have something to offer and make sure you sell it at a price that is higher than your costs.

It is a matter of common sense. The issue is how to make it happen. Common sense, sound judgement, instinct, intuition, insights and wisdom are stressed in the

---

[33] Castells (1996; quotation from p. 168).

handbook-type marketing literature; in the scholarly literature they are often treated with contempt. I feel inspired by the way common sense is defined in *Brewer's Dictionary of Phrase & Fable* from 1870:

> Common sense does not mean that good sense which is common ...
> but the point where all five senses meet, supposed to be the seat of the
> soul, where it judges what is presented by the senses and decides the
> mode of action.

Let us widen the five senses to include experience, intelligence, emotions – even referred to as 'emotional intelligence'[34] –, masculine and feminine instincts, and extrasensory perception if we have it. The complexity of today's markets and organizations, the advanced technology, and the ongoing changes conceal the obvious and we get lost in a maze. Companies grow and employees cannot overview the meaning of their job. We need to go 'back to basics' – or rather, 'forward to basics' – as it is not a matter of regressing to a past society but of adapting to the present and the future. When Scandinavian Airlines (SAS) commenced its turnaround in the 1980s, one of the instruments was 'smile courses'. Among other things, people were taught that it is important to smile to customers; they will then like you more than if you look gloomy and disinterested. Common sense and sound judgement had to be reinstated. They had got lost in the red tape and standardized mass production of the industrial society. Nordstrom, an exceptionally successful US chain of department stores, says in its *Employee Handbook* under the heading 'Nordstrom Rules': 'Rule No. 1: Use your good judgement in all situations', and adds: 'There will be no additional rules.'

Many have stressed 'management by walking around', leadership through presence where and when it happens. The concept 'rapid reconnaissance' is used in science and refers to the scientist's need to quickly assess a situation or a problem.[35]

This is not the kiss of death of research and science. It only means that we must enhance our ability to utilize *both* systematic analysis *and* personal experience and insights.

The rules of the marketing game are rewritten through political events and changes in values, consumption patterns and technology. Marketing reality requires living with complexity, paradoxes, uncertainty, ambiguity and instability. Many markets are perceived as chaotic, but chaos holds opportunities for those who can see them and use them better than the competition. Chaos is not chaotic *per se*, there is order in chaos,[36] but we fail to

---

[34] Goleman (2006).

[35] Patton (2001) mentions this as a research strategy in social sciences when a qualitative, inductive approach is deployed.

[36] Prigogine and Stengers (1985).

see the underlying pattern. It was an uncertain venture when, more than a century ago, European companies took their new products to South America. Many of these ventures succeeded and spawned today's global corporations. Currently, the former Soviet Union nations are chaotic markets having gigantic potential; Hong Kong – once the epitome of capitalism – has become part of China which is transforming into a market economy together with India and other Asian nations; and membership of the North American Free Trade Agreement (NAFTA) or the EU offers new conditions. We may wish to reduce uncertainty, but the market economy is built on dynamic change, which is only partially predictable.

As theory and scientific literature only cover fragments of reality, it is crucial to add knowledge from the *reflective practitioner*. Business leaders, marketers, consultants and others disseminate their experience in action by running corporations as well as through lectures, interviews, articles, handbooks and memoirs. Sometimes, professors of business schools have practical experience of business or government. Furthermore, we shall not forget our lifelong and daily experience of being buyers and consumers, perhaps *reflective customers*. All this knowledge can be integrated in research and contribute to more dynamic and rich progress beneficial to both education and practice. Knowledge, experience, compassion and reflection – the *pre-understanding* of the individual – are grounds for enhancing the *understanding* of marketing. The personal experience and the practitioner's gut feeling are not always welcomed in the parlours of science. There is, however, a growing tendency to take better care of *tacit knowledge* or *knowledge by acquaintance*. This kind of knowledge has not found a language and a theory, but is used by the insightful both in practice and research.[37]

If international research in marketing was less obsessed with surveys and statistical techniques and less committed to received theory, we would have more *reflective researchers* who contribute more valid knowledge to the development of more comprehensive and useful theory.

What do we see through the relationship eye-glasses?

We need new approaches that reflect today's markets and help us find our way in these markets. There is no general marketing theory that makes us see everything at the same time. New categories, concepts, models and theories work as lenses through which we perceive the world. If the lenses are wrongly curved, the world will look blurry. If they

---

[37] The reflective practitioner is discussed by Schön (1983); understanding and pre-understanding are central in hermeneutics (see Gummesson, 2000, pp. 57–82); tacit knowledge is treated by Polanyi (1962) and Nonaka and Takeuchi (1995); and knowledge by acquaintance by Russell (1948).

are tinted, it may look sunny when in fact it is cloudy. Certain lenses improve our vision at close range, others at a distance. As marketing is a complex field, a single pair of glasses is not sufficient. There are bifocals that allow two perspectives, but we need more than two. This book offers the *relationship eye-glasses*. If we look through these glasses we can only see relationships, networks and interaction. RM is about what you see through these glasses.

New concepts, models and theories can very well be the emperor's new clothes and only the innocent child dares say the obvious: 'But he doesn't have anything on!' I have, however, come to the conclusion that RM and CRM provide a new costume which is both visible and tangible. RM offers more common sense in marketing, and it makes important phenomena visible in the confusing world in which marketers search for meaning. CRM offers systems to implement RM strategies. It is then up to the readers to try RM and CRM on their own reality and draw their own conclusions. If marketing executives or salespeople either get a feeling of *déjà vu*, or are made aware of something they might already have sensed or even used but were unable to articulate, it means that the text is close to reality and has validity.

My conclusion is that a radically new thinking in marketing – a paradigm shift – is necessary.[38] But it is not enough to think in new ways to claim a paradigm shift; it must also materialize in action.[39] Research and experience have contributed with general properties of relationships which can help us understand and evaluate individual aspects of relationships and networks. These properties are presented in the next section. An overview of the 30 specific relationships which I have found applicable in marketing-oriented management follows.

Properties of relationships, networks and interaction

In studies of relationships, networks and interaction, a series of general properties have emerged. In the network approach of B2B, a distinction is made between three types of connections which together form a relationship between buyers and sellers:[40]

- *Activity links* embrace activities of a technical, administrative and marketing kind.
- *Resource ties* include exchanging and sharing resources which are both tangible, such as machines, and represent intellectual capital, such as knowledge.
- *Actor bonds* are created by people who interact and exert influence on each other and form opinions about each other.

---

[38] For criticism against RM, see Blois (1996); Bliemel and Eggert (1997); Fournier, Dobscha and Mick (1998); Snehota and Söderlund (1998); Brown (2000); and Möller and Halinen (2000).

[39] RM as a tool for implementation is treated by Gummesson (1998b).

[40] Håkansson and Snehota (1995).

The interaction can also be approached as a hierarchy where *activities* (lowest level) together form *episodes* which form *sequences* which form *relationships*. The relationships constitute the *partner base*, the organization's total network.[41] *Relationscape* has been suggested as a designation for all the relationships that are included in a network.[42] These relationships may be active and visible; they could also be invisibly embedded in the network by being passive and unobtrusive, yet still be influential.

It is also feasible to list the properties or dimensions which a party may perceive in a relationship. In a study of consumers, as many as 45 properties were identified.[43]

The general classifications and properties of relationships can be useful in RM for decision-making and planning. In Chapters 2–5, where 30 relationships, the 30Rs, are presented, applications of these properties will be continuously examined.

The following sections summarize important general properties of commercial relationships.[44]

Collaboration

Collaboration has already been claimed to be the fundamental property of relationships between suppliers and customers, competitors, consultants, government agencies and others. It is stressed in S-D logic as co-creation. The collaboration can be linked to a single deal or be continuous. The degree of collaboration could be combined with the degree of competition.[45] A situation with little competition and little collaboration between two or more companies can be a good start for expanded collaboration. A high degree of collaboration and a low degree of competition provide a base for a long-term and harmonious relationship. Relationships can also thrive in a situation of both extensive collaboration and competition. If the collaborative part is insignificant and competition takes over, it becomes imperative to either divest in the relationship or to consciously work for a reinforced relationship.

Power

Power is an undervalued concept in the marketing literature. The formation of gigantic global groups today is a matter of power. Brands give power. The Internet as a medium

---

[41] Holmlund (1997); see also Liljander and Strandvik (1995).
[42] Strandvik and Törnroos (1997).
[43] Ward, Frew and Caldow (1997).
[44] This section is a synthesis from research within the B2B network approach; studies within sociology and psychology (see Granovetter, 1973, 1985; Boissevein, 1976; Scott, 1991); practical business experience; plus some specific references in the text.
[45] According to Wilkinson and Young (1994).

for information and interactivity gives the customer more power. Power in a relationship is only rarely symmetrical, meaning that each party has the same amount of power. An asymmetrical relationship means that one party is weaker and may feel used, but the relationship can still be functional if there is no better alternative for the weaker party. It can also be perceived as unfair and at the first opportunity the weaker party exits. Patients with toothache are left to the discretion of dentists and their willingness to serve them; they may be left at the mercy of an emergency clinic where patients must wait long hours. The symmetry of power can change. A company in a booming market may be short of components and the supplier has the power, but when the market turns downward the customer can negotiate cuts in prices and delivery times. To use one's position to the extreme is detrimental to sustaining a relationship; a certain amount of goodwill and helpfulness is demanded from all parties.

Longevity

It has been stressed that the long-term relationship is a pillar of RM. This is in opposition to transaction marketing, which is characterized by single deals and customer promiscuity. The concepts of duration, retention and defection have been defined above. Long-term relationships can be more effective for all parties, especially if it takes a long time to build them, a common case in B2B. Switching costs may be high and no relationship should be broken because of negligence or lack of interest. The parties learn how to handle the relationship and utilize it to their benefit. Sometimes it is rational to break a relationship. It may have become obsolete or lost its zest. For example, it is reasonable to change advertising agency at times in order to stimulate creativity.

Commitment, dependency and importance

If a relationship is important, we are dependent on it and we must then commit ourselves to making it work. If a delivery is delayed, a whole factory or construction site may stop, particularly if they are part of a just-in-time (JIT) production system. Dependency is dramatically obvious when emergencies occur, for example, when an ambulance or fire-fighters are needed. There are also daily and trivial dependencies on the telephone, the newspaper, and public transport to and from work. Three levels of dependency and commitment have been proposed.[46] On Level 1, customers are primarily attracted by low prices. The effect of this attraction quickly fades away if the competition also lowers its

---

[46] Berry and Parasuraman (1991, pp. 136–142).

prices. Level 1 is often easy to copy. On Level 2, the relationship has deepened. There is no longer just a price relationship, but also a communication with the customer that may consist of face-to-face contact or personally addressed direct mail. Level 3 adds a structural dimension which means that the parties have pooled resources and are therefore highly committed to making the relationship work. The Procter & Gamble and Wal-Mart production–sales–delivery system is such an example.

Trust, risk and uncertainty

The success of closer collaboration between customer and supplier is often credited to trust. Consumers can trust an airline, a plumber or a doctor, but also a certain brand. A company can have a trusting relationship with a bank which facilitates credit decisions. Management consultants live on their clients' trust for them; to 'objectively' measure their performance is usually not feasible or meaningful. Individual lawyers and accountants can be important to a person and they must be available when needed; the client may not want to turn to other professionals, even if they work in the same firm. Often we only know partially what we are buying – we do it on trust – for example, when our dentist performs root canal surgery. We only know the value of an insurance policy when a claim is made; we have probably not quite understood the fine print and legal conditions of our home insurance or retirement plan. This ignorance creates uncertainty. Alliances represent a risk; there may be arguments, one party may pick the other party's brain without giving anything in return. The degree and significance of trust varies widely between cultures and nations, which has been analysed by Fukuyama (1995). He points out that the mom and pop business, embracing the next of kin and friends, has its own rules and a tight social control, whereas large-scale operations require trust in the society as such. He makes a distinction between high-trust societies and low-trust societies.

Frequency, regularity and intensity

Certain relationships are frequently and regularly active, such as travel to and from work or bank transactions. Following a fixed timetable, which is part of a long-term contract, the Swedish railways transport rolls of paper from Sweden to newspaper printers in London every day. Other relationships are rare, such as engaging a funeral parlour or estate agent, but loyalty to a specific provider can still be strong. Education can require an intense relationship during several years, heart surgery an intense relationship during a few days. The relationship to a convenience store can be sustaining and frequent, but not particularly intense.

Adaptation[47]

In long-term relationships the parties must adapt to one another. In B2B this adaptation can be far reaching as the years pass by and termination of the relationship can be very costly for one or all of the parties. Adaptation can mean large investment which is customized to the needs of other parties and that cannot necessarily be used for anything else. It can concern manufacturing, finance, information systems and knowledge, but it can also be mental and social. Also, in B2C/C2B consumers adapt to a system and procedures. For example, most consumers want paying bills to be an effortless routine. When payment systems are changed, as currently customers transfer to Internet banking, it requires you to invest in a computer, an Internet subscription and installation of software. The system requires you to learn the job of a bank teller and to comply with inconvenient, yet non-robust, security procedures. For some, this may be a positive adaptation; it may offer more flexibility and the customer may save time. For others, such as the elderly, adaptation may not even be an option.

Attraction

In the marriage metaphor of long-term relationships, attraction between the parties is a dominant factor. The predecessors of the EU were alliances and mergers between countries, and matrimony between princes and princesses were a major instrument of securing sustainability and peace. When, in 2001, Norwegian Crown Prince Haakon married Mette-Marit, a girl of the people with a past, it was not because of political, economic or social convenience, rather the contrary. Attraction – love – took over. In a similar vein, studies have shown that attraction between companies may require a combination of rational financial motives and psychological factors.[48] Even in business, a partner should be cool and sexy. This also applies for the image that companies convey through their brands (see R13 on parasocial relationships). The importance of attraction for establishing relationships both within industries and to customers is perhaps nowhere more protruding than in entertainment, sports, tourism and politics.

Closeness and remoteness

Closeness can be physical, mental or emotional. The physical proximity facilitates mental and emotional contact. Companies that want to do business in a foreign country often

---

[47] See Hallén, Johanson and Seyed-Mohamed (1993).
[48] Halinen (1997, p. 270f).

have to be continuously present in order to obtain credibility. Cultural differences exist between countries, and ethnic and religious groups may build mental distance despite physical closeness. Certain relationships become truly personal, especially if you meet often and even associate privately. Others are remote in the sense that the conduits are machines, such as automated teller machines (ATMs). The Internet and email create a virtual closeness, but there is still a physical distance. Closeness strengthens the feeling of security. The majority of relationships thrive on tacit understanding between parties and only a minority are regulated in contracts. Consumers are often far away from manufacturers who must rely on distance information through intermediaries, such as reports from market research institutes.

Formality, informality and transparency

Commercial relationships are usually more informal than formal. As consumers we rarely have a contract or any other written obligation, but there are exceptions. As members of a golf club we have consented to abide to strict rules and we cannot usually just move to another club; to be effective a retirement plan may force us to stick to the same insurance or finance company, and the payments and contracts are formal and regulated. If we break the rules we may be punished or even be dropped as customers. The better we know the people in a small store, the more informal the relationship may be. They may let us in after opening hours or give us credit if we have left our purse at home. In B2B, informality is an absolute necessity as a supplement to formal agreements. Problems are solved over the telephone and the parties trust each other. Negotiations and exchange of information may occur at the golf course or in a hotel bar, sometimes leading to major deals with long-term effects. The formal aspects must be heeded, however. One such aspect is the degree of transparency. For example, how much are we obliged to reveal to the other parties concerning our own cost and revenue?

Routinization

A common complaint in marriages is the lack of romance and excitement; after a period of passion the relationship turns into routine. Although it sounds dull, routine procedures may be conditional for efficiency and cost effectiveness, both in commercial and marital relationships. Banking today is routinized through computers and telephones, and the days when you went to your local branch office and were greeted by a bank teller, with whom you had a chat, are numbered. Even if you think you telephone your local bank branch, a digital switch will select a free line to a call centre, which can be located anywhere in a country, even abroad. In B2B, routines are established for deliveries, and both the customer and the supplier follow rituals and standard procedures. Increasingly, these routines are handled by machine-to-machine interaction. However, customers also abandon suppliers who show no interest in them. So there is a trade-off between routines and standard procedures for speed and low cost, and the feeling that the relationships develop and live.

Content

The content of a business relationship is traditionally described as economic exchange. One party provides goods and services and the other provides money; streams of goods or services go in one direction and financial streams go in the other. In this sense marketing is exchange. In new marketing and management theory, the relationship is increasingly seen as interaction and co-creation of value. The content of a relationship is often knowledge and information. This is a rationale for alliances, for example, for product development or for a hotel to join a room reservation network. This way a company 'can become bigger without growing'. Co-ordination and utilization of resources for manufacturing and distribution can be important, for example, competing newspapers who share a printing plant and the distribution to subscribers in order to slash costs.

Personal and social properties

These are age, gender, profession, education, ethnicity, personality type, geographical and social mobility, as well as personal traits such as lust for power, or an ability to create trust and confidence. Charm, charisma, good vibes and chemistry belong here, all phenomena that are difficult to analyse but which we recognize when we encounter them. In social network analysis, efforts are made to identify patterns of relationships: cliques, clusters and blocks. The analysis offers matrices and descriptions of structures of personal relationships. The sociogram is a graphical technique to show patterns of relationships between individuals. Relationships can be of the first degree concerning friends, of the second degree concerning friends of friends, of the third degree, etc. The relationships can be direct or can be arranged through a mediator.

Properties of properties

It is often asked which properties are the most important. The idea then is to be Pareto optimal and to zoom in on the properties that account for the lion's share of the benefits of RM. Collaboration must always be in the core of a relationship. Some claim that power is always decisive, others that commitment and trust are the key.[49] I am inclined to

---

[49] About power, see Thorelli (1986, p. 38); about commitment and trust, see Morgan and Hunt (1994).

agree that power, which can come in the form of financial power, social power, monopoly power, power through a superior or scarce value proposition and so on, is more important than commitment and trust, but power is not always present. Most of the properties are fuzzy entities which overlap in several respects and they do not readily lend themselves to clear-cut definitions. General rankings are misleading, as the importance of a property is always relative to a specific situation and its constellation of properties. For example, trust is taken-for-granted in some business cultures. It is only when trust is abused that the property stands out as pivotal and something else is needed, such as superior social contact or a formal contract.

The general properties of relationships can contribute to the evaluation of a relationship and its development or liquidation. But they cannot alone serve as a basis for marketing decision-making, planning and execution. Even if each of them highlights an interesting phenomenon, they must be put into context. I have therefore chosen to define types of relationships which are composed of many properties and which can be recognized in the management of marketing.

The 30Rs of RM: introductory specification of the 30 relationships

The philosophy of RM/CRM has to be converted into hands-on relationships that can become part of a company's marketing and business planning. This has been done by defining 30 relationships – the 30Rs – which embrace a mix of relationships between parties and specific marketing properties. These are listed and briefly characterized in Table 1.1. With the exception of the first relationship (R1), the relationship between a supplier and a customer – which is the foundation of marketing – the Rs are not in ranking order. Their significance varies between companies, markets and specific situations. In reading the text, keep the vantage points of RM in mind by posing the question: If we view marketing through the relationship eye-glasses, what do we see and how can we use what we see?

The relationships are grouped in the following way. The first two types are *market relationships*. These are relationships between suppliers, customers, competitors and others who operate in the market. They constitute the basis for marketing; they are externally oriented and apply to the market proper. Some of them concern relationships to both consumers and other organizations, others are focused on either consumers or they are *inter*organizational relationships. The market relationships are:

- *Classic market relationships* (R1–R3): The *supplier–customer dyad*, the *triad of supplier–customer–competitor* and the *physical distribution network*, which are treated extensively in general marketing theory.

Table 1.1 The 30 relationships of RM – the 30Rs

Classic market relationships (Chapter 2)

R1 The classic dyad – the relationship between the supplier and the customer

This is the parent relationship of marketing, the co-creation of value which constitutes the basis of business.

R2 The classic triad – the drama of the customer–supplier–competitor triangle

Competition is a central ingredient of the market economy. In competition there are relationships between three parties: between the customer and the current supplier, between the customer and the supplier's competitors, and between competitors.

R3 The classic network – distribution

Traditional physical distribution and modern channel management, including goods, services, people, information and whatever consists of a network of relationships.

Special market relationships (Chapter 3)

R4 Relationships via full-time marketers (FTMs) and part-time marketers (PTMs)

Those who work in marketing, sales departments and customer service departments – the FTMs – are professional relationship makers. All others, who perform other main functions but yet influence customer relationships directly or indirectly, are PTMs. There are also contributing FTMs and PTMs outside the organization.

R5 The service encounter – interaction between customers and suppliers

Traditionally, production and delivery of services often involve the customer in an interactive relationship with the provider. In light of the S-D logic the service encounter can be broadened and service is seen as co-creation of value; it is not limited to services in the traditional sense.

R6 The many-headed customer and the many-headed supplier

Marketing to other organizations, B2B, often means contacts between many individuals from the supplier's and the customer's organization.

R7 The relationship to the customer's customer

A condition for success is often the understanding of the customer's customer, and what suppliers can do to help their customers become successful.

R8 The close versus the distant relationship

In mass marketing, the closeness to the customer is lost and the relationship becomes distant, based on surveys, statistics and written reports.

R9 The relationship to the dissatisfied customer

The dissatisfied customer perceives a special type of relationship, more intense than the normal situation, and often badly managed by the provider. The way of handling a complaint – the recovery – can determine the quality of the future relationship.

R10 The monopoly relationship – the customer or supplier as prisoners

When competition is inhibited, the customer may be at the mercy of the supplier – or the other way around. One of them becomes prisoner.

R11 The customer as 'member'

In order to create a long-term sustaining relationship, it has become increasingly common to enlist customers as members of various loyalty programmes and clubs.

R12 The e-relationship

The electronic relationship, the e-relationship, represented by the Internet, email and mobile telephony and other IT applications is set against the h-relationship, the human relationship. The concept of high tech/high touch becomes increasingly more crucial to watch in RM and CRM.

(Continued)

Table 1.1 Continued

R13   Parasocial relationships – relationships to brands and objects
        Relationships do not only exist with people, but also with objects and mental images – symbols – such as brands and corporate identities.

R14   The non-commercial relationship
        This is a relationship between the government sector, NGOs (non-government organizations) and voluntary organizations on one side and citizens/customers on the other, but it also includes other activities outside of the profit-based and money-based economy, such as those performed in families.

R15   The green relationship and CSR
        Environmental and health issues and corporate social responsibility (CSR) in general have slowly but gradually increased in importance and are creating a new type of customer relationship through legislation, the voice of opinion-leading consumers and politicians, and changing behaviour of consumers and citizens.

R16   The law-based relationship
        A relationship to a customer is sometimes founded primarily on legal contracts and the threat of litigation.

R17   The criminal network
        Organized crime is built on tight and often impermeable networks guided by an illegal business mission. They exist globally and are growing but are disregarded by marketing theory. These networks can disturb the functioning of a whole market or industry.

Mega relationships (Chapter 4)

R18   Personal and social networks
        Personal and social networks often determine business networks. In some cultures, business is solely conducted between friends and friends-of-friends.

R19   Mega marketing – the real 'customer' is not always found in the marketplace
        In certain instances, relationships must be sought with governments, legislators, influential individuals and others, in order to make marketing feasible on an operational level.

R20   Alliances change the market mechanisms
        Alliances mean closer relationships and collaboration between companies. Thus, competition is partly curbed, but collaboration is necessary to make the market economy work.

R21   The knowledge relationship
        Knowledge can be the most strategic and critical resource and 'knowledge acquisition' is often the rationale for alliances.

R22   Mega alliances change the basic conditions for marketing
        The EU and NAFTA (the North America Free Trade Agreement) are examples of alliances above the single company and industry. They exist on government and supranational levels.

R23   The mass media relationship
        The media can be supportive or damaging to marketing and they are particularly influential in forming public opinion. The relationship to media is crucial for the way they will handle an issue.

Nano relationships (Chapter 5)

R24   Market mechanisms are brought inside the company
        By introducing profit centres in an organization, a market inside the company is created and internal as well as external relationships of a new kind emerge.

R25   Internal customer relationships
        The dependency between the different tiers and departments in a company is seen as a process consisting of relationships between internal customers and internal suppliers.

R26 Quality and customer orientation: the relationship between operations management and marketing
The modern quality concept has built a bridge between design, engineering, purchasing, production and other technology-based activities and marketing. It considers the company's internal relationships as well as its relationships to the customers.

R27 Internal marketing: relationships with the 'employee market'
Internal marketing can be seen as part of RM as it gives indirect and necessary support to the relationships with external customers.

R28 The two-dimensional matrix relationship
Matrices are the simplest form of networks and exist in all large corporations, and above all they are found in the relationships between product management and sales.

R29 The relationship to external providers of marketing service
External providers reinforce not only the marketing function by supplying a series of services, such as those offered by advertising agencies and market research institutes, but also in the area of sales and distribution.

R30 The owner and financier relationship
Owners and other financiers partly determine the conditions under which a marketing function can operate. The relationship to them influences marketing strategy.

■ *Special market relationships* (R4–R17): They represent certain aspects of the classic relationships, such as the interaction in the service encounter or the customer as member of a loyalty programme.

The next two types are *non-market relationships*, which indirectly influence the efficiency of market relationships:

■ *Mega relationships* (R18–R23) exist above the market relationships. They provide a platform for market relationships and concern the economy and society in general. Among these are *mega marketing* (lobbying, public opinion and political power), *mega alliances* (such as the NAFTA, setting a new stage for marketing in North America) and *social relationships* (such as friendship and ethnic bonds).

■ *Nano relationships* (R24–R30) are found below the market relationships, that is, relationships inside an organization (*intra*organizational relationships). All internal activities influence the externally bound relationships. Examples of nano relationships are the *relationships between internal customers*, and *between internal markets* that arise as a consequence of the increasing use of independent profit centres, divisions and business areas inside organizations. The boundary between the externally and the internally directed relationships is sometimes fuzzy; it is a matter of emphasis. For example, the physical distribution network (R3) is part of a logistics flow, concerning internal as well as external customers.

In her book *From Tin Soldiers to Russian Dolls*, Vandermerwe (1993) uses the metaphor of tin soldiers and wooden dolls to describe the management of an emerging service society.

The tin soldiers, who represent an obsolete management paradigm based on strict army hierarchy, are neatly placed in rows; they follow orders and regulations. The dolls represent the new paradigm of the network. A Russian doll is composed of dolls enclosed inside each other and mutually dependent in a never-ending series. Her book inspired me to use the metaphor of 'the relationship doll', with layers of relationships that are interdependent but yet of different character. The dolls in the middle represent the market relationships. The nano relationships are the inner dolls and together with the mega relationships, the outer dolls, they constitute the necessary conditions for market relationships. The metaphor points to connections and dependencies that must be considered when a company organizes its marketing. The doll becomes a symbol of the network organization where the borderline between organization, market and society is not fixed as in traditional organization theory and economics.

Summing up: total RM is more 'total' than ever

The concept of total RM sums up what has been presented in this chapter, and what will be explicated in more detail in the remainder of the book. It is defined in the following way:

Total RM is interaction in networks of relationships, recognizing that marketing is embedded in the total management of the networks of the selling organization, and its nano, market and mega relationships. It is directed to long-term win–win relationships with individual customers, and value is co-created between the parties involved. It transcends the boundaries between specialist functions and disciplines. It is made tangible through the 30 relationships, the 30Rs. Total RM represents a paradigm shift in marketing.

RM is more total than ever. S-D logic and the integration of goods and services into service and value propositions; the growing importance of the customer in co-creation and C2C; CRM as part of a company's business system; many-to-many marketing addressing the whole network of stakeholders; and the value-creating network society – they all point in the direction of a more systemic and complete view on marketing.

IN BRIEF

The 30Rs will be further presented and explained in Chapters 2–5. The principal idea of each relationship is treated and practical examples are given. The purpose of the classification into 30Rs is to make RM operative, that is, useful for planning and implementation of marketing activities. All Rs are not applicable to each company and each situation; it is a matter of selecting a specific relationship portfolio for the marketing plan.

In reading the book it is essential to recall its vantage points. You have to wear the relationship eye-glasses and pose the question: If we look at marketing as relationships, networks and interaction, what do we see and what can we do with it? The relationships need not necessarily be read in chronological order, but the reading should rather be guided by relevance for the reader's interests and situation.

QUESTIONS FOR DISCUSSION

1 Write a small case based on your own experience where relationships, networks and interaction have played a role. You can either take it from your work experience or from your experience as customer.

2 Define RM, CRM and many-to-many marketing. Discuss how these definitions relate to the new definition of marketing suggested by the American Marketing Association, AMA.

3 What is meant by C2C interaction and why has it increased in importance?

4 What are the major characteristics of S-D logic?

5 The book is critical to the marketing concept and customer centricity as guiding principles for companies:

   a What do these principles entail and why could there be reason to be critical?

   b What is meant by 'balanced centricity'?

6 Which are the fundamental values of RM?

7 Do you ever feel that you are exposed to marketing tricks?

8 Give examples of where transaction marketing is likely to be more important than RM.

9 The book lists and explains general properties of commercial relationships. It is common to rank such properties in order of importance but the book claims that such rankings are misleading. Why – and do you agree?

Chapter

2

Classic market relationships

In this chapter

The first three relationships are marketing classics, although here they are observed through the relationship eye-glasses. The relationship between the customer and the supplier (R1) – the classic dyad – constitutes the foundation for commercial exchange and interaction; it is the parent relationship of marketing. It is supplemented by a third force, competition, which is a necessary element of a market economy; the relationship between a customer, its present supplier and the supplier's competitors constitute the classic triad (R2). Physical distribution has always been central in marketing. It has broadened into channel management and here it is viewed as a network of relationships, the classic network of marketing (R3).

The classic dyad – the relationship between the supplier and the customer

The relationship between the one who sells something, the *supplier*, and the one who buys something, *the customer*, forms the *classic dyad of marketing, a two-party relationship*. It is the parent relationship of marketing.

Customer usually means *external customer*. The notion of the *internal customer* has become widely accepted and is defined as one of the nano relationships (R25). The supplier can be represented by a salesperson. In personal selling there is usually a face-to-face relationship like in a store. It can also be a relationship via telephone, letter, email, the Internet or other media. In individual market relationships a customer interacts with a salesperson or another employee of the selling organization. Market relationships also exist between companies, industries, regions, countries and groups of countries. When the selling situation is more extensive and complex, the selling activity turns into *negotiations*, and especially in B2B these are often handled by a team from either side.

For a long period *caring for existing customers* was second to *attracting new customers*. The salesperson who acquired new customers was considered dynamic, while the guy who 'just' took care of old customers was seen as old and tired and frightened of the new. Today, keeping, caring for and developing existing relationships is more in balance with the need to attract new customers. The strategy is: court your own customers before you start courting somebody else's customers.

The case of Christer is a practical illustration of the implementation of these RM basics.

CASE STUDY   **Christer**

Christer Roth brought the Ulla Winbladh Inn, Stockholm, Sweden, to fame. He was always there and his presence was felt. He kept a close watch on guests and employees and sensed the atmosphere, making sure that everything ran smoothly and that the food was top class. He quickly got to know guests who came back, and he made them feel special. 'You must like your guests', he said. 'If you don't, the job is impossible.' He was not servile, constantly smiling to guests. He could argue with them but he did it in an open and sincere way that created respect. Before joining the restaurant he worked in a rehabilitation centre for drug-addicts. My immediate reaction was that this must have been very different. 'Not really', he said. 'In both cases you have to be interested in your customers and show a genuine concern.' Christer was right – both jobs are in the hospitality business. Commitment and a positive attitude are absolutely essential in business and public service alike and Christer did not make a distinction among production, delivery and marketing; it was all there as part of the restaurant's value proposition. When the Ulla Winbladh Inn was sold in 2006, Christer accepted to help turn a run down restaurant, Josefina, into a popular spot for lunches, dinners and drinks. Although he is approaching retirement, he is equally committed and applies his service formula with great success.

Before we go further I am anxious to establish that RM is applicable to all types of marketing, be it B2B or B2C/C2B. The case of Christer is B2C/C2B if a family has a private dinner in his restaurant but B2B if a company entertains customers there. Retailing has a B2C/C2B relationship downstream but buy its products from upstream B2B, that is from wholesalers, manufacturers or farms. I mention this because I often hear sweeping statements from those in B2B that RM/CRM is 'just consumers'. In the end anyway, B2B merges with B2C/C2B.

A rationale for investing in existing customers is that customers are often the most scarce resource of a business; another is that getting new customers is costly. Consequently, long-term and stable relationships come into focus. Most RM definitions emphasize the establishment, maintenance and sometimes termination of customer relationships. The first stage, to acquire a customer and establish a relationship, is always of importance, but the second stage, to maintain a sustaining business relationship, may be the more demanding part of marketing.

The terms *retention marketing* and *zero defection*[1] emphasize the relationship to existing customers. The latter term is paraphrasing the 'zero defects' quality strategy which says that

---

[1] The term 'zero defection' is taken from Reichheld and Sasser (1990).

a company should continuously improve its quality until it can deliver defect-free goods and services. Zero defection means a defect-free relationship, reducing the loss of customers to zero. This strategy does not imply that customers should be kept at all costs. If a customer has no need for our offering or the customer will remain unprofitable, defection should be encouraged. There should be an ongoing *customer migration*; customers immigrate to us, or emigrate from us to other suppliers or they don't buy any more. This is a freedom factor in a market economy. What the zero defection strategy really says is that customers should not leave because of disinterest from the supplier, late delivery, sloppy service or wrong pricing.

A key question is: To what extent is it profitable to keep a relationship, and when should we accept that a purchase is just an one-shot deal? Among marketers we often hear that it is 5 to 10 times as expensive to make a new customer than to keep an old customer. I do not know how well this is proven, but it has become a buzz axiom.

A salesperson adage says that 'real selling isn't making sales but making customers'. This strategy has been taught at sales courses as a practical experience. It is more uncertain how many understand and live the strategy. Carl Sewell in Dallas, the world's most successful Cadillac dealer, has understood and follows the advice. Long ago he estimated that each customer was worth US $332 000; it must be considerably more today. That was what a Cadillac customer was expected to spend on purchasing and servicing cars during a lifetime. As one strategy to strengthen the relationship, Sewell keeps the auto repair shops open on Saturdays and evenings. He has explained his relationship credo as follows:[2]

- If you're good to your customers, they'll keep coming back because they like you.
- If they like you, they'll spend more money.
- If they spend more money, you want to treat them better.
- If you treat them better, they'll keep coming back and the circle starts again.

It's hard to argue this credo, it's solid common sense.

A major question is whether it is possible to create a relationship if you have thousands or even millions of customers as can be the case, particularly in B2C/C2B. The B2B companies can also have numerous customers but often they have a limited number of key customers to whom they establish a close personal relationship. A smaller operation with regular customers like a restaurant or a store have a limited number of customers, both B2B and B2C/C2B. Christer's restaurants are such a case. With numerous customers, isn't mass marketing through advertising and supermarket distribution the only possibility? In mass marketing, the customer is anonymous. The contact through 'mass communication' is *indirect*, *impersonal* and *one-way*. In fact, it is deceptive to call it communication, which should be a two-way street.[3] At best it is *information*, at worst it is barely *noise*.

---

[2] Sewell (1990, p. xviii).
[3] Edfeldt (1992, p. 100).

In the rationalistic mode of the Western industrialized world, the cost of keeping personal relationships is too high, especially if the value proposition includes a low price or is exposed to fierce price competition. Therefore, relationships are made mechanical, which is possible by means of large-scale mass marketing, supermarkets and self-service. Personal relationships are substituted for packages which carry product and price information, and the consumers themselves fill carts and bags with goods.

The transfer from an individual relationship to a mass relationship offers many intermediary forms. The notion of *customized mass marketing* may appear to be an oxymoron, but is an increasingly viable marketing strategy made possible through modern technology. It can also be implemented in a traditional setting like a store, provided an ability of the supplier to free itself of established tradition and see things through the customer's eyes. Slater Menswear is such a successful case.

CASE STUDY   **Slater Menswear**

Slater Menswear is an example of customized mass marketing. Its first and flagship store in Glasgow, Scotland, is the world's largest men's store and the entrance displays a diploma from the *Guinness Book of Records* to prove it. The store guarantees at least 12 000 suits in stock including well-known fashion brands and a price level 25–40 per cent lower than in the average store. As a customer you are quickly attended to by a sales assistant who is helpful but leaves you alone if you prefer to look around on your own. You can turn to any sales assistant, they do not need to protect you against their colleagues because they are not paid commission. They advise you on colour and fit. Measurements for changes are taken immediately, are offered without extra cost and are ready the next day, or if you are pressed for time, within an hour or less. If you are from overseas, they complete the documents for a sales tax refund and they do it without you even asking for it. Everything is smooth, quick and easy. It is large scale, but the personal service is high. It is difficult to leave Slater without buying. In 2007, Slater had expanded to 23 large stores located throughout the United Kingdom and they keep expanding. Slater locates its stores at shopping centres but off the main street, and the stores are on the first or second floor of the building. There is a modest street-level entrance but no shop-frontage to show their clothes. In this way rental cost are kept to a minimum. According to owner Paul Slater, an additional reason for the low prices is the purchasing and payment policy: 'We buy large amounts from the manufacturers and pay them within 3 to 5 days of delivery, allowing us to pass on discounts to

> our customers. Experience has shown that we are very easy to deal with and we have succeeded in building up very successful relationships with some of the large fashion houses over the years. Slater creates a positive relationship to vendors as they are not spoilt with speedy payment. This in turn makes Slater more competitive to consumers. However, low price is not enough; the staff also quickly establish a relationship with the customer.'

Marketing attempts to create an impression of a personal relationship to customers even if the supplier does not know the customers or even meet them. It is a *pseudo-personal relationship*, but, all the same, it could be an efficient one. There are, however, quality differences in the personal relationships between a family doctor and a patient, or a restaurant keeper and a regular dinner guest, and the relationship between a consumer and a newspaper advertisement or a poster in a train station.

Direct marketing has long worked with personally addressed letters to enhance the impression of a close relationship. Computers can repeat the name of the customer in the text of the letter and the order card. The tone can be personal: 'Dear Mr Smith: You have been selected …' Once this was a sensation, but was frowned upon by many suppliers and advertising agencies. Even if most consumers intellectually understood that the letter was not genuinely personal, the individualized letter increased the response rate dramatically. *Reader's Digest* was a pioneer in this field.

CASE STUDY   ***Reader's Digest*[4]**

> Within the RM spirit, the Reader's Digest Association says that 'Our business is more than publishing or direct marketing – it's about building lasting customer relationships in everything we do'. Although the modern terminology was not invented, the Reader's Digest Association has done RM/CRM since its inception in 1922. The magazine *Reader's Digest* established advanced relationships with its subscribers by building a customer database and using it for direct mail. It was early in deploying new techniques in its large-scale international operation for individualized direct mail. When the company broadened to books and music, its address list – the customer base – became its most valuable asset. The new products were sold to existing magazine subscribers through personally addressed letters. The mailing lists were divided into segments: subscriber, subscriber and buyer of one (two …) books, subscriber and

---

[4] For the history of the *Reader's Digest*, see Heidenry (1993).

buyer of one (two ...) music albums, and other combinations. It turned out that the more products a consumer had bought, the higher the probability that he or she would buy yet another product. The long-term relationship between *Reader's Digest* and the consumer determined future sales. It was clearly established in sophisticated statistical tests that socio-demographic variables for segmentation, such as age, gender and income – which are routinely recommended in marketing textbooks – added no value whatsoever. In 2007, the *Reader's Digest* monthly magazine was printed in 21 languages reaching 85 million readers. Apart from the original magazine, the Reader's Digest Association publishes 25 other magazines and sells 50 million books a year. It is primarily targeted to the specific markets and affinities of food and cooking, health, home, gardening and language learning.

Still, with this kind of rather obtrusive marketing, customers may easily miss that they have ordered ongoing delivery until they cancel, and delivery mistakes are made by the supplier. This leads to irritation and the feeling that the supplier deliberately tries to push something on you. If it leads to complaints the supplier can correct it, but the majority of customers suffer in silence – and may be lost forever.

Not least through websites, mail-order has grown in importance but is increasingly combined with stores and home-parties. L. L. Bean started with boots but now offer clothing, outdoor equipment and 'outdoor discovery schools' including, for example, kayaking, fly fishing and adventurous vacations. Its main store in Freeport, Maine, has been open 24/7 since 1951. It has some 10 stores and factory outlets in the United States and 9 retail stores in Japan. Like Land's End, retailers in clothing, luggage and home furnishing, the customer guarantee is the basis for customer loyalty and retention. Land's End say 'The world is full of guarantees, no two alike. As a rule, the more words they contain, the more their protection is limited.' So they have decided to make it simple: 'Guaranteed. Period.' Compare this to the pages of unintelligible small print that banks, insurance companies, airlines and others throw in the face of the customer! *Direct selling*, such as Avon, Nikken, Oriflame and Tupperware, is also a viable way of marketing certain value propositions. It includes face-to-face interaction through home-parties and visits to consumers, and it further stimulates C2C interaction. In the United States and Western Europe it holds a modest market share but in developing and growing economies it can be a significant supply network, even 20 per cent of retail.

Direct marketing is increasingly using the telephone and media other than mail; that is the reason for changing the name from direct mail. *Telemarketing* has become a major industry. For example, Teleperformance, an international telemarketing service, claims that 70 per cent of marketing and sales communication is handled by telephone, that a telephone contact is 5 to 10 times as efficient as mail contact and is often as effective as a face-to-face visit but costs 5 times less.

CRM has already been defined as a systematic way of applying RM in practice, particularly when it comes to customer relationships. CRM means active work to handle customer relationships on a large scale with long-term profitability and survival in mind. The steps in one-to-one summarize well what it takes:[5]

- *Identify* individual customers and establish how they can be reached.
- *Differentiate* customers by their values and needs.
- Interact with customers, establish a *dialogue.*
- Customize, treat every customer as an *individual* through personal contact or an automated process.
- Make the relationship a continuously *learning relationship.*

There is an addendum: 'These steps are tough.' They may sound simple, even trivial, but they require persistence.

One useful distinction is in operational, collaborative and analytical CRM.[6] *Operational CRM* provides support to sales and customer service in the form of the customer's history with the supplier and customer data. With the large number of contact and call centres today and when the customer is allocated to a different person each time, access to previous contacts is necessary. It does, however, only partially replace the contact needed with the same person, especially if something goes wrong and requires repeated contacts to be fully sorted out, sometimes in a brief but intense period. Then *collaborative CRM* may be necessary, that is, interaction with a customer, through face-to-face contact or phone, email, webpage or text messaging.

Finally, *analytical CRM* refers to a large variety of activities to collect, use and manipulate customer data. The purpose can be a targeted sales campaign for customer acquisition and customer retention but also to try *cross-selling* (get an Amazon book customer interested in buying music) and *up-selling* (get a customer of Toyota Yaris interested in buying the bigger Corolla model).

All this requires computer software. Preferably a company works to integrate a series of specialized systems into a general business system. This may sound rational enough, but data collection, storage and processing are complex operations and data keeps changing. Computer software is therefore not complete; it is only an enabler. The high tech/high touch balance is absolutely urgent. Complex and dynamic marketing does not work by itself through an automated machine. If it did, we would not need to educate marketing people.

---

[5] Rogers, in Newell (2000, p. xiv).
[6] According to the META Group, now part of Gartner; late 1990s.

In the narrow sense of CRM, the supplier only zooms in on the customer relationship and the application of IT. To make CRM a winner, however, two things are needed:

1 To set the customer–supplier relationship in the context of the company's whole network of relationships, such as the relationships to competitors, governments, media and internal customers, that is, both market, mega and nano relationships. If not, the customer–supplier relationships will just hover among the clouds and never touch the ground of reality.
2 To balance IT with human contact. The human aspects have been exemplified here together with IT support and applications. R12, the e-relationship, will further deal with this issue.

The foundation of CRM is the RM philosophy and to develop goals and strategies within its spirit. To execute the strategies, system and IT support are needed. It is tempting to follow the ostrich strategy and put your head in the sand, not face reality and install systems, software and consulting packages, hoping that these will clear up everything.

But this is myopic, naive and costly. New technologies, least of all the Internet, cannot solve any problems automatically. *Problems are solved by people who understand the new, have incentives to implement the new and have resources to do it – and who understand customers.* Only then can the CRM arsenal of techniques and consultants be effective.

When companies have many customers, especially in B2C/C2B but also in many cases of B2B, CRM is dependent on *data warehousing*, a process to search, store and integrate data from all available sources, systems and organizational units. The data warehouse is a more advanced form of database, often supplemented by mini-bases, *data marts*. It is not so easy to execute the RM ideas and integrate everything, particularly not during a pioneering phase. In the era of mass marketing, new sales were often solicited among old and prospective customers in a mess. Large companies had, and most still have, tens, sometimes even hundreds or thousands, of databases without contact between each other. Insurance companies had several databases on the production side (registering policies, invoicing and settling claims) and others on the sales and marketing side (different product lines and different regions). The waste with resources became gargantuan in sales calls, mail and advertising. In the old times, insurance was often sold by part-time agents as an extra source of income. The agents operated in a local market, a part of their home town or in their workplace, and they knew their customers and prospects. Successful agents handled their databases through personal relationships, a box of cards, curiosity, local gossip, daily observations, charm and a nose for business. Good agents saw the use of good customer relationships. That was hCRM, where 'h' stands for human but the agents did not know it in those terms; it was their use of common sense, experience and a desire to add income.

The thought behind *permission marketing* is that customers have scarce time and do not want to be disturbed unnecessarily. Therefore, customers are asked for permission, something that an interactive relationship makes possible. Surely the number of prospects goes down, but each prospect holds a better potential.[7] Permission marketing is preventive and constructive as compared to the negative messages on letterboxes: 'No advertising, thank you!' Or even: 'No junk mail!'

In a technical sense, data warehousing can now integrate information about customers and other stakeholders in our networks of relationships. Data become accessible and can be used in more advanced combinations. If the goldmine of today's economy is a rich database, the gold has to be extracted and refined. This occurs in *data mining*, a systematic process which may use advanced models and techniques. The mining process can be statistical and automated as the computer searches for patterns and pools data on customers and their purchasing behaviour, and develops hypotheses and suggestions for strategies. Data mining offers an opportunity to see structures and links that might be converted into implementable knowledge. With this knowledge, a company can better customize and target its value propositions, boost its competitive power and increase customer retention.

Now that everything can be done by computers, what then is left for the marketer to do? In fact, the most important is still there. Decisions need to be taken on what data to store, how to store it, and what models and software to use, which proposals from the data mining process to execute, and how the outcome shall be monitored. The proposals shall be assessed in relation to business missions, objectives, experience, common sense, intuition, instinct, social and emotional intelligence – all easily concealed behind the facade of IT tinsel. The demands on the person grow as more advanced technology is used.

The new includes *call centres*. They have taken over more of customer service and customer contact, especially in enterprises with many customers in both B2C/C2B and B2B. A call centre is a specialized unit where the employees talk to their customers over the phone or email to provide assistance and information, and handle complaints and suggestions from customers. What's new is the specialized role and that mass customization has been brought one step forward. Although the toll-free 800 number was opened in the United States in 1967 it took until the 1980s for companies to realize its potential for a dialogue with consumers. In most other countries similar telephone services are quite recent.

It is also new that the call centre employee has access to information about the caller on his or her computer screen; that customers – within the spirit of RM – are encouraged to call; that self-service has been made possible through the digital push-button phone; that the telephone system can be optimally utilized through automatic direction of a call to a free line; and that the call centre is not predistined to be in a certain physical location.

---

[7] Godin (1999).

The call centre business is now a major industry comparable in size to many of the pillars of the industrial economy, such as textile or ship-building. Unfortunately, statistics lag behind, still with their feet in the industrial era more than in the value-creating network society.

However, there are snakes in the technological paradise. To make the quality of automatic phone calls and call centres certain, there must be an option to speak to a real person if the customer needs it. For example, when an issue goes beyond the knowledge and power of the employee, the call must be quickly transferred to someone else. It is not satisfactory when companies and governments still today – in the spirit of the Soviet Union commissar – put the caller on hold: 'Right now many people are calling but ...'. It does not help to design a website which is loaded with banners, advertising, peripheral information and on top of this is hard to interpret. There will be growing pressure on call centres and their staff when they come more in use and serve many needs, all the way from standardized matters to advice on how to order on the provider's website, to smooth complaints handling.

In Europe, the leading Norwegian insurance company Storebrand has implemented a comprehensive CRM programme to establish a correct and complete customer database. 'Had we known the hardships we had in front of us we would never have dared to begin', said Alfred Bakken, then senior vice president and in charge of Storebrand's 'dialogue concept'. For an insurance company it is a production necessity to keep records. The novelty is that the database is now actively used for marketing and the maintenance of closer and long-term relationships; marketing and production have entered wedlock. Getting the customer database in order was found to be a mammoth undertaking. Founded in 1767, Storebrand has gone through many passages and changes during its lifespan and been able to adapt. The database contained a high error rate, including people who died long ago. The oldest 'customer' who still received mail died the same year as Napoleon Bonaparte, which was in 1821. Talk about caring for old customers! In 2007, Storebrand can boast record profits and also that during the past 4 years it has won the Norwegian award for 'most satisfied pension fund customers'.

In a market economy, a company must make a profit to survive. An excellent relationship with customers is no goal in itself; productivity in marketing must be kept up. Sales staff and others who negotiate deals must know how to close a deal within a reasonable time and with reasonable prices. The customers must offer a reasonable profit potential. For example, Storebrand found that 100 000 of its customers were not reasonably profitable. Some qualities of the horse salesmen and the poker player are needed, but must be weighed against the ability to cement long term, professional and trusting relationships with customers. Short-term greed is not a viable RM strategy.

Even if they breathe a certain manipulative attitude with affinity to the Duveen legacy, there are classic books that advocate much of what RM stands for – long-term relationships, win–win and personal contact. The number one bestseller in this field is probably Dale Carnegie's *How to Win Friends and Influence People* from 1936. It is reputed to have sold thirty million copies since then. What it says is generic; there has not been any need to revise it except for some references that are not known by today's readers. Heinz Goldman's *How to Win Customers* from 1958 has sold 2.5 million copies. Both books are translated into most languages and are reprinted continuously. The old type salesman followed the same guidelines as CRM but without IT support. Even if selling and sales management have been part of marketing textbooks, they have usually been treated just as a subgroup of the third of the 4Ps: promotion. But there is also literature on consultative selling (the salesperson investigating needs, informing and giving advice rather than trying hard pressure sales techniques), team-selling and negotiation techniques. Although personal selling is important in B2C/C2B its heaviest application is in B2B.

A value proposition is a *promise* from the supplier to the customer.[8] The customer reciprocates by promising to pay. Promises create expectations which must be met for the relationship to be sustained; it is a part of business ethics which makes both parties trust one another. A trusting relationship is rational as it reduces red tape and the risk for litigation. An European businessman, long settled in Japan, has portrayed the Japanese business relationship as follows:[9] 'The Japanese customer demands personal contact with his suppliers. He does not buy on the basis of sales letters, catalogues, brochures and the like. He wants to speak to the seller ... These personal promises must of course later be confirmed in a written document, but this is usually very brief. It is of primary importance that the buyer has contact with one particular person at the selling company, one who feels totally responsible for the contract ... The human being plays the lead role – not long and complicated contracts on paper'.

For small businesses – and most of them do not want to grow – the relationships can be a goal *per se* for the owners. In a study of small hotels in Scotland, it turned out that the 'familial unit' – the nuclear family, relatives, friends, regular customers, employees, suppliers – came first and the hotel second. The same pattern was found among small businesses in a ski resort in Sweden.[10] The network and the interaction was a personal goal, a lifestyle which was beyond financial goals. This attitude and behaviour is poorly considered in economic theory, where the supplier is expected to rationally pursue economic self-interest, usually meaning growth and maximization of net income.

Person-to-person contact with consumers is common, especially when selling expensive and complex products like cars, homes and retirement plans. In small stores, hotels, restaurants and schools, the personal interaction can also be extensive. Sales to households via the telephone or door-to-door has decreased in many countries but is important in others. The milkman is an institution in the United Kingdom; in The Netherlands the retailer brings a whole store in his van. From its start, Electrolux based its success on selling vacuum cleanersdoor-to-door. Their most successful salesman sold 14 000 cleaners during his career.

---

[8] See Calonius (2007).
[9] Delaryd (1989, p. 25).
[10] The study from Scotland is by Lowe (1988); the Swedish study is by von Friedrichs-Grängsjö (2001).

He made an average of 5 per day; 3 is enough to bring the salesperson into the star class.[11] He points to the importance of the minute details in the interaction with the customer:

- You have 20 seconds to develop a positive contact.
- Do not ring one long demanding signal but two short, merry signals.
- Stand back five feet from the door and a little to the side so that the customer must open the door completely.
- Shake hands with the customer to improve contact.

Systematic work with these and other details, together with continuous learning and testing, have a decisive influence in situations where the salesperson must quickly establish a relationship.

The transition from person-to-person contact to person-to-machine contact has reduced the personal relationships in areas where they used to be ubiquitous. Banking is a current example where the dealings with a bank teller are replaced by an automated teller machine (ATM), a telephone or a computer. The social interaction has transformed into e-interaction, which involves a radical shift in the bank–customer relationships (see R5, the service encounter, and R12, the e-relationship).

Production and marketing have moved through several stages during the past century and developed more options:

1 Everything was *customized* in the crafts society, both goods and services. The technical quality of the products was usually high; they were expensive but lasted a long time, sometimes a lifetime. There was no shortage of people to provide household services but it was hard to find good ones. Every customer was a segment of one – it was one-to-one – and marketing was thus individual and personalized.

2 *Mass manufacturing* in the industrial society lowered prices but offered the same product to everyone with ensuing misfit between the product and individual needs. All individuals belonged to the same segment and were exposed to heavy advertising, that is, *impersonal mass marketing of standardized goods*.

3 *Crude segmentation* through the mass marketing of mass manufactured products by means of socio-demographic variables such as age, sex and income, and sometimes previous buyer behaviour, allowed a limited number of product variants.

4 *Refined segmentation* and more subtly defined *niches* of lifestyles and previous buying behaviour catering for specific, individual needs.

5 *Customized mass production* of both goods and services unites large-scale advantages with individual needs. We are not back to square one of the crafts society, but we have

---

[11] From an interview with Ove Sjögren (Ohlson, 1994).

recovered one-to-one treatment. It becomes *surgical marketing*,[12] which requires a diagnosis of the current market and precision in our efforts to reach the right customers with the right offering. *Economies of scale* have also become *economies of scope*.

The circle is closed. The stages take us 'forward to basics', to the individually and community customized offering. We have broadened the scope of options through new production, distribution and promotion techniques. These stages are not mutually exclusive, rather co-existing supplements. We will still need craftspeople, and soda drinks will be produced in mass quantities and be partly mass marketed. But the dominance of the industrial mass manufacturing and mass marketing society is broken.

Identifying marketing's parent relationship is not enough and R1 can be divided into several special types of market relationships. R1 only shows the tip of the iceberg, whereas the 30R approach attempts to show the whole iceberg. Marketing is also dependent on the supporting nano and mega relationships. The following relationships highlight interaction between parties in networks of relationships and different facets of the interaction process.

The classic triad – the drama of the customer–supplier–competitor triangle

A cornerstone of the market economy is the presence of several suppliers in each market. Competition arises, consisting of a triad of players: *the customer, the customer's present supplier* and *competing suppliers*.

The treatment of competition in this section assumes an RM perspective; it is not an orthodox overview. There is extensive literature on competition.[13] At the same time as the interest for RM and collaboration is growing, the interest in competition is growing. The well-established recommendation to create a sustainable competitive advantage through product differentiation, lowest cost or niche marketing is being challenged, and so is market share as a driver of growth and profit.

Marketing warfare was once a recommended strategy and later followed by *hypercompetition* defined as '... a series of actions designed to stun or confuse competitors, disrupting the status quo to create new advantages and erode those of the competitors ...' and '... to harass, paralyze, induce error or block competitors'.[14] Within this spirit a strong player in the market is one with superior ability to manoeuvre in constant turmoil. Mega mergers and mega acquisitions that take place in various industries such as media and financial

---

[12] Frankelius (1997).

[13] Porter (1980, 1985, 1990); Hamel and Prahalad (1994); Hunt and Morgan (1995); Moore (1996); Hunt and Madhavaram (2006).

[14] D'Aveni (1994, p. 34).

service build muscle. Large, global and aggressive companies such as Coca-Cola, Wal-Mart and McDonald's only accept total dominance of markets; all else is failure.[15]

The value of hypercompetition and aggressive market behaviour is rejected by Kim and Mauborgne (2005) in their book *Blue Ocean Strategy*. With one million copies sold in just a few years it shows the same appeal to businesspeople as *Harry Potter* to children. But they do not recommend witchcraft and wizardry. The 'blue ocean' is a metaphor for clean waters and 'untapped market space' which are competitor-free for you to navigate. Instead of going for the 'red oceans' which are crowded with competitors, companies should go for 'value innovation', be entrepreneurs and explore the new. The Body Shop did and explored the blue ocean and opened up the market for 'green' cosmetics.

These ideas are further supported by Simon, Bilstein and Luby[16] who urge companies to learn to compete peacefully: '… business is not warfare. Business and war differ in two critical aspects: first, war always ends, but competition never does; second, there are no customers on a military battlefield … You are trying to attract and keep customers, not capture fugitives or disable opponents'. They are also passionately critical to market share as a goal for businesses. Although RM does not exclude red ocean competition, blue ocean and peaceful values are closer to its heart and closer to corporate social responsibility. It echoes S-D logic and the co-creation of value.

Even in its brief version below, Airbus and Boeing exhibit many of the the complex aspects of competition.

| CASE STUDY | **Airbus versus Boeing, Europe versus America** |

If you want rivalry and drama, you don't need to watch a Shakespeare play. You can follow Airbus, the European manufacturer of passenger aircraft, and its competitor the American Boeing. The business media offer continuous deliveries of new episodes which not even the *Merchant of Venice* can top.

There are innumerable dimensions of the developments of Airbus' new and problem-ridden A380 superjumbo that seats 555 passengers in its standard version – but 853 could be packed in. It flies 14 800 kilometres non-stop. Airbus and Boeing are in tight competition for aircraft orders; each has a market share of close to 50 per cent. During 2004, Airbus had the lead in new orders but Boeing passed Airbus in 2006 and 2007. While Airbus is running at a deficit, Boeing is making a profit. Both have a broad product range and together they can offer aircraft from 100 to over 500 seats. They simultaneously confront each other and

---

[15] Klein (2000); Quinn (2000); and Hertz (2001).
[16] 2006, quotation from p. 27.

try to position themselves as unique with models a bit smaller or a bit bigger than the other. The Airbus A380 is bigger than Boeing's 747 jumbo jet. It is anticipated to reduce sales of the Boeing 747, gaining Airbus a growing market in very large aircraft. Frequent delays in A380 deliveries – several years – have caused irritation among airlines. Media report that 'they have stopped yelling and just sit there and stare, speechless'. It has made many cancel orders and instead consider the refreshed Boeing 747-8. Airbus has also proposed the smaller A350 XWB to compete with the fast-selling and fuel-efficient Boeing 787 Dreamliner. Airbus planes in service are outnumbered by Boeing 4 times. What goes on in the sales negotiations we don't know. But Airbus is owned and manufactured by several EU countries, among them France, Germany, the United Kingdom and Spain. The US administration and EU leaders are in a fight, both sides claiming that the other benefits from illegal subsidies. It is thus not only a market relationship but it has mega overtones and has spawned a political battle between Europe and America. The battle also spills over into the labour market where 50 000 jobs in Germany, France and the United Kingdom are dependent on Airbus success.

In market economies, competition is hailed as the driver of economic evolution and a necessary condition for wealth. This is a traditional view advocated by the business community, and also by governments in countries where deregulation and privatization have become forceful strategies.

However, the 'capitalist' societies are *mixed economies* in which market forces and regulations have entered into wedlock. In totally unregulated markets many destructive forces set in. Only a few may be able to obtain the necessities of life; price competition may become cut-throat with streams of bankruptcies; quality may be impaired and dangerous products will be sold freely; powerful corporations offset competition; and criminal networks flourish. The opposite extreme – total regulation – leads to rigidity but there is no general formula telling us in what proportions freedom and regulation should be mixed. Every market and period have to search for their own specific solution.

Competition is desirable whenever it is efficient, but it is certainly no panacea. Through competition, relationships are formed between customers and many possible suppliers. It gives rise to the types of relationships other than a monopoly (see R10). The customer is given a choice, and a supplier can never be sure to have the customer in its pocket. Nor can a customer be sure to have a supplier in his or her pocket.

In its idealized and theoretical form, the market functions through the 'invisible hand' provided by supply and demand and refereed by competition and price. Every moment millions of purchasing and selling decisions are made, and millions of activities are performed by individuals, and today also by computers. These decisions and activities are accumulated and – according to neoclassical economics – strive in the direction of a *long-term market equilibrium*. In the terms of network theory, the economics view offers a market of a *random network* of events caused by consumers, suppliers, politicians, the media and so on. Marketing on the other hand sees events as *planned networks* involving the visible and active hand of numerous actors with purchasing and selling strategies. In B2C/C2B marketing the net outcome is caused by decisions made by millions of households and competing suppliers. In B2B the numbers are usually lower, sometimes there are even just a few major actors as in the Airbus–Boeing case.

I propose a pendant to market equilibrium from economics, namely *marketing equilibrium*, composed of three forces: *competition*, *collaboration* and *regulations/institutions*. My thesis is that:

> | INSIGHT | The focus on collaboration is the most important contribution from RM, with an impact on both marketing management and economics, and that collaboration in a market economy needs to be treated with the same attention and respect as competition.

But collaboration will not be efficient without the other two forces. In order for regulations, through government resolutions, laws and rules, to operate in practice, institutions are needed. Institutions inform, facilitate execution and check obedience. They can range from very formal institutions like the courts and the tax authorities to religious creed, family values, accepted practice, moral codes, professional ethics, and a shared, tacit understanding of good manners. Although both collaboration and regulations/ institutions are mentioned in the marketing literature, they are not in its core and they are often treated as impediments to competition.

Here is an example of a B2B network organized by competing hotels to support each other and collaborate on the common interest of attracting visitors to their destination, at the same time as they have to heed institutions and regulations.

| CASE STUDY | **The Hotel Group**[17]

In the beginning of the 1990s, the hotel sector in Sweden suffered a reduction in room reservations. The hotels in the town of Östersund were hit hard and the managers of two of the largest hotels decided to start a local hotel network, the Hotel Group. There were 12 hotels and 2 guesthouses in Östersund

---

[17] Based on von Friedrichs Grängsjö and Gummesson (2006).

varying in size from 7 to 177 rooms with 10 different owners, all but one being privately owned, and 7 belonging to chains. All the hotels in town joined the Hotel Group. In addition, the Tourist and Congress Office, operated by the local government, became part of the group. The network has been successful in balancing the interests of its members to jointly market Östersund as a destination, but at the same time keeping individual freedom to compete for guests. The members agree that three basic principles are vital for the network: show enthusiasm, give time and participate actively, and contribute to financing. The outcome was increased reservations of available rooms from 48 per cent in 1996 to 54 per cent in 2001 and 57 per cent in 2002, considerably more than in the rest of Sweden. In 2002, the Hotel Group was awarded the local prize "Businessman of the Year" because of their success in attracting tourists to the destination to the benefit of all local businesses.

Even if RM puts emphasis on collaboration, I would like to see RM as the synthesis between competition, collaboration and regulations/institutions as is shown in Figure 2.1. The issue is which combination of these three forces will best contribute to an optimal and dynamic balance – a marketing equilibrium – in each specific situation?

The global wave of privatization and deregulation is a reaction to markets that have become stifled. The bureaucratic–legal values led to a misguided interference by politicians and an unreal belief in centralized control of society. Inadequate and obsolete formal regulations/institutions were allowed to rule.

Figure 2.1 The three forces of the market economy which together can create marketing equilibrium

Deregulation does not mean abandoning all regulations. It is a search for more adequate laws and institutions which are supportive to constructive forces of society and hold back destructive forces. *In fact, it is not deregulation but re-regulation.* Today this is a global strategy with few exceptions – but it's not easy.

Collaboration, hypercompetition, privatization and re-regulation create new relationships between customers, their current suppliers, competitors and other parts of society. How these relationships should be handled we only know to a limited degree. For example, the deregulation of the financial sector caused chaos in many countries.

The extreme belief in the automatic blessings of competition is just as naive as the dream of the total, planned economy where 'experts' with the 'right' knowledge and armed with regulations and institutions survey a country's economy and through 'facts' and 'analysis' engineer an equilibrium in a completely integrated system. There is no known market that has functioned without regulations and institutions, nor one that functions without competition and collaboration. In the former Soviet Union and its colonies and now in China, the socialist extreme – the total regulation of the market – was replaced by the capitalist extreme – completely free competition. The outcome not only means economic growth and an emerging middle class, but also a widening gap between rich and poor accompanied by chaos, injustice, bribery and violence. 'Good institutions' that support economic activity are required, both the formal ones and those inherent in the informal culture and collective consciousness of a people.

There are necessary elements of the market economy that competition and the free market forces do not master. They can be worded in two paradoxes. The *first paradox* says: *Regulations are needed to secure that free competition will not be curbed.* In spite of all the sweet talk about competition, every individual company or industry prefers to be spared the hazards of competition. But they consider it essential for other companies and industries. The *second paradox* says: *The goal of competition is to get rid of competition.* Being competitive means that a company attempts to reduce the influence of other suppliers through barriers to entry and disruptive hustle and bustle.

Regulations therefore are not the same as restrictions. They can also be dynamic influences by forcing slow companies to take action, for example, to declare the content of their products, and to make environmental considerations. The EU is designing institutions and regulations, among others courts to handle discrimination and contract disputes. It is a formidable task as both differences in national politics, tradition, language, culture, ethics and legal premises are being thrown into a melting pot. Whether a dinosaurian bureaucracy – big, with a small brain and in reality extinct – is being born in the EU 'capital' Brussels, Belgium, or whether the EU is succeeding in constructing institutions that make markets more functional, is yet to be seen.

One of the winners of the 1993 Nobel Prize in the Economic Sciences, Douglass C. North, has studied the significance of institutions and regulations in a market economy. In his Nobel Lecture, North (1993) proposed that the study of economic development 'ignored the incentive structure embodied in institutions [and] it contained two erroneous assumptions: one that institutions do not matter and two that time does not matter'.

North continued: 'Institutions form the incentive structure of the society and are the underlying determinant of economic performance.' Being an economic historian with a longer time perspective than marketers, he claims that it takes 500–600 years to implant a functioning institutional framework in a society; it is the outcome of the collective consciousness of a people. The possibilities of creating 'instant capitalism' are consequently no more than daydreams which many African countries and Russia have verified.

There are signs that the interest in collaboration is gaining ground not only in real business life but also in marketing theory. Alderson[18] long ago complained about the economists' lack of interest in cooperation: 'Cooperation is as prevalent in economic activity as competition. Marketing cries out for a theory of cooperation to match the theory of competition.' Solomon[19] says that 'business life, unlike life in the mythological jungle, is first of all fundamentally cooperative.' According to Mattsson and Lundgren,[20] 'competition and collaboration are not antipodes but two different dimensions, one being a condition for the other'. Brandenburger and Nalebuff (1996) introduced the term 'co-opetition', a combination of co-operation and competition; Doz and Hamel (1998) use the term 'co-option' for turning competitors into allies. Gray points to collaboration as a solution to the multiparty problem and says: 'Despite powerful incentives to collaborate, our capacity to do so is underdeveloped.'[21]

In the same spirit Senge, in his treatise on learning organizations and the need for dialogue, says:[22] 'Interestingly, the practice of dialogue has been preserved in many "primitive" cultures ... but it has been almost completely lost to modern society. Today, the principles and practices of dialogue are being rediscovered and put into a contemporary context.' The word dialogue comes from the Greek and literally means 'thinking together'.

A company's result and behaviour may be more dependent on its partners in long-term relationships than how it is positioned to competitors or mass markets. Viewing the company and its market as part of a network is important in RM and the central issue of many-to-many marketing. Consequently, the classic triad of a buyer, a supplier and a few competitors is naive and too simplistic. An important general conclusion for competition is that *competition occurs between networks of firms rather than between individual firms.*[23]

Neoclassical economics is based on the existence of anonymous mass markets, while in reality these markets are far from anonymous. In B2B each customer and each competitor

---

[18] Alderson (1965, p. 239).
[19] Solomon (1992, p. 26).
[20] Mattsson and Lundgren (1992–1993, p. 9).
[21] Gray (1989, p. 54).
[22] Senge (1990, p. 10).
[23] Thorelli (1986).

are often personally known. This is often true in B2C/C2B as well; for example, a restaurant's relationships to loyal guests illustrated by the Christer case, and the dentists' relationships with their patients. Consumer goods can be bought and sold on a scale ranging from total anonymity to the consumer and the retailer being buddies. Retail outlets may be small and intimate or be huge 'hypermarkets' that resemble the impersonal and standardized assembly line of a factory.

Competition usually refers to rivalry between suppliers. In times of shortage there is also competition between buyers, and buyers have to court sellers by queuing, appealing to personal relationships, exerting pressure and power, or paying under the table. In many countries housing, higher education, legal service, day care and health care are in short supply – and for some strange reason these shortages are accepted as inevitable. In a similar vein, the official institutions of the Soviet Union accepted that soap, bread and cars were scarce commodities. In the former East Germany, the waiting time for the Trabant car was 12 years before the Berlin wall was knocked down. Trabant was obsolete and expensive, was reputed to cause throat and breathing disorders, and had a highly variable manufacturing quality.

If networks of relationships become completely stable over the long term, true competition ceases to exist. A new supplier stands little chance of entering the market; the door is locked.

Nothing of all this is new but it still seems to come as a surprise to marketing theory and it is not acknowledged in economic theory except as an anomaly. Long ago Arndt wrote about locked and domesticated markets: 'To an increasing degree, transactions are occurring in "internal" markets within the framework of long-term relationships, not on an *ad hoc* basis.'[24] Collaboration sometimes knocks out competition, and marketing becomes a political game.[25]

In Japan – where long-term relationships are institutionalized in the culture – it happens that a new supplier gets an order from a customer and the regular supplier may perceive this as a failure in his relationships with the old customer. It is not necessarily a failure, the customer just wants to stimulate competition and make sure the regular supplier stays alert: don't take me for granted! Japanese companies use more than one bank to secure excellence in service and to create an incentive for banks to be continuously interested in their customers.[26]

In quality management, competition is considered through such goals as becoming 'world class' or 'best in class' in order to grow or survive. *Benchmarking* refers to a comparison with the very best – not the average or the mediocre. It requires comparison,

---

[24] Arndt (1979, p. 69).
[25] Arndt (1983); Stern and Reve (1980).
[26] Delaryd (1989, pp. 30 and 98ff).

not only with competitors but also with best practice in whatever company or industry it can be found.

Competitive bidding is demanded by law in certain instances, above all in government purchasing. A purpose of the bidding procedure is to make markets mechanical and impersonal. Tenders must be delivered before a specified hour and competitors are expected to submit their bids independently. This does not always work in practice. The building and construction industry lives with continuous bidding contests. From time to time secret cartels are uncovered where competitors have split the market and design bids to help an elected 'colleague' win a contract. Industrial espionage in order to learn about competitor bids is not uncommon. Bribes exist: pleasure trips; parties with 'hostesses'; help to build a summer house; and lots of other ingenious variants. Even if the intentions and the logic are good, bids are not always rational. They tend to get stuck on price comparisons as price is the easiest variable to measure. A value proposition is a composite service characterized by quality, security, trust, commitment, joint development and flexibility – which are in the core of long-term relationships – but are difficult to pinpoint in simple short-term indicators. For example, customers of the Airbus superjumbo are now left with an unexpected 3 year postponement of deliveries.

At the same time, it is common that a supplier gets a first order in competition and if this order is successful, new orders will follow through negotiations without a bidding procedure. The first order is often not profitable but a precursor to future profits. Competition in its entirely free and price-based version may cause excessive *switching costs* (costs to change to another supplier) as well as excessive *transaction costs* (costs of handling the purchase and the sale).

Blumberg has pointed out that the strength of the market economy – competition and the profit incentive – encourages fraud.[27] It pays to cheat! He calls this *the paradox of the market economy*. Everybody is familiar with this from jobs and private consumption, but it is neglected in marketing theory. The official image is idealized: competition as the driver to create customer satisfaction and in its wake profitability and long-term success. Customers are asked about the quality they get, but their knowledge is limited. In 1271, St Thomas Aquinas stated that it takes great knowledge to assess quality and that most consumers lack this knowledge. This is just as true today, maybe even more true as the complexity of society and its value propositions has grown. A cynic is reputed to have said: 'Customers are not as stupid as you think. They are much more stupid.' Maybe this is not just a cynicism but is sometimes true and is explored by suppliers. For example, prices are sometimes raised before a sale and then reduced – '25 per cent off!' – meaning the same price as before

---

[27] Blumberg's (1989) study is based on 700 essays written by sociology students who had worked in different industries. From their job experience, they have told about systematic methods to swindle their customers.

the raise; some taxi-drivers tamper with meters; and some suppliers exploit customer stress, confusion and helplessness.

Can good customer relationships emerge in spite of such behaviour? Yes, it seems so to a degree as customers, especially consumers, must buy on trust. If consumers believe they have been given the right product and the correct service they feel satisfied. Or they lower their expectations and accept the imperfections of life; they become 'happy slaves'.

Markets show ongoing efforts to find a marketing equilibrium. When companies and whole industries experience restrictions from regulations, they attempt to circumvent them. This may occur legally (but not seldom illegally) by creating new networks through alliances, new technology, or influencing politicians through lobbyists or exerting outright pressure. Competition thus takes new forms and the effects of existing regulations are nullified; re-regulation become imperative, and so forth.

Could it be that hypercompetition is the real driver of the upsurging interest in RM, that there is a need to neutralize the effects of increasingly faster, more fierce and ruthless rivalry and to create one's own blue ocean? If competition becomes hypercompetition, collaboration must become *hypercollaboration*.

The classic network – distribution

Physical distribution is the most obvious network in marketing; it constitutes a classic network. The common designations today are *supply chain, channel management* and *logistics*. In RM, a network view is preferable to sequential and linear thinking that the words chain and channel indicate. In line with RM and many-to-many marketing I will therefore talk about *supply networks*.[28] These distribution networks are numerous, complex and interwoven. Sometimes they are efficient and fast, following the shortest route to market. Sometimes they are slow, inefficient and replete with detours and broken chains. As consumers we are surrounded by them. We are unpaid workers in the distribution networks when we shop for food, walk to the postbox with a letter or drive our car to work.

When traditional marketing literature deals with distribution, its domain is physical distribution of consumer goods, although a major share of distribution concerns industrial goods as part of B2B. But supply networks handle all sorts of service from value propositions other than just physical goods: information, security, people, other living organisms and so on. This is clearly visible in modern retailing. Traditionally, the core mission of retailing is to make goods conveniently available. The Tesco case shows ongoing changes in consumer supply networks.

---

[28] See also Christopher (2004) who approaches distribution from an RM and network perspective; and Skjott-Larsen et al. (2007).

CASE STUDY **Tesco**

Tesco is the third largest grocery retailer in the world and the largest retailer in the United Kingdom. It is a strong and profitable company. It has diversified to discount clothes, consumer electronics, consumer financial service, Internet service, consumer telecom, car fuel, and the housing market. The mix of value propositions cuts across the traditional goods/services divide and established sectors. Through elaborate marketing research, observations by being close to consumers and business acumen, Tesco has made sure it knows what consumers want. It has picked up the ideas of lean production from quality management and extended it to lean consumption. One important source of customer information comes from its Clubcard with 13 million active holders in 2007. The card offers points to its club members and in return Tesco can use customer data to develop its value propositions to consumers. As the examples above tells us the consumer is in focus, not traditions or established business sectors. In this sense it is clearly customer centric. When the Internet became widespread in the 1990s grocery retailers started to offer shopping services; you ordered on the website and got the groceries delivered at your doorstep. Very few of those online services survived more than a year or two. But Tesco did; in 2006 it was the only online grocery retailer in the United Kingdom that made a profit.

Goods distribution channels are well developed in most countries and industries, but there were exceptions. At the time of the dissolution of the Soviet Union, the state was unable to organize the distribution of a loaf of bread. Waiting lines were part of daily life in Moscow and eventually you needed an ID to be allowed to buy bread. It was not the lack of grain that prevented the supply of bread, but the lack of functioning networks and institutions/regulations.

The relationships between the parties in the distribution network vary for many reasons. If a store is part of a chain, the producer often sells to central buyers. The goods are sent to a central warehouse or regional warehouses, or direct to the store. Many stakeholders can influence the deals in the supply network. The goods are bought by a consumers but if a household consists of several individuals, the buyer represents a network organization where family members play different roles in a similar way as in B2B buying (see further R7, the relationship to the customer's customer).

If a few actors in the daily goods distribution are big and powerful, the relationships between the producer and the central buyers may become predominant and the B2B aspect takes over. The producers risk having no relationship with consumers and cannot monitor the changes that take place in attitudes and buying and consumption behaviour. The producers try to compensate for this through market surveys and visits to stores, whereas retailers link consumers to the stores through cards and membership (see R11, the customer as 'member').

Producers can circumvent the traditional wholesaler–retailer networks through telemarketing, mail order, and the opportunities that are increasingly offered by TV, personal computers, modems, the Internet and World Wide Web. Here are some examples:

- By cutting through the established distribution network and sell computers via direct mail, Michael Dell become one of America's richest men and his computer company quickly made the Fortune 500 list. The mainstream idea was that computers were too complex and too costly to sell without face-to-face interaction. But they weren't, neither to consumers not to businesses.
- Companies can set up chains of one-product shops. Factory outlets – each selling their own brand at substantially reduced prices – began to gather in outlet villages during the 1990s. In 1997, the Great Western Designer Outlet Village with some hundred stores was opened in Swindon, UK, including global brands such as Iceberg, Burberry, Gap, Ted Baker and Nike.
- Direct selling, also referred to as multi-level marketing (MLM) or network marketing, is a system for marketing value propositions based on contacts with friends and friends-of-friends. It offers a network of collaborating small firms and individuals who support each other and are in turn served by a supplier. It has been expressed as 'You are in business for yourself, but not by yourself.' Often these firms are operated out of the owner's home at minimal overhead and investment.[29] Tupperware is an example of successful party selling of household goods. Every two and a half seconds a new Tupperware party is set up. You cannot really get closer to your customer. When recruiting new salespeople, Tupperware says: 'More than Just Parties. The location is never a problem. Perhaps you would prefer a demonstration during a lunch hour or after work. Maybe you'd like to invite a few friends for coffee at a nearby restaurant.'

Distribution of goods – things – are a service but so is the distribution of activities – 'services' in conventional statistics. Examples are restaurants, insurance companies, hairdressers, consultants, electric power companies, water suppliers, telecoms and stock exchanges. Important, but often badly managed, is consumer service of repair and maintenance of homes and household equipment.

---

[29] Serious direct selling and MLM should not be mixed up 'pyramid selling'. There a company persuades independent salespeople to buy big parcels of goods which they in turn sell to other distributors who sell to others and so on, in each instance at a cost plus price. They do not build on the existence of a consumer in the end. These pyramids have sometimes just become a gamble with most of its participants as losers.

It is the availability of potential activities for co-creation which makes marketing possible. One example is the infrastructural networks of post offices, postboxes and postal deliveries. Post offices were early global network builders. Through bureaucracy and monopoly, they long lagged in adjusting to contemporary society. Under pressure from deregulation and competition, mail services have undergone changes. Two examples of innovators are FedEx and DHL, both started by students around 1970. FedEx has a hub and spokes system which means that all mail is flown to Memphis, Tennessee, where it is sorted during the night and delivered the next morning. DHL uses Brussels, Belgium, as its main hub in Europe. Both have aircraft of their own, and pick up and deliver with their own vans. The mail is marked with a bar code and can be traced quickly. Time of delivery is guaranteed and ancillary service has been developed.

Distributions of people and information are also services, for example, being able to travel by train but also to call Deutsche Bahn or Amtrak or enter their websites for information on train departure, arrival and fares. The service of a forwarder is to direct physical goods through a transport network. Whereas goods must be lifted and stored, people usually walk themselves or drive their own cars. Consumers are feeders to an institutionalized system, like when they walk endless concourses at airports, carrying heavy luggage. Transportation is seldom associated with do-it-yourself but it may be the largest do-it-yourself system in existence. Destination marketing – including tourism, conventions, business travel, hotels and other facilities – is growing fast. Travelling consists of fragmented components, centred around a transportation technique such as aviation. Gradually, the understanding for more integrated systems has emerged – the seamless service – where the customer is in focus and not the technique or tradition. As Scandinavian Airlines (SAS) advertised: 'We used to fly aircraft. We now fly people.' Packaged vacation tours have assembled the pieces of the trip and the stay in order to make holidays hassle-free.

Different means of transportation are increasingly being perceived as complementary rather than competitive. Fast railroads connect city centres with airports. In Sweden, the domestic and international airline re-designed malfunctioning ground transportation to and from airports, and implemented a functioning system despite the disinterest from local transport companies; the fight for the air passenger at one stage was not in the air but on the ground. The reconstructed Union Station in Washington, DC, which was ready in 1988, is an example of how different transport techniques meet in symbiosis: train, bus, taxi, rental car and closeness to the national airport via the 'metro'. The station is also a service centre with restaurants, shops and movie theatres. I have even participated in a banquet held on the main station floor. Travellers are still inconvenienced by transfers from one means of transportation to another.

Other living organisms are also the object of transportation and quite extensively so. In recent years weird and cruel animal transport has been exposed, that is, large B2B distribution networks from farms to butcheries to consumers. Studs are flown from Ireland to Australia and after completion of their task they fly back; race horses are being transported regularly; hearts and kidneys are transported express to hospitals for transplants, involving several types of vehicles and strict handling procedures. Fresh food such as fish, newly shot deer and moose, flowers and vegetables are distributed locally through personal contacts, but sometimes pass a multitude of actors from where they were caught or grown to towns and cities.

Excellence in after-sales service in B2B is an antecedent to future sales and is often a matter of distribution of people. On the world market, exporting companies often have difficulties in the distribution of service people; keeping them on the spot is often judged to be too costly. To fly out personnel for troubleshooting can work in certain markets but not in others. In Japan, it is considered unsatisfactory; it is too slow and the personal relationships become shallow.[30] IT has partly made travel redundant because for example, software can be repaired or re-designed over the Internet and repair work can be led from a distance.

Distribution of speech and data via electronic media are not part of the distribution systems as they are presented in marketing theory. The e-relationship has many unique properties and is treated as a separate relationship (R12). Physical and electronic distribution supplement each other. By converting physical transportation into electronic transportation, the speed can be accelerated, for example, a letter being replaced by Internet transmission. On the other hand, it will hardly be feasible to dispatch parcels or people unless the IT-based virtual reality and cyberspace machinery can act as a surrogate for actual physical presence.

The concept of *logistics* concerns the flow of goods, all the way from the extraction of raw material, manufacturing of components and assembly, to finished goods made available to the buying organization or household. The goods flow is accompanied by an information flow via documents and computer transmissions. Logistics cuts across functional and hierarchical borders. The idea of logistics is in tune with the efforts to organize along processes instead of functions and thus strive to produce seamless service. The consumers' transport of goods to their homes and their treatment of the goods is also part of the logistics flow. Increasingly, environmental laws require recycling, which is why logistics are stretched even further (see R7 and the case of the dead enduser).

Logistics requires a holistic understanding of a business operation. It is a matter of making processes more effective, so that manufacturing and delivery are performed straighter and faster and on time, keeping costs and capital employed down. The slower the logistic process, the more capital is tied up and the longer the time before the customer pays. Logistics is also a marketing strategy. One strategic decision concerns

---

[30] Delaryd (1989, p. 73ff).

the scope of the suppliers' offerings: Should the supplier offer a complete systems solution or a partial solution, or enter into alliance with other companies who provide elements of the system?

Kiichiro Toyoda, founder of Toyota Motor Company, coined the concept *just-in-time* (JIT) as early as in the 1930s. 'Just' and 'time' are equally important; only what was absolutely necessary should be delivered, and this should be done at the very minute when it was needed.[31] The Toyota factory stops after 30 minutes if scheduled deliveries of components do not arrive. In comparison, the traditional auto factory strategy was to order large quantities of components and store them for several weeks.

Logistics and JIT influence quality, productivity and profitability. They establish regular and close relationships between supplier and customer. They must make plans together and connect their systems into a fluid process which requires investment and continuous maintenance and improvements. It becomes a co-creating partnership, an alliance, rather than a supplier–customer relationship. The earlier strategy for organizational buyers was to use multiple suppliers and to play them against each other and press prices. The trend has gradually turned in the direction of fewer and closer supplier relationships, with less weight on price and competition and more on collaboration. During the 1990s, Sundstrand in Germany, has gone from 550 suppliers to 120 and Ford in the United States from 6000 to 2000. IKEA decided to cut the number of subcontractors in Northern Europe from 400 to 300, demanded cost reductions of 15 per cent from the remaining suppliers, but also offered assistance with the implementation of the reductions. One of the issues was the closing of a central warehouse and introducing JIT deliveries direct from a factory to the furniture stores.

Although JIT is usually discussed for goods delivery, it is equally applicable to service in general. As service is partly co-created and consumed simultaneously, it must be produced when needed. Extreme examples are emergency services performed by the police and paramedics; it's JIT that counts.

Waiting lines have not been particularly investigated in marketing. In its early days FedEx (the overnight package delivery service) noted in advertisements that 'Waiting is frustrating, demoralizing, agonizing, aggravating, annoying, time consuming and incredibly expensive.' Unfortunately it's easy to agree – the claim is equally true today. From a customer point of view, I would like to propose the following definition: *A waiting line is an inventory of customers waiting to be served*. A waiting line contributes no 'value-added', only 'value-reduced'. A delivery system stores capacity to perform service, but the service itself must be delivered JIT. Waiting lines are treated in queue theory but primarily as a short-term optimization and cost issue based on perception of an 'average' customer.

---

[31] Womack, Jones and Roos (1990).

ABB once got famous for its T50 project to reduce cycle time. It is an example of time-based management or speed management. T50 meant reducing cycle times by an average of 50 per cent. Some results: the processing time for an order via telephone or fax was reduced from 3 hours to 2 minutes; an order for an axis to an electric engine that took 4 weeks and cost €200 to process was reduced to 2 days and €30; and a proposal for an electric transformer that required 7 man weeks can now be delivered in 24 hours based on the customer's own design, which required 10 minutes using ABB software.

To have access to a distribution network can be the most critical element of marketing. Distribution networks are often blocked by those who have established themselves in the networks. It may be difficult or costly to set up a new network. Although US companies have a competitive advantage on the Japanese market concerning lifestyle and youth products they have had difficulties in getting into the Japanese distribution. The Japanese 'keiretsus' have made up impermeable business networks, based on regulations, cross ownership between members of the network, and social and personal relationships. Habits change, however. In the wake of globalization, catalogue and Internet sales by Land's End and L. L. Bean direct from the United States have gained market share in Japan. Internet shopping will continue to shake up national, locked distribution networks.

Looking at distribution through the relationship eye-glasses, we see networks of partnerships between manufacturers, intermediaries, customers and others. This requires trust more than power-based control mechanisms, contracts and formal vertical integration. Negotiations between manufacturers and retail chains often have a strong social content, where in the end personal relationships, joy and enthusiasm are crucial ingredients.

Collaboration in distribution networks is a requisite for success:[32] 'Marketing channels cannot function without sustained cooperation in which each party knows what to expect from his opposite number.' An example of this is *efficient consumer response* (ECR). Consumer goods manufacturers enter into partnership with retailers. In collaboration they try to reach consumers with the right product line in order to increase revenue and slash cost. This leads on to *category management*, to handle categories of products linked to specific consumer needs and consumption behaviour. One category could be 'breakfast'. Managing this category means arranging products in a retail outlet around the breakfast need, not around the type of product. The breakfast category can consequently include yoghurt, fruit, jam, bread and cereals. It is an example of going from product centricity to customer centricity and from lean production to lean consumption opening up for a broader consideration of all stakeholders as the concept of balanced centricity postulates.

---

[32] Alderson (1965, pp. 239–258; quotation from p. 239).

By looking at distribution channels and channel management in the light of RM, we are provided with a different focus:

- RM sees distribution as a complex supply network of interactive relationships rather than a sequential chain. Many-to-many marketing further puts emphasis on the network and stakeholder aspect.
- The supply network is part of a value proposition in which goods are just one component. The RM focus should be on the total proposition and the customer's combination of components and interaction with providers and others.

QUESTIONS FOR DISCUSSION

1 Why is it natural to make the relationship between the supplier and customer the first relationship and why is it called 'the parent relationship of marketing'?

2 It is common to say in marketing that better service means higher prices. The case of Slater Menswear revokes this claim. Have you encountered any businesses where price is low and service is great? Or where prices are high and service is lousy?

3 Explain the content of the CRM idea.

4 There is a widespread belief these days that a free market economy is superior to a planned economy. The book says that this is too simplistic and introduces the concept of 'marketing equilibrium'. What does it mean and what is the rationale behind it?

5 What is meant by (a) hypercompetition; (b) the 'blue ocean strategy' versus the 'red ocean strategy', and (c) 'peaceful competition'?

6 Why is 'supply network' suggested as a better term for what is usually called 'distribution system' or 'supply chain'?

7 Are waiting lines necessary or are they just a token of disinterest in customer needs and wants, sloppy management or badly designed systems?

3

Special market relationships

> **INTRODUCTION**
>
> Chapter 2 presented classic marketing issues interpreted through the relationship eyeglasses. This chapter deals with special market relationships. They are all rooted in R1, the parent relationship of marketing. The focus of the relationship eye-glasses allows us to see other aspects of marketing, those which do not stand out well in general marketing management but are of current significance for marketing success (R4–R17).

RELATIONSHIP 4

Relationships via full-time marketers (FTMs) and part-time marketers (PTMs)

Marketing cannot survive in isolation from other functions. This has been pointed out in Chapter 1 and in the treatment of logistics and just-in time (JIT) in R3. Marketing management theory does not specifically address the dependency between functions, although many have over the years pointed to the inadequacy of functional silos. In practice, the marketing function is spread throughout the firm, and the marketing and sales departments may even play a limited role in the total marketing effort. Perhaps there is not even a marketing and sales department. Instead, each and everyone is involved in marketing. This may be perceived as an organizational dilemma, but should be seen as a possibility to enhance marketing resources.

We can identify two types of marketers: *full-time marketers* (FTMs) and *part-time marketers* (PTMs). These are not only found within a company, but also in its environment. They are defined as follows (Figure 3.1):

> **INSIGHT** FTMs are those who are hired for working with marketing and sales tasks. PTMs are all others in the company and those in its environment that influence the company's marketing.

Role as marketer	Resources Internal	External
Full-time marketer (FTM)	Marketing and sales staff	Distributors, advertising agencies, etc.
Part-time marketer (PTM)	All those who are not FTMs	Customers, investors, media, etc.

Figure 3.1 Internal and external FTMs and PTMs

FTMs are found in *the marketing and sales departments* and among *external suppliers of marketing service*. Outsourcing in general has increased and external suppliers are reinforcements to the marketing function. Distributors offer transportation, wholesaling and retailing, all strategic and crucial for success in marketing. The marketing function also engages external professionals such as advertising agencies, market research institutes and Internet consultants (see R29). At the time these suppliers are engaged, they can be viewed as FTMs for their client company.

Salespeople are professional contact people who build relationships; they are FTMs. But they can never make it on their own. *FTMs can often not be at the right place at the right time with the right customer contact and right knowledge, but the PTMs can!* Unsuccessful marketing is not solely the responsibility of the marketing and sales departments, but also of the marketing function as a whole and its lack of integration with other functions.

The distinction between FTMs and PTMs has extensive consequences for the approach to marketing. It makes legitimate and imperative for everyone to influence customer relationships. CRM, by furnishing the organization with more data, easier access and opportunities to combine data, supports not only the FTMs but also facilitates the role of PTMs.

Two cases will be shown, one from manufacturing and one from services. The first concerns the marketing organization of a large manufacturing company which sells primarily to other companies and governments (Figure 3.2).

FTMs are found in the marketing and sales departments and in the group of reinforcing specialists, PTMs, in the other boxes:

- *Management* spends time on designing marketing strategies, negotiating major contracts and entertaining VIP visitors.
- *Product development*, including R&D, design and engineering departments, has to understand the needs of customers, design quality into the specifications and blueprints, and prepare for the user-friendly operation of the finished equipment.
- *Production* influences customer relationships by fulfilling specifications and keeping delivery times. Organizational customers visit plants for inspection to get a first-hand impression of a potential supplier, but also for continuous quality assurance.
- *Purchasing* affects customer relations as the end supplier has the responsibility of equipment sold – irrespective of who manufactured single components – and for outsourced services connected with the product. Even if an independent transport company causes damage to the goods and is formally responsible and the supplier declines responsibility, such incidents will damage customer–supplier relationships.
- *Finance* is often an important – sometimes *the* determining factor in major deals – especially for major customers in strained financial circumstances. Those customers

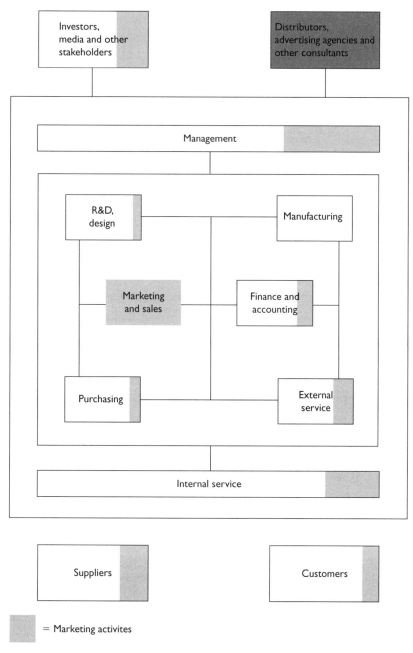

Figure 3.2 Principal components of the marketing function of a manufacturer of industrial equipment

may be forced to buy from a supplier who offers an attractive financial solution rather than looking at the quality of the equipment or services.

■ *External service* is important as facilitator and as augmentation of equipment. It contributes to differentiation and uniqueness, and ultimately competitiveness. There are a large number of services connected with industrial equipment, both *before-sales service* (such as custom design, solutions offered in a tender and demonstration of equipment) and *after-sales service* (such as installation, training and education of customer personnel, operations support, updating of software, emergency support and maintenance), and *general services* such as the telephone exchange.

■ *Internal service* shall be supportive to marketing. It must not be 'administrative routines' or rituals that rigidly adhere to regulations as the bureaucratic–legal values prescribe; it must be sensitive to needs. Internal service consists of secretarial service, computer service, legal service, canteen service, health service and service from the accounting department, such as handling invoices and the salespeople's travel expenses.

These are PTMs *within* the organization. The case also includes several groups of *external PTMs. Customers* may be the most important marketers. They influence the image of the supplier and they can recommend or criticize the supplier. Our *suppliers* have opinions about us and let others know, and so do *investors, media*, and *other stakeholders and opinion leaders*. The advantage of the external PTMs is that they are not on our payroll, but the disadvantage is that we cannot prescribe what they will say about us.

The second case concerns professional services such as management consultants, certified public accountants (CPAs), lawyers and architects. It is common for professionals to see themselves as producers of qualified service, negotiating contracts during a limited part of their time. In small professional firms, partners and senior professionals are PTMs and they often perceive marketing as a nuisance that steals time from 'productive' work. In large professional service firms, there is usually also a specialized marketing and sales department. This department has to include experienced professionals who have a gut feeling for the service delivery process. In order to get leads and introductions to prospective clients and information about competitors, the department has to draw on the skills and contacts of those professionals and assistants who are carrying out assignments and have inside knowledge from the field. As was spelled out in the case of PA Management Consultants in Chapter 1, they have to rely heavily on the professionals creating long-term relationships with clients leading to extended assignments. The marketing and sales departments, if they exist, are populated by FTMs, while other employees are PTMs (Figure 3.3).

Just as in the case of the manufacturing firms, there are external marketers. Present and former clients are instrumental in enhancing or degrading the image of the professional service firm. But above all, *former employees* become influential PTMs. Consultants who take up positions in existing or potential client companies will buy consulting services in the future. It is therefore essential that 'beautiful exits' are offered so that departing consultants are treated well and leave gracefully, keeping a positive relationship with their former employer. Remarkably enough, many consulting firms behave naively from a

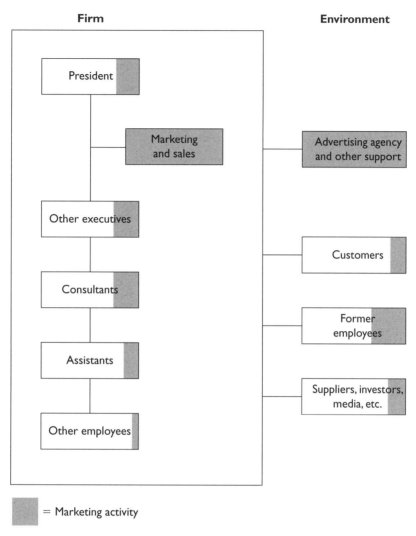

Figure 3.3 FTMs and PTMs in a consulting firm

marketing point of view, and make it difficult for employees to leave or to start their own business. The employer considers the consultants as owned assets and want to be compensated for damages. Other consulting firms see departures as part of their marketing strategy. The management consulting firm McKinsey & Company, located in 51 countries, is such an example. They offer opportunities for consultants both to make a career inside and outside the firm. When consultants leave they are offered membership in an alumni association, in 2007 with 18 000 former consultants, become subscribers of a newsletter and are invited to various events:[1] 'McKinsey keeps in active contact with its alumni.

---

[1] Quoted from a McKinsey recruitment brochure.

Wherever they go, there remains a strong bond between McKinsey and its alumni, with most people maintaining close personal and professional relationships for a lifetime.' It's a dynamic network of lasting benefit. There are consulting firms who get half or more of their assignments from former employees; they have become the most valuable marketers although they are unpaid PTMs.

These were B2B examples but the FTM/PTM distinction is equally applicable in B2C/C2B as the cases of Christer and his restaurants and Slater Menswear have shown.

The PTM concept dissolves the boundaries for marketing responsibilities to embrace not only the marketing and sales departments (and probably never did in successful companies). The job of creating and maintaining market relationships is being shared between the professional FTMs and the ubiquitous 'amateurs', the PTMs. The network of contacts inside the firm, the formal and the informal, the professional and the social, become part of the marketing function.

INSIGHT   Everybody is either an FTM or a PTM. Those employees who do not influence the relationships to customers full-time or part-time, directly or indirectly, are redundant.

RELATIONSHIP 5 — The service encounter – interaction between customers and suppliers

The service encounter – a cornerstone in service management and marketing the way it developed over the past 30 years – used to refer to the meeting between a buyer of services (as distinct from goods) and the service provider. The service-dominant logic (S-D logic) has broadened the service encounter to concern all types of suppliers and all aspects of value propositions. It embraces the customers' contacts with sales staff, but all types of contacts with supplier personnel, equipment and systems during production and delivery and during the customer's future value actualization process. And it acknowledges C2C interaction. To repeat once more: the supplier and the customer co-create value. In B2C/C2B the service encounter can be brief (lunch at a restaurant) or extended (buying and using a car). In B2B it can also be brief and shallow but it is often very close for years or decades. The marketing that takes place during the interaction is often the most important, sometimes the only marketing a supplier does. Although FTMs are in the core of a firm's marketing and sometimes handle most customer contacts, the PTMs sometimes account for the major share of customer contact.

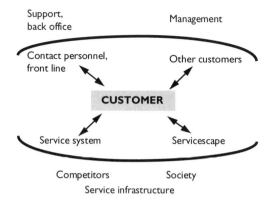

Figure 3.4 The service encounter: the customer perspective. Adapted from Gummesson (1993)

The service encounter is thus central to all types of enterprises, both those who are habitually called manufacturing companies and service companies. ABB, General Electric and IBM are examples of manufacturers who now see themselves as service organizations.

The following interactive relationships can be defined in the service encounter, as seen from a *customer* perspective (Figure 3.4):

■ *Interaction between the supplier's contact personnel (the front line) and the customer*: This can be a traditional contact between a sales representative and a B2B buyer; a contact between a store-keeper, who is both a salesperson and a producer of the goods delivery service, and a consumer; a doctor and a patient, an advertising agency's account manager and a marketing manager; or a firm's engineering department and a buyer of machinery. Only if the customer and the personnel co-operate will the quality of the value proposition be secured.

■ *C2C interaction*: The customers partly produce the service together if the supplier offers the right system, environment and personnel. An obvious example is the dance club. In order for its core service – dancing – to be produced, the guests must dance with each other. The supplier can only make sure that the arena for interaction is inviting. Customers who wait in line or listen to a concert interact and influence the production of service value, including influencing each other's purchasing. When a local or national sports team wins a major championship, streets will be blocked with enthusiastic fans who celebrate the event and this is an essential part of the quality of the event. Unfortunately, sports games attract hooligans and trigger destructive emotions leading to vandalism. A limited group of customers can ruin the quality of the event for all the other customers and some may not come back but watch the TV in the future.

- *Interaction in the servicescape,[2] between the customer and the supplier's products and physical environment*: One example is the supermarket, where the location of the products, the way in which they are exposed, the layout of the store and the convenience of the parking will affect the customer's behaviour and their relationships to the store. The marketing director of a hamburger chain considered the most important people in his marketing function to be six architects. They designed the physical surroundings – the buildings, signs, tables, colours, light – which all add to the relationships with customers in the service factory of the fast-food restaurant. The staff are scarce and the physical environment, the servicescape, becomes a prominent part of the service. Through S-D logic the servicescape takes on a broader meaning and could include a factory in a B2B deal.

- *Interaction between the customer and the supplier's service system*: This interaction between human beings and systems is just as important as between people, for example, between a potential travel and an airline website which offers information but also takes orders for tickets and issues tickets on the customer's printer; between man and banking systems (manual service, cash machine or Internet bank); or a taxpayer and the tax system. The system should be customer friendly and educational in its construction or the customers will perceive the relationship with the supplier as strained. Unfriendly systems scare customers away and even if they do not leave there will be constant hassle and fire-fighting. Through IT, systems takes over from servicescapes.

In the view of Cova,[3] the Northern School (Northern Europe, North America) advocates organized and tightly controlled customer interaction in clearly designed systems and servicescapes. The purpose is 'user value', a no-surprise service that complies with customer expectations. In contrast, the Latin School sees a supplier's service as a carrier of 'linking value', getting people together in communities where they can express individual needs as well as tribal identity, C2C. The supplier, then, should offer 'wilderness servicescapes',[4] which '… reintroduce recesses, corners and curves, fuzziness, enabling people to meet, to get together in a part-open and part-closed space that favours community encounters …' with opportunities for '… micro-events, incidents and happenings …'. The C2C interaction becomes especially pivotal, outweighing much of what is commonly referred to as superior service quality, such as short waiting time and predictable delivery.

Four roles for personnel can be discerned which together shape the marketing, production and delivery system. Considering their role as co-creators, the customers should be

---

[2] A term used by Bitner (1992).
[3] Cova (1997; quotation from p. 663).
[4] According to Price, Arnould and Tierney (1996).

Figure 3.5 The service encounter: the contact person perspective. Adapted from Gummesson (1993)

treated as members of the service-providing organization, as part-time employees. *The contact staff* or *front line* consists of those who have the immediate contact with the customer, salespeople as well as others who produce and deliver service. The *support* or *back-office staff* are found backstage; these employees are not visible to the customer but interact with the front line. Furthermore, there is *management*. By focusing on each of these roles separately it is possible to see the service encounter from different perspectives.[5] The relationships are also influenced by the activities of the *competition* and by *society in general*. For example, and after the infamous September 11 attacks on the World Trade Center in New York and the Pentagon in Washington DC by tighter security controls at airports. The *service infrastructure* includes such things as roads, hospitals and access to news reports. The most recent infrastructural additions are email, the Internet, broadband and mobile telephone systems.

Figure 3.4 showed the customer perspective of the service encounter. In RM, it is vital to see more than a one-party perspective, at least address the two-party issue. Merely calling it 'the supplier' is to vague; suppliers consist of people in different roles with different personalities. We can't chart personalities here but we can identify aspect of their roles. Therefore Figure 3.5 shows the service process from the perspective of the contact person (front line).

Front-line staff are, for instance, exposed to waiting lines and, like the customers, they may experience stress when lines are formed. They may feel that the customer is too slow or asks too much. In the case of turnaround times of an aircraft at an airport, the contact staff—the staff at the gate and the cabin crew—have the job of speeding up embarkation and disembarkation without upsetting the passengers. Slow passengers who block the aisle are irritating and the irritation is reinforced by the fact that on short flights the crew is responsible for embarkation and disembarkation almost every hour during their work day.

---

[5] For a discussion on different perspectives of relationships in a service organization and the roles of the individual, see Gummesson (1993, pp. 94–112). See also the discussion on contextual matrices in the same source (pp. 108–110).

Figure 3.6 The service encounter: the support staff perspective. Adapted from Gummesson (1993)

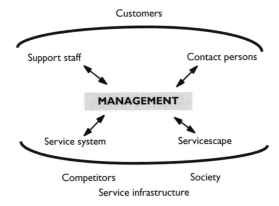

Figure 3.7 The service encounter: the management perspective. Adapted from Gummesson (1993)

The contact staff also form an *internal customer relationship* with support staff (Figure 3.6). Internal relationships are further dealt with in Chapter 5. Support staff at a hospital, for instance, include laboratory staff, medical secretaries, purchasing staff, and cleaning staff. They rarely have direct contact with the customer and are generally behind the line of visibility. Insufficient support from back-office or management will lead to difficulties for contact staff in maintaining quality.

Management, with which the front line staff interacts in different ways, can be found at many levels (Figure 3.7). Management often help to even out the work load and are frequently on the premises, thus meeting contact staff and customers on a continuous basis. One restaurateur may choose to be highly visible to customers – like Christer in Chapter 2 – and establish personal relations with them, whereas another might prefer to remain invisible.

If these roles are strictly assigned to employees and never rotate, a major problem arises. Those who never meet an external customer get no opportunity to confront customer behaviour and needs. This lack of experience makes employees hallucinate and develop phantom images of customers. It does not result in empathy. Technology can change the relationship between the supplier and the customer with ensuing consequences for marketing. Banks have gradually moved their relationship from face-to-face to a *faceless relationship* via cash machines and Internet banking. Instead of going to the bank to pick up cash we go to ATMs. Bank cards connected to a credit or debit system allow you to withdraw money outside the branch office of another bank than the one where your salary is deposited or where you have your mortgage. Therefore, you may not even notice at what bank you are withdrawing your money. Little personal contact will be left with the bank. The only contact person who can charm you or scare you off is represented by a call centre telephone voice, the one that happens to be available when you telephone. This means that if you need to telephone several times to settle an issue you are sent off to different people each time. These people are rarely empowered or enabled to complete more than standardized machine-like tasks. The relationship has become mechanically neutral, even sterile. The service encounter has moved from the bank office – the money retail store – to the street, the telephone, the laptop on your kitchen table, and a standardized 'human' voice. The servicescape has entered a new climate zone.

During service production and delivery, the interaction process offers many touch points which in turn are marketing and sales opportunities – *points-of-marketing*. Good encounters encourage the customer to speak well of the supplier and eventually to become valuable PTMs. These points-of-marketing can occur in all the encounters between the customer and the supplier's organization. A viable strategy is to establish the points which make an impact on the customers' relationship to the company and decide how to best handle them in order to cement the relationships, improve retention and stimulate positive word-of-mouth and referrals.

If the interaction works well, customer perceived quality will increase. The customer's *style of participation* – behaviour, lifestyle and mood – becomes important as customers are co-creators. It is particularly important in *the intensive phase*, which embraces the interaction with the customer during the production of the core service.[6] The supplier's ability to design and produce the service and its production and delivery system is equally crucial. The job of the customer must be deliberately matched with the job of the supplier. This has led to *service design*, manifested in techniques for making drawings and specifications of a service.[7] Considering that every value proposition consists of both things and activities,

---

[6] Participation style and intensive phase are concepts taken from Lehtinen (1985).
[7] See Shostack (1981); and Kingman-Brundage, George and Bowen (1995).

the drawings resemble flow charts over the process during which service is produced and consumed, and the organizational structure and the systems which are engaged in the process. What is new and differentiates the traditional administrative flow chart from the service drawing is the fact that the customer's behaviour and perception provide the vantage point, not the producer's systems and organizational structure. They are a type of lean consumption charts.

The relationships between the consumer and the supplier can be of different character. The following 10 bonds have been found.[8] The first 5 – legal, financial, technological, geographic and time-based – can be controlled by the supplier and it can be difficult for the customer to leave the relationship. If you have your mortgage with one bank, legal and financial dependencies are there, maybe also geographical. The remaining 5 bonds – knowledge-based, social, cultural, ideological and psychological – are primarily tied to the personalities of the consumers and their perceptions of the customer.[9]

I once learnt about the doctor–patient model in which the doctor–patient relationship is '... the voluntary and trusting submission of the patient for treatment, and the essentially prescribing role of the doctor'.[10] The doctor establishes the patient's symptoms and prescribes a therapy and the patient follows the doctor's orders. It is a stereotype interpretation that doctors are know-all experts and patients are ignorant amateurs. It is a highly asymmetrical relationship with all the power on the doctor's side. A close look at the roots of the word 'patient' in an encyclopaedia also uncovers a bundle of obsolete, bureaucratic–legal values. A patient is a miserable creature, passively undergoing treatment, suffering, waiting and not complaining. The reverse is also possible in service encounters if there are, in Lovelock's terminology, 'jaycustomers', those who misbehave and, for example, bully the staff.[11]

These types of relationships do not develop quality in its commonly used sense. Quality is the outcome of interaction between equal parties, where each party contributes with his or her knowledge and activities. The doctor represents a competence for setting a diagnosis and recommending a remedy. The patients should rather be called medical consumers and be treated as co-creators. They have knowledge about themselves and motivation to contribute to the right outcome quality, that is, eventually to become well or at least improve their health. Through googling, chatting and blogging the medical consumer of today can quickly learn about symptoms and their illness, ask questions and get tip-offs from others.

---

[8] Liljander and Strandvik (1995).

[9] Although studies routinely compare differences between male and female views and behaviour, it is only recently that gender differences have entered research in marketing on a relational and more fundamental level. An early study was by Palmer and Bejou (1995) but there are probably more studies now.

[10] Cang (1976, p. 4).

[11] In America, 'jaywalkers ... are people who cross streets at unauthorized places or in a dangerous manner', and 'jay' is slang for stupid; see Lovelock and Wirtz (2007, p. 250).

The Ritz-Carlton hotel chain was one of the first to win the Baldrige Quality Award.[12] Its credo is 'We Are Ladies and Gentlemen, Serving Ladies and Gentlemen.' It proposes that the hotel staff and the guests are equals and both have a role in the service production. This is very different from the roles of master and servant or expert and amateur which still prevail in many encounters, backed by either or both parties.

The intensity of relationships and interaction can vary considerably. The front-line staff who have continuous but brief contacts with customers – the cashier in the supermarket, the receptionist, the waiter, the ticket collector in the cinema – can experience emotional strain. At the Disneyland Paris hotel, New York, I found a poster in my room with Disney's 'Ten Standards of Excellence'. Number 3 reads: 'We smile. It's contagious. Remember: we create happiness and memories'. This seems an excellent strategy, but a demanding one. In all intense or frequent interactions with customers, the strain on personnel is high. The natural smile can lose its warmth and turn into just showing your teeth. Service is often concomitant with emotions, insecurity and severe stress for the customer, for example hospitalization, fear of flying, making certain that the craftspeople do a proper job in repairing your house, and engaging a lawyer in a divorce case.[13] Two Australian resorts can serve as cases of service high up the interaction intensity scale.

| CASE STUDY | **Australian resorts** |

Lizard Island, a reservation in the Great Barrier Reef, has one hotel with 32 rooms. Its strategy is high-quality service and a premium price level. All front-line employees address the guests by name. Meals are served at the tables and the guests take their time; the dinner offers a 5-course menu. The days are filled with sports activities, among them snorkelling, diving and boat excursions. The guests interact both with the staff and with each other, but guests who prefer to be on their own are left alone. Camp Eden – a health spa off the Australian Gold Coast – goes even further up the intensity scale. Thirty guests form a group during one week. They all arrive at the same time and in the welcome speech they are informed that there are two options: 'Either you are here and stick to the programme or you are not here.' Apart from health food and physical exercise there is mandatory training in emotional development and group relations. A guest's interaction with staff and other guests is sometimes so intense that conflicts occur; they may even be evoked as part of the service, and there is no chance for a guest to be left alone.

---

[12] The Malcolm Baldrige National Quality Award is the prestigious US quality prize which has become a role model for quality prizes throughout the world.

[13] Goodwin (1994).

In B2C/C2B service encounters include people with differences in life situation, demands, social status, age, gender, language, and other physical, cultural and social aspects. These are also present in B2B but then in a professional role and therefore B2B service encounters are often very different as will be spelled out in R6 about the many-headed customer and the many-headed supplier.

In brief service encounters the parties have little opportunity to develop empathy. One example of a delicate and often irritating interaction in the service encounter is tipping. Shamir (1984) asks: How does tipping influence the relationship between service personnel and customers? How does a firm, which attempts to standardize its service in large-scale or multiple operations, handle this tacit, uncontrollable and individualized method of payment? Tipping – which is not dealt with in the marketing literature, but has a significant effect on pricing of many service situation – is part of the value proposition. Tipping is the outcome of economic, social and psychological elements in the interaction between supplier and customer. In the 1933 edition of the *Oxford English Dictionary*, a tip is defined as 'a small present of money given to an inferior, especially to a servant or employee of another, for a service rendered or expected'. Note the word 'inferior'! In some countries, tips were the only 'salary' for the staff. They became related to performance; those who did a good job and were pleasant could earn more. Then, in some countries, a certain percentage gratuity was added automatically to the bill; the customer was forced to pay whether the service was excellent or lousy and behave irrationally. It is not clear for the customer what is included in the price of the service and what is extra service. A subculture develops in which the employees, the supplier and a whole industry make customers feel uneasy. For many who travel between countries, tipping is a constant nuisance. You can pay extra everywhere to get rid of the issue and take the cost as a necessary evil, or you can feel a constant irritation and insecurity. In some cultures, tipping has degenerated into organized begging. To me it creates a relationship of disrespect between contact personnel and me as customer. Is tipping just accepted out of tradition and not tried for functionality, a sign of the happy slave syndrome? In Europe tipping is declining but is still expected in parts of the United States. What is its correspondence in international B2B? Bribing? Furthermore, where does tipping end and become bribes in the relationship with government officials? Or with 'facilitators' in major international purchasing? (see R17, the criminal relationship).

INSIGHT Once the service encounter was limited to what is traditionally named 'services' or 'service sector' in official statistics. In this treatise of the service encounter it includes all companies and all value propositions and is thus of general interest to marketing.

The many-headed customer and the many-headed supplier

When we leave the simple dyad, we quickly enter into increasingly more complex networks. In B2B – including marketing via wholesalers and retailers to reach a consumer or citizen – both the customer and the supplier can be many-headed. Companies are made up of individuals, and relationships between companies have to be tied to people in order to become real; the company as such is an abstraction (see Chapter 7). A company does not buy and sell, individuals do. IT offers exceptions and the buying and selling are sometimes delegated to computers; the Procter & Gamble and Wal-Mart examples have already been mentioned. Even so, behind the computers are systems generated and maintained by people.

In more complex B2B deals, it is not a single person selling to a single person. Both the customer and the supplier are many-headed, meaning that one network meets another. This is exactly what many-to-many marketing puts emphasis on. However, this is valid also in B2C/C2B. If, for example, a wife buys groceries for her whole family, she is influenced not only by family members but also by friends, people she admires and so on, thus representing a network. The store is also part of a network of suppliers, employees, other customers and so on. So two networks meet.

We have had many examples with consumers so far, so this one will focus on B2B. Let us start with models of organizational buying behaviour which emerged in the 1960s and 1970s. These models are presented in marketing textbooks and often constitute the ground for the presentation of B2B. The models have obvious merits and contribute to RM. However, additional approaches are needed in order to understand the network in which value propositions are conceived, produced, marketed and bought.

In the network where the many-headed customer and supplier relationships are formed, with people representing a variety of functions and expertise on both sides participate in the marketing and purchasing process (Figure 3.8). In order to find one's way in such a network, guidance is needed by concepts, systematic studies, long-term strategies plus stubborn endurance. Knowledge of the network becomes an asset, an investment in marketing.

The complexity of the network increases if the core of the value proposition is high-tech equipment and if the market is global. In this sense, Ericsson is an obvious case. Its products are telephone systems, switches and cellular telephones. Its largest customers are major telecom operators around the globe. Ericsson has 60 000 employees and many of their key customers are of the same size or often bigger. Both parties are large and powerful organizations. A deal concerning a new telephone system – which often is a matter of several hundred million US dollars – emerges in stages. Several employees are involved both from the supplier and buyer side. The following stages for such relationships have

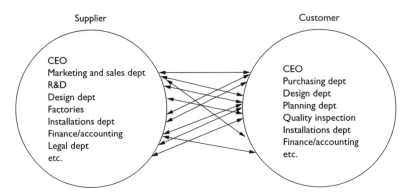

Figure 3.8 Relationships between the many-headed supplier and the many-headed customer

been discerned and the division in stages of the customer–supplier relationship are based on my own studies of Ericsson:

1 *Establishing contact and credibility*: If the customer is new, the supplier must start by establishing an initial contact with the customer and create credibility. The first objective is to be considered for tendering. Professional and personal relationships need to be established with key personnel in the buying organization, usually on several organizational tiers and in different functions.

2 *Competitive bidding*: During this stage the tender is made and presented to the customer. The idea behind tendering is Darwinean: survival of the fittest and may the best man win. As was discussed in R2 on competition, marketing and purchasing are reduced to an allegedly 'objective' and 'unambiguous' presentation of price, technical quality and other clearly measurable requirements which have been specified by the buyer. To advance their competitive position, suppliers circumvent the 'rational' bidding procedure; it simply becomes too burdensome. There can be intermittent contacts for clarification of specifications. Illegal means through facilitating payments may be tried (R17). Mega relationships with lobbying activities can play a role (R19), and so can the formation of alliances (R20).

3 *Evaluation*: Usually the law demands that evaluation of tenders must be made without contact between bidders and buyers. However, efforts to circumvent the rules of the evaluation procedure can initiate further manoeuvring than at the bidding stage.

4 *Contract*: This may be preceded by a 'letter of intent', which is a declaration that the customer is inclined to buy from the supplier. The design of the formal contract may require final negotiations and the complete deal can consist of several subcontracts.

5 *Planning, engineering and market adaptation*: Provided the contract is landed, this stage embraces planning the execution of the contract and fitting the equipment to an individual customer's specific technical requirements. It means an ongoing relationship between Ericsson personnel and customer personnel.

6 *Production*: The relationship continues, partly with other people involved. Quality inspectors from the buyer may show up without appointment to check quality levels, to make certain that delivery dates will be kept, and to prevent problems with potential delays before they become acute.

7 *Delivery and installation*: Deliveries are made during a long period of time, sometimes several years. There is collaboration between the installation team of Ericsson and the customer's employees to make certain that the equipment and systems function according to requirements. Only when an 'acceptance test' has been completed does the customer take over the responsibility.

8 *After sales*: In this stage the supplier must make sure that the customer is satisfied. If not, problems must be cleared up. These can be technical, but can also concern, for example, payment. This stage is an opportunity for further sales. If relationships are successfully cemented, future business will follow. The next contract goes through the same stages as before but often in a much simplified form. The buyer may not ask for bids from others, and the evaluation of the offering from the supplier is negotiated without direct competition, albeit with the threat of potential competition.

9 *Conclusions and evaluation*: It is desirable to reflect over a completed deal and learn for the future, both what was good and bad. Unexpectedly, and almost in shock, Ericsson lost a prestigious deal with the national telecom of Norway. ITT, a then major competitor, won. In retrospect it was clear that Ericsson neglected to establish credibility on the mega level, among politicians and the general public, while ITT devoted considerable resources for this. ITT had hired a public relations firm and one of its tasks was to design the final bid to communicate properly, and not just become a technical document. Ericsson took for granted that its reputation in Norway was superior to that of other suppliers. An analogous pattern of events had occurred in Mexico a couple of years before, but organizational learning had not taken place as the same individuals were not involved in both deals.

During these stages, Ericsson is represented by individual members of management, sales engineers, designers, operations management staff, educators (to train customer employees to use new equipment), financial officers, lawyers and others. Some of these come from corporate headquarters, others from local subsidiaries. On the customer side, relationships are established with individuals from management, technical departments, planners, financial officers, lawyers, installations people and those who receive education from Ericsson. The marketing and the whole production process become a joint project; the parties are producing value together. Both professional and social interaction is essential on these occasions.

Figure 3.9 shows a case of a complex network of relationships where the key players were Atlas Copco, an allied supplier, and a customer in Ecuador. Atlas sells equipment for

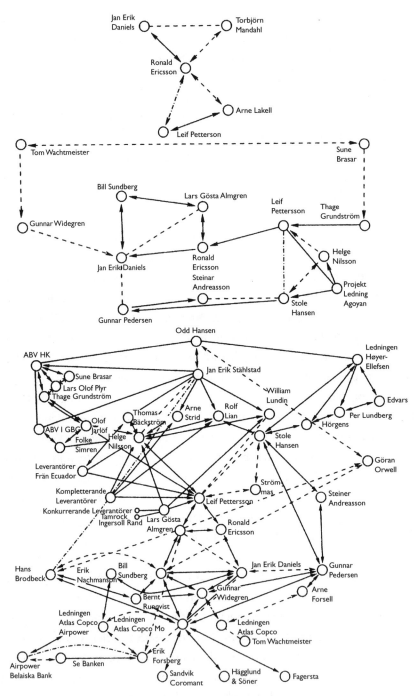

Figure 3.9 Networks of relationships. The figure shows three stages in negotiations between Atlas Copco, an allied partner, and a buyer in Ecuador. The lines denote: ——— regular and active relationships; ---- existing relationship which is irregular and passive; --·--·-- new relationship. Source: Liljegren (1988, pp. 174, 243 and 255). Reproduced with permission of the author

drilling to be used in the construction of, for example, tunnels, and its ally represents the building and construction industry. Liljegren[14] has made a thorough analysis of the relationships and interactions in this deal. He speaks about the complex networks of relationships to the internal organization of the customer as 'customer-in-customer relationship'. Within Atlas, there were 3 units who wanted to deliver the whole or part of the equipment. The allied partner had 3 units that considered themselves in charge of the whole or part of the deal. Some 30 diagrams were used to show how the network of relationships changed during the negotiation process. Figure 3.9 shows 3 of these: an early stage, a middle stage and the final stage.

It is a recurrent problem in sales management how many-headed a relationship should be. The prevailing strategy of reducing the number of suppliers and integrating their activities more closely requires organizational adaptations. The organization on either side must facilitate the processes of a smooth, ongoing partnership.

Key account management (KAM)[15] is a concept to provide just that, as it is specifically geared to the management of relationships with strategic B2B customers. For example, a supplier of mobile phone systems, equipment and handsets serves a handful of big international mobile network operators. In 2007, the 5 biggest were China Mobile, Vodafone, Telefónica, China Unicom and América Móvil, varying in size from 350 million subscribers to 150 million. The supplier had better handle these accounts with care.

KAM raises a series of questions, none of them new or with a simple and general answer. Should a supplier who sells different products use different salespeople for these, even if those employees who do the purchasing in the customer organization are the same? A company may have several different product lines which are somehow related, but which are bought by different people in the customer organization. An insurance company can sell retirement plans, life insurance and fire insurance. Retirement plans and life insurance for employees may be bought by a financial or human resource department or the individual employee, while fire insurance is bought by the property management department. A management consulting company might offer many types of service – company audits, cost reduction, quality management systems, market research, executive search – and the purchases are decentralized to the users. The consultants who sold the first assignment may wish to continue, since they have established relationships and trust. Another individual consultant may consider himself or herself to have excellent contacts in the company through other channels. Selling to a customer's head office may be handled by one of the offices of the consulting company. The sales to a subsidiary in another district could be handled by the first office or by the office where the subsidiary is situated. We are confronting an eternal dilemma: Who 'owns' a relationship?

---

[14] Liljegren (1988, pp. 244 and 250).
[15] McDonald, Millman and Rogers (1997).

R6 shows the necessity to think in terms of networks of relationships in B2B marketing. Up-to-date knowledge of the networks and an ability to interact and manage in these networks become the foundation for marketing strategy.

 ## The relationship to the customer's customer

In B2B, customers are using received deliveries as input to deliveries to their customers. It can be the same product, which is sold onward, or a delivery that goes into further manufacturing or assembly; it can be equipment or service such as office supplies or security.

Every supplier has a relationship to the customer's customer. It is there even if it is indirect and not recognized. Many products pass through several stages before they reach the user. The stages can represent different companies, more or less related to each other. Iron ore becomes steel and then sheet steel, which becomes components which are assembled into a car which is then sold to a consumer. In between, there can be different types of distributors. This creates a dilemma: Who is the customer and whose needs and specifications should be satisfied?

The dilemma has been expressed in the following way: 'It is also possible that the properties sought by the customer may not be the same, or may even be at odds with those properties required by the user further downstream. In this respect the injunction to match the product not only to the needs of the immediate client, but also to those of the user further downstream is worth recording even if this is difficult to achieve in practice.'[16] Sometimes a new product may be neutral to the intermediary, but of special value to the user. Should a supplier then turn directly to the user? This may seem rational but at the same time it means a disturbance in the relationships to the middlemen, who feel that their positions are threatened. The intermediaries in turn may protect their business by withholding information and blocking personal contact between the manufacturer and the user. If the trade is international the distance grows not only physically but also culturally through, for example, differences in language and legislation.

The suppliers can choose their mission to be 'helping customers to do business with their customers'. They must then understand the customer's customer. They must understand that if a delivery does not arrive on time, the workers and the machines in the customer's factory will be idle, and the customer's customer is put in the same predicament. Chain reactions occur which may not be obvious to the first supplier in the chain. This was pointed out in R3 in connection with physical distribution, logistics and JIT.

---

[16] Quotation from Smith and Laage-Hellman (1992, p. 47).

Even if Ericsson delivers systems to telecom operating companies it should understand how telephone subscribers think and feel. The question is what type of relationship they should establish with their customer's customer. Ericsson's long-time strategy was not to interfere with the subscribers' behaviour or problems for fear of disturbing the relationship to the telecoms. Unfortunately, most of these were state monopolies, and several of them did not feel they should put the subscriber, above all not the household or the small firm, in focus. With deregulation and new technology, smaller and more customer-centric telecom operators have emerged. The cellphone has opened up a new relationship to consumers. With its roots in B2C/C2B, Nokia had experience of televisions sets, toilet paper and rubber boots, an experience which Ericsson lacked. Sony Ericsson, the joint venture on the mobile side, needs to understand how the phone itself is used as a lifestyle product where design and a stream of new features are far more important in some age niches than the basic telephone function. Even though both Ericsson and Nokia market mobile phones to consumers this is primarily done through a network of independent retailers. The daily contact with users is therefore not a natural part of their day (see further R8 on the close versus the distant relationship).

The importance of understanding the customer's customer is also imperative when it comes to consumer goods and retailing. A brewery uses the distinction between customers (wholesalers, retailers and restaurants) and consumers (the beer drinkers). In retail chains, the central buyers for these chains have been endowed with power over the manufacturers. They are intermediaries between manufacturers and consumers, and they are closer to the consumers than the manufacturer is. The manufacturer risks not knowing enough about consumer needs and behaviour and how these change. They lose the opportunity for consumer interaction. To mitigate the power of the intermediaries, manufacturers take marketing action towards consumers by means of image and brand advertising and sales promotion in stores. Their representatives travel to the stores to inform, deliver promotion material, offer samples to consumers, and help to fill shelves even if ordering is increasingly computerized and online.

Efficient consumer response (ECR) has been mentioned as a strategy to create a mutually beneficial partnership between manufacturer and retailer. Manufacturers also do their own consumer research, for example, through consumer panels who meet regularly to discuss tastes, fragrances or new products.

In the previously mentioned study of Atlas Copco,[17] it turned out that changes with the customer's customer influenced the delivery of drilling equipment from Atlas to the construction and building industry. Atlas' customers had local and regional governments as well as factories and estate owners among their customers. Their projects varied over the years from increased production of housing, roads and bridges during the 1970s to

---

[17] Liljegren (1988, pp. 399–401).

more individual homes and large international projects at the end of the 1970s, to repair and maintenance during the 1980s. Atlas had to keep track of these changes and if possible predict them. In S-D logic and seen through the eye's of the customer, Atlas delivers value propositions although a central part is heavy equipment.

By viewing the market as a network of relationships in which interaction takes place we get a coherent picture of marketing and how it is interwoven with production and consumption and the whole functioning of society. The next case study shows an example from convenience goods as seen through the many-to-many eyeglasses.

| CASE STUDY | **Products die hard**[18] |

The upper left of Figure 3.10 shows a network of a raw materials producers. A producer sells to manufacturers of convenience goods, and each can be viewed as the hub of its own network. It can be corn which is delivered to a mill to become flour and proceed to a cookie producer. It can be chemicals and other ingredients which are part of the cookies, and packaging material. It's all B2B. But instead of seeing each actor as an isolated node, each specific buyer/ seller is present in a network of relationships to suppliers of material to other products, transportation, computer support, finance, the media and others.

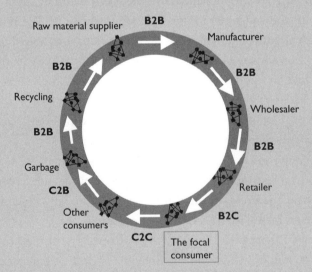

Figure 3.10 The death of the enduser, the endless networks of relationships between suppliers and customers. An example from convenience goods. Source: Gummesson (2008)

---

[18] Adapted from Gummesson (2008a).

Production is followed by a series of B2B relationships in the distribution to wholesalers and retailers. If the goods proceed to retailers, these exist in a context of own networks of relationships, for example, including other suppliers.

The retailer's customers are consumers who buy, pay and consume. It's B2C/C2B. But the focal customer is also part of a network, a household, where we can distinguish the roles of buyer, payer and user.[19] The situation can be further complicated if you look closer at what happens when a household makes decisions and interacts in C2C relationships. We are now gradually leaving the value proposition stage which merges with the value actualization stage. And if everything is working smoothly we go from the lean production in the supplier's value chain to lean consumption in the customer's value chain. Raw ingredients enter into a food preparation process in the consumer's or restaurant's kitchen and are cleansed, cooked and combined with other ingredients; the table has to be laid and later cleared; the leftovers are thrown away or saved; and plates, knives and forks are put in a dishwasher; and finally put back in their cabinets. It is an extensive production, delivery, consumption, and clearance process. It is production by consumers, partly simultaneous with consumption. There are many variants. In the US many families cannot prepare food but pick something out of a can or a bag or put a ready made dish into the micro oven. During the whole process with the meal, there is C2C interaction where the food is assessed through words or behaviour (take more of a dish, take nothing).

The garbage is first sorted in the household, then goes into a B2C/C2B relationship when the consumer throws it into garbage cans, returns it to the retailer and gets a refund, or delivers it at a garbage dump. Then it can move into a new cycle. Durable goods like books might get into the second-hand market, C2C, or sold and bought through an intermediary, an Internet bookstore like Amazon or online auctions at Ebay. And so it goes on and on. There is simply no enduser.

In RM, interaction and dialogue in two-way relationships are emphasized, while in mass marketing relationships are primarily one way. Consumers have an active relationship to suppliers but the degree of co-creation varies. The general notion of the seller being the aggressive party and the buyer, the passive party, is erroneous which is emphasized in S-D logic. Just as often an organizational buyer or consumer is the active and aggressive party;

---

[19] See Sheth and Mittal (2004).

the initiative can go in both directions. Consumers wish to have pleasant relationships to their retailer, gas station, hairdresser and doctor. In times of ample supply of goods, the relationships can be dependent on a store or gas station having a courteous staff, being located in a good spot and having a system that is known by the customer. With doctors it can be different. Through the relationship it becomes easier to get an appointment; the doctor already knows much about the consumer, who can count on being well taken care of. The consumer's behaviour becomes part of the service production and the interaction determines the quality.

The construction of a supply network differentiates one supplier from the other. The power, management and leadership of a network becomes important in marketing as was discussed in R3, the classic network. It can be located with a manufacturer, a wholesaler or a retailer, or any other type of distributor.

Even if you can see the consumer as the terminal link of a chain, there is reason to point to the distribution and logistics relationship in R3 and the green relationship and corporate social responsibility (CSR) in R15 in which the fact is considered that production–consumption are increasingly viewed as an ecological cycle. Then there is no terminal point as the manufacturer or distributor becomes liable for closing the circle and recycling the product.

INSIGHT It is easy to lose sight of the relationships to the customer's customer or not even make an effort to look one step beyond. The relationship is there whether you care to acknowledge it or not. As our customers live by their customers, it is an intelligent marketing strategy to help our customers help satisfy their customers.

 The close versus the distant relationship

Both marketing literature and managers can give the impression that market surveys and research techniques, particularly the use of quantification and statistical formulas, provide first-class knowledge about customers and the effect of marketing activities. Closeness to the customer seems to be of little significance.

In my view it is the other way around: the interaction with customers is the single most important source of marketing knowledge and the cry for more market research is often a sign of failure. Top management and marketing executives may have such limited contact with customers and the front line that they do not understand what is going on in the minds of customers and competitors. They are forced to hire someone to ask their customers for help and to make historical reconstructions. History is reported in seductive multimedia presentations where the design of coloured graphs, animations and music offer an illusion of knowledge. In reality such decision-makers drive into the future with a steady glance in a dimmed rear-view mirror.

This was the dark side of market research. It might have sent shock waves through the minds of some readers. Sometimes market research techniques are required as certain data are difficult to access in the daily operations through presence and interaction. Access to the customer or the data is sometimes both physically and mentally barred. If you need certain quantitative customer data – how much, how many, how often – or macro data, you need systematic and statistical research. Statistical and computerized customer satisfaction surveys have been polished since George Gallup's polls in the 1930s. The early focus on attitudes and opinions has been supplemented by more interest in actual behaviour and the link between satisfaction and profitability.[20] CRM with data warehousing and data mining offers new possibilities to use customer data and statistical connections. Despite these developments, my conclusion is as follows:

> Market research, with the use of 'approved' techniques, is a
> supplement to the knowledge which comes naturally through customer
> relationships, interaction and active reflection but it is not the prime
> source of marketing knowledge.

The basic problem is *access* to customers, competitors and others. The relationship to the customer can be *close* or *distant*. The close relationship is *direct* and *personal*. The distant relationship is *indirect* and *impersonal* with market survey reports as intermediaries (Figure 3.11).

The current trend goes in both directions: increased distance knowledge and increased knowledge through proximity to the customer. This is not an oxymoron. It is simply that the interest in the customer has grown dramatically in marketing practice; in the

Figure 3.11 The physical proximity to the customer versus the distant relationship via market research reports

---

[20] Johnson and Gustafsson (2000).

marketing textbooks it has always been there. This is of course commendable. However, market research and the techniques are often better suited to the mass manufacturing and mass marketing of the industrial era. In current and future society, with more customized production and marketing, mass marketing research techniques – in which individual differences are concealed and evened out – do not play the star part.

In search of access, I have found it essential to discriminate between *understanding at first hand* via personal experience and involvement, and *understanding at second hand* via intermediaries.[21] 'Experiencing customers' – through discussion, observation, participation, working at the front line and continuous reflection – renders deeper understanding than can be reached through research performed, reported and interpreted by others. Mass marketing largely builds on second-hand understanding and recommendations based on the interpretations of intermediaries. This is sometimes advantageous, because an outsider to the firm or the industry may see things in a new light. But it can only be supplementary. Despite the fact that techniques for market research are becoming more sophisticated, for example, in search of the multiple characteristics of lifestyles, it is difficult to present valid and useful studies of consumers and the cause and effect of behaviour. Proximity, the pulse, the richness of variation – it is all degraded to standardized statements and simplistic conclusions. The customer becomes a number, an average, a distribution, a probability, a percentage and sometimes just a couple of decimals. The personal relationship has turned into a *statistical relationship*.

The closeness to the customer deteriorates when a company grows and gets thousands or millions of customers. At least, it may seem so. Small companies can get their knowledge about the customer through close relationships, but only if they are sensitive to the knowledge. This is true for stores as well as hotels and factories. R6 defined relationships between many-headed customers and many-headed suppliers where representatives of both parties can have close contact on several levels and build knowledge about one another. Alliances between suppliers and customers are often formed with the purpose of facilitating knowledge transfer (see R21, the knowledge relationship).

In hotel rooms, we find questionnaires asking guests to assess the hotel and its services. They could have a function, provided that the guests fill them out and the hotel uses the responses. Seldom do these forms tell you more than how much the hotel values your views and nothing about what they intend to do with them. I often make a list of things I am not satisfied with, but I rarely tell the hotel management, especially if it is a large hotel belonging to a global hotel chain. They do not give the impression that they really want to know and the risk of standing out as an odd grumbler holds me back. Despite the physical

---

[21] The concepts access, understanding and pre-understanding are treated in Gummesson (2000, pp. 25–54 and 57–72).

proximity that exists between a hotel guest and the staff, the mental proximity may not be present and the 'communication' is left to a questionnaire.

In 2007, Ingvar Kamprad, the founder and owner of IKEA, had 260 giant furniture stores with 600 million visitors. As long as the stores were few, the management could keep in close touch with customers and personnel. The management of each separate store can uphold this contact, whereas international corporate headquarters in practice cannot. In order to compensate for the relationship difficulty, 'antibureaucracy weeks' were introduced. During these weeks, staff from the corporate head office work in the stores. In an interview, Kamprad said that he does not trust statistics or reports; he wants to be directly confronted with reality. Now in his eighties and one of the richest men in the world, he constantly makes visits to his stores around the world, currently a lot in Russia and China. It is usually quite informal and he mixes with employees and customers, discusses and jokes with them – and sometimes hugs them. In addition, he visits 20 stores a year with his executives, managers and associates, who observe and take notes during the 12 hour tours. He pays attention to detail and gives instructions for improvements. It is hands-on research, and whenever feasible instant implementation.[22]

The old expression 'all business is local' also concerns today's global – or 'glocal' – society. Joshua Tetley & Son in the United Kingdom, now owned by Carlsberg and the world's largest brewer of cask ale, used to control some thousand pubs. In order to strengthen the personal relationship to the consumer, the '100 Club' was established. Eligible for membership were personnel who knew the name and habits of a minimum of 100 guests. A misgiving was expressed that no one would qualify for membership, but the outcome was staggering: 250 employees knew the names of 500 customers or more; 50 could address 1000 customers by name; and the champion could address 2000 customers.[23]

The Italian Benetton family, merchants of clothes and accessories, is best known for casual clothing branded the United Colors of Benetton. In 2007, they had 5000 stores in 120 countries. Its founder, Luciano Benetton, travels to the stores to exercise leadership and collect his own impressions, as do 200 of his staff. Furthermore, the Benetton shops are part of an online computer network, which enables global monitoring of current sales. This is both a close and distant relationship, based on personal contact, utilization of state-of-the-art IT and streamlined logistics. Benetton raised a controversy when they considered using radio frequency identification chips (RFID) on clothes to monitor inventory. The 'spychips' raised issues of privacy and the plan was abandoned. 'How would you like it if, for instance, one day you realized your underwear was reporting on your whereabouts?' California State Senator Debra Bowen asked at a hearing in 2003. How intimate

---

[22] See further Enquist, Edvardsson and Petros Sebhatu (2007, p. 394).
[23] According to Tetley's then Personnel Director, Terry Lunn (1990).

a relationship do customers want with their suppliers? Increasingly, however, RFID, cameras in shopping areas and streets, satellite controlled GPS (global positioning system) for navigation, tracking of mobile phone calls, and other technologies will be used to provide suppliers and governments with behavioural customer and citizen data.

Instead of measuring customer relationships at a distance, a company could engage the customers in interactive improvement and development work. When the Swedish Railroads launched the long-distance rapid train service X2000, the introduction was a 6-month test period and this was explained in the advertising. Business travellers were offered free tickets to make them test the train as an alternative to flying. Personal interviews were made on board the train with a sample of passengers, and questionnaires were distributed to all passengers.

The staff was selected for those with the capacity of listening, observing and suggesting improvements. The train crew convened before departure and after arrival to plan and assess the journey. They also had regular meetings with management. The 'product manager' of this particular train service also travelled on the train several times per week. Taken together, the railway company deployed both the personal face-to-face relationship and systematic, standardized and continuous information as support. Moreover, the interactive research became a way of engaging and influencing the customers – it became an important part of the promotion.

All these sophisticated research techniques, however, are overshadowed by the mindset and attitude of individual employees and the collective consciousness inherent in the corporate culture.

The examples show that it is possible to keep close contact with the front line – both staff and customers – even if the operations are large scale. The real impediment is not size, it is soiled relationship eye-glasses and lack of innovation. Supplementary input from other sources such as the deployment of market research techniques can add to the knowledge.

Social and psychic distance are key concepts in RM. The further we are apart the greater the risk for misunderstandings. This can be particularly disturbing in international trade, where not only physical distance but also culture and language raise obstacles.[24] If customers are kept at arm's length and are only percentages and anonymous masses, you do not apply the same ethical standards as if you are close to the customer. Anthropological studies have given rise to the hypothesis that honesty in exchange relationships is inversely related to the social distance.[25] Studies of fraud show that staff do not feel as much hesitation to cheat an anonymous customer as they would a person they know and meet.

---

[24] Hallén and Widersheim-Paul (1979).
[25] Czepiel (1990).

Blumberg sums up his conclusions in the following way: 'The injury done to others is often impersonal ... People die in automobiles far from those who have designed them. Smokers die quietly far from those who manufacture and advertise cigarettes ... in a large bureaucratic organization people abandon their role as full moral human beings.'[26] Individual consciousness is not the same as collective consciousness.

Management and personnel can hide in large organizations and systems, and rarely have to take direct responsibility for the relationship to the customer. Through size and distance, large scale promotes inferior ethics and inferior relationships. However, the distance can be reduced in many ways and several of the 30Rs concern the reduction of social and mental distances.

| INSIGHT | My conclusion is unequivocal: You can only understand customers by regularly meeting them, training your empathy, and reflecting over your observations. |

The relationship to the dissatisfied customer

According to Hirschman (1970) dissatisfied customers have the following options:

- *Exit*: The customers leave for a competitor, or stop buying the goods or services temporarily or permanently.
- *Voice*: The customers speak their mind and demand correction.
- *Loyalty*: The customers remain loyal for lack of alternative suppliers or prohibitive switching costs, inertia, ideological reasons and others, at least within limits.

All these options are used by customers. The feelings behind them, however, are largely a black box to suppliers. When British Airways commenced a quality improvement programme they were surprised by the reaction from customers: 'Recovery was the term we coined to describe a very frequently repeated concern: if something goes wrong, as it often does, will anybody make a special effort to set it right? Will someone go out of his or her way to make amends to the customer? Does anybody make an effort to offset

---

[26] Blumberg (1989, pp. 106–109).

the negative effects of the screwup? Does anyone even know how to deliver a simple apology?'[27]

Recovery is more than settling a claim, it is the restoration and strengthening of a long-term relationship. The course of action must be constructive, not just mechanical or routine. *Complaint management* has become a discipline of its own. Stauss and Seidel[28] argue that complaint management is the heart of CRM. They list 5 prejudices about complaints:

1 'Our customers are satisfied. The low number of incoming complaints proves it!'
2 'The number of complaints should be minimized!'
3 'Customers who complain are adversaries!'
4 'The majority of customers who complain are either grumblers or grousers!'
5 'Complaints only lead to greater costs!'

The reaction to all of these is of course an emphatical outcry: WRONG! These complaints are the tip of an iceberg, they contain valuable data from customers and they are evidence that a relationship exists to the customer.

In the spirit of quality management, a zero-defects strategy – always doing it right at the first time – should be pursued. Errors will occur despite the strategy. A positive way of dealing with the error must be designed into the customer relationship. In brief: 'Combine ultra-reliability with excellent recovery.'[29] The conclusion builds on research which says that 'reliability' is the central quality dimension – the machine should not break down, the computer should be free of viruses, the train should leave on time, the customer must be able to trust the hotel room reservation.

An often suggested strategy, particularly in the United States and Japan, is 'customer delight', not only meeting customer expectations but giving a little extra. Applied to complaint management it would mean being generous, overcompensating the customer. It is a delicate balancing act between giving just enough and giving too little or too much. To add to the dilemma, customers have individual and changing expectations and demands. A study of Norwegian consumers indicated that it was not necessary to delight customers in order to regain their confidence and loyalty.[30] The requirement was compensation for actual cost, ascertaining that the customer perceived the treatment as fair. The study further showed that single negative experiences – properly settled – did not make customers defect.

---

[27] Albrecht and Zemke (1985, p. 34).
[28] Stauss and Seidel (2004); quotations from pp.18–19.
[29] Berry (1989, p. 27).
[30] Andreassen (1997, pp. 209–213).

Two cases from a study of critical incidents in the relationship between consumers of retail banking may serve as illustrations to alternative treatment of dissatisfaction:[31]

1 A customer wanted to withdraw money from an ATM but only received a fraction of the amount. The customer telephoned the bank who promised to make an instant investigation. Staff were sent to the ATM and they found that banknotes were stuck in the machine. The incident has not impaired the relationship with the bank as the bank took the customer seriously and quickly solved the problem.

2 A man and a woman had standing orders for payments coupled with their accounts. They later opened a new account together and informed the bank that the standing orders now should be charged to their joint account. The woman later received a letter which claimed she had overdrawn on her account and that continued overdrafts would ruin any possibility of future loans. She concluded that the bank had erroneously proceeded to withdraw money from her old account and told the bank so. The bank clerk promised to correct the mistake, but nothing happened. After further contacts with the clerk and with others in the bank no correction was made. The customer lost her trust in the bank and transferred to another bank; she 'didn't want to nag any more'.

In the first case the bank acted correctly although not with any particular generosity. In both cases the banks caused the customer costs, trouble and insecurity, in the second case maybe even sleepless nights and depression. The demonstration of social, mental and physical distance – a tradition of many bank managers and clerks to shield themselves from mismanaged relationships – obstructs the application of RM/CRM. From the bank perspective the customer is a free utility. When banks charge for their service, they should naturally pay 'fees' when they cause customers extra work. The production of bank service is an interaction where the customer does part of the job; with Internet banking all of the job. If the customer has power over the bank by being a major corporation or a wealthy individual, the customer can influence the conditions and 'voice' compensation. In many places the bank culture is so uniformly uncooperative that 'exit' is no actual alternative for consumers or small firms; the grass is not greener elsewhere.

The inability to understand the customers' lack of power in a relationship when a bank has failed, when passengers miss their connection, or when a hospital gives a patient the wrong therapy, is no less than tragic. Most of us have encountered situations of this kind. Why do they arise? I have never been able to grasp why the same mistakes must be repeated over and over again, so that eventually you believe that's the way it must be. Nor have I been able to reconcile with it. Is it incompetence, deficient systems, indifference, lack of empathy, arrogance? Perhaps all of these explanations have validity.

---

[31] From Olsen (1992, p. 369), who reports 272 critical incidents in his study.

Figure 3.12 Alternative relationships to the dissatisfied customer

Usually members of the front-line staff cannot correct mistakes themselves, as these are designed into products, service, systems, organization and resources. Therefore, management should promote both vertical interaction between the layers of the hierarchy and horizontal interaction between departments and functions (see further R25, the internal customer relationship). From the quality awards that have been introduced around the world, it is obvious that quality can never be made certain unless the whole organization is geared towards quality. According to one of the best-known quality crusaders, Edwards Deming (1986), the operating staff can only correct a small percentage of defects; the majority are built into the systems and organizational structure.

In the same way as in R8 – the close versus the distant relationship – dissatisfaction can be handled through direct contact with decision-makers or indirectly through middlemen (Figure 3.12). Companies have established customer service departments and call centres to handle customer relationships, concerning service, information and complaints. The ability of a member of a call centre to relate to dissatisfied customers is strongly dependent not only on personality, but also on the organizational culture. Sometimes call centres are outsourced to telemarketing companies. If their contact staff have been both empowered and enabled to solve complaints when and where they arise, disputes can be settled quickly and smoothly. Unfortunately, at the same customer department you can encounter anything from empathic employees who graciously set things right to hibernating Soviet commissars.

There can be several reasons for establishing call centres.[32] An increasingly more important reason within RM/CRM is to stimulate more customer contact, not least to build individual profiles and learn continuously. Another is to unload people in the organization from continuous disturbances caused by calls, emails or letters from customers. A third is to keep customers at arm's length, a fourth to get away by stalling. At the same time as a call centre is established, a natural access opportunity between customers and managers is abolished. The good intention of proactive complaint management turns into a vicious circle. Customer service staff can experience difficulties with their internal relationships to support staff, such as middle managers. The experience and knowledge that piles up at customer service may never reach the bosses; if customer service employees

---

[32] See also Fornell and Westbrook (1984); and Fornell and Wernerfelt (1988).

become too obtrusive in their efforts to get internal response, they may get into trouble. The messengers of bad news risk getting their career paths blocked.

It is imperative to separate what is right from strictly legal considerations and technicalities, and what is right from a long term and ethical relationship perspective. If a customer has bought machinery and made modifications, which in turn cause disturbances, the supplier is probably not legally responsible to repair the machinery. In Japan and many other countries, the correct relationship strategy is often to offer assistance to the buyer without charge. The production manager who initiated the modifications may be criticized by his superiors. He comes out of this predicament if the supplier takes the blame. As a consequence 'he owes you one', which opens up for future deliveries. It is not a matter of the repair cost; it is a matter of investment in long-term relationships. It is RM investment, not a manufacturing cost.[33]

Being both employees and consumers, many of us have noticed that a customer complaint resolved well creates a solid relationship, sometimes even better than it was before the incident. There are companies that do not take performance too seriously, but are very prone to settle disputes in a generous way. There are even stories about companies which deliberately make mistakes just to be able to show how good they are at correcting them. I am not sure, however, that this is a commendable marketing strategy.

Frequently, the customer does not know whom to talk to. The person who receives the complaint is often badly trained, has low status in the organization and little chance of contacts higher up in the hierarchy. Silly replies and explanations should therefore not in the first place be attributed to front-line staff but to their president and top managers. Furthermore, consumers in many cultures are too timid to ask for recovery. Japanese consumers raise their voices, although politely, and the supplier makes apologies. The important thing is to restore trust, or the Japanese customer will be quick to inform authorities and others.

Consumer activists and vigilante consumers takes personal action against bad products and dangerous value propositions. The two most publicised themes are genetically manipulated food – or GMOs, modified organisms as the industry prefers to call them – and the dangers of radiation from new technologies, above all mobile phones and masts. The activists become lobbyists for consumers, usually without money to run campaigns, and they are up against superrich corporations and professionally trained lobbyists and PR officers. But millions of consumers can vote through their wallet in the stores or voice their discontent in the web. The media reports on both sides but often randomly and with doubtful quality of the reporting (see further R15, the green relationship and CSR; and R23, the media relationship).

---

[33] The Japanese example is taken from Delaryd (1989, p. 69).

In the United States, the consumer can sue companies for damages that are totally out of proportion; this is hardly a reality in other countries (see further R16, the law-based relationship). Apart from directly criminal operations, the worst sinners are found in the government sector. Officials have been able to hide behind locked doors, lawyers and stalling tactics. Whether the situation has improved during the past 20 years is doubtful, despite all the quality programmes, awards and ISO certifications. In a sustaining spirit of bureaucratic–legal values a plethora of government agencies have seen the light, but they are often difficult, sometimes next to impossible, to benefit from, for example for a maltreated patient. Consumer organizations have been established on a voluntary basis to support citizens in distress. It is a bizzare situation where the citizens – who own the state – have to establish their own organs to fight the state. It's a lose–lose situation.

Offering a guarantee is a way of preventing customer dissatisfaction. Richard Chase, professor at the University of Southern California, Los Angeles, introduced a course guarantee. The students who were not satisfied were promised $250 plus reimbursement of course material expenses. How many have evoked the guarantee I don't know but no one did during the first years of its existence.

Warranties for goods have been there a long time, even if they often imply extensive extra work for the customer. The fact that there is a guarantee can exert pressure on a company to do a better job, as evoking the guarantee is an indicator of failure. Unfortunately, it is often inconvenient for customers to use a guarantee. A good guarantee shall fulfil the following requirements:[34]

- be unconditional and free of the fine print in legalese, and not make exceptions for everything of importance;
- in clear and simple terms, state what the customer needs to know;
- focus on customer needs;
- be meaningful both to the customer and the supplier;
- easy to evoke;
- the customer should not have to beg for its implementation.

The customer and the supplier front-line personnel face a particularly loaded moment when a customer is dissatisfied. According to one study, a customer whose complaints have not been solved well will tell 10 to 20 people; one who gets well treated will tell only 5.[35] This shows the merciless revenge that can be taken by dissatisfied customers in their role of PTMs, and the value of the satisfied PTMs. Furthermore, it is claimed that research shows that few consumers raise their voice when dissatisfied. On the other hand, they punish the supplier by exiting, now or later.

---

[34] Based on Heskett, Sasser and Hart (1990, pp. 89–90).
[35] TARP (1986, p. 50).

Initially, the options of exit, voice and loyalty were quoted. In the spirit of RM/CRM I would like to add a fourth option – *collaboration*. The parties solve a problem together – in interaction – with the purpose of co-creating value out of the current situation. It has already been advocated that collaboration is the most significant contribution from RM to general marketing.

The monopoly relationship – the customer or supplier as prisoners

This section is about *monopoly* and how monopoly affects the relationship to customers, suppliers and other interacting parties. Economic theory talks about monopoly when there is only one supplier, and *monopsony* when there is only one customer.[36] The term monopoly will be used here to denote any party who has power over another in a relationship; monopoly is accepted jargon for power and sometimes for power misuse. It is an asymmetrical relationship, where one party has unlimited, or almost unlimited, control over the other party.

But we don't have so many monopolies in today's deregulated and privatized market economy where the buzziest of buzzwords is competition and choice, do we? Let's start with the case of Microsoft.

CASE STUDY   **Microsoft monopoly**

In 2004, EU found Microsoft guilty of abusing the near-monopoly of its Windows PC operating system and it was fined a record €497 million. The European Commission reached a unanimous decision, finding Microsoft in violation of EU competition law. The EU's antitrust authority observed that the illegal behaviour was still ongoing and demanded changes. In 2006, Microsoft was fined a further €280 million for its failure to comply with the antitrust ruling from 2004. It will cost Microsoft a total of €800 million or $1.2 billion. Microsoft was the first company to be punished for not abiding by a European Commission ruling. EU competition commissioner Neelie Kroes said to the

---

[36] Monopoly and monopsony come from the Greek '*monos*' (alone), '*polein*' (sell) and '*opsonein*' (buying food).

media that 'It is now more than two years since the Commission's March 2004 decision that found Microsoft to be in violation of the EU's antitrust rules by abusing its dominant market position. The European Commission cannot allow such illegal conduct to continue indefinitely. No company is above the law'.

The causes for pursuing a monopoly strategy are manifold. A monopoly can be benevolent when for instance the government runs schools to make sure that everybody gets education irrespective of income. It can be predatory when it gets stuck in bureaucratic–legal values and knows that the customer/citizen has no alternative supplier. There can be lack of empathy and a desire of one party to dominate over the other and misuse power, and there can be short-term greed and overpricing.

I would like to introduce the concept of *power organization* or *power network* for a company or public agency that has power, either as a traditional monopoly, or by being in a relationship where the customer or any other party is in practice imprisoned. We are involved in more such monopoly relationships than we are aware of. In several of the 30Rs abuse has been brought to the fore, leading to captivity instead of freedom. Table 3.1 features a sample of these.

A subcontractor can be in the palm of a single customer. The customer demands reports of the subcontractor's costs, and the price is set by the customer. The subcontractor's business becomes customer controlled, most evident in a JIT system. When IKEA demanded

Table 3.1 Examples of power organization effects on relationships

R9	The relationship to the dissatisfied customer	Quality fails and the supplier makes it difficult for the consumer to evoke the warranty.
R11	The customer as 'member'	It can be expensive for the customer to change supplier (high switching cost) through negative pricing (penalty for leaving).
R16	The law-based relationship	Legal technicalities are misused; the power organization dictates 'justice'.
R18	Personal and social networks	Can require unwanted social adaptation, but not being in the network can make business impossible.
R20	Alliances	Alliances can create power industries where every supplier behaves uniformly and no genuine alternative remains for the customers.
R22	Mega alliances	Misgivings that the EU will force small member countries to accept rules and activities that impair their economy.

a price cut from suppliers by 15 per cent, suppliers had two choices: comply and face a challenge, or go bust. Finding a new large customer in a recession is next to impossible, but the demand from the buyer may be an incentive to cut fat out of the organization and its processes. Power can be used constructively for a symbiotic rather than a parasitic relationship. By being dependent on a big and responsible customer, the small supplier enjoys a certain security and stability. A big customer can also be dependent on continuous delivery. If the switching costs are sizeable, a small supplier has power. This is particularly so if the adaptation process has made the companies structurally dependent after having integrated their systems and product or service development, or if the supplier offers a unique strategic component or service.

'Power corrupts; absolute power corrupts absolutely', Lord Acton wrote in a letter in 1887. There may have been rapid development in technology but the development of human behaviour is remarkably slow. Corruption in business is usually associated with *financial corruption*, that those in power are paid unofficially or enjoy freebies. The 'nomenklatura' of former communist countries – the upper class of the classless society – was corrupt in this way and a large number of them survive today in the new economies, retaining similar or even better privileges.

There is also *mental corruption* in which you imprison both others and yourself. Morgan's (1997) metaphor of the company as a psychic prison can be transferred to the customer's and supplier's propensity to handcuff themselves. The American auto industry became inmates of its own escape-proof cells built on its historical record of success. When the small car arrived – first the German Volkswagen and later Japanese cars – the auto industry could not absorb the information or adjust to the new competition. It did not understand the small car concept. It did not want to understand the combination of improved quality and lower price of the Japanese car. When consumerist Ralph Nader suspected General Motors' Chevrolet Corvair to be defectively designed and that this was the cause of hitherto unexplained accidents, the manufacturers did not listen and examine the suspicion. They knew. In industry conventions, the car-makers determined that such accidents were caused by 'driver error', a catch-all concept for unexplained events that was erroneously perceived as an explanation. The design could simply not be deficient.[37]

Government agencies can only plead the prerogative of making authoritarian decisions when such power is called for and adds value to society and its citizens; only then should they be allowed to act as power organizations. Those who travel by air are often imprisoned by airport authorities and sometimes by airlines. An airport authority must have full and undisputed authority in air traffic control. But it should not impose this power on service in general. Authorities too often embrace bureaucratic–legal values which are

[37] Nader (1965).

in direct confrontation with RM. An airline has a certain market share protection through 'slots'; these are the permits to traffic the airport at certain hours. If they have concessions and the attractiveness of the destination is growing – like Brussels because of the EU headquarters – airlines will continue to get more passengers, irrespective of the quality of their service. One reason why the Belgian state-owned airline Sabena collapsed was just this: it was fed passengers with a spoon, despite bad service at Brussles airport and in the air.

If you have installed oil heating in your house, you are forced to buy oil. The installation is so costly that the sacrifice in money, time and trouble provides an insurmountable switching cost. Same thing if you have your mortgage in a bank and a long-term contract, or if you live in a place with no choice of convenience stores. Hotels increasingly include a self-service buffett breakfast in the room price but in some hotels premium prices are asked, the customer has to wait to be seated, wait for service and be expected to enjoy somebody else's idea of a standardized breakfast. The breakfast customer is captive and treated like a prisoner. Remarkably enough a majority of guests succumb to this treatment, probably being under the impression that this is the way it must be.

It is possible to order, for example, theatre tickets by giving your credit card number over the telephone. As no ID and no signature are required, it opens up the possibilities for fraud at the same time as it is convenient for both the theatre and the customer. When credit card companies try to create relationships with customers through the legal system (see also R16) by utilizing force and the customer's lack of power, they become power organizations. They do not constructively exploit the benefits of RM. Such behaviour is not only unethical, it represents a stupid marketing strategy.

Official monopolies are not the same as real monopolies. Nor is the presence of several suppliers a guarantee for absence of power organizations. If all companies in an industry belong to alliances, social networks and trade associations they become power organizations, even if they seem to compete. Together they constitute *power industries*. From the customer's point of view, there is no actual competition when the suppliers are primarily protecting each other. There is no choice, everybody is as good or bad as the other. The relationship between the competitors has then become too collaborative, they have become colleagues instead of rivals. They meet in the industry association to unite against the ugly customers, authorities and other 'threats'.

Many successful upstarts have clashed with the accepted practices of the trade, set up by an established power industry. In its early days, IKEA was perceived as a threat to the traditional furniture stores and as it turned out rightly so. The reaction, however, was less effective. Instead of improving themselves, the members of the industry used the hypercompetition strategy to harass manufacturers and threaten to blacklist them if they delivered to IKEA. Eventually, IKEA had to turn to suppliers behind the Iron Curtain, which proved to be a brilliant strategy that opened up for today's presence in East European market. Finland managed to keep IKEA out for 30 years through the lobbying of the local retailers.

Within some areas of expertise, competition is curbed with reference to 'scientific requirements' and 'scientific evidence'. We can call these *expert monopolies* protected by *expert power*. Within these restrictions, they can do a lot of good in certain areas. It is when they believe that their expertise is the one and only approach, and they begin to fight competition based on rival approaches and new developments, that they become a menace to the free market. Health care is an obvious case. The medical establishment and its perception of what science is puts limitations on the development of medicine. This is sometimes for the benefit of customers and citizens, sometimes not. For example, ordinary patients and practising dentists have observed and suspected that fillings, primarily amalgam based on poisonous mercury, could cause severe disorders. In many countries this was stamped as nonsense by the representatives of dental research and the dental problem became a mental problem; the patients were referred to psychiatrists. The reason is 'lack of scientific evidence', a declaration so devastating that consumers and practising dentists are knocked out. Lack of scientific evidence, however, only means that nothing has been discovered through the application of narrowly delimited experiments and double-blind testing, not that an observation is untrue. More innovative and adequate research techniques could show different results. It may even mean that the results have not been published in a recognised medical journal. Evidence-based medicine is above all adapted to the needs of the pharmaceutical industry to sell more pills. 'Truth' had become the monopoly of a power industry. Until 1997, with reference to 'science' and legal technicalities, a united power industry claimed that cigarette smoking did not cause lung cancer and was not addictive.

When the Consumer Cooperative was founded in 1844 in Rochdale, England, the customer was truly a prisoner. The factory owners ran the stores, set the prices and let the workers buy on credit. As long as the workers were in debt to factory owners, they could not leave their jobs, they were imprisoned. The co-op released the prisoners.

In the cases where a company has a real monopoly, it can disregard customers. Monopolies therefore become complacent, fat and lazy, taking their privileges for granted and getting extremely upset when they are taken away. There can be exceptions, however, provided that customer-oriented values prevail. In some countries – among them Finland, Norway and Sweden – spirits, wine and strong beer are only sold in state-owned monopoly stores. The purpose is to keep excessive drinking down. The Swedish retail monopoly on alcohol has a demanding mission: lower the consumption of alcohol by promoting sounder drinking habits, develop a taste for wine at the expense of hard liquor, and offer an attractive product line in high-quality and high-productivity stores. How much of the alcohol consumption that goes beside the monopoly is difficult to assess; a monopoly is rarely absolute. Buying alcohol in other countries with lower prices or at tax-free stores at airports and on ferries are options for the traveller. Because of the freer regulations prescribed by the EU, European citizens can now privately transfer large quantities across national borders.

If competition grows because of deregulation the monopoly must either adjust or close down its operation. Public agencies that have a monopoly react in different ways, sometimes by adjusting to new conditions, sometimes by demanding more protective legislation.

According to the original bureaucratic–legal values, it is a virtue to be inaccessible. Personal contact is replaced by impersonal 'systems contact'. People should have positions, be easy to substitute, go by the book and handle each case 'objectively'. This, in practice, only works for extremely simple and standardized matters. A more customer-centric approach has been introduced in some niches of the public sector. After having been a dirty word, marketing has gained acceptance, and has in some cases even become a fashionable buzzword. Government organizations and authorities have been forced to obtain revenue from sources other than taxes, which requires marketing. Unfortunately, they often mistake marketing for colourful advertisements, glossy brochures and a fancy logo, and do not introduce a changed mode of operations with the customer and citizen in focus.

Organizations also have *internal monopolies*. Forrester expressed this succinctly more than 30 years ago:[38]

> On a national level monopolies are forbidden because of their
> stultifying influence on economic efficiency. Yet within corporations
> monopolies are often created in the name of presumed efficiency and
> are defended as avoiding duplications efforts. For most activities the
> economies of scale are not as great as commonly supposed … It should
> be a principle … that every type of … service must exist in multiple.
> No person is limited to a single source for his needs. No person is
> dependent on a single user of his output.

A rationale for the decentralized organization is to provide profit centres with the choice between insourcing and outsourcing (see R24, 'market mechanisms are brought inside the company').

In conclusion, a power organization and power industry can lock an economy into a permanent marketing disequilibrium. Sometimes, though, monopolies and unrestricted power are required for security and human reasons. In general, however, the market economy works best when there is an ongoing search to balance competition, collaboration and regulations/institutions.

---

[38] Quoted from Forrester (1993).

The customer as 'member'

If you buy a Harley-Davidson, the king of motorcycles, you become a member of Harley Owners' Group (HOG), with more than a million members in 2007. It is spread around the globe through almost 1200 local chapters. The club offers insurance, emergency assistance, contests, magazines and, most important, the opportunity to make friends and hit the road with other Harley fans.

HOG is an example of a growing marketing strategy: 'membership' for commercial purposes. Membership usually means being a member of an association for idealistic reasons, personal development, sports and leisure activities. *Genuine membership* is non-commercial or commercial in a co-operative sense; it is not there primarily for a profit reason. We are also 'members' of a nation or a mega alliance such as the North American Free Trade Agreement (NAFTA) or EU, but there we are not just customers, we are also *citizens*.

Membership is used commercially to reinforce customer loyalty and to promote long-term relationships. There are combinations of genuine membership and commercial purposes, for example through affinity cards. Affinity credit cards are issued to members and supporters of a special organization and cause, for example, the World Wildlife Fund and the protection of endangered species. They require a relationship between a credit card company, an affinity group that gives the issuer access to their membership list for marketing purposes, and the members. In return the issuer makes payments to the affinity group, the size being dependent on the number of cards issued and the frequency with which they are used.[39]

Club membership can be part of CRM systems, combining customer benefits with data on customers. Tesco does so systematically and have to balance their commercial interests against the customer's interests and need for privacy. They explain it to customers in this way: 'Clubcard is about helping you get more out of your shopping at Tesco, as well as enjoying what our many partners have to offer. It's important to us that you're happy with the service that you receive. That's why, when it comes to your privacy, we created the Tesco Customer Charter to show you exactly what we do with your personal details.'

Membership can be demanding or non-demanding. The customer who wants to visit a 'private' nightclub might be able to enlist at the door, maybe only for a single night. Membership of golf clubs may cost thousands of dollars per year, and there are even exclusive clubs that charge US $100 000 or more. The strategy of subscription is close to membership; you pay as long as you do not cancel your relationship to the telecom

---

[39] See Worthington and Horne (1993).

provider, the *Wall Street Journal* or the bank.[40] If everybody can become members with a simple qualification and the relationship is commercial, it is a *pseudo-membership*, not a genuine membership.[41]

The following way of classifying pseudo-membership has been suggested:[42] *full choice* for the customer (the customer can choose to be in or out, but can use the supplier in either case), *price-driven membership* (offers lower prices), *earned membership* (you must spend a certain amount of money to qualify for benefits) and *access membership* (only members get access to the service). If membership is easy to copy, it loses some or all of its impact on the market. The relationship gets thin with little customer commitment.

The idea behind a co-operative is that the members themselves own and run the operations as an economic and democratic association. The consumer co-operative emerged in the nineteenth century because the retailing, banking and housing industries were mismanaged. In the spirit of the original co-operative idea, the consumers shopped in their own stores and were genuine members. This turned into a pseudo-membership when the co-ops grew in size and members became anonymous and lost their individual influence on the stores. The members became just customers and the strong loyalty advantage, which differentiated co-ops from other stores, was lost.

IKEA with its 260 stores in 45 countries, a growth rate of 20 stores a year, and with 1350 suppliers of 9500 different products, develops and maintains a complex network of relationships. The most intimate relationships between the customers and IKEA are established in the stores, where 600 million visitors encountered individuals among its 120 000 employees in 2007. The relationships must also be kept alive from a distance in between visits. The catalogue is one way; its annual distribution in 2008 approaches 200 million copies in 27 languages and 56 editions. Another is membership in IKEA Family, which gives benefits such as discounts, pre-sale invitations and newsletters. Members account for 60 to 70 per cent of sales and pay 3 times as many visits to the stores than non-members.

'Warehouse clubs' have grown quickly in America. With some variation between the clubs the strategy includes:

- membership fee of US$ 50–100;
- bulk-packaged and marketed primarily to large families and businesses;
- low price and strictly for members;
- low-cost locations but still accessible;
- concentration on the most popular brands;

---

[40] See Lovelock's (1983) classification of 'membership relationship' and 'no formal relationship'.
[41] Björn Lindvall has drawn my attention to the risk of commercializing genuine membership by appointing the members 'customers'.
[42] For an overview see Gruen (2000).

- rapid turnover of goods;
- no advertising;
- other cost saving measures.

Frequent flyer loyalty programmes are the technically most advanced attempts to create long-term individual relationships through membership. The next case explains why.

| CASE STUDY | **Frequent flyer programmes** |

With its AAdvantage, American Airlines pioneered frequent flyer programmes in 1981 and it is still the largest programme in the airline industry. The basic value for the customer is that loyalty is rewarded in a useful way. As member you get points for every mile you travel and can convert these into free tickets. Today it is part of the value proposition of airlines and taken for granted. The airline can increase share of customer, that is, the ratio of a customer's total purchases of a specific service that goes to a specific supplier. It is common for travellers to join several programmes, but the real pros stick to one or two airlines. One of the best relationship strategies has proved to be the upgrading of members to elite status: silver, gold, platinum cards. For each level you can make you get extra benefits, for example, that every mile is counted as two miles, access to special airport lounges and priority in stand-by waiting lines.

The AAdvantage regime quickly spread to other airlines and those who believed it was just another marketing gimmick had eventually to give up. In 2007 there were more than 70 programmes in operation with 100 million members worldwide. Today, no major carrier can exist without a loyalty programme. These were made possible through deregulation of the industry – and IT. It's a CRM system for getting knowledge about passengers, tracking them and rewarding their loyalty. The use of certain data may conflict with laws on privacy. In applying for the Scandinavian Airlines (SAS) EuroBonus membership you have to sign an agreement to the following: 'SAS will register the information you give in this application and use it as a base for marketing communication. SAS will record when you order a ticket. This is necessary in order to calculate the points that give you the EuroBonus benefits.'

Through the alliances in the airline industry, a member of a bonus club can use the benefits of membership in one club on all allied airlines, including earning mileage points. For example, being a member of SAS Eurobonus and SAS being a member of the Star Alliance, I have access to a network of almost 30 airlines including Lufthansa, Singapore Airlines and United. Finnair is part of OneWorld and as a member of the Finnair Plus club, I can benefit from access to American Airlines, British Airways and others.

AAdvantage involved hotels and car-rentals from the beginning, having in mind the customer value chain and desire for lean consumption. If you stay at certain hotels and rent a car from certain firms the expense renders points as well. Airline programmes have also been joined by credit card companies, local florists, supermarket chains and others.

A requisite for success is that a traveller can evoke the benefits and reserve a free ticket without too much hassle. An average of 5 per cent of seats are allocated for free tickets. However, some airlines have made it a strategy to raise obstacles – or perhaps it is just the outcome of sloppy systems. To reserve an earned ticket on KLM, now part of Air France, requires many contacts for the customer with different information given at each contact and a requirement to book – from Europe to America – 11 months ahead! In such cases the free tickets enter the league of dilutes guarantees.

Information about individual customers has been used in the practice of marketing long before the advent of IT, but marketing theory has been pre-occupied with averages and masses. USAA was founded in San Antonio, Texas, in 1922 by a group of US Army officers to self-insure each other when they were unable to secure auto insurance due to the perception that they were a high-risk group. It entered a blue ocean and became quickly successful. It has since broadened its service to people and families that serve or served in the military of the United States and other selected federal agencies. It now offers a full range of property and casualty insurance, banking, life insurance, and investment and financial planning. It became a pioneer of direct marketing and most of its business today is conducted over the Internet or telephone.

For USAA it is advantageous to insure a homogeneous group, characterized by an economy in good order. The company takes service quality seriously, for instance by calling customers after a claim has been processed to make certain that they are satisfied. Its success is reflected in the fact that it is now a Fortune 200 financial service company, and in *Business Week's* 2007 ranking of 'The Customer Service Elite' puts USAA in first place.

There is no doubt that pseudo-membership provides benefits to customers. But it also requires work from the customer. The supplier and the customer are co-creators of a win–win relationship, although the many and sometimes intricate membership regulations can make customers behave irrationally. For example, upgrading on flights has proven attractive for business people. Instead of arriving just before check-in and boarding time, surprisingly many come even 2 hours before to line up for a possible upgrade. The customer may become imprisoned in a rat race for benefits. Furthermore, being a member in too many commercial clubs makes it difficult to keep track of all the cards, codes and offerings.

In summary, membership serves the following purposes for the supplier:

1 It has the potential to increase retention and share of customer.
2 It provides more information about customers, and CRM makes it possible to build a database of any number of customers, thus replacing blunt mass marketing with targeted communication and customized offerings.
3 If the competition offers membership, an individual supplier may have to join in order to stay in the market.

The e-relationship

Electronic relationships or e-relationships embrace relationships, networks and interaction based on IT. Like eCRM, e-relationships have appeared throughout the text, naturally as today they exist in some form in all company, consumer and citizen activities. Under R12, a more comprehensive review will be given, discussing strengths, weaknesses and question marks. R12 is focused on relational issues and does not attempt to give a state-of-the-art or futures account of IT – who can overview that anyway? And even if one could it would soon be obsolete. Even how it affects relationships is difficult as generations of people use it so differently and IT has such different impact on social behaviour.

IT introduces a new infrastructure in our economies and offers new opportunities for marketers. In the United Kingdom in 2006, on average 65 per cent of households owned a home computer and 55 per cent had an Internet connection. In the highest income group these figures were 95 per cent and 93 per cent respectively though in the lowest income group just 29 per cent of households owned a computer and 17 per cent had an Internet connection. Ownership of mobile phones followed a similar pattern. On average, 79 per cent of UK households owned a mobile phone though only 56 per cent of households in the lowest income group reported owning a mobile phone, compared with 92 per cent in the highest income group.

To understand what happens in the value-creating network society requires a great deal of creativity, reflection and experimentation. IT is presented as the saviour, the pill that combines penicillin, Viagra and Prozac, and is prescribed to every company, government, consumer and citizen. The dotcoms were bestowed upon us as the fast lane to wealth in mushrooming stock with the World Wide Web as its vehicle. But the steering system turned out to be defective, at least it was not yet ready.

Whereas the *Harry Potter* stories are sold as fiction, witchcraft and wizardy, the digital events are sold as reality. It is inevitable to be influenced by the sensations offered by corporations and the media; they shape our reality. IT companies, finance institutions, consultants, stockbrokers and the media have self-interest in hyping the information to maximum decibels. The urgency for common sense is nowhere as evident as in IT. There is a Pareto optimality; 10 per cent of what is communicated is useful, 90 per cent is garbage. But the embarrassing question remains: *Which* 10 per cent is of value?

A book on RM can contribute to put the e-relationship into a context and thereby renew marketing theory. Just like in RM, the heart of IT is relationships, networks and interaction. We cannot, however, just hook on to extant marketing management. When introducing websites and CRM systems, a company must convert to a true e-business with strategy, organization and systems which take advantage of the new opportunities and let them loose with full power.

To give context and theory to marketing with IT we should give history a chance without regressing to conservatism and nostalgia. Somebody has said that 'the only thing we learn from history is that we do not learn from history'. We find that IT promises often become reality, but not within the same decade as they are proclaimed. Sometimes the news becomes swiftly obsolete and sometimes there is no need in the market. Next to the industry of politics, no industry litters the road with so many unfulfilled promises as the IT industry. Its value propositions are launched on visions, at worst illusions. Personally I have fallen into many of the IT pits, both as consumer and businessman.

IT offers a complement to other networks – roads, railways, canals, airlines, post, telephony, radio and TV – which have long formed an infrastructure for business and marketing. The networks meant great changes in our ways of communicating and doing business. Some are very old. Printing gave rise to the first mass medium in the fifteenth century.

The predecessors of today's telecom, the telegraph and the telephone, have been there long. Alexander Graham Bell patented the first usable telephone in 1876 and Ericsson has celebrated its 130th anniversary. Electronics and its practical applications have grown with progressive speed during the past 40 years. IBM launched mainframe computers in the 1960s, and Apple Macintosh made the personal computer user friendly in the 1980s. The fax got its breakthrough in the late 1980s. It took over a large part of postal services, but 10 years later it had been marginalized by the Internet, email and mobile telephony.

Today's IT integrates the telecom, computer and media industries, all with different histories and cultures. A new wave in communications and relationship building has seen the light of day. The Internet is an electronic network of relationships, and links market, mega and nano relationships. And it is all growing more mobile. In the West almost everybody has a mobile phone and in countries like China, Pakistan and Peru where few people had access to phones before they went mobile, 50 per cent now have mobile phones and the number grows every minute.

Contrary to the popular talk about faster and faster development and changes, IT is not an instant revolution, it is a slow evolution. Lennstrand puts the philosophical question: 'Why does it move so slowly when it moves fast?' What happened to distance work, e-learning, navigation systems in cars, e-publishing and e-commerce?[43] These questions and their doubts are corroborated by Microsoft's Bill Gates, who has said that companies must view the use of the Internet and the web as long-term investment which demand redefined marketing strategies. The Internet and the web will not reach their full potential until after 10 or 20 years. The profits will not come immediately.

From having primarily offered *information* – an electronic brochure and a billboard – the Internet and its websites have become a *market* where you buy and sell, and an *arena for experiences and social contact*. All three tasks will remain, but they need to mature and develop further. All have a role in RM/CRM.

The traditional physical *marketplace* is being supplemented with the *e-market, the marketspace*. For example, the spot market for oil was once in Rotterdam, the Netherlands. Today it is an e-network, spread around the clock and the globe. It is everywhere, but yet it is nowhere. 'Any time, any place' is becoming a real marketing strategy with the assistance of the e-relationship.[44] Time and space perceptions are invalidated. The customer and supplier scripts are rewritten. Through the Internet, tickets can be ordered and Internet banks can process bills when it suits the customer. Call centres can be physically placed anywhere.

The Internet offers a break for C2C interaction which is not constrained by the physical marketplace or a phone call between two people. It offers enhanced interaction between people with similar interests and lifestyles; you find new friends on the web. Electronics build informal and self-organizing networks, small communities in the large society with little chance for politicians and governments to exert control. Chat groups can exchange views on the quality of suppliers. If you are ill you can seek medical information not only in databases, but also from fellow patients around the world. You can be well equipped before the high touch meeting with a doctor.

There is more high-tech news: *the search agent, the artificial customer*. The machine can function as a proxy for the real customer both within B2C/C2B and B2B, searching for information according to customer profiles and needs, and execute purchases. In many cases B2B has already turned to M2M, machines selling to and buying from machines. The customer gets a butler, available for the ordinary person and not just for the rich and famous. The artificial customer may grow in importance but does not exist in economic theory.[45]

---

[43] Lennstrand (1998/2001).

[44] Davis (1987, pp. 12–89).

[45] Gatarski and Lundkvist (1998); and Gatarski (2001).

Electronics is not just an aid for mass processing, storing and transportation of data. It is a tool for strategic marketing, which is epitomized by eCRM. It creates new markets which are missing among the classic of market types in economics. If the company does not appear in a certain e-network, it is out of the market. If farmers did not appear at the town square – the original physical marketplace – they did not exist in the local networks of those days and could not sell their carrots and eggs. This market, just like that of today's brick-and-mortar grocery store, was physical and tangible. Now there are global market squares where the computer screen is the stand; it has been called click-and-mortar. The e-markets will not replace other markets – there are still local markets at the town square – but the proportions between marketplace and marketspace will change.

Although IT is presented as conveying and processing information in a richer and faster way, it offers primarily *media – conduit – but not better content*. A letter does not improve in content because it is written on a computer or sent via the Internet. On the other hand, there is a link between content and media. Even if we do not entirely subscribe to Marshall McLuhan's famous thesis that 'the medium is the message', the chosen medium influences the receiver's perception of the content. It partly offers a new context. Davenport (1997) speaks of information *ecology* instead of information *technology*. Ecology stresses the social context and relationships. To become meaningful, he states, data need to be converted to relationships. Consequently, e-networks should be designed to manage relationships; only then do they offer meaningful information.

IT is high tech that can, under certain circumstances, be a rational tool to make things quicker, cheaper and simpler. The major contribution, however, is that IT creates blue oceans, new relationships and new roles. IT would not be given a prominent place in RM if it were only a matter of technology and faster data processing. The interactive role of the customer, as well as customer power, grows. But IT is a secondary enabler; the real enabler is the human being. IT offers no markets if there is no one to organize them, and consumers and companies must be connected to the networks to explore their potential. IT must find its place in the daily life of the consumer, not just in the plans of executives. IT supplements our achievements just like the crane spares our backs and the car speeds up transportation. The e-relationships are technically relationships at a distance that sometimes translate into a totally new type of close relationship.

IT has gradually influenced the structures and processes of companies. eCRM can contribute to glue together activities which are taken from different parts of an organization, from different legal units with different owners, and from different geographical locations. IT can mean enhanced ability to act and reduced cost of customer contact. This may only be the overture to a new type of company where the future possibilities of electronics are now being explored: databases with rapid access to customers, rapid networks of communication and standards that allow rapid application of new knowledge.

IT plays a prominent part in CRM, but did so in direct mail and direct marketing as well. CRM is not just the Internet, websites and email, it has a human side too. Today, we talk about electronic CRM, eCRM, and human CRM, hCRM.[46]

A reason why IT forecasts and applications have frequently shot off the target is the inability to combine *high tech* and *high touch*, where high touch represents human contact. I encountered high tech/high touch in Naisbitt's book *Megatrends* as early as 1982. Going back to the book 25 years later, I find that the idea is more alive than ever.[47] High tech/ high touch builds on the need to balance '... the material wonders of technology with the spiritual demands of our human nature' and Naisbitt's conclusion was: 'The more high technology around us, the more the need for human touch.'

The establishment of an accurate and useful database has been made possible through IT. But eCRM takes you nowhere unless you adapt your efforts to RM values and manage them properly. At the Ritz-Carlton hotels, each employee is trained to note a guest's likes and dislikes. The data are entered into a computer database which includes the guest history of Ritz-Carlton's 240 000 repeat customers: credit card number, corporate rates, previous hotel visits, non-smoker, etc. It is a practical measure that creates a bond with the guest. It smoothes the interaction between the customer and hotel staff at reservations, check-in and check-out, and it helps to make each visit a memorable visit. The disadvantage of impersonal treatment caused by large-scale operations is partly offset, and IT, in combination with personal customer contact, makes relationship maintenance efficient.

Instead of *substituting* technology for human contact, technology can become an *impetus* for more human contact, partly in new forms and partly in old forms. The urgency of human contact is obvious; for example, the face-to-face contact between the elderly and a nurse.[48] To make care 'efficient' by replacing high touch with alarm systems and TV screens is absurd and irresponsible; technology can at best be a complement.

Downsizing has become a euphemism for firing people. Automation is good in certain applications and for certain individual customers, and can lead to improved service and less work. For other customers it can be a burden, for example, for the largest segment in our economy, the senior citizens. To train yourself to take over the job of a bank teller or a travel agency clerk is presented as 'knowledge development', but for many it is just deteriorating service. The customer is expected to invest in a computer, and Internet subscription and software, learn how to operate the system, and carry the hassle of unintelligible instructions and pig-headed computers, and bad support from the supplier. Customers undertake the larger share of IT development, the correction of faulty programmes and systems that are down. Over the long term this may or may not stand out as rational. The customer is

---

[46] See Gummesson (2001a).

[47] Naisbitt has followed up the idea with a book called *High Tech/High Touch* in 1999. The quotations are from Naisbitt (1982, pp. 42 and 52).

[48] Mattsson and den Haring (1999).

thus a co-creator, co-investor and a co-producer, sometimes voluntary, sometimes through crude force from the companies.

Many observations support the mutual dependency between technology and human action. One example is the Bay Area in California, where two cultures were nurtured: IT with its heartland in Silicon Valley, and the alternative lifestyles of New Age hippies and the gay community in the neighbouring city of San Francisco. One observation is that there have never been so many international conferences with so many delegates as it is now, coinciding with the breakthrough for the Internet, email and mobile telephony. Why don't these delegates, in the name of economic rationality, meet in Internet conferences? They do not need to leave their homes of offices, pay airline tickets and hotel nights. Despite a setback after the 9/11 2001 attacks against the World Trade Center and the Pentagon, the growth of travelling has never been so rapid. This has led to congested air space above airports with delays and inferior service quality, not least caused by tighter security control to prevent terrorism. The e-relationships have spawned a need to meet in real life, not, as was postulated, a reduced need.

A possible explanation is that faster and simpler communication prepares for more productive human encounters, both to work more efficiently and to mingle socially, for example, play golf, share adventures like white water rafting, and enjoy a concert. It is a yin and yang relationship where the tension between the extremes and an ever ongoing effort to strike a balance is the vitalizer. If one extreme takes charge, life will come to a standstill. Yin and yang are often quoted but misunderstood concepts. They say that the opposites are dependent on each other, that life is a matter of both – and not of either/or. It is not either IT or human touch, it is not either competition or collaboration, but both. In this sense the opposites are not adversaries but partners.

Parallel to high tech we can see the need for experiences and kicks. We have the dedicated consumer, the experience junkie, relentlessly chasing trends, challenges and adventures. Whereas Amazon.com has grown and broadened its product line, the traditional bookstores have become experience centres. Barnes & Nobel and Chapters keep their store open until 10 or 11 p.m., and offer cafés and restaurants and evenings with authors. The mobile phone has become a social toy where 5-year-olds send text messages and play games, and compare features and models rather than talking. As an Italian woman in her mid-thirties said to me when I expressed irritation over her constantly ringing cellphone: 'But Evert, this is my social life.' Perhaps this is the future way of never being physically and mentally at the same place. Presence 'here and now' is replaced by an infinite compulsion to have multiple and simultaneous experiences.

Even if high tech may be felt as cold, it is not given that personal contacts are friendly and passionate. The lack of knowledge and social intelligence among front-line service staff is one of the most frequent causes of customer dissatisfaction. As a customer you often have no desire for contact; you want to be left in peace and prefer a machine or self-service. High tech can even add human dimensions that do not exist in the physical world. The computer enables employees to remember and consider the habits and needs of loyal customers.

The e-networks thus build relationships between suppliers and customers and other stakeholders. Here are some examples of applications.

B2C/C2B

Great expectations have been tied to home shopping, that is, retailing via the Internet; 'retailing' became 'e-tailing'. Instead of visiting a store, the consumer visits a website and gets the goods delivered at home. There are advantages with e-markets: speed, global reach, access to current information and online purchasing with credit card. There is also reason for shopping for daily goods on the Internet: less dependence on the hour, price can sometimes be lower, price comparisons may be facilitated, easier to shop globally. It may be a relief to be spared inevitable C2C interaction. New consumption patterns that can, for example, augment the value of bookstore service has emerged of e-commerce.

As the case of Tesco explained it has been successful with its home shopping where other retailers have failed. In the beginning of 2000, the average market share of home shopping in Europe was 0.2 per cent and in the United States 1.2 per cent. This has increased substantially and keeps increasing but the penetration varies greatly between different goods and services. For example in 2006, 42 per cent of Finnish consumers bought travel and holiday accommodation on the Internet, 37 per cent bought clothes and shoes and 35 per cent books and magazines. But only 1 per cent bought food and beverages! Ordering goods is not new and that was more efficiently done 60 years ago. You called the grocer, left a note in the store or just told what you needed. After an hour or so a little sweating errand boy came biking with the goods and was given a few pennies as a gratuity. Internet shopping becomes more expensive today as the distribution work done by the customer must be done by others, but it is not clear if it is more convenient for the customer. There is little sense in being able to send an order via the Internet if the goods are still distributed with traditional logistics: pick the goods from the shelf, pack them and deliver them. There are also other obstacles: technical hassle, impersonal, unsafe payment, and goods missing at delivery. A study of consumer Internet shopping in the United Kingdom showed that 40 per cent of the deliveries were late, 17 per cent were not delivered and 5–10 per cent were sent back by the customer.[49] This may have improved by now.

B2B

Of all e-commerce in 2000, B2B accounted for almost 90 per cent. In the United States this meant $157 billion (against $22 billion for B2C/C2B).[50] It has grown many times since

---

[49] According to a study by UK Trading Standards, reported in the media in 2000.
[50] According to a study by Merrill Lynch, reported by MSI, Marketing Science Institute (2001, p. 1).

then. Retailers order their goods via portable terminals in the store or online with the manufacturer's factory or warehouse. In R6 (the many-headed customer and the many-headed supplier) it was clarified that it is not companies but individuals who buy and sell. This is no longer the whole truth as M2M trading is made possible. The documents and the logistics are programmed for recurrent delivery between firms who have established a long-term relationship, and the effect is reduced cost. One application is simplified public purchasing. The government sector – such as defence and health care – is one of the largest markets in every country. Within the mega alliance of the EU, government purchasing is gargantuan.

Information-based products

Software, financial information and tickets are examples of offerings that are particularly well suited for the Internet. For these, there is no need for physical transportation but the information can be downloaded from the web to the customer's computer. The Internet is perfectly suited for e-tickets loaded into your credit card or airline bonus programme. IATA (International Air Transport Association) has decided that e-tickets shall replace conventional tickets.

Other media products such as books and records can be sold in two ways, either to be downloaded from the Internet or to be physically distributed. ABBA exists physically as the nostalgic musical hit 'Mama Mia', but the group has been dissolved for 25 years. Their CDs sell and they exist as a website. The downloading of music and movies from the web has changed entirely the market conditions for the entertainment industry. IT has stimulated C2C interaction, 'peer-to-peer technique', meaning that without cost, customers swap, for example, music files with each other.

Much of e-commerce is mail order, which is now advertised on the Internet and ordered there instead of being advertised in magazines and ordered by coupon, phone or fax. The majority of Amazon's 7500 employees are busy picking, packaging and dispatching books, records and their non-media products, just like any mail-order business has been doing for a hundred years.

Money

In the financial sector – banks, insurance, stock exchanges, brokers, finance and accounting departments, consumer transactions – membership of an e-network is a *sine qua non*. The historical date when the London Stock Exchange went electronic (8 March 1987) is referred to as 'the big bang'. The traditional, elderly London City banker and broker, dressed in bowler hat, umbrella and with a Rolls-Royce, was replaced by the computerized yuppy dressed in Italian fashion suits, with credit cards and a Porsche. The old boy network of British gentlemen, held together through their fathers' social relationships, the school tie, the club and title, lost its grip. Computer knowledge, youth, action and a stream of financial innovations became the hallmark when the marketplace transformed to marketspace. In buying shares, you no longer become the owner of a tangible certificate on paper, it is an intangible 'electronic share ownership' in a 'certificate-less society'. Today, the broker relationship is on its way to becoming a broken relationship altogether. This is so because customers can open accounts with an e-brokerage service and do the trading themselves. It is quicker and cheaper, but it lacks the personal advice and assistance, whatever that is worth. Through its speed, however, it offsets a healthy type of inertia of the traditional system which allowed better control and held back premature reactions.

These were instances of current marketing practices involving e-relationships. Those who did not grow up in the digital world may have difficulties in utilizing the potential. There are cognitive and emotional walls to knock down and the users need to adjust their behaviour and attitudes. Yet it is amazing how quickly some IT developments strike a cord with the customer – despite the hassle to use them especially in the beginning – catch on and can grow from nothing to millions of users in a matter of months.

But every IT service is not taken to the hearts by consumers. Electrolux and Ericsson started a joint venture to turn the kitchen into the 'brain' of the 'intelligent building'. The refrigerator was supposed to order new orange juice for me before I ran out of it. The president of Electrolux replied to the question why the project was not a smash hit: 'The consumer is more conservative than we thought.'[51] I wonder if the reactions of consumers are not rather signs of common sense. 'Make my day,' Clint Eastwood and Ronald Reagan would have said.

The e-markets give rise to a series of questions. Will a new type of social and commercial relationship be established between people who grow up with the Internet? What type of business cultures will IT create? What happens to the high tech/high touch balance? What happens when h-relationships – the close face-to-face or ear-to-ear relationships – are replaced by distant e-relationships? When the bank moves to your mobile phone or laptop, the bank will only 'know' its customers as transactions and statistics, not as human beings. How can one company get its customers to its website when it is so easy to surf from one site to another? How do we learn to design customer-friendly sites that really work and where customers do not get fed up by all irrelevant 'information' and demands on filling in time-consuming profiles and forms? How do we make money from websites and how do we make payment safe? And finally, the eternal question

---

[51] Interview with Michael Treschow (*Svenska Dagbladet*, 23 September 2001, p. 5 in the business section).

for marketers: timing! When is the time ripe to do what? And a question for scholars: When is the time ripe to enter the marketspace and e-relationships into marketing theory, and not just add them as anecdotes? When will the artificial agent become part of buyer behaviour theory?

> **INSIGHT** Whatever the answers to these questions are, IT will change market, mega and nano relationships. *e-relationships will create new markets and new ways to run a business.*

Parasocial relationships – relationships to brands and objects

In her controversial bestseller *No Logo*, Naomi Klein directs severe criticism against global brands. She points out that industry now understands that '… successful corporations must primarily produce brands, as opposed to products'.[52] Branding is old, and the core of politics and the church has often been symbols – the crown, the coronation, Buckingham Palace, the White House, the cross, the communion, the Vatican – rather than content, such as a promise or a message. Industry, however, has been more oriented towards manufacturing products and has seen brands as a form of advertising. Increasingly, the brand has become the 'real' output, and manufacturing has become a network of partners and subcontractors.

How brands fit into S-D logic is not quite clear. Previously branding was considered something for products and companies but not for services, then service branding was presented as different. If the two are now treated as value propositions, integration of resources and the co-creation of value by two or more parties, what role will branding have?[53]

We usually think of relationships as personal and the 30Rs are primarily relationships between people. But there are also *parasocial relationships*,[54] which are relationships to objects but also to symbols like brands and other less tangible phenomena. Our relationships to corporations and their value propositions are often impersonal but yet important through the *image* they convey to us. These relationships are manifested in the connotations

---

[52] Klein (2000; quotation from p. 3).
[53] For a discussion on S-D logic and branding, see Brodie, Glynn and Little (2006).
[54] '*Para*' is Greek and means 'beside'; parasocial relationships then are relationships beside the relationship between individuals. For a discussion of its meaning for RM, see Cowles (1994).

of company names, brands, trade marks, logotypes and well-known business leaders or other people who symbolize a business. Just like a person, a product or a company has a soul, a personality and a body language. A limousine and French champagne have a different appeal than a taxi and beer. Russian caviar, oysters and red roses symbolize festivity, romance and wealth.

The established term 'brand' emerges from a product tradition and agriculture; a symbol was burnt into the hide of cattle to mark ownership. The brand can be represented by a word, an acronym, a token or a graphic design such as a logotype. It can also be a human being whom you do not meet, or who may not even exist. Companies have signed direct mail with genuine-looking, yet fictitious, names and if a consumer has asked for the name on the phone, someone has answered with this name. Tobacco companies use healthy-looking beauties and tough cowboys on horseback to spread the blessings of smoking. It is embarrassing to the manufacturer, the media, consumers and society in general that some of the best-known models have died of lung cancer. The tobacco companies of course want to limit the dissemination of such information and are quite successful in doing so.

The importance of brands and *brand identity* has become all the more emphasized during the past decade. The value of a company's stock has become its *brand equity*, the capital it represents. It reflects how well known a company is, how satisfied the customers are, customer loyalty and the connotation that it sparks off. A comprehensive literature on branding has been published.[55] R13 is not focused on the brand as a general phenomenon but on its role as a relationship-booster, something which is less prominent in the literature.

All value propositions have certain inherent properties, but just as important are the properties we as individuals or groups allocate to them. Companies, goods, services and celebrities become surrounded by myths. 'Reality' can be seen as a social construct in which goods and services are consumed for their symbolic meaning. In a broader social context, consumption not only includes the relationship between the supplier and the customer, between the customer and the product, but also between the supplier and the product. *Positioning* is a strategy for allocating a position – a cell in the consumer's brain – to a product or service in order to make the consumer think of a special brand when a purchase is pending.

Linn[56] was an early proponent for the *meta product* which he defined as 'the whole of the invisible world of perceptions which we link to a branded product'. He proceeds: 'Every object has its metaphysical properties. It is sufficiently strong in symbols like the

---

[55] For an overview, see Keller (2007) for an American version; and Keller, Apéria and Georgson for a European version (2008). A discussion on brand relationships is found in Stenbacka (1998).

[56] Linn (1985; the quotations are compiled from pp. 9, 26 and 28).

Christian cross, the David star or the hammer and the sickle for people to sacrifice their lives ...' He takes the example of the classic Volkswagen, the 'Beetle': 'It was so personal that it was almost provocative ... people established a relationship to the car. You had to react, it was hard to be indifferent ... If we want to see the whole in which the marketed product thrives, we must look more to men and their relationship to the products than we do today.' The perceived reality is not constituted by the product and service as independent objects, but by the relationships and interactions between the beholder and the product/service.

DeBono (1992) said that offering *integrated values* is the third stage of a firm's development. It has been preceded by a product-oriented stage when goods were scarce and manufacturing was the overriding issue. In stage two, competition was in focus. We are now approaching the third stage and begin to see the whole picture of value and the customer's role as a resource, as S-D logic proposes. Value propositions and service are replacing the divide between goods and services. Competition has been discussed with reference to the peaceful competition in the blue ocean versus the hostile competition in the red ocean. But the insights of thought leaders is one thing, actual practice is another.

Taking a closer look at image, brands and quality, it is easy to find examples when the 'reality' is in the customer's eye, heart and brain, and does not exist in an objective sense. In an essay on pop art and restaurants, its author says:[57] 'There is any number of Pizzeria Napoli around the world and often these are more "original" than the "original" in Naples. By the way, is there an original at all? Isn't it so that Pizzeria Napoli rather imitates a popular image of what a pizzeria in Naples should look like? If there is no original, there can't be any copies.'

It is both an opportunity and a risk to use aesthetic gimmicks such as imaginatively designed and animated Powerpoint presentations, fancy logotypes, glossy brochures and beautifully decorated premises to make the market believe that you are something you are not. Rationality – that if you cannot live up to your image, customers will unmask you after some time and exit – should not be taken for granted. One example is the cosmetics industry, which can deliver very little of its promises – youth, beauty, happiness and romance – but the consumer wants to believe it.

In entertainment and culture, mass production is often a goal; the bigger the audience of your show or circulation of your book, the more successful you are. The relationship between the entertainer and the consumer is rarely a personal friendship. Celebrities such as rock groups or sports champions become symbols of lifestyles, beauty, strength and smartness. Sometimes an actor's charisma, star quality, visibility and private life are equally important or much more important to the fans than his or her professional performance. People know them from their appearances but also from news media and

---

[57] Nilsson (1993, p. 27).

gossip columns. The fans can come close to their idols in their imagination. *It is a personal relationship for one party, and a mass relationship for the other; the fans 'know' their stars as individuals, but the stars usually know their fans as anonymous audiences.* The role and the stage personality are perceived as real, and get mixed up with the private person. The fame of the star can be used to add credibility and popularity to products and services, and to boost images.[58]

In 2007, 10 years had passed since Diana, Princess of Wales, died in a Paris car accident. The strength of the parasocial relationship became blatantly obvious. Her beauty, love affairs, and care for the less privileged, combined with her own vulnerability, captured the minds of people around the world. They genuinely mourned her as a close friend. Her relationship with the paparazzi and reporters included mutual dependency, but an inability to turn it into win–win relationships. After 10 years her star status has not faded and she remains the world's most famous Briton. Is it just because she looked pretty, wore designer clothes and fed the tabloids with celeb gossip? No, she also became an active agent in the modernization of the British monarchy; she supported AIDS victims and helped to tear down prejudices; she gave eating disorders a face; and she raised her voice against land mines.

A new generation of exotic brands have seen the day on the IT stage and they have changed relationships and given birth to new ones. Amazom.com, Yahoo! and eBay were early ones that survived; those who disappeared in the dotcom crash around 2000 we don't remember any more. These brands created a very special relationship in that they rose quickly, their mushrooming stock price and brand equity being based on thousands or millions of Internet customers who have an interactive and ongoing relationship with them. Being one of these millions when I revised this book, I was constantly checking data on Google. I could call my friends free on Skype through my computer and we could see each other through a webcamera. Soon I can use Skype on my mobile phone. Anyone can submit a video to YouTube and anyone can access it. Advertising agencies look for these amateur films to get ideas, even to buy them and use them as they are.

Rapp and Collins[59] point to new types of brands, *relationship brands*:

> ... with the ability to identify prospects and customers by name
> and address, learn more about them, and interact with them in an
> ongoing relationship, a new form of branding is evolving: 'relationship
> branding'. You no longer simply brand or promote what you sell. You
> brand and promote the relationship as well.

---

[58] See also Rein, Kotler and Stoller (1987).
[59] Rapp and Collins (1995, pp. 197–298); and discussion with Stan Rapp in 1997.

In a similar vein, Duncan and Moriarty offer an RM model claiming that 'communication is the primary integrative element in managing brand relationships', with brand equity as the goal and core category.[60] A relationship brand has a name, a logo, offers membership, is advertised and includes continuing involvement.

HOG, has already been presented as an example of a customer club, established to increase customer retention. But it is more than that, it is also a successful relationship brand. Customers do not only have a relationship to the Harley-Davidson brand and its motorcycles. HOG is in itself a brand that represents a relationship to a community of people, an affinity group. Harley owners rarely used their bikes – it was no fun hitting the road on your own – and consequently did not buy more than one motorcycle in their lifetime. With the HOG clubhouses, strategically located in the dealerships, Harley owners consume their product as part of a community. They have not just bought a product, they have joined a group. They further identify with the group through branded Harley merchandise. And the HOG members are extremely loyal, with a 95 per cent repurchase rate. The parasocial relationship to the Harley-Davidson brand has spawned the HOG social relationship.

Monopoly means that the market is ruled by a single supplier. When there is competition, companies differentiate their offerings. One strategy is to achieve a *value monopoly*.[61] There are many cities, paintings, movie directors, cartoons and awards, but only one Venice, one Mona Lisa, one Ingmar Bergman, one Donald Duck and one Nobel Prize. Patents give a temporary, innovation-based value monopoly. A corporation can dominate its industry, like IBM ruled over the computer industry up until the 1990s. Then Microsoft took over the star role and its president Bill Gates became the symbol for the new and exciting IT future.

The cost of breaking a value monopoly can be so excessive that no competitor will succeed. A handful of such brands are known throughout the world – Sony, Mercedes, Kodak, Disney, Luis Vuitton, Microsoft, Starbucks, Nestlé, Toyota, IBM – we recognize them all. They are ranked annually and their brand equity is estimated.

Some brands have become so well known that they degenerate as brand names and are identified as synonymous with the generic product. 'To Xerox' now means to take copies even if the brand of the machine is Canon, and Caran d'Ache, the Swiss pencil manufacturer, is used as the word for pencil in Russian. When New Zealand growers launched the kiwifruit on the world market, it became such a success that other countries began to grow the fruit and profit from its formally unprotected name. Here is what happened.

---

[60] Duncan and Moriarty (1998, p. 1).
[61] DeBono (1992).

CASE STUDY   **From kiwi to ZESPRI**

The kiwi is a local bird on New Zealand with a peculiar behaviour. It is shy, it only comes out at night and does not fly, just runs. It has become a national symbol and New Zealanders are colloquially called Kiwis. A fruit called Chinese gooseberry was growing wild and was not really on the market. New Zealand farmers started to grow it and sell it on the export market under the name of kiwifruit. In 1997, the New Zealand-grown kiwi was renamed ZESPRI, a name that research showed to have the desired connotation: fun, energetic, effervescent and nutritious. ZESPRI is a co-operative of 2500 New Zealand kiwifruit growers. They are as determined to continue to attain and improve the quality benchmarks that consistently earn ZESPRI products a premium position with retailers and consumers. A network of global market offices are managed from its headquarters in the heartland of kiwifruit, the Bay of Plenty on the North Island. The company employs 200 people and the brand and its staff champions are very much in evidence around the world. 'We're not mere buyers, sellers and distributors – from orchard to market, we're team players, ready to back up, build combinations with and support other equally dedicated partners', they say on their website.

An intriguing issue is the ratio between price and the symbolic values of a parasocial relationship. What does it take to break a relationship between a customer and a brand? As it is a commercial relationship, it has a price. In England, the major retail chain Sainsbury introduced a new brand for a cola drink, Classic. The price was set 25 per cent below the price of branded colas which it soon surpassed in sales. In Canada, a similar development occurred when Loblaw introduced President's Choice, PC. PC also sells cola in the forms of both major competing brands, *PC Cola* in a red can and *PC New Wave Cola* in a blue can to look like the two biggest brands. The PC brand embraces a wide variety of food, drinks and consumer products, and services, such as President's Choice Financial Services. Many store brands including Loblaw's own *no name*, provide low-priced versions of branded products. But many PC products are marketed as being on the same level as brand name products, or even, for some food products, as a premium or luxury product. The PC brand is used as a 'unity brand' across the many food store chains operated by Loblaw under different names.

When Nestlé bought Rowntree-Mackintosh and the brands After Eight, KitKat and Quality Street, the price exceeded the tangible assets by 300 per cent. The price reveals brand equity – the financial value of these brands. It was a purchase of both tangible product values and abstract values. In traditional accounting terms, goodwill is not registered as an asset unless a certain amount of money has been paid for its acquisition. There are also negative connotations of the global brands. They may be perceived as the new colonialists who through sheer power threaten national independence and destroy local cultures.[62] Companies choose different strategies in building an image and value monopoly:

- Unilever, one of the world's largest corporations, does not advertise its corporate name to consumers but has invested in strong brand names, such as Cornetto ice-cream, Lipton's tea, Surf detergents and Lux soap. All these are well-known convenience goods brands throughout the world.
- BSN, the third largest producer of branded food in Europe after Nestlé and Unilever, do it the other way around. In 1994, it changed its name to Groupe Danone. This was its brand for dairy products and the second largest brand in the food stores. The company chose to invest in corporate image rather than in brand image. The urgency of a corporate name change was felt; BSN was unknown and in Spain there was a bank with the same name, in the United States a textile firm, and in Japan a TV channel.

Marketing via symbols can be seductively low-key. I should like to introduce the term *subtle marketing*, as opposed to the usual obtrusiveness of television commercials and other types of promotion. One example is the doctor and the 'health and illness industry'. By creating an air of divine powers – the rulers of health and disease, of life and death – medicine has built an almost invincible image. The connotation of the white coat and the characteristics of the hospital environment have become strong symbols, which govern the relationship to the customer, the patients. It probably inhibits the interaction process and the co-creation of health. Through laws and membership to associations the industry has monopolized alleged abilities. According to the American Medical Association, only members are allowed to claim that they *cure* disease. If others so claim, they will be taken to court. The expert monopoly becomes a reality, a unique and timeless 'patent' supported by a veil of 'scientific' jargon. As no monopoly is free of leaks, alert patients look for alternative treatment and seem to be doing so increasingly.

With the diversity in value propositions to consumers, branding becomes elaborate. Tesco seems to have managed to address every segment and wallet in the market and it is clear to the customer who he or she is buying from. How about airline alliances when you

---

[62] Klein (2000).

use two or more differently branded carriers to get to your final destination? And even with small companies this can pose a problem as the following case explains.

CASE STUDY   **Who am I a customer to?**

To a consumer it is not always obvious who the supplier is. A consumer needed a new toilet. A plumber was contacted to deliver and install it. He bought the equipment from a manufacturer with a well-established corporate brand. The toilets profited from the halo effect of the manufactures product line of pottery and glassware, which was reviewed in newspapers and exhibited in art galleries. The toilet did not work after installation. It leaked when flushed and the lid could hardly be lifted. When telephoning the plumber, he referred to the manufacturer as the one responsible for the guarantee, but with whom the consumer had not had any contact whatsoever. When contacting the manufacturer – a large, anonymous and disinterested organization – they told the consumer to wait for a fortnight. They considered it only natural that the bathroom was out of order for two weeks! The consumer called a member of his Rotary club – the local club is a network of members with different professions – who was president of one of the major plumbing firms and asked for advice. 'Call the head of the division and refer to me,' he said, 'we are one of their biggest customers.' After several calls – the division manager was not too keen on consumer contact – he finally answered. Just as uninterested he tried to get out of it, but afraid of disturbing his relationship with the consumer's Rotary friend, he promised to fix it. All the same it took two days. The consumer felt he was the customer of the plumber, whereas the plumber felt he was only an intermediary without responsibility and without customers. The manufacturer was not prepared to handle consumer relationships. Needless to say, they both lost one customer for good.

The issue of brands and image is not new, but is currently stirring up more interest than ever. By approaching the issue through the relationship eye-glasses, new marketing insights can be generated. We even find relationship brands. There is no doubt that parasocial relationships belong in RM. In the global economy, brands and logos '... by force of ubiquity, have become the closest thing we have to an international language, recognized and understood in many more places than English'.[63]

---

[63] Klein (2000, p. xx).

RELATIONSHIP
14

The non-commercial relationship

Marketing is primarily about the commercial part of our economy. It applies to companies that are run on market conditions with profit as the yardstick of success and survival. Economies are also based on non-profit organizations. The public sector, which is mainly a non-commercial service sector, has gradually begun to understand that marketing – in an adjusted form – is necessary. There are also other huge non-commercial sectors which are poorly described in official statistics, notably the voluntary sector – NGOs (non-governmental organizations) – with associations and clubs. And where do households and do-it-yourself fit, although they are fierce competitors in, for example, care and repair service and are gradually taking over service tasks from government by means of the Internet?

In marketing we tend to make everybody who is offered a value proposition a customer. I would like to repeat that citizen is a broader concept. The non-commercial sector has some fundamental properties, which separate it from the commercial sector and give rise to relationships of a partly different character. One is that it is citizen centric rather than customer centric. Pricing is another. *In public service, pricing and payment are not part of the same system as production and delivery.* It is often not the same person who pays and benefits from the services. Even if it is, payment and delivery do not coincide in time. Payment can be a general insurance cost via the tax bill, for example against illness, or it can be a help to the less privileged, such as unemployed people. The citizen does not perceive a tangible connection between price, cost and such public service as health care, education and the police. Payment – the tax – disappears into a black hole; when you benefit from taxes, the money appears as windfall. The service may easily be perceived as 'free', which from an individual standpoint is true at the time it is needed. This may lead to excess consumption or inability to value the service: 'Those who are offered a free meal do not go to McDonald's, they go to the Ritz'.[64]

In commercial marketing, payment and performance belong to the same system and are largely simultaneous. But even here it can be difficult to see the connection between price and performance if, for example, daddy pays and kids consume.

R5 dealt with the service encounter and the individual's relationship to a supplier. The notion of the service encounter is also applicable to public service. Public agencies, however, offer two types of service. One type could also be private and both private and public alternatives may exist, for example, in education and health care.

The other is the authority that public agencies are allowed to exercise. From the individuals' point of view, there is a positive side when authorities assist them. There is also

---

[64] Based on Albinsson-Bruhner (1993).

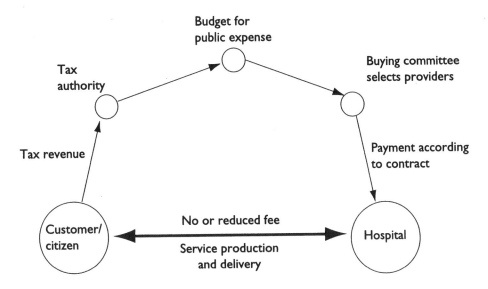

Figure 3.13 The relationship between payment of taxes and public services and the customer/citizen

a negative side to contacts with authorities, a *service collision* rather than a service encounter. Authorities provide both service to the community of all individuals, and to the single individual. Some authorities have the monopoly of using force against the individual for the benefit of the whole of society. Those who get arrested or are forced to pay additional taxes are not inclined to see this as a service; the encounter becomes a collision. There is also a collision when authorities fail because of disinterest, inertia, sloppiness, legal technicalities or red tape. The criminal is let loose and the victim is offered no help; the little guy is harassed while the big crook is left alone. The 'values' of the legal and bureaucratic establishment are often far apart from what citizens perceive as fair.

Figure 3.13 shows one possible pattern of a purchasing procedure for public service, in this case public health care. The service is produced directly between the customer/citizen and the hospital staff. The payment goes via the taxes to a budget for public expense. In this case, hospitals offer their service in competition through bidding, a committee selects the winner and payment follows a contract.

The terms customer and supplier are now being used in non-commercial operations too. It is an effort to change the relationship between, for example, the customer/citizen and the tax authority, and to make the tax authority both an *authority* and a *service organization*, not just an authority. The two roles of authority and service provider have been mixed up when publicly owned organizations behave like an authority in instances when they should be performing ordinary service. This attitude has created an unhappy relationship to the customers/citizens and low quality and productivity. By handling service tasks well it becomes easier to exercise authority. The tax agency must ascertain the revenue from taxes. At the same time, the citizens and the companies perform service when they fill in tax forms and deliver money. Laws and regulations are frequently difficult to understand intellectually. They are sometimes ambiguous and sometimes not even passed before they are supposed to be applied. No wonder that the taxpayer makes mistakes or cheats. A majority of the mistakes can be prevented or smoothly corrected if the authority enters into constructive interaction with the citizen. This requires that the authority informs in a way that is comprehensible to the citizen and is available for consultation. In most countries availability is a major hurdle even if authorities in some countries have realized the need for change of attitude and work procedure. Through websites and email, contact with public authorities can sometimes be facilitated.

Unfortunately, many of those employed by authorities do not realize that they are there for the citizens, but believe that the citizens are there to serve them; the organizational culture inverts the roles. The citizens' perceptions of relationships with authorities have been characterized by the French author Anatole France as 'the State is a surly old man behind a window'. In service research we had predicted that a new generation of officials would emerge, representing relationship and service values, thus replacing the bureaucratic generations. It is sad to have to say it, but even if many changes have taken place, the historically bureaucratic–legal values are still predominant.

It is difficult to draw a line between what types of consumption should be a human right, and what should be the effect of own work and earnings. Much of the political tensions between different economic systems are caused by conflicting opinions about a fair trade-off between rights and own performance.

Public authorities and service agencies increasingly become 'borderline organizations'.[65] They live in a fuzzy zone between public and private, between the non-commercial/tax financed and a competitive market economy. Deregulation and privatization have been international strategies for many years. An airport authority may be state operated. It exercises authority over certain aspects of the airport such as air traffic control, and operates service such as parking and tax-free sales.

While the public sector is paid via taxes, the voluntary sector receives its means through donations and unpaid work and to some extent through public funds and taxes. According to Drucker, the voluntary sector, which he calls the third sector, has been the fastest growing economic sector in the United States; it engages more people than the private and public sectors together.[66] Churches, scouts and environmental groups, such as Greenpeace, belong in the voluntary sector. Their work neither fits the market economy and its price mechanism, nor the tax-based public sector institutions and the political

---

[65] Winai (1989).
[66] Drucker (1989).

system. In spite of its size, the voluntary sector becomes a residual in official statistics and is neglected by management and marketing theory. It lives on conditions other than the public sector. Its missions have been unnoticed or mismanaged by the private or public sector, or they lack the capacity to handle them. Voluntary work is often pioneering, often scorned and actively opposed by the establishment, one example being environmental protection. The third sector has a long tradition and is used to handle many of the issues which were later transferred, at least in part, to the public sector. We could also add a fourth sector which embraces what we do for ourselves, our family and friends.

The board of directors has a special role in voluntary organizations, namely to be the driver in the collection of funds.[67] This is an additional role from the board in a commercial enterprise or a public agency. An important part is building relationships with donors for fund-raising, or better: *fund development*. The change in terminology is essential for RM. To *develop* funds is more long term and more intimate than to *collect* funds. According to Dudley Hafner, then head of the American Heart Association: '... your true potential for growth and development is the donor ... someone you want to cultivate and bring along in your programme. Not simply someone to collect this year's contribution from.'

The quotation stresses that long-term relationships must be cultivated through a programme, as compared to the transaction, the occasional gift. One strategy is to engage the donor in actual work in the organization. Hafner continues: 'Someone who pays taxes does not think of himself or herself as getting involved in the welfare programme. But if they become involved in a Salvation Army activity or the Visiting Nurses programme, they *are* involved. They are involved spiritually and they are involved monetarily. That makes a difference.' If an organization consists of members – real members and not pseudo-members – these can be both recipients of the organization's offerings and producers for themselves or for others. This way of looking can be expanded to seeing nations as organizations of 'members', the citizens. To regard members or citizens as customers requires the insight that their role is only partly commercial.

Companies are increasingly developing strategies for their donations by funding long-term projects.[68] This corporate philanthropy aligns self-interest with doing good for society, the companies becoming corporate citizens. Examples of causes are increasing literacy, AIDS prevention, school reforms and environmental programmes. It does not only include cash, but also advice and the use of their technology and human resources.

A large share of the cultural sector is non-commercial. A museum must target its relationships in four directions.[69] One is to *visitors* and, in order to reach them, the museum

---

[67] This and the next paragraph are based on Drucker (1990; quotations from pp. 85 and 88).
[68] Smith (1994).
[69] Bradford (1991, pp. 93–96).

needs *intermediaries*, like tourism organizations and the media. Then there are those who support the operations through *contributions*, such as corporate sponsors, local governments and grant committees. The fourth is *inward bound*, the organization of the museum and those who propose exhibitions, plan them and implement them. All this is tied together; it is three perspectives of the marketing of a museum.

The following case shows a private initiative to take care of a market need in which neither the commercial sector nor the public sector took an interest. It is a dive into the blue ocean, not to become rich but to do good.

CASE STUDY   **Then savings banks, now Grameen Bank**

When I was born, savings banks presented newborn babies with a bank account and a small deposit. When I started school, I received a savings box, which was emptied regularly under the supervision of the schoolteacher, and the money was deposited in the savings bank. This was seen as community work without a profit motive. The savings banks had an assignment from society, just like the schools had. Saving was a virtue: 'Save First, Buy Later!' The mission of the savings banks was to give the less privileged a chance to improve their financial situation, go to college and acquire their own home, and to let small farmers and firms develop their operations. The savers were members and citizens rather than customers.

Grameen Bank ('Bank of the Villages') was founded in 1976 in Bangladesh by Muhammad Yunus, a PhD in economics. Yunus understood that the poor needed loans to get a small business started *and* could be good customers. It was a blue ocean, but he did it out of social responsibility, not for personal profit. He challenged upfront the conventional banker's thinking. The bank gives small loans, 'microcredits' to impoverished people without demanding collateral. Every loaner buys a share and becomes an owner and there is a 'peer review' when someone applies for a loan: customers assess each other, a type of close C2C interaction. The bank also accepts deposits and runs development-oriented businesses including fabric, telephone and energy companies. Grameen Bank and its founder were jointly awarded the Nobel Peace Prize in 2006. Now the big commercial banks have discovered the blue ocean and jump into the water. The question is if conventional banks can handle these types of credits and customers. Grameen bank had 7 million borrowers in 2007, 97 per cent were women and the loan recovery rate was 98.85 per cent. The bank has expanded around Asia and to Latin America and North Africa.

The non-commercial relationship is ever so important for the commercial economy and the marketing equilibrium. What cannot be handled through market mechanisms must be handled by the public sector and the political system – including setting up adequate regulations and institutions – and by the voluntary sector and NGOs. Relationships between customers, suppliers and other stakeholders are important all the same, but are of a different character than in ordinary business markets.

The green relationship and CSR

> Dear Guest: Try to imagine how many tons of towels from all hotels around the world are washed unnecessarily. Think of the enormous amount of detergent and water, which thereby contribute to the strain on the environment. Please note that if you put the towel on the floor it means that you would like it to be replaced. However, if you leave it hanging on the rack it means: I can use it again – and help protect the environment.

This type of message is often found in hotel bathrooms. It is an instance of a growing phenomenon – the green relationship. Hotels are trying to establish a relationship with guests and engage them in environmental issues. They want interaction and co-creation with the customer. The ulterior business motive is to slash cost and enhance profits, but there could also be a genuine desire to protect the environment.

The green relationship concerns the company's way of handling environmental and health issues in its value propositions and how to use this to strengthen the relationships that are created to specific individuals and communities. Environment and health have been in focus for public debate for decades and they have spawned a special type of relationship between business, consumers, citizens and society. *Green marketing* has become a subdiscipline of marketing.

The green relationship in a broader sense is ethics and corporate social responsibility, CSR. *Cause-related marketing* has become a term for 'doing good in society'. The primary business reason for supporting a good cause is to boost public image and brands. Promoting a cause is more effectively done through sponsorship, events and public relations than by advertising. These strategies involve relationships, networks and interaction which advertising does not and are therefore in line with RM.

There could be a genuine desire from a business to do good, to be a good corporate citizen. But a business has to make a profit to sustain and the big question then is: Can green marketing and CSR be made profitable? In 2007, two of the most circulated business magazines carried feature articles with contradictory conclusions on the profitability of going green.[70] *Fortune's* headline was 'Go green. Get rich' and *Business Week's* 'Little Green Lies'. *Fortune* lists the 7 biggest environmental and health problems – global warming, hunger and malnutrition, waste disposal, dirty water, dirty air, epidemics and overfishing – and present companies addressing each of these profitably. *Business Week* features Auden Schendler, an environmentalist who has been guided by the belief that green issues can be in the core of a profitable business mission, but has now given up. Where is the truth? Or is it just that some green value propositions are viable, others are not, just like in ordinary business? Or has it got to do with long term versus short term? Today's CEO is driven by short-term results and has difficulties convincing shareholders that future profits will come. Is it green versus greed, or idealism versus realism? More examples will follow.

Environmental aspects are embraced by the ISO quality certification system (ISO14000) and by the quality awards that now exist around the world. As the following case shows the *Baldrige Quality Award* considers societal responsibilities, including environmental improvements which appear under several of its other quality criteria. A presentation of the general features of the Baldrige is found in R26, 'quality and customer orientation'. Reference is made to green technology and green manufacturing, health and safety, emission levels, waste stream reductions, by-product use and recycling. According to former Baldrige chief executive Curt Reimann, the importance of environmental issues for the applicant is weighed against a company's potential impact on the environment. Consequently, a producer of chemicals is judged by tougher standards than, for example, a life insurance company.

CASE STUDY   **Social responsibility in the Baldrige Quality Award**

Green issues and CSR in the Baldrige award are integrated and described as follows:

An organization's leaders should stress responsibilities to the public, ethical behavior, and the need to practice good citizenship. Leaders should be role models for your organization in focusing on ethics and protection of public health, safety, and the environment. Protection of health, safety, and the environment includes your organization's operations, as well as the life cycles of your products and services.

Also, organizations should emphasize resource conservation and waste reduction at the source. Planning should anticipate adverse impacts

---

from production, distribution, transportation, use, and disposal of your products. Effective planning should prevent problems, provide for a forthright response if problems occur, and make available information and support needed to maintain public awareness, safety, and confidence.

For many organizations, the product or service design stage is critical from the point of view of public responsibility. Design decisions impact your production processes and often the content of municipal and industrial waste. Effective design strategies should anticipate growing environmental concerns and responsibilities.

Organizations should not only meet all local, state, and federal laws and regulatory requirements, but they should treat these and related requirements as opportunities for improvement "beyond mere compliance." Organizations should stress ethical behavior in all stakeholder transactions and interactions. Highly ethical conduct should be a requirement of and should be monitored by the organization's governance body.

Practicing good citizenship refers to leadership and support—within the limits of an organization's resources—of publicly important purposes. Such purposes might include improving education and health care in your community, pursuing environmental excellence, practicing resource conservation, performing community service, improving industry and business practices, and sharing nonproprietary information. Leadership as a corporate citizen also entails influencing other organizations, private and public, to partner for these purposes.

Managing social responsibility requires the use of appropriate measures and leadership responsibility for those measures.[71]

---

[71] Quoted from the Malcolm Baldrige National Quality Award (2007), *Criteria for Performance Excellence*.

The Baldrige takes a demanding and holistic approach. But how has it worked out in practice? Green advocates have had a strained relationship with companies and governments which have denied the urgency and been reluctant to take action. I have heard a series of objections: 'Our company does not cause pollution! It's fad and fashion among confused idealists and will soon pass! It costs too much! There is lack of scientific evidence! The customer does not want to pay for it! We will lose our competitive edge!' Legislation has often not been enforced and companies have been granted temporary exemptions that have turned permanent. Those who have been appointed responsible for environmental issues at corporations often lack power. It has turned out to be difficult to enforce effective agreements on the environment and health with the UN, WTO (World Trade Organization), EU and other supranational organs.

There are several dilemmas. How much can and should a business enterprise interfere with national and local habits that are supported by governments or at least not prevented by them? What are the boundaries? For example, the green car has had its breakthrough during the past few years. It has been led by Toyota Prius, a hybrid running on petrol and self-generated electricity in combination. Etanol has become a popular green fuel with low emissions but its production process is costly and non-ecological. Further, being manufactured from farm products it has caused substantial price increases on food, which hits ordinary consumers in the West but especially those in poor countries. It shows that the supply network and the many B2B touch points have to be part of the final value proposition. The message of network theory that everything is connected has to be accepted and lead to implementation.

Although IKEA owner Ingvar Kamprad is a hard-nosed businessman with no special knowledge about green issues to start with, he saw them coming. He took them seriously and continuously adapts to a more ecological product-line, prevention against child labour among suppliers and so on.[72] The green activities are an integral part of the company's daily and long-term operations.

Tesco's policy for stimulating green consumption and link it to their Clubcard is a practical case of its efforts to implement a green policy in interaction with customers. They can collect Green Clubcard Points when they recycle old mobile phones and inkjet cartridges but also on an inconspicuous item – the carrier bag.

CASE STUDY   **Tesco's Green Clubcard Points for reusing bags**

We all know we are using too many carrier bags. That's why from now on, we'll give you a Green Clubcard Point every time you reuse a bag. It really doesn't matter what kind of bag it is. As long as you're helping the environment by not using new carrier bags, we'll give you Green Clubcard Points in return.

Tesco.com are now offering to have your grocery order delivered without carrier bags where you can collect 1 Green Clubcard Point for every 10 items ordered.

As part of this we hope to cut Tesco carrier bag usage by 25 per cent over the next two years.

---

[72] Enquist, Edvardsson and Petros Sebathu (2007).

> You can spend Green Clubcard Points just like any other Clubcard Points. And this is just the beginning; we'll soon be introducing other initiatives to make Tesco and Clubcard greener.
>
> Along with helping customers reuse their carrier bags we have also taken the following steps:
>
> - From September all our free carrier bags will be degradable.
> - Most of our larger stores have carrier bags recycling units, so when your carrier bag is worn out bring it back and we'll recycle it.
> - Our 10p 'Bag for Life' is a great way to carry shopping home, if this wears out bring it back and we'll replace it with a new one for free.

In the mid-1990s, US consumers spent over US $100 billion on products from companies that they perceive as environmentally and socially progressive.[73] One focus of Wal-Mart's Live Better Index concerns green products and attitudes. It concerns, for example, extended-life paper products, compact light bulbs, organic milk and reusable shopping bags. A survey in 2007 showed that only 11 per cent of American consumers see themselves as 'extremely green', but 43 per cent that they will so in the next 5 years.[74] It is both surprising and discouraging to note that in the early 1990s, 84 per cent of all Americans considered pollution a serious problem getting worse, 75 per cent that the air was getting more polluted and that 80 per cent of lakes and rivers were more polluted than 20 years ago.[75] Even if a lot is happening, why has not more happened and why do companies seem so reluctant to engage in green issues? Perhaps the time is ripe now?

One of the most successful marketing campaigns in this millennium has former US Vice President Al Gore at the steering-wheel. He is marketing a mega message that affects each and everyone on earth. He has long taken an interest in green issues and CSR. Due to global warming, the green-house effect and melting icebergs – expressions that suddenly have become everyday words – we all have to take action. Gore has used a mix of mass marketing through a book and a film, his celebrity status, and his relationships with powerful people, to make sure his message reaches out. In a short time the campaign led to global awareness. He was even awarded the Nobel Peace Prize in 2007 together with the UN's Intergovernmental Panel on Climate Change. Apart from the money involved, all the publicity surrounding the Nobel ceremonies adds credibility to the campaign.

---

[73] Entine (1996, p. 31).

[74] Based on Appliance Magazine. com, 'Wal-Mart Says More Consumers Buying "Green"' October 25, 2007.

[75] The data in this paragraph are quoted from Ottman (1992, pp. 3, 8 and 13).

A basic impetus for businesses must be that going green will not only mean higher costs but also has a revenue and profit side in the long run. The hysteria of stock market gambling and quick profits which is widespread in the financial sector is counterproductive to this. The Body Shop has shown that a green business mission can be viable, and has been so for 40 years. It has long been held up as the role model of environmentally friendly business that also makes a profit. The charisma and common sense of its founder Anita Roddick has made business and consumers listen.

When Bill Gates, who has become of the world's richest men on Microsoft, shares his wealth for good causes such as AIDS relief in Africa, his contribution is welcomed. Although of an unheard-of grand scale it is more like traditional charity – the rich give to the poor. Green issues and CSR do not stand out as part of the Microsoft marketing strategy. Microsoft is more perceived as practicing hypercompetition and marketing warfare than competing peacefully as the case in R10, the EU fines Microsoft, showed. Another of world's wealthiest man, financial wizard Warren Buffett, has joined forces with Gates' good causes. Buffett has demonstrated long-term responsibility in his investments which is a contrary strategy to what Wall Street is known to promote. CSR stands out as an integral part of his business.

The group of green consumers who take an interest in the environment and health is growing. Previously, protests against environmental destruction were most visible in demonstrations and efforts to boycott companies. Consumers also 'vote' through their purchases, and a growing share of 'voters' refuse to buy products which are detrimental to health and the environment.

Figure 3.14 shows green market relationships – to individual consumers and middlemen – and relationships on a mega level, to citizens as a group. Companies sell their goods or services to customer segments or individuals who can be more or less environmentally and health conscious. There are communities of people dedicated to green issues. Children began early to accept the messages and have begun to influence their parents' purchasing habits.[76] Producers of daily goods establish closer relationships to supply networks in order to solve environmental problems – for example with packaging – and to explore the sales opportunities provided by the increasing green interest. Investment in good relationships with authorities, environmental organizations and the media can be supportive to marketing. During its 160-year history, Church & Dwight in the United States, makers of Arm & Hammer baking soda, have worked with both the product and its package to make it more environmentally friendly and applicable for new uses where it can replace toxic products. They did so based on common sense and CSR when this was rarely talked about; it became a natural part of their business mission. Its representative says: 'Building coalitions with all stakeholders keeps the company abreast

---

[76] Ottman (1992, p. 146).

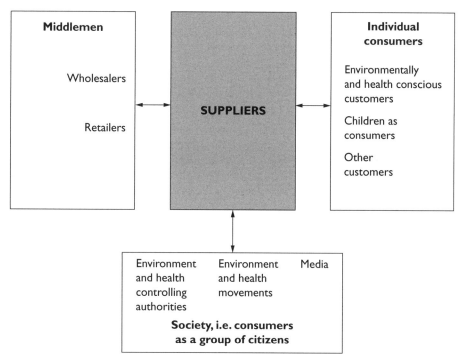

Figure 3.14 The company and its relationships in the green network

of environmental regulations, issues, debates, technology, and attitudes ... [which] results in a dialogue ...'[77]

Companies and consumers alike are in continuous interaction with the environment. The consumer might not notice much of this, as a large share of environmental destruction caused by production and consumption appears with delayed effect and away from the consumer's location. The general environmental destruction, which we cannot do much about as individuals, hits back at us as citizens of a nation and increasingly as global citizens. The products we consume have an impact on our individual well-being. This is obvious with food, a choice we can partly control. If wrongly combined, it impairs our general health status and immune defence system and causes disorders. We incur costs both directly as consumers and indirectly as citizens. The bulk of health care cost, which is one of the largest costs for society amounting to 8 per cent of GNP in most Western countries but skyrocketing to 16 per cent in the United States, is caused by lifestyles, not least through inadequate nutrition and polluted food. The interest in health food, fruit and vegetables has got a kick forwards through BSE ('mad cow disease'), foot and mouth epidemics, and the negative media exposure of animal transports and slaughterhouses. We can expect more of *functional food* with a focus on health effects in the future.

---

[77] Ottman (1992, p. 146).

Marketing as a discipline is primarily dealing with issues of a micro and short-term character. Companies endeavour to maintain long-term profitability and survival, but in practice short-term considerations are given priority. Survival this year is a necessary condition for long-term survival. The consumer is often focused on satisfying momentary needs. In a macro perspective and over the long term, both companies and consumers have a responsibility as citizens which are partly in conflict with the individual's immediate self-interest.

Reasons for a delayed breakthrough for green marketing and CSR are therefore found in the conflicts between our responsibility as individual consumers, suppliers and citizens. There are *short-term* and *long-term* effects, as well as *direct* and *indirect* effects.

Individual consumers

In our role as *individual consumers* we can choose to buy certain goods and services. We demonstrate environmental and health awareness through our consumption habits. This requires that the products we want are available at a reasonable price or the green considerations will become too much of a burden of daily life. One obstacle is the lack of infrastructure such as distribution networks based on ecological concerns. If consumers want to buy organically grown food, they usually find that availability is low, both in stores and restaurants. If consumers want to patronize manufacturers that use recycled material, reliable information is difficult to obtain. Much of what we do as individuals has a direct, predictable and short-term impact. Indirect and long-term effects are vague and provide weaker incentives.

Suppliers

In our role as *suppliers*, we can choose to create value propositions as long as we live within the law – or, more realistically, do not risk to be discovered and punished – and as long as it pays. Today, environmental costs incurred by companies are passed on to others and society at large, even to other countries via air and water. Even worse, pollution and the consequent destruction of natural resources has a more general consequence. It is stored in molecules, which are then distributed through the ecological cycle. We get 'molecular rubbish', the invisible rubbish which is 10 times the amount of the visible rubbish[78] and affects hormones and genes. In the long run, we cannot dodge payment of these anonymous costs; they will hit us as consumers and citizens.

---

[78] Robért (1992).

Citizens

As *citizens* – that is *us*, the same people as those mentioned above but in a different role – it is comfortable to hide in the collectivity of society. We may not see ecology as our responsibility, and as single individuals we may feel we cannot do much as long as authorities do not take action. This is also a neat excuse for doing nothing. Politicians are squeezed between a will to act on issues which have not matured in public opinion and to become popular and attract votes. A more developed collective consciousness is a necessary antecedent for more far-reaching and sustainable change.

GMO, gene manipulated food, was on its way to establishing itself, particularly through the aggressive actions by Monsanto. Consumer and political protests in the United States and most of Europe were lame, probably because Monsanto and other actors used a scientific front to impress the public and assure that GMO had only advantages for the consumer. As an exception, the UK debate went high from 1999 and onwards and many of the sophisticated 'promises' were exposed. The president of Monsanto eventually had to publicly admit that the company could not live up to its claims.[79]

It would be easier if environmental and health hazards could be clearly identified by mainstream scientific research. In many cases there is overwhelming evidence both from science and common-sense observations; no more research is needed. In other cases treating green issues as part of an ecosystem requires new scientific mindsets. With the profits and stakes involved, however, it is tempting to modify green issues to greed issues; changing just one tiny letter changes the whole strategy, just like changing one tiny gene changes a whole organism – and the effects are unknown.

Table 3.2 shows that companies are driven by different motives in their environmental and CSR considerations. *Law driven firms* heed environmental issues only when forced to by court orders. They often try to escape the issues through massive use of lawyers and stalling techniques. Lobbying organizations have been formed to discredit environmental efforts and to spread disinformation, even demanding free use of nature for the benefit of short-term business profits. No doubt, environmental enthusiasts have sometimes gone too far, not accepting any kind of human interference with nature. The 24 kilometre (15 mile) bridge between Sweden and Denmark had been the object of environmental studies and controversies for decades before the actual construction could start. This has forced the proponents of the bridge to consider – and reconsider – its effects on the flow of the water and the living conditions for fish and organisms. Any change, however, will have some effect on nature, and the question is how much is acceptable and how the harm can be reduced.

---

[79] Hertz (2002).

Table 3.2 Drivers to deal with green and CSR issues

Law driven firm	Public relations driven firm	Value driven firm
Defensive strategy	Opportunistic strategy	Offensive strategy
Cost to be avoided	Image enhancement	Basis for revenue
Consumers do not really care	Consumers want it to some extent	Consumers demand it
Resistance	Cosmetic add-on, green-washing	Inherent in their business mission
Threat	Faddish	Opportunity for sustaining competitive advantage
Let the court decide what is a good citizen	Efforts to be perceived as a good citizen	Genuine desire to be a good citizen

Public relations driven firms seem to constitute the most prevalent species. For them, green issues and CSR are trendy and if consumers seem to want them, firms offer them in order to enhance sales and image. They apply a 'green-washing strategy' rather than implementing fundamental changes. This is in line with the values of the 4P approach with promotion, persuading the customer to view the company in a positive light, a matter of 'information'. A study in the United States showed that 87 per cent of consumers thought that less than half of all companies took environmental issues seriously.[80]

Value driven firms – those who understand and believe – are still a minority. Green products are often manufactured and distributed by voluntary organizations based on personal beliefs and values, such as those of anthroposophs and biodynamic farmers. Some of the companies that have seen the business opportunities in environment and health are e-cover in Belgium, Ben & Jerry's Ice Cream in the United States and The Body Shop in the United Kingdom. More traditional companies have sometimes spent large sums on green programmes and made certain improvements, but the larger share of their operations continue as before. It is hard to uncover if there is, besides the voluntary and idealistic organizations, any commercial enterprises that fully embrace green and CSR values, not only in rhetoric but also in action. We would like to believe their claims and some companies have received extraordinary media coverage for promoting green issues.

Particularly in Europe, where consumer and producer co-operatives used to have large market shares in food retailing, one could have expected leadership in green marketing. The explanation may be simple: management never understood that environment and health could be part of a business mission. A survey of advertisements from the period 1950–1985 indicated that companies did not reveal any growing awareness of green opportunities, although the arguments for health increased somewhat during the 1980s.[81]

---

[80] According to *Marketing News* (Schlossberg, 1992).
[81] Feurst (1991).

| CASE STUDY | **The Body Shop** |

The Body Shop's products seem to sell themselves through unique perceived qualities and consumers constitute the sales force as voluntary PTMs. The company has never advertised but claims to get 10 000 favourable mentions in the media per year. It was founded in 1976 with one store in Brighton, England, and in 2007 there are 2200 stores in 54 countries. The official strategy is to make both the products and the packaging as environmentally friendly as feasible. They are based on natural ingredients and must not be tested on animals. The Body Shop has introduced a rolling 5-year rule in its relationship to the suppliers. Twice a year, suppliers must sign a confirmation that the ingredients or the finished product have not been tested on animals during the past five years. Companies that currently practise animal testing but cease to do so can become suppliers to The Body Shop five years later. Bottles are standard plastic bottles used by pharmacies and consumers can get them refilled. Plastic has been a major problem, and the company has worked systematically to recycle the material; this is now beginning to succeed. Every individual store has an environmental programme, a requirement in the franchise contract. The Body Shop establishes relationships with environmental organizations, among them Amnesty International and Greenpeace. Ten years after that The Body Shop was introduced on the London Stock Exchange the value of the stock had increased by 10 944 per cent. The growth, which has taken place through franchising, is exceptional. Obviously there is no contradiction in marketing green products and running a profitable operation, as has incessantly been claimed by traditional companies.

Its founder and president, Anita Roddick, expressed her business philosophy in the following way:[82]

> ... [M]any trading companies are now fighting to clamber on to the bandwagon and are loudly proclaiming their brand-new, shining green products and policies. I would be happier if I thought they were motivated by real concern for the environment.

> ... [A]t first media and the politicians ... categorized environmentalists as brown sandal freaks with a screw loose. They sneered at them.

> The Body Shop is, and has always been, an unshamedly green company ... it was a simple expression of our core values and beliefs, values that are constantly policed by our customers and staff ...

---

[82] Roddick (1991, pp. 220–221).

It has been argued by Entine (1996) that there are flaws in the green Body Shop facade, the image being glossier than the reality. And by selling the company to French cosmetics giant L'Oreal in 2006 the Roddicks have been accused of abandoning their core values. A totally new situation has arisen and its consequences are yet to be seen. Anita Roddick died suddenly in 2007 and we will miss her comments on future developments.

The traditional task of companies is production and marketing, the task of consumers is to consume, and it is the task of local governments to dispose of the rubbish. In an ecological perspective, however, the whole must be considered. Rubbish disposal and recycling must be designed into the product and the delivery systems; it must be a natural part of the logistics. A major share of environmental pollution is directly coupled to daily consumption, how the raw material was produced, how the products were manufactured and transported, and how they are taken care of as rubbish; 60–85 per cent of household waste could be recycled or composted.

In the future, producers will be responsible for their products all the way to scrapping and wasting, which means a role after sales and consumption. Figure 3.10 showed how intimately B2B, B2C/C2B and C2C are knit together in supply networks of consumers, intermediaries, manufacturers and others. This will require a dramatic redesign of the logistics of the producers. While only a fraction of all packaging is recycled today, 90–95 per cent might be a future goal. Car manufacturers have developed systems for recycling. In the Italian Fiat cars, plastic material is going to be used up to three times. Counting the life expectancy of a car to 20 years, the material will be around for 60 years. Security details such as bumpers are made of new plastic, which will be recycled and used for less critical components. Manufacturers recycle toners for copying machines and printers, and ask the customer to return them to retailers. For the future, the distribution system needs to be as efficient *from* the consumer and retailer as it now is *to* the customer and retailer. Recycling requires a whole new infrastructure. This strategy is 100 per cent different from the 1960s, when throw-away and 'no deposit–no refund' was considered the most efficient production and consumption strategy.

The trends in production and consumption, however, are puzzling and contradictory. The consumption of junk food and alcohol is on the increase and withstands anticampaigns; a more liberal view towards drug abuse is being adopted by politicians and the police; drug abuse is romanticized by the music industry which exerts a heavy influence on young people; elite sports are contaminated by performance-enhancing drugs; the breeding of animals and the growth of plants are increasingly more artificial with pesticides, hormones and penicillin; and gene manipulation is sneaked in through the back door to avoid the consumer noticing it.

There are also signs that a changed and more constructive view on green marketing and CSR is coming forth at a more rapid pace, even if the degree of awareness varies considerably between consumers, industries and countries. In order to break through among consumers, green products have to be as easily accessible as a soda drink. Marketers begin to see opportunities, eloquently epitomized in the following words: 'When the boss got green glasses, the red numbers disappeared.'[83] Let's hope these words are true.

The law-based relationship

'When ITT came to the customer for final negotiations and to sign the contract,' an international businessman told me, 'the delegation consisted of 9 lawyers and 1 engineer. When Ericsson came, they were 9 engineers and 1 lawyer.'

This anecdote uncovers two very different relationships. For one company, it is first and foremost a legal relationship with the courts hovering over the negotiations. For another, it is a professional and even personal relationship focused on technology, with some provision for legal features.[84]

The formal regulations/institutions of the marketing equilibrium are partly found in the law-based relationship. It involves three objectives:

1 *Quality assurance through prevention*: Law for preventive purposes, during negotiations and in contracts, is used to avoid potential misunderstandings and install a certain protection against a party that does not fulfil its obligations. The work of legislators and lawyers then is quality assurance. As in all quality work, prevention should be maximized. If relationships are good, parties usually solve a dispute without taking it to court. Oral and informal agreements where people trust each other are continuously being made in business and are a necessity for the market to operate smoothly.

2 *Quality inspection and solution of disputes*: Prevention is always more effective than measures taken after the problem has arisen, not least if the goal is long-term relationships. The world is not perfect so legal procedures are also needed for quality inspection and rework, as a ground for settling a dispute and for dealing with outright dishonesty. Misunderstandings can occur, however; if the parties cannot reach an agreement through a benign and constructive effort, they may be forced into a law-based relationship. The outcome of legal procedures can solve a problem, but there are dark sides. Winning a war is not the same as winning the peace; even the winner of a case becomes a loser if the cost of litigation in money, time and psychic effort is substantial. The outcome can also be random or controlled by technicalities, obsolete legislation, ruthless

---

[83] Karpesjö (1992, p. 9).
[84] For a discussion of contract law and its transactional and relational qualities, see Macneil (1983, 1985); and Paulin, Perrien and Ferguson (1997).

smartness of lawyers, and ignorant courts. Unfortunately, sometimes prevention can be an antecedent to a win–lose relationship; the stronger party makes certain that it is exempt of all responsibility and only has rights.

3 *Manipulation*: Law is also used to deliberately trap another party. Within the marketing mix and the 4Ps, law ought to have its own P for the art of using legal technicalities to exploit and fool another party, thus winning a 'victory' over a customer, supplier, ally or employee. This type of law application is counterproductive to RM/CRM and can only function in transaction marketing and situations where the customer, or other party, has little power; it is also unethical. Notorious examples are fine print in contracts, which cannot be understood without the assistance of lawyers and courts. In hypercompetition though, manipulation of the law is part of the ongoing marketing warfare and win–lose values.

The law-based relationship to the customer is partly an indirect relationship. It goes via a 'repair crew' of law firms, prosecutors, courts, juries and judges. They work as intermediaries – wholesalers, retailers, agents – who are distributors of decisions about who is right and who is wrong. They also function as the refuse collectors of broken human relationships; they are expected to clean up where others have littered. The fact that legal institutions have to be activated is a sign of relationship failure (Figure 3.15).

Although rarely mentioned in marketing texts, *bankruptcy* is a natural ingredient of the market economy. It is a way of tidying up in the marketplace, a Darwinian selection, the survival of the fittest. Through periods of snowballing bankruptcies in many countries, they have become a more obtrusive part of the relationship between supplier and buyer. Suppliers are vulnerable in a customer bankruptcy; little is usually left to pay invoices. Tax authorities and sometimes banks can have preferential right to remaining assets. This is remarkable as banks boast about being professional credit assessors, while a supplier seldom has a chance to foresee the failure of a customer company. A failure has a domino

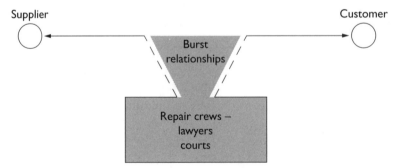

Figure 3.15 The law-based relationship as a substitute for burst social and business relationships

effect: suppliers go bankrupt because their customers did and they cannot pay their debts to their suppliers, and so forth.

Bankruptcy often leads to legal proceedings where fraud and unethical practice are uncovered. Some bankruptcies are a deliberate and systematic abuse of the legal system and a way of making money. Most failures, however, are not deliberately criminal, but formal mistakes are often made in the confusion that precedes the failure. In either case, bankruptcy leads to law-based interaction.

In the airline business there has been a partial switch from a bureaucratic–legal paradigm to a service and relationship paradigm. It has been a well-known secret that airlines overbook. Promises are given but the airlines do not know if they can deliver. It was quite common that they refused to admit overbooking, blamed the passenger, the airports or the weather, and disclaimed all responsibility. Today, serious airlines acknowledge overbooking, or 'denied boarding' as they prefer to call it. There are financial benefits and airlines have statistics to show just how much in each type of flight makes 'sound' overbooking. Ways of compensating passengers for the inconvenience have become more customer friendly. Some airlines ask for volunteers to give their seats to a traveller with an urgent need to be on the flight. They promise the volunteer a seat on the next flight and offer a free ticket for a future flight or cash compensation. The value of a free ticket for a customer usually exceeds by far the cost for the airline. The failure is turned into recovery, a win–win relationship flavoured by customer delight, the little extra, which is often recommended in modern quality management.

From a strict, legal perspective, airlines could probably waive the responsibility or make it burdensome for passengers to claim compensation. Compared to goods transportation, passenger transportation used to be neglected by the legislators. Airlines and many others have realized the importance of long-term relationships and understand that legal tricks spoil relationships. Instead, they volunteer to solve problems and the outcome is reinforced relationships.

The number of lawyers in the United States has trippled during the past 30 years and in 2007 they were well over 1 million. This is twice as many lawyers *per capita* as in the United Kingdom, 3 times as many as in Germany and 25 times as many as Japan. The United States has 5 per cent of the world's population but at least 25 per cent of its lawyers.

All these lawyers must find work. By tradition or formal regulation, lawyers only got jobs through personal relationships and professional networks. This is not enough today and US lawyers indulge in fierce hypercompetition and innovative marketing in the red ocean. There are 'ambulance chasers', looking for traffic victims, helping to sue as many parties as possible in the vicinity of the accident. They encourage citizens to sue each other. In some countries lawyers take on cases on speculation and the customer does not take a monetary risk; the lawyer's fee may be a third or half of the settlement if they win.

It can therefore pay to speculate in law just like in a lottery. They have also found new markets, blue oceans which at least stay blue for some time.

Frivolous suits in the United States have become a problem in the relationship between customers and suppliers. Frivolous in a strict legal sense refers to lawsuits that are unfounded and unreasonable. In colloquial language it also includes the claim for excessive damages. These lawsuits are a speculation in the imperfections of the law, shortcomings of judges and jury members, and the other party's frailties or lack of power. It is not a matter of who *is* right, it is a matter of who *gets* right. Law can both support security and cause insecurity.

Another strategy of securing the future of the legal profession has the character of mega marketing. By making sure that new legislation is continuously passed, the market keeps expanding. A good political support for the future is the fact that 40 per cent of the members of the US congress and 60 per cent of the senate are lawyers. Going to law school is considered a road to a bright future.

The threat of litigation, together with the bureaucracy and complicated interstate regulations in the United States, is a major hurdle experienced by overseas companies. Here are some legal cases from the US market showing the strains on customer–supplier relationships:[85]

- Electrolux, with 30 per cent of its sales in the United States, had 8 lawyers at its American headquarters dealing with some 400 legal cases. At its international headquarters there were 4 lawyers dealing with the rest of the world, but with no case taken to court for several years.
- According to US law there is a strict product liability. It is enough if a product is present when an accident occurs – not to have caused the accident – to make the manufacturer potentially liable. A Volvo owner in California filled up with contaminated petrol and after a while the engine stopped. The driver parked the car by the kerb and walked across the street when he was hit by another car and broke a leg. He sued Volvo. The strategy is 'Go for the deep pocket'.
- Two of the most publicized instances of punitive damages[86] in the United States concern a doctor and a granny. The doctor managed to get $4 million in compensation and punitive damages for bad paint on his BMW car. A granny, departing from a McDonald's drive-in, spilt hot coffee and burnt herself severely. She needed 8 days

---

[85] The examples from Electrolux and Volvo, as well as some of the background material for this section, are taken from Ramsey (1991).
[86] Punitive damages, termed exemplary damages in the United Kingdom, are the part awarded to make the supplier understand that it has to change its behaviour. The amount is set in relation to the size of the supplier. Compensatory damages are paid to compensate the claimant for loss, injury or harm.

in a hospital. At that time the hamburger chain made its coffee extremely hot to get more out of the coffee bean. The reason she sued was that the chain refused to give any compensation at all for her costs. If it had, granny would have gone unnoticed by the public. Now she was awarded $2.7 million by a court although the amount was later reduced to $400 000.

- Betty Bullock started to smoke at the age of 17. In her forties she contracted lung cancer and sued cigarette manufacturer Phillip Morris. She was awarded US$850 000 in compensation and a whopping $28 billion (yes, billion) in punitive damages, that is to punish Philip Morris. The previous record was held by smoker Richard Boeken who was awarded 3 billion. Bullock's claim was later considered excessive and reduced to 28 million. As her lawyer said, the tobacco company had lured her into a life-long habit knowing that it was selling death.

These examples sound like fabrications for a TV sitcom – and they are funny until you discover they are for real. It is common knowledge today that smoking causes disease and death and excessive compensation does not change your life. Both smokers died of lung cancer before they could enjoy their new fortunes – but their heirs became filthy rich! It is against common sense as long as the tobacco industry is not illegal. And how do you compensate for an early death and bodily suffering beyond medical help and help to improve your comfort? Life is full of risks. In the same spirit a serious and devastating attack on legal and bureaucratic systems – with the striking title *The Death of Common Sense: How Law is Suffocating America* – is offered by Howard (1994), himself a lawyer. The randomness of the courts' decisions where a jury of lay people are influenced by the sued company being rich, domestic or foreign, and how pitiful the prosecuting party stands out, adds no value to the market or society. They are lawsuit lotteries.

Mass torts, where a large number of customers simultaneously sue a company, are becoming a special type of litigation. When customers experience that a product has been damaging to their health, they have no other chance than to unite. Injuries caused by a herbicide and asbestos fibres each had a quarter of million claimants; Dow Corning and other manufacturers of breast implants had almost half a million claimants; and in 1997, the tobacco industry agreed to set aside funds for the victims of smoking, to the amount of $350 billion, that is, the staggering sum of three hundred and fifty thousand million dollars!

Compared with business contracts in Europe or the United States, those in Japan are short and vague.[87] The Japanese rely on relationships rather than legalities; the latter are felt as an intrusion. Many of the key elements of a business deal are left for later

---

[87] Based on an Asia Society presentation by Carl J. Green, Hitachi, in Washington D.C., March 14, 2001. 'Japan: The Rule of Law Without Lawyers Reconsidered'.

determination as circumstances develop. The parties often agree just to negotiate their differences in good faith. Japanese like to think of their business deals in terms of human relationships; it is RM.

Consequently business in Japan has little use for lawyers but legal contracts are important in dealings with foreigners. The inward orientation of most of Japan's industrial establishment poses a problem in globalisation, and it inhibits venture capital and entrepreneurship. Doing business with a friend who you trust, and who confesses to the traditional institution of Japan to honour trust, is one thing. Doing business with someone you don't know becomes difficult and legal protection is necessary. There is a gradual movement towards the use of more Western-style written contracts among Japanese businesses, but it is still the exception. Law is described with the metaphor of a sacred sword: It is kept and occasionally displayed, but never used. Underpinning this is Confucianism and its tradition of 'benevolent paternalism' and Japan's adoption of Western law is a result of foreign pressure.

To be forced to go to court in Japan is considered a defeat for all parties. Those who break a business agreement will not be seen as trustworthy in the future and will be excluded from the business community. In US business life it is considered smart to trap counterparts; in Japan a trial has only losers.[88] On the other hand, Japanese business can be ruthless to foreign companies who have to sue them and be persistent to secure, for example, patent rights.

The way legislation has mushroomed in America creates a strained relationship between customers and suppliers, such as between patients and hospitals. Both health insurance and hospital insurance rates rise, in turn burdening the patient's cost. Doctors have to be on guard every moment. There is also a positive side; the insights into the secluded guild of doctors are improved. The United States has gone to a ludicrous extreme and fantasy damages can be awarded to people who are in a legal sense maltreated. In other countries, for example Sweden, you must have robust health in order to survive if you challenge the health and hospital systems; the damages for malpractice are no more than an insult to the consumer.

I can speculate in two explanations for these developments. One is that the bureaucratic–legal values have taken over from common sense and human empathy. The other is that citizens have got so fed up with the treatment they have received as consumers – unfulfilled promises in advertising, low-quality products and services, little or no willingness to settle complaints, monopoly behaviour – that they are now hitting back.

Suing someone is a natural part of marketing in the United States, but it is not mentioned in marketing texts: 'This is business. We're not doing business out of love.'

---

[88] The Japanese examples are based on Delaryd (1989, pp. 57–59).

According to Blumberg:[89] 'It is an elementary sociological fact that as the social fabric of society unravels, shared values and norms that once guided behaviour break down and are replaced by formal codes, regulations, and laws. As the sense of community withers further, social conflict intensifies and litigation proliferates as each person seeks advantage at the expense of others.'

New forms for mitigation are sought, however. In the United States, 95 per cent of all cases are solved in the last minute before a trial. Legal systems – or rather a set of loosely linked components – are extremely closed and tied to rituals. One practical solution is a private American company organized around a network of 2000 retired judges who solve disputes faster and more simply than the courts do.[90]

In a thesis on the significance of contractual law for organizing companies and markets, an article from 1931 by Karl Llewellyn is quoted:[91] '... transactions come in a variety of forms and ... a highly legalistic approach can sometimes get in the way of the parties instead of contributing to their purposes. This is especially true where continuity of the exchange relation between the parties is highly valued.' The statement is equally applicable today; it shows that RM as a phenomenon is an old common-sense practice. The author further points out that a transaction which is unambiguously defined in a contract and which is then fulfilled in each and every detail is unusual, and that we deceive ourselves by believing otherwise.

In the spirit of RM, we could speak of *relationship contracts* which include legal aspects as well as negotiations to solve a problem, an assessment of the long-term consequences for future collaboration, and high ethical standards. It seems like a merger between the United States and Japanese extremes would be optimal for the future.

 The criminal network

Many have asked whether I really consider criminal networks to belong in a book on RM. My question is rather: How long can marketing textbooks pretend that organized crime and financial fraud do not impact on marketing strategy and the functioning of the market? Organized crime wipes out the blessings of sound competition and has an effect on customer relationships in many markets. It is growing and it infiltrates governments on all levels as well as legitimate enterprises. Even a financially well-established and sophisticated country like Switzerland has found mafias from one of the least sophisticated countries, Russia, intruding on a large number of Swiss corporations.

---

[89] Blumberg (1989, p. 209).
[90] Based on Harper (1993, p. 10).
[91] Quotation from an article by Karl Llewellyn and reproduced by Williamson (1981).

Crime is such a diverse area; it is several economies that need their own theories to be understood and kept back. Here I can only give glimpses of relational issues, especially stressing the import of networks. Today's crime on a large scale cannot exist without the support of extremely strong ties between criminals, their victims and institutions in society, such as governments, certain sectors like finance, and specialists like accountants. Being treated as a necessary evil with marginal impact in developed countries it has not earned its place in marketing and economics texts. Its been a matter for the police and the law. But this is a false picture. It is equally much a matter for satisfying needs and wants in the market.

The criminal relationship takes its stance in organized crime but the broader concept of 'systems-threatening criminality' is perhaps more adequate.[92] It includes all types of criminal activity that disrupts the market, irrespective of whether it emanates from an organization dedicated to crime, or takes place inside an otherwise legitimate corporation.

I would like to make a distinction between crimes from a strictly *legal* standpoint and those from and *ethical* standpoint. By using the law and being supported by groups of lawyers, the biggest criminals are often acquitted. There is lack of evidence, witnesses have been silenced and there may be legal technicalities and corruption in the judicial system. From an ethical standpoint it is still a crime.

Nowhere are networks more closed and less transparent than in organized crime. The networks are frequently reinforced by ethnicity and are tightly kept within families. Organized crime can consist of a global mafia, but also of a long-term relationship between a local thief and a fence. The presence of criminal networks impacts the relationships between the triad of suppliers, customers and competitors, and impairs the marketing equilibrium. Economic crime disturbs and threatens the functioning of whole economic systems as well as single markets. The networks comprise organizations built on a criminal business mission such as trade in narcotics, fencing and 'protection'. It can also comprise legal trade which, behind a respectable facade, is using bribery, murder and threats to get orders. Within originally legal trade there are also false promises, illegal use of brands, tax fraud, computer crimes, and the misuse of shareholder and customer assets to augment the wealth of management and board members.

The epitome of corporate crime in recent years is Enron, originally a legitimate United States corporation that turned criminal. In its new shape it was hailed for its entrepreneurship and growth. It was audited by the accounting firm Arthur Anderson, one of the largest in the world. It worked with the prestigious management consulting firm McKinsey and with the biggest banks and financial institutions. It gradually based its operations on fraud, both in the stock market and, for example, by obstructing the functionality of the electricity market. It is not an isolated example.

---

[92] Hartelius (2007).

Financial crime has become IT-based; it is more comfortable to rob a bank and its customers with a laptop at home than with guns at a bank branch. No doubt independent hackers are involved but it is also organized. It needs skills and knowledge about financial systems and money laundering possibilities through the financial sector and offshore banking. It requires employees with IT and business school education. The criminal networks are fast, authorities are slow; the networks think as entrepreneurs and adjust to change, authorities think as bureaucrats that maintain status quo.

I particularly want to show two things. First, networks of relationships are a condition for sustaining criminal business operations. Second, if the good market forces in certain industries or geographical areas are obstructed, the rules of the competitive game are set aside and the existence for law-abiding businesses is jeopardized and consumers are defrauded.[93] Obviously the reason for detailing criminal relationships is not to teach unethical and illegal behaviour. The reason is that illegal networks are widespread and that it is important to demonstrate their effect on legal marketing. For the same reason, the University of Buenos Aires introduced courses in the mechanisms of corruption and other illegal procedures.[94]

When monitoring professional journals and news media for organized crime and other illegal acts by companies and governments, I found the subject to be treated daily. It stands out clearly that organized crime and corruption are not limited to a few countries and regions; they are omnipresent, although their 'market share' and influence vary. A report on corruption in the world,[95] based on the experience of businesspeople and country analysts, puts Finland, Iceland and New Zealand as the least corrupt (score 9.6 on a scale where 10 is best) and not surprisingly some of the poorest countries as the most corrupt. Out of the 163 countries included in the report 98 score 3.5 down to 1.8. The United Kingdom scores 8.6, France 7.4, the US 7.3 and Italy 4.9.

Even with the top score, Finland, is struck by economic crimes. In one study on 'outlaw marketing' Lindqvist (2006) surveyed criminal relationships in a region of Finland. It revealed that economic crimes, including the black market for labour, accounted for 4 per cent of the GDP. He notes that the criminal groups tend to be ahead of the police in forming new networks and inventing new techniques. The importance of a network of authorities, political life and family is demonstrated by a policeman who was also a member of a town council. He was sentenced for drug trafficking but after having served time in prison he continued with counterfeiting dollar bills, and later a relative took over his drug business.

In countries with a low rate of domestic corruption, major cases have been reported to surface from global companies. In their efforts to increase smoking in a situation

---

[93] For an overview of economic effects of organized crime, see Fiorentini and Peltzman (1995).
[94] From *Time* (1993, p. 16).
[95] According to a survey by Transparency International reported in the media in 2006.

where countries prohibit cigarette advertising and smoking in buildings, Philip Morris and R. J. Reynolds are accused of organizing large-scale cigarette smuggling. The former Director of Research at one of the large tobacco companies has revealed how ingredients were added to escalate nicotine addiction. His experiences have been exposed in the movie *The Insider*, a drama documentary from 1999 with Al Pacino and Russell Crowe.

Organized crime is reported through official investigations, research institutes, investigative journalism and memoirs, and it is a pet theme in novels and entertainment. Scholarly research on organized crime is limited. It is a matter of surveying closed and protected networks; talk about proprietary information! Even if ongoing criminal activity is publicly known, people are frightened of speaking out or taking action. Research can be done as covert action research where researchers infiltrate an organization under disguise. It can also be done through people who have defected and are willing to talk, and through criminal investigators and courtroom proceedings. The story by Italian judge Falcone about his war on organized crime, told just before he was assassinated, has credibility as a report from the inside.[96]

Except for the godfather, no one is supposed to be able to overview the cells and relationships of the network. A family is often in the core and social ties are strong. Telling on someone produces a clear feedback; you are not fired, you are fired at.

The shadow economy of a country – its unofficial economic sector – consists of the black, illegal economy, and of household and voluntary activities which are not registered in the GNP. All statistics of the shadow economy are uncertain, but assessments of 10–20 per cent of the economies of industrialized countries are often reported in the media. The abandoning of the border checks within the EU and the dissolution of the Soviet empire offer new 'business' opportunities, and so do value added tax and subsidies within deficient control systems. The turmoil and ignorance of this new situation, and gaps and differences in legislation and institutions between countries, are taken advantage of. The 'four freedoms' of the EU – free movement of goods, services, labour and capital across national borders – and the common currency, the euro, not only facilitate for legitimate businesses but also facilitate illegal trade and money laundering.

Covert price cartels are another type of illegal networks. Representatives of the largest companies in some industries meet once or twice a year to fix world market prices and decide on markets and market share. They meet in an airport hotel, different each time, and leave no written records behind. Bidding cartels – competitors that agree on who is going to give the lowest bid and thereby get the order – kill competition in certain areas of the building and construction sector. These illegal forms of RM also occur in companies where everything else is operated according to laws and regulations.

---

[96] Falcone and Padovani (1992).

Money laundering is an important part of illegal trade. Black money which can be traced must be turned into white money. If 70 per cent of black money from the drug trade is laundered, US $15–60 billion of 'dirty money' will be passed through the international financial systems. Parlour offers the following description of the laundering process and the network, which is required to perform the process, follows a certain pattern.[97] First, the money must be deposited (placement). Then the money is separated from its source by a series of confusing and complex financial transactions which make it hard for accountants and police to trace (layering). Eventually, the money is placed in legitimate funds (integration). He forecasts '... further sophistication of money laundering techniques, greater investment of dirty money into established businesses, further internationalization of money laundering networks and intensified involvement of criminal organizations'.

A disquieting but long-term trend is that legitimate and illegitimate practices are woven together into a fabric of relationships. They become invisible power organizations – like octopuses stretching out their many arms into all corners of markets and society. Organized crime increasingly establishes itself behind respectable fronts, investing in companies on the stock exchanges, using IT and sending their staff on executive training programmes. The establishment of mega relationships in order to involve people in high places is a necessity for organized crime. It cannot thrive without the support of a network of government officials, police and courts, and specialists such as lawyers, accountants, chemists and physicians. Crime becomes embedded in the power centres of society. In the Russian parliament, the douma, it has been estimated that 40 per cent of the members have organized crime connections. A seat in the douma is a strategic investment as its members used to have immunity from the law and could not be the object of criminal investigation or prosecution.

In order to be competitive, organized crime indulges in a series of most effective acts, such as physical threat, bribery, kidnapping, blackmailing, assault, murder and arson, and legal technicalities are used to obstruct justice. These marketing tools are never mentioned in marketing textbooks. It is hard to tell how frequently they are used, but there is no doubt that they are crucial for marketing 'success'. All the same, organized crime can run into financial difficulties. In 1995, an accumulation of events led to red figures for Italian mafia organizations. Some 4000 bosses, 'employees' and affiliates were in prison; lawyers' fees skyrocketed, as did the monthly salaries guaranteed by the mafia to its inactive staff; property had been confiscated by the police; and operations in their most lucrative market – bidding for building and construction contracts – had been halted by the authorities.

---

[97] Parlour (1993; quotation from p. 66).

'Facilitating payments' can be a euphemism for bribes but they may be a condition for certain types of business. Such payments appear under various disguises. It is hard to uncover what is behind certain consulting fees and commissions. The borderline between corruption and legal dealings is unclear and each country has its own laws and customs. The arms contract between Bofors and India became a sensitive issue at the end of the 1980s and 20 years later the dispute is still not settled. Prime ministers and other officials from both sides were involved in exercising pressure, and facilitating payments were suspected. Corruption among Italian politicians and civil servants has been continuously reported. These have been given *'tangenti'* – kickbacks – which means that to make a buying organization accept a supplier's offer, a percentage of the order sum has to be returned as a personal gift to those who handle the purchase. A scandal in Milan showed that *tangenti* were a *sine qua non* to getting orders for building, construction and service contracts for the subway, airport, railroad, sports stadium and theatre. In defence of competing suppliers, it was established that there was no realistic way of getting an order without facilitating payments.

Organized crime is a challenge to the 'violence monopoly of the state'. One definition of organized crime is 'violence-based private protection operations in conflict with the state violence monopoly'.[98] The inertia of bureaucracy and its red tape, outdated regulations, and a lack of leadership and institutions open up a market for organized crime. When a state cannot handle the protection against muggings and shoplifting, criminal groups can provide the protection for a fee and do it efficiently. The boundary between legal regimes and authorities and illegal organizations then becomes subtle. A legal system can be designed in a way that it is next to impossible to do business. Established gangs, *'yakuzas'* in Japan, work more or less overtly. If *yakuzas* are left with their trade – primarily gambling and betting – they help the police to keep other crimes down. They can also be hired for special assignments, such as intimidating competitors or people who refuse to sell a company or a house.[99] In some areas of the world, the majority of small stores and restaurants are forced to pay for 'protection' in order not to become victims of violence.

Here are some examples of how criminal networks operate on a national and global scale with crime as business mission:

- *Italy*: The revenue of organized crime in Italy was estimated at $120 billion in 2006 which makes it Italy's biggest business. Mafia networks have diversified into all sectors of the economy. Partly it is in strictly illegal businesses such as narcotics, car theft, hijacking of trucks and their loads, pirate copies, extortion and loan sharking. Partly it is illegal action within legitimate sectors, among them garbage disposal where they

---

[98] Lappalainen (1993).
[99] According to Rossander (1992).

dump dangerous garbage that destroys the environment; food products such as cooking oils, mozarella, parma ham and beer produced with unsuitable ingredients; and building and construction where they are awarded contract through extortion and threats. The majority of the money is laundered and lands on the official financial market and so they can buy stock in legitimate corporations. They are strongest in the otherwise poor southern Italy where 80 per cent of shops pay a monthly sum to criminals to be able to conduct their business undisturbed; in northern Italy it is 20 per cent. The four largest 'corporations' are *La Mafia* (Sicily), *'Ndrangheta* (Calabria), *La Camorra* (Naples) and *Sacra Corona Unita* (Puglia), all in the south. In the richer and industrialized northern Italy, says a business person, 'you can still say no to corruption, in the south they shoot you'. Increasingly big business seems to turn a blind eye to their crimes and find it easier to negotiate with the mafia then to report their rackets to the police. According to Lilley[100] '... the Italian Mafia are creating strategic alliances with other international organized crime groups, together with successfully exploiting new channels such as Internet stock trading'.

■ *Russia*: The former Soviet Union is an exemplar of how difficult it is to change from one economic system to another, from a planned commando economy to a market economy. During the communist hegemony for over 70 years and during the czar era before that, black markets grew strong. So there was already a professional group of black market businesspeople with long experience. Low-salaried civil servants had to take bribes to survive, so the system of corruption was well developed. The excessive bureaucratic power of the 'nomenklatura' epitomizes the famous lines from George Orwell's 1945 satirical allegory *Animal Farm*: 'All animals are equal but some animals are more equal than others'. They took over state assets for little or nothing. They were used to handle it for the state and now they did it for themselves. Competition did not exist and was not accepted meaning that foreign investment and entrepreneurship were punished by 'comrad criminals'. In other words, institutions and regulations to support crime were already in place, but institutions to support the new market economy were non-existent. For example, there were no shareholder's rights and there was no experience in handling economic crimes. As North said (see R3) it takes several hundred years to establish functioning institutions, such as legislation and courts. As much as 70 per cent of Russia's business is estimated to be criminal, with up to 5800 crime syndicates. Soviet organized crime was divided among different 'corporations'. The Krasnodar mafia ruled the tourist trade in the Crimea, the Uzbekistani mafia the cotton trade and the Azerbaijani mafia the petrol industry. A string of organizations had conquered niches of the market, such as fruit and vegetables, collection of customs

---

[100] Lilley (2000, p. 177); see also Lappalainen (2007) and Savioni (2008).

tariffs and foreign trade. The political power and organized crime were united in securing privileges for the communist elite. Today, largely the same people, together with trained members of former 'security' organizations, constitute the core of organized crime. A particularly profitable service industry is prostitution, both in domestic and foreign markets. According to statistics from the Russian Ministry of the Interior, prostitution is Russia's third largest industry after the weapons and drug trades. The largest threat to the creation of a market economy in Russia is probably organized crime and the lack of adequate institutions and regulations. Foreign companies that establish themselves in Russia and many of the former Soviet Union states have to pay special attention to organized crime. The gas stations of Statoil, the Norwegian oil corporation, were exposed to car bombs. The objective of Statoil was to open 40 stations in the Baltic States by 1998. Two security companies were hired for 24-hour surveillance of stations, offices and the residences of key staff. The infiltration of organized crime among authorities led to brutally executed tax raids in companies.[101]

These two countries serve only as examples. Organized crime and corruption are integral parts of every economy. Here are some examples reported in the media:

- Pirate products are 5–7 per cent of global trade.
- British companies annually loose 6 per cent of its revenue as a consequence of corporate crimes.
- The World Health Organization (WHO) estimates that 10 per cent of all medication is pirate copies that are useless or dangerous; in Africa it is 40–60 per cent.
- The World Bank considers corruption as the biggest obstacle to economic and social development.
- The amphetamine exports of The Netherlands are claimed to be bigger today than its well-known trade in tulips and bulbs.
- Bolivia, Colombia and Peru account for 98 per cent of the world cocaine trade.
- According to the Italian mafia prosecutor Caselli, organized crime worldwide had a global revenue of US $700–1000 billion in 1996. It has grown considerably since.
- The narcotics trade alone is the second largest industry in the world after arms, but before oil; it could amount to 8 per cent of world trade.
- Globally organized crime corresponds to 15–20 per cent of the GNP of the United States and is 8 times the GNP of Switzerland.[102]

---

[101] See also Bagelius (2003).
[102] Lilley (2000, pp. 28–29).

We should note that these numbers are generalised and show averages. In markets such as building and construction and in certain regions, criminality controls the majority of economic activity. The bulk of criminal phenomena are hard to catch, not least because they are deliberately hidden. So statistics give a deceptive and incomplete image of reality and the rest has to be found out through unorthodox qualitative methods.

Let us recall Blumberg's (1989) paradox discussed in R2, claiming that the strengths of the market economy – competition and the profit incentive – encourage fraud. In economic theory and its limiting assumptions about market mechanisms, violence is not included. In reality it is different; in crime-controlled markets violence is the number one marketing tool. Both marketing theory and economics are treating criminal market mechanisms with naivety. Both white collar economic crime and organized violence distort the functionality of the marketplace and obstruct the dynamics of the marketing equilibrium.

There is little doubt that criminal networks gain more power and that they gain it through alliances with companies and governments, through infiltration, pressure and bribery. A provocative hypothesis – and not a very agreeable one, but probably true – is that a certain element of illegal action is necessary to make an economy work. Weak governments and inadequate official institutions/regulations and competition open the market for illegal entrepreneurship and disrupts the marketing equilibrium. RM, however naively, persists on a belief in win–win value creation both from a commercial and a societal perspective.

QUESTIONS FOR DISCUSSION

1 Discuss the statements 'Everybody is either an FTM or a PTM. Those employees who do not influence the relationships to customers full-time or part-time, directly or indirectly, are redundant'.

2 In R5, two issues should especially be noted. In line with S-D logic, the service encounter has been broadened to embrace all value propositions and their service, and not just services as opposed to goods. It is further shown that those involved in and around the service encounter perceive the encounter from a different perspective than the customer. Do you have any comments to these two issues?

3 What is your personal attitude to tipping? Is it a good incentive for an employee to establish long-term relationships with customers? And how do customers feel about it?

4 RM is usually described as creating long-term relationships between a supplier and a customer, one-to-one. But both in B2B and B2C/C2B reality requires a many-to-many approach where the supplier and the customer are many-headed. Give some examples of this from the book or from your own experience.

5 Why should a supplier pay attention to the customer's customer?

6 Why is the close relationship to the customer important in RM? Isn't it enough to get statistics on customers through a survey?

7 In R9 '5 prejudices about complaints' are listed. Why are these 5 prejudices?

8 Despite the increasingly heavier emphasis of competition and free market economies, monopolies remain in many areas. Should we or could we abolish all monopolies?

9 Customer clubs are everywhere. Which are their strengths and weaknesses in creating relationships with customers?

10 The e-relationship has penetrated everybody's life. Why is the high tech/high touch balance important?

11 Branding is an effort to create a parasocial relationship with customers. What is your personal stance to brands? Do feel you have a special relationship to any specific brands?

12 How do commercial and non-commercial relationships differ?

13 Is charity a good way of showing CSR?

14 How strong is really the green relationship? Despite the unprecedented attention that is being given to green issues these days, the majority of customers, companies and governments seem reluctant to take action. What does the green relationship mean to you personally?

15 R16 presents the 'Law-based relationship' showing that legal action sometimes is an important parameter in marketing, sometimes not. Especially in the United States, litigation is common and consumers can be offered astronomic compensation from companies. Do you think the United States 'I'll sue you' attitude' is a good or bad thing?

16 Why bring up 'The criminal network' in a marketing book?

Chapter

4

Mega relationships

INTRODUCTION

Chapters 2 and 3 dealt with market relationships, the relationships to suppliers, customers, competitors and others who operate in the market and certain properties of these relationships. This chapter is about mega relationships, located a step above the market relationships, in society in general. The mega relationships (R18–R23) set conditions for market relationships.

RELATIONSHIP 18

Personal and social networks

In many cultures, business is not conducted with strangers and where business with strangers is accepted, the preference is usually for people one knows and likes. This is often perceived to be the typical case in Asia and some other areas. But personal and social networks carry weight in Western Europe and the United States, too. Even in the age of the Internet and e-relationships, the h-relationship remains pivotal. Personal and social relationships are the most stable part of business life and can even help to mitigate recessions.[1] The formation and maintenance of social networks are important tasks for top management, marketing and sales. Sometimes social networks may even be more important than professional relationships and a supplier's competence.

As Figure 4.1 shows, personal relationships and social networks have emerged from different areas of life, and they mostly have an origin other than business. It is therefore justified to approach them as mega relationships.

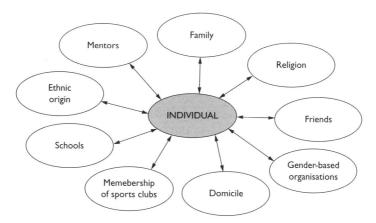

Figure 4.1 Different types of relationships that constitute an individual's social network

---

[1] McKenna (1985).

Personal networks – the old boy network, invisible colleges – are locked for non-members. It may be just as appropriate to speak about old girl networks, as those can be strong through family, friendship, ownership and class bonds, and their power is probably underrated.[2] Gender-based networks have attracted growing attention, particularly as women have formed their own networks against the suspected conspiracy of male networks. Rotary, composed of 'prominent representatives' from different trades and professions, used to be open only to men, but since the end of the 1980s it has also been open to women.

It is possible if not always easy to establish new business relationships in the United States, but it is just as easy to break the relationships. In Japan it is difficult to be accepted, but relationships last. 'Keiretsu' is the designation for long term, personal and financial relationships between companies. The good side is the potential productivity of a stable relationship, the bad side is that others are locked out which inhibits competition. In the 6 largest keiretsus, firms are 15 times more likely to borrow capital within their own group and 3 times more likely to trade with members than with outsiders.[3] The president of the US Chamber of Commerce in Japan once claimed that keiretsus, bidding cartels and personal networks are formidable obstacles for US firms in Japan, whereas Japanese firms in the United States do not encounter similar resistance.[4] At the same time, a study concludes that 94 per cent of large multinational corporations established in Japan are doing very well.[5]

According to Nakane:[6]

> In scope and density of personal relationships and in availability,
> 'school clique' relationships function more effectively than kinship
> … those educated outside Japan are handicapped in their careers.
> On the other hand, a foreigner who has been educated in Japan is
> accepted in the group and can enjoy and make use of in-group
> feelings … the sharing of experience during the critical period
> of the teens and twenties has life-long effects.

In Japan, both presidents of large corporations and government organizations come primarily from the University of Tokyo and some of the other leading universities.[7] Together with corporations, government agencies and politicians, they form a comparatively closed system within which a power elite is produced. Only when there is need to refill the systems are new members let in. It is common that an official of a public agency, at the age of

---

[2] Kahn and Yoshihara (1994).
[3] Gerlach (1992, pp. 121 and 144).
[4] From an interview in *Fortune* (Faltermayer, 1992).
[5] According to Kahn and Yoshihara (1994).
[6] Nakane (1981, p. 134).
[7] This and the following paragraph are based on Taira and Wada (1987); the example of the steel industry is taken from p. 271.

40 to 50, transfers to industry and becomes a colleague with his fellow students who entered a business career. In the meantime, their sons grow up and enter the system and social alliances are formed through marriage. Clans and dynasties are established. The German word 'Schicksalverbundenhei' – to be linked through a common destiny – has been adopted by the Japanese language. An example is found in the case study below.

CASE STUDY   **Japanese friendships**

Yoshihiro Inayama and Shigeo Nagano were both graduates from the University of Tokyo, one in 1924, the other in 1927. Nagano began his career at the private steelworks Fuji, and Inayama at the state-owned steelworks Yawata. In 1935, the two corporations merged into Nippon Steel. Nagano became section manager of the purchasing department and Inayama received a position in the sales department. After the Second World War, US General MacArthur broke up the merger for antitrust reasons. Nagano advanced to chief executive of Fuji and Inayama to chief executive of Yawata. In 1963, Nagano was elected chairman of the iron and steel industry organization, and was succeeded by Inayama some years later. The two again merged Fuji and Yawata into a new Nippon Steel with Nagano as chairman of the board and Inayama as CEO. Nagano later became the leader of Nissho, a powerful coalition of chambers of commerce. Ten years later, Inayama became head of Keidanren, another coalition between businesses. The two friends now headed one of the world's largest steelworks and the two mightiest business coalitions in Japan. Taira and Wada conclude that '... the two close friends ruled Japan's business community and indirectly governed Japan itself'. The behaviour of the whole steel market was controlled by the personal relationship between two school friends.

Networks based on friendship and family bonds are highly stable but require the members to adhere to tacit regulations/institutions. The team feeling is highly developed in Japan and it is almost a capital punishment to be excluded from the family, company or university alumni association. It is practically impossible to exist in business if you are out of favour with the group.[8]

The ties to family and friends are grounded in strong feelings and values, not restricted by national boundaries or current domicile. Kotkin (1993) claims that 'the global village' is

---

[8] Delaryd (1989, p. 175).

built of tribes, people with the same ethnic and religious roots. Their bonds outrank national industry policies and traditions. He lists several such networks: Jewish families have, since the Middle Ages, engaged in trade and finance; the Anglo-Saxon tribe consisting of Calvinists who emigrated from the British Isles to America spread their accounting system and trade law, and English as the international business language; Japanese expatriates who left their resource-poor home country see loyalty to their countrymen as the number 1 priority; and Chinese and Indian clans control global networks of finance, and manufacture and market textile products, jewellery and IT products. The swift rise of the Chinese market economy has been made possible through relationships with Chinese expatriates. This 'bamboo network' favours relatives at the expense of Western investors.[9] Western business people getting into China are at a disadvantage as they lack social bonds with key informants and gatekeepers.[10] There is strong distrust towards strangers; they do not get access to information on potential customers, for example on upcoming tenders. The 'guanxi' network is highly personal; social relationships come first – they are on a mega level – and they can be followed by market relationships and form the basis for new network organizations.[11]

Social relationships and personal networks also play an important role in European and American societies. In his study of trust, Fukuyama[12] says that:

> … if Americans were traditionally as individualistic as they think they
> are, it would be hard to account for the rapid rise of giant corporations
> in the United States in the nineteenth century … These supposedly
> individualistic Americans have also been, historically, hyperactive
> joiners, creating strong and durable voluntary organizations from Little
> Leagues and 4H Clubs to the National Rifle Association, the NAACP,
> and the League of Women Voters.

Here is a case from Europe.

CASE STUDY   **Mærsk McKinney-Møller**

In a recent 'Reputation Quotient' study in Denmark, its largest company A.P. Möller-Maersk conquered the No. 1 reputation rank, reflecting how visible a brand is.[13] It is somewhat surprising as the company is mainly in B2B and Bang & Olufsen, which is primarily B2C/C2B and well known for its cutting-edge

---

[13] Apéria, Brönn and Schultz (2004).

---

[9] Wiedenbaum and Hughes (1996).
[10] Björkman and Kock (1997).
[11] See further Fang (1999).
[12] Fukuyama (1995, pp. 270–272).

design of high-end audio products, television sets and telephones, only ranked No. 4. A reason could be Denmark's grand industrialist, the now 95-year-old Arnold Mærsk McKinney-Møller. He mixes with kings and queens, presidents, government members and the world's most powerful business leaders. It gives him high visibility in the media, but his brand name of Maersk is visible on ships and containers in harbours around the world. As a personal friend of Thomas Watson – the man who once made IBM the world's leading computer company – he served for many years as the only non-American on the board of directors of IBM. His personal and social relationships on a mega level made it possible for him to direct conditions in the market in his favour. The members of his 'non-market network' are socially empowered to influence regulations, provide financial assistance, bypass gatekeepers and expedite bureaucratic procedures. They have access to privileged information. Maersk McKinney-Møller shows social responsibility by sharing his wealth with society through several foundations, which further boosts his standing in a mega context. In 2005 a landmark building, the new Copenhagen Opera facing the Royal Palace, was inaugurated. He funded it and very actively spent time getting his ideas implemented. He was demanding, committed and focused; it is rumoured that he was the architects' nightmare.

Network membership can also fool you. Membership based on position alone is lost if the position is lost. Presidents of important corporations often draw their power solely on their position. I have met a number of ex-chief executives who have been forced to leave their job because of a merger or disagreement with the owners, sometimes also because of failure. They are forced to find a new job, or start their own business, or become consultants. They often claim that they have contacts everywhere, but their 'friendship' was based on position. When the position is snatched away, the 'friends' quickly leave the sinking vessel.

The US ex-presidents are asked for as advisers and board members as well as speakers. Former Secretary of State Henry Kissinger established Kissinger Associates, Inc. The business mission was exploitation of Kissinger's experience and personal network, and the unique knowledge and power that followed. His capital was personal access to government members and other key leaders throughout the world. He sold informed advice on international affairs, access to the powerful elite and the opportunity of hobnobbing with Henry Kissinger.[14] Among his 30 customers have been GTE, Volvo and Montedison.

---

[14] *Newsweek* (1990, pp. 34–35).

The borderline between social and professional relationships is partly erased; work may become an around-the-clock lifestyle. Membership in professional associations gives an opportunity to meet competitors and have informal discussions, sometimes of great significance. Playing golf has long been considered a key to informal but crucial business decisions.

Friendship is characterized by people speaking to each other, helping each other, trusting each other and spending leisure time together.[15] This can also happen in a commercial relationship which gradually changes character into genuine friendship: 'In communal relationships, members have a special obligation to be responsive to one another's needs, whereas in exchange relationships they do not'.[16] It can, however, result in abuse, and 'the friendly thief' is born.[17] Home-party selling thrives on the feeling that when you are there you should buy – but you know this before you go there so it is really your choice. The salespeople are usually housewives who arrange selling parties with invited neighbours and others. At the same time the party fulfils a social need which you as friend/customer may value and be willing to pay for.

It is hardly news for marketing practitioners that social networks exert influence. Sometimes they are critical, sometimes of little significance. Their role has not been taken up in the marketing and economics literature, especially not when the focus is directed to anonymous mass marketing, which used to characterize marketing management and still does in economics.

Mega marketing – the real 'customer' is not always found in the marketplace

Apart from the relationships between individuals in the seller's and buyer's organizations and their social networks, there are other relationships that open or close the presence in a market. This requires *mega marketing*.[18] It is marketing above the market proper which addresses public opinion and political power. Without the initial mega decision there is no market to address. This type of marketing seems to be growing in strategic importance. The social network of Mærsk McKinney-Møller in R18 is a strong platform for mega marketing.

Often the real battle for the market is not fought in the market. *The real battle is about being in the market at all*. Only after *mega decisions* have been taken in the non-market network – above the market relationships – it is wise to start building market relationships.

Through the lenses of economic theory, markets are seen as intensely competitive and rational. The invisible hand – the ability of the market economy to strive in the direction

[15] According to Goodwin (1994).

[16] Clark (1983, p. 282).

[17] Cialdini (2006).

[18] Kotler (1986; definition on pp. 117–118).

of equilibrium between supply and demand – is not just an abstract and self-regulating phenomenon. It is also a hands-on intervention by powerful agents whose influence is not visible from the outside.

For example, the market system in Japan is partly out of function through centralized control, disguised to give the impression of competition.[19] Former students from prestigious universities, industrial heads and government representatives make the decisions. If you are not accepted by them, you have little chance of success. It is essential to exploit both the market mechanisms and the central control: 'Successful Japanese businessmen who are adept at utilizing the rules of the marketplace are also generally good at the use of the nonmarket network of kinship and marital ties.'

Mega marketing is often the most important part of marketing for companies producing goods and services of infrastructural character, like telephone systems, military equipment and nuclear power plants, but it can be the concern of any product and market.

The principal idea behind mega relationships is shown in Figure 4.2, which is an extension of Figure 3.5. The figure illustrates B2B of a complex offering, but the same notion can be adjusted to B2C/C2B.

Although it has been discussed, mega marketing has not previously made its way into mainstream marketing theory. One early example is the financial wizard Ivar Kreuger, who built an empire during the beginning of the twentieth century. By merging factories in many countries, Kreuger became the world market leader in safety matches and was granted a monopoly in several countries where he offered favourable credits to governments. At most he had an 80 per cent world market share. Despite the financial crisis that

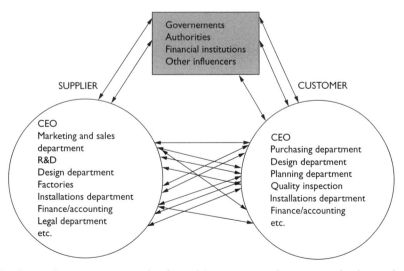

Figure 4.2 The real 'customer' can be found in a non-market network above the market

---

[19] The paragraph is based on Taira and Wada (1987; quotation from p. 288).

followed Kreuger's sudden death in 1932, the foundation was laid for a monopoly-like market status that has been sustained in some markets until late. The relationships on the mega level made marketing possible.

There are also general instances of locked networks on the mega level such as the 'military–industrial complex'.[20] Buyers are national military organizations and suppliers are domestic and foreign manufacturers of weapons and defence systems. Within the military–industrial network there is an extreme need for mutual trust. Suppliers design specifications that must not leak to the enemy. The belonging of the seller and buyer countries to defence pacts can determine the outcome of the negotiations. Doctors can also be a locked network and it can be difficult for the supplier to establish credibility. Mega marketing may be the solution as the next case shows.

CASE STUDY   **Healon**

Healon is injected into the eye during surgery and gently lifts and stabilizes the eye tissues. The substance dramatically enhanced the quality and productivity of common cataract surgery, but it required a revised surgical procedure. Healon could not be launched through the ordinary sales force, as the sales representatives did not have credibility among eye surgeons. Instead, the 10 most respected eye surgeons in the world were selected as the target group. If they converted to Healon, others would follow suit. Getting through to the megastars was not easy, it had to be achieved on a mega level. In one case, an effort was made to establish a relationship with a top Spanish surgeon who refused to meet vendors. A meeting was suggested with the Spanish Minister of Health, an ambassador, the president of Pharmacia-Upjohn and the surgeon. The purpose of the event was to perform surgery together under the guidance of the surgeon – on eyes from dead cows, though. The status of the event was such that the surgeon agreed to participate.[21]

Lobbying is increasingly a necessary mega marketing strategy. The term lobbying comes from the US Congress and its lobby, in which people waited to get an opportunity to speak to congressmen. Lobbying has developed into a profession. It is performed by trade organizations and interest groups as well as by single corporations. When FedEx were about to start, changes in the regulations for postal services were needed, and the company

---

[20] See Arndt (1979).
[21] Based on discussions with the executives in charge of the launching of Healon.

managed to get these thanks to lobbying in Washington DC. Corporate contributions to presidential campaigns are on the increase. What comes under the eyes of the public is more likely just the tip of the iceberg. More aggressive research, more lawsuits, deeper investigative journalism, clamour for transparency, and citizen movements with demonstrations and open conflicts are making the abuse of lobbying more exposed. Washington DC, harbours 15 000 registered lobbyists and several tens of thousands who are not registered. Among former members of Congress, 128 worked as lobbyists. A stream of detailed regulations has been introduced – no golf or ski weeks together, legislators can be asked to lunch no more than twice a year, to eat in somebody's home is allowed as long as people are not seated – but innovative loopholes are found continuously.

For a decade or more one of the largest lobbying projects concerns public opinion and political acceptance of gene manipulated food. One important objective was to introduce the new designation 'gene modified organism, GMO', which sounds less menacing than manipulated, and this introduction has been successful. The marketing of GMOs is implemented with the help of consultants; the establishment of networks of 'friends' among politicians, public administrators and scientists, the latter group renumerated indirectly through research grants; by whisking seemingly harmless but mandatory decisions through parliaments and supranational organs; by planting articles in papers and journals; and through advertising disguised as documentaries. The misgivings of the consumer are belittled or met with silence, and active opponents are labelled eco-terrorists. One strategy is unobtrusiveness and leave the consumer with no choice in the end. Hazardous to the health and the environment or a means to boost health and solve ecological problems – those who run the campaigns are taking on a huge responsibility for the future but they feel confident they will not have to face the consequences personally.

Close relationships to a certain political group or individual politician can provide a strong marketing edge. If these 'friends' lose power and popularity, however, the intimate relationship can backfire. Business generally tries to be non-political and sell to everyone, irrespective of political colour. The skill of maintaining relationships with many political parties may be the ground for future business.

In marketing terms, lobbying has been characterized as a decision market, the place (or space) where decisions are bought and sold. The need for lobbying is an effect of representative democracy not being, in practice, representative. Its evil sense, powerful economic interests can surpass the interests of society and citizens so that decision-makers dare not act, or are misled. In order to prevent the misuse of lobbying, several regulations have been introduced in the United States. For example, top officials and politicians are forbidden to work as lobbyists within 5 years of leaving office, thereby preventing them from 'selling' their administrative and political networks to external clients. In other countries there are no such regulations as the following case shows.

CASE STUDY   **The revolving door and support networks**

The 'revolving door' phenomenon is a designation for former politicians who are hired by lobbying firms. The firms want to profit from the politicians' celebrity status, get access to their network of high-level contacts and ability to open closed doors, as well as their knowledge of political decision processes. It is tempting as it is well paid. Recent acquisitions are the former member of the EU Parliament and former chair of the Dutch Social Democratic Party who was hired by the international PR and lobbying giant Burson-Marsteller, and the Swedish former Prime Minister Göran Persson hired by JKL, a leading firm in 'strategic communications' in Northern Europe. Both of these moved from representing the citizen to representing big business. There are also moves from public functions to civic pressure groups and NGOs. Harold Burson, co-founder of the world's largest PR firm, Burson-Marsteller, explains on his blog that the question most often asked me by both students and interns is: 'Mr. Burson, based on your experience, what is your best advice for us as we start out careers in public relations?' His answer is networking. You have to build a 'support infrastructure' that you can continuously tap into. But there is also a word of warning: It's not enough just to know people. There must be a strong relationship built on shared experiences and trust.

The mega relationships involve customers, suppliers and others more deeply into the societal mega networks, not only in market networks. Approaching the customer with the traditional marketing mix and its 4Ps is meaningless unless the basic conditions for marketing exist. There must be a stage to perform the play. In the examples above, the real 'customers' have been politicians, presidents, government members and famed eye surgeons. None of these were accessible for a sales force. These real decision-makers are not identified in marketing theory as being part of the market.

Marketing seems to be increasingly dependent on mega relationships, as the following example indicates. It concerns complex products of importance for the buying country's infrastructure:[22]

- *1950s* – Direct exports and imports.
- *1960s* – Buyers stipulate that the sellers manufacture a small part of the delivery in the buying country.

---

[22] Based on the author's study of Ericsson.

- *1970s* – Demands on local manufacturing, national co-ownership and support with financial solutions for the purchase.

- *1980s* – Additional demands include: performing part of design and engineering in the buying country; supporting the exports of part of their production; establishing R&D projects together with the supplier; and barter.

- *1990s* – Through deregulation in the industrialized world and the rapid development of technology the buying countries press their demands further. The Swedish defence negotiated the purchase of tanks from American General Dynamics. One stipulation was that the supplier should make sure that ABB would get a major order for rapid trains from Amtrak, the US railroads company. According to US law, a minimum of 50 per cent of the trains had to be manufactured in the United States, which was feasible through ABB's network of subcontractors.

- *2000* – The previous requirements will be even more important.

A study of the relationships within Japanese business and between business and the public sector came to the conclusion that:[23] ' … business and government in Japan are like two major divisions of a well-run organization – Japan itself … the personal networks and contacts of the public officials and private business leaders render the formal structural distinction of government and business almost meaningless in Japan'.

As should be obvious from the examples, *mega marketing requires different skills than those usually existing in marketing and sales departments*. Marketers are not trained to play a political game on a mega level. Top management involvement with the aid of politicians, diplomats, lobbyists and others is required. My contention is that *lobbying and other mega influences will increase in importance and should consequently be explicitly accounted for by marketing theory*. As lobbying builds on networks of relationships within which interaction takes place, it has a central role in RM/CRM.

Alliances change the market mechanisms

Alliance is a designation for organized and agreed relationships between parties, for example, between suppliers and customer and competitors. Companies can enter a large variety of dependencies which do not stand out in the traditional classification used in economics, such as monopoly and oligopoly. Alliances are part of corporate strategy and exist above the market relationships and the daily marketing routine.

---

[23] Taira and Wada (1987, p. 264).

While competition means that companies oppose each other, alliances mean collaboration. The incentives to enter into alliances vary. Alliances also vary in intensity and duration: they can be one-shot projects; imply limited but continuous collaboration; or take the parties so close that they may lead to a merger or acquisition. For Corning, the US global designer and manufacturer of specialty glass and ceramic components, alliances are so central that the corporation has described itself as 'a network of organizations'. Its partnerships are based on technology, products, non-technology and non-product deals with different types of partnering such as licensing or marketing; in addition they make mergers and acquisitions.

Five types of actors on the competitive arena have been identified: *present competitors*, *potential competitors*, *competitors that offer substitutes*, *customers* and *suppliers*. Between these, *competitive forces* develop as threats and power to bargain and influence.[24] Interpreted within the spirit of RM, these competitive forces could also be perceived as *relationship forces*, giving birth to alliances. A current example is how China gets established in its exploding domestic car market.

CASE STUDY · **Chinese–Japanese car alliance**

In 2007, China has become an exploding market in passenger cars and other vehicles. With 1.3 billion inhabitants China is the biggest market all times. The Chinese are used to the bicycle and some to motorbikes but now that wealth is growing they want cars. To establish itself in the market, European, American and Japanese automakers needed to get into alliances with Chinese industry. The early entrants were Volkswagen, General Motors and Honda. The more recent ones are Toyota and Nissan and they have chosen to ally with Chinese manufacturers FAW and Dongfen. Nissan had already established a trusting relationship with Dongfen in the 1980s when they formed an alliance to manufacture diesel trucks. Nissan could now offer its brand, technical skills, an extensive product line and management know-how. Dongfen contributed with its brand, customer knowledge, sales network and production facilities. For Toyota being the biggest car manufacturer in the world – in 2007 it passed GM in size – China was an unexplored market until 2003 when its alliance with FAW was established. Toyota could offer its production system with the lean production process which today is a global standard for manufacturing. Joint manufacturing facilities and a joint sales company have been set up.[25]

---

[25] Based on Lee and Fujimoto (2003).

---

[24] Porter (1985, p. 5).

Alliances appear in many costumes:

- In the United Kingdom, American Xerox started out in 1956 with a joint venture between Xerox and The Rank Organisation and became a wholly-owned subsidiary of Xerox in 1997. In Japan and India, Xerox joined forces with Fuji and Modi. Thanks to these alliances, Xerox became the global market leader in the copier market.
- Apple Computer established an alliance with Japanese Sony to develop its new Macintosh laptop. Apple could not mobilize enough designers, nor did Apple have experience in miniaturizing products, which Sony had; the laptop was to become a 2-kilo variant of a 7-kilo Macintosh, and Sony wished to learn more about laptops. Sony took it from the design office to the factory and assembly line in just over a year.
- In 2007, the Microsoft Business Process Alliance was announced. Its purpose is to make business process management available for more types of customers as well as to improve its functionality for existing customers. Large companies have the resources to handle the processes themselves but smaller companies don't. A small company must install and maintain the same processes as the large companies even if the scale is smaller but it lacks the personnel and money for doing so. The alliance includes 10 leading software companies working with business process management based on the Microsoft platform.

Collaboration *per se* is not new. It partly occurs in all buying and selling. When relationships are aiming for longevity and continuous development, outsourcing and network organizations emerge, and the relationship comes closer to formal alliances. The 'make or buy' choice has long been an issue in manufacturing, using different strategies. Auto manufacturers outsource the larger part of its manufacturing and focus on assembly, brand management, finance and service. Reebok develops and markets technically advanced and trendy shoes for sports and leisure. It has no factory of its own but outsources the manufacturing to Taiwan, South Korea and other Asian countries. Among service that is contracted to other providers are transportation, cleaning, property maintenance, computer support, call centres and canteens.

There is yet another link between companies that I have found little observed in the literature. We can call it *tacit alliances*. These emerge through industry consensus and mean that all industry members behave in the same way. In an industry association, for example, good 'bedside manners' develop. These can grow slowly over a long period. A positive side is that they can instil ethical behaviour; a negative side is that they uphold the past at the expense of the future. Competitors – who have been converted to colleagues – protect each other and assume a hostile attitude to change, or at least pursue a wait-and-see strategy. Innovation then requires revolution, breaking with the tacit alliance.

> INSIGHT   I would like to introduce the concept of the *alliance market* with the following definition: an alliance market consists of companies which at a certain point in time are possible partners for an alliance.

The concept has similarities with a market for matrimony, with the difference that polygamy is allowed, even recommended. The alliance market operates at a corporate strategy level, above the market relationships. The first step is to find partners in the alliance market, the next to address the customer market.

When the major air carriers in Europe began to look for partners, only few attractive partners were available and everybody knew everybody else. Scandinavian Airlines (SAS) is one of the oldest alliances in the world; it has been in operation since 1946. It is made up of 3 companies from 3 countries – Denmark, Norway and Sweden – and owned fifty-fifty by the 3 states and private enterprise. In spite of this long experience of keeping an alliance together, SAS was initially not successful in extending it to other airlines. In the late 1990s, SAS, Lufthansa, United Airlines, Thai, Air Canada and Varig announced the birth of the Star Alliance covering 700 destinations and 95 per cent of all airports with regular passenger traffic. The alliance has since expanded considerably. For the passenger it means better more frequent flights and a more complete network of destinations timetables, easier check-in and better use of a bonus card. For the airlines it means improved competitiveness, increased sales, increased revenue and lower cost through co-ordination of destinations, timetables, reservations systems, ticketing and staffing.

In the United States, the number of formal business alliances increased by an average of 27 per cent per annum in the 1980s and the growth has continued since.

In a study of the globalization of hotels and restaurants, four groups of formal alliances were defined: strategic alliances, franchising, management contracts and joint ventures.[26] Strategic alliances can vary from a common reservation system to complex networks including not only hotels, but also travel, holiday packages and conference service. The European reservation system Amadeus and the American Sabre are of this character. Franchising is used by, for example, companies in the InterContinental Hotels Group, among them Holiday Inn with 1 500 hotels around the world. Those who run a Holiday Inn are independent firms but work strictly according to the concept of the hotel chain. The chain is entitled to a fee based on a percentage of the revenue. Management contract is an undertaking by someone to run a hotel for the owner, by applying skills, knowledge and systems, but also to offer well-known names such as Hyatt or Hilton. SAS's earlier

---

[26] Based on Tse and West (1992, pp. 126–132).

expansion in the hotel market together with Intercontinental Hotels and Saison of Japan, and later with Radisson, is an example of joint ventures.

It is estimated that the largest 500 companies have 60 alliances on average. In a study by McKinsey one-third of the alliances failed. Short-term alliances to achieve quick results, such as cost reduction through downsizing, did not pay off; alliances should be strategic and long term.

Another study showed that 70 per cent of all strategic alliances were discontinued or do not live up to expectations.[27] Alliances may look good on paper but may not work in practice. Here follows comments on two issues, values and management, which are frequently reported to cause problems with alliances as well with mergers and acquisitions.[28]

Values

Making relationships between two corporate cultures work is known to be hazardous. Confrontations between value systems and cultural shocks are the rule rather than the exception. Time and patience are required to build relationships. There must be mutual trust. Trust cannot be assured through contracts, and those who believe that lawyers can prevent the risks and hurdles of collaboration are bound to be disillusioned. As compared to many other cultures, the US business tradition seems to have a weakness in handling the more subtle aspects of relationships. The RM values discussed in Chapter 1 become clearly tangible in alliances. Alliances must be win–win, parties seeing each other as equals, as partners. Otherwise the parties will act covertly, trying to outsmart one another and thus pursuing hypercompetition strategies rather than RM strategies. It is not the formal structures – for example, that each partner owns equal shares of the alliance – which are crucial, but the spirit of the alliance. There are also obstacles in antitrust legislation, patent laws and the right to intellectual property, degradation of the other partner's ability, and the tradition to work alone rather than together.

Management

It is not easier to manage in a network of collaborating individuals and organizations than to manage a traditional hierarchical organization. Doz and Hamel[29] claim that 'Managing the alliance relationship over time is usually more important than crafting the initial formal design.' Management is definitely different, although it offers more opportunities and varieties. If disputes arise, these cannot be settled by an executive in the same way as in

---

[27] Kanter (1989).

[28] See, for example, Lorange and Roos (1993); and Lowe's (1998) study of a merger.

[29] Doz and Hamel (1998, p. xv).

the single enterprise. Managing an alliance jointly is not recommended; the risk of coming to a deadlock is pending. You either turn the alliance into a separate corporation which answers to its board, or you let one of the partners run it. The latter is recommended for an alliance where one partner possesses unique expertise which is crucial for future success. Giving the alliance full autonomy can be necessary for several reasons. The alliance must adjust to conditions prevailing in its market and not be drenched by its parent's financial control system and a standardized reporting format unfit for the operations of the alliance.

The advice provided by a marriage counsellor is surprisingly well suited for the advice needed for a company entering an alliance – choose your partner carefully, invest in a win–win relationship, stay attractive to your partner, develop a sound economy, and search for a division of labour that works for all parties. Good vibrations are needed, even if it is not passionate love. Still we know that decisions on co-habitation are taken under uncertainty with no guarantee whatsoever of the outcome.

Alliances lend opportunities for a company to achieve both economies of scale and economies of scope and yet stay lean and flexible; alliances are important elements of a network organization. In order to cut down time to market and become more competitive – to create 'the fifteen minute advantage' – companies can work together in constellations, concurrently performing several operations and, via computer networks, do this in real time. Spellbound by the promises and potential of the e-relationship and eCRM (R12), it may be easy to forget the importance of h-relationships and hCRM manifested in the closeness to the customer (R8) and social relationships (R18).

Alliances give birth to power networks, which in themselves create partly locked markets. The complex networks of relationships which exist in markets create multifaceted interaction patterns between buyers, sellers and others. These patterns become institutionalized and limit the space for the market mechanisms. Within the spirit of RM and the marketing equilibrium, however, it is equally as important to utilize collaborative forces as it is to utilize competitive forces.

 The knowledge relationship

Knowledge can unite and divide. Established knowledge can inject stability and professionalism; if it becomes obsolete it will stifle operations. New knowledge can initiate change, dissolve established industry definitions and create new ones, transcend geographical borders, and create novel technological conditions. According to S-D logic, knowledge and skills are what makes a value proposition. Interpreted in this broad sense it may sound only natural to claim that knowledge is frequently the basis for alliances. The daily applications of knowledge may be part of the market and nano relationships, whereas new combinations of knowledge and new ways of commercializing knowledge largely exist on levels above market relationships.

In order to explore the knowledge relationship, we can ask the following question: 'If we look at the corporation from a knowledge perspective, what do we see that is pertinent to RM/CRM?'

Companies need knowledge to develop, produce and market goods and services. Knowledge is progressively perceived as the core driver of competitiveness. In some organizations this is so evident that they are called knowledge-based organizations or intelligent enterprises.[30] Current society is often referred to as the knowledge or information age. We hear more often these days that the future corporation is a learning organization – IBM presented this as one of its most prominent strategies for reorientation – and its most eminent resource is intellectual capital.[31] The marketing of professional services has long been treated in the literature, but a more general interest in knowledge and its meaning to organizations and profitability has been steadily growing. The Internet has added yet another dimension to network-based knowledge.

A company can be viewed as consisting of three knowledge processes:[32]

- The *generative* process, in which knowledge is created.
- The *productive* process, transforming knowledge into value propositions.
- The *representative* process, handling the relationship to customers.

In terms of traditional corporate functions, the generative process comprises R&D, design and engineering and not least innovation and entrepreneurship; the productive process production and purchasing; and the representative process marketing and sales. But emphasis is on knowledge, its content and significance. In alignment with modern thinking in product development and the launching of new products – concurrent engineering – the generative, productive and representative processes are synchronous and reciprocal, not sequential steps. These processes embrace internal and external relationships that differ from those of the traditional hierarchical organization. The relationships are not tied to a certain structure or function; they constitute elements of a network organization.

Knowledge can either be *migratory* or *embedded*. This division has relationship consequences.[33]

Migratory knowledge is explicit and portable, it can emigrate and immigrate. In order to succeed in this transfer, the knowledge must be packaged in drawings, specifications, books and various IT media. Furthermore, migratory knowledge can be a physical product which performs what an individual cannot; a computer and a crane are such examples.

---

[30] See Drucker (1988a); Quinn (1992); and Sveiby (1997).
[31] See Senge (1990); and Edvinsson and Malone (1997).
[32] According to Wikström and Normann (1994).
[33] The following two paragraphs are primarily based on Badaracco (1991, pp. 79–81; quotation from p. 79).

A product can be seen as 'frozen knowledge', and a skilled person can dismantle a machine and learn how it is constructed or make a chemical analysis of a substance. This is 'reverse engineering'; you start with the product and then make the drawing and specification instead of the other way around. Knowledge can also be moved when people leave one job and bring it to the next or start a new business. A necessary condition is that somebody can open the 'knowledge package' and has an incentive to do so. Patents and other methods of protecting inventions are insecure, particularly if the knowledge can easily migrate.

Embedded knowledge cannot be transported as easily; it is tacit, often non-verbal, and dependent on first-hand experience. It is embedded in '... specialized relationships among individuals and groups and in particular norms, attitudes, information flows, and ways of making decisions ...'. Embedded knowledge is found in the skills of the master and the master's environment.

By being difficult to transfer, embedded knowledge offers a sustaining competitive advantage. In order to acquire this kind of knowledge, companies must have close access to those systems and relationships in which the knowledge is embedded. In their alliances with banks in the West, Japanese banks have insisted that the Western banks hire Japanese staff who can access the embedded knowledge of their allies. This is reported to have caused an asymmetric relationship. Instead of the mutually beneficial strategy of 'you show me, and I'll show you!', the strategy has become 'you show me, and I'll show my boss!'[34] It has also been pointed out that the ability to make tacit knowledge explicit is a strength with Japanese companies.[35]

Knowledge is not only embedded in an individual, group or corporation, but also in the relationships between companies and – on a mega level – between companies, universities and governments and between nations, and geography. Silicon Valley reached a critical mass of companies and innovative people within IT; knowledge was embedded in the community. In a similar vein, Switzerland acquired fame for clocks and watches and Wall Street for financial knowledge. In an extensive study of the competitiveness of nations, the geographically concentrated networks between companies in the same and supplying industries is emphasized:[36]

> Once a cluster forms, the whole group of industries becomes mutually
> supporting. Benefits flow forward, backward, and horizontally ...
> Entry from other industries within the cluster spurs upgrading by
> stimulating diversity in R&D approaches and providing means for
> introducing new strategies and skills ... The cluster becomes a vehicle
> for maintaining diversity and overcoming the inward focus, inertia,

[34] According to Wright and Pauli (1987, p. 63).
[35] Nonaka and Takeuchi (1995, p. 11).
[36] Porter (1990, p. 51).

inflexibility, and accommodation among rivals that slows or blocks
competitive upgrading and new entry.

Here is an old example which could have written today, only it would not be about
violin but about IT.

| CASE STUDY | **Stradivari** |

An example of embedded knowledge is Stradivari (1644–1737), who built
violins with a sound quality and beauty that has not been surpassed since.
This is not only explained by the skills of the master in using tools, wood and
varnish, but also by his network within which others developed raw material,
designed violins, experimented with new strings, invented techniques for
treating wood, composed music, bought his instruments and played on them.
Stradivari worked in Cremona, Italy, where there was a century-long tradition
of building violins, and he was the student of the master Nicolo Amati. This
way of working is not outdated or limited to the crafts and odd products like
violins. It applies to all activities that require skills and knowledge, to high-
tech activities such as the design of software as well as the performing arts.

Embedded knowledge can be moved by moving its holders and offering them a
supporting environment.[37] French cuisine was created by Italian cooks. The technological
and cultural development of the United States was partly the work of German intellectuals
who fled the political persecutions during the 1930s and 1940s. Creative processes and
knowledge advancement require interaction between individuals and professions in
tightly knit networks. They need a meeting place in order to interact. It is inherent in the
nature of creativity that planned control in a rigid structure is not feasible and the meeting
places therefore are often informal. In Vienna and Paris people met in cafés, in Silicon
Valley in bars, in Manchester, UK, at the Chamber of Commerce, and today the encounter
may occur on the Internet.

Embedded knowledge requires a different strategy than migratory knowledge. It
requires extensive relationships and networks. These are influenced by the globalization
of knowledge and its fragmented specialization to many individuals in many locations.
The concept of learning organizations has been revived in the 1990s. Senge[38] lays stress

---

[37] This section is based on Törnqvist (1990, pp. 49–51).
[38] Senge (1990; quotation from p. 10).

on five 'disciplines' necessary to succeed in continuous learning: individual learning; guiding concepts and mental frameworks; leadership, shared values and visions; team learning; and finally the ability to see the whole, how everybody's contribution constitutes a system. Team learning makes possible knowledge development that individuals cannot achieve on their own, today like in the age of Stradivari: 'The discipline of team learning starts with "dialogue" ... To the Greeks, *dia-logos* meant a free flowing of meaning through a group, allowing the group to discover insights not attainable individually ... Interestingly, the practice of dialogue has been preserved in many "primitive" cultures ... but it has been almost completely lost to modern society.' He further says that the requisite for team learning is the ability to interact.

Interpreted within RM, the team is more than the closest colleagues. It becomes a network of relationships which outgrows functional and hierarchical boundaries. It outgrows the organization, and extends to customers, competitors, suppliers, scientists and others. It is a matter of handling the dialogue – the interaction – constructively in order to make the network stay alive. Dialogue means not only availing oneself of existing knowledge, but also creating new knowledge. But Einstein is reputed to have said that 'imagination is more important than knowledge'. Furthermore, you must teach others what you have created and the learning organization therefore has its counterpart in the teaching organization.

Knowledge not only creates and dissolves geographical and organizational borders, but also traditional industry borders. Cars, which are basically mechanical, contain more and more computer technology, and a new type of knowledge has intruded the auto industry. Until the end of the 1960s, offices could purchase purely mechanical calculating machines and these were supplemented with electromechanical machines. At the beginning of the 1970s, these technologies were rapidly made obsolete by electronics, an entirely new concept which caused successful manufacturers to go bankrupt; they could not cope with the transfer from one technology to another.

Alliances between companies used to concern migratory knowledge, but the trend has changed.[39] From having been self-contained citadels, companies developed alliances through product relationships in order to transfer migratory knowledge and these then become knowledge relationships for the transfer of embedded knowledge. Knowledge relationships have four characteristics:

- Learning and knowledge creation are increasingly the purpose of alliances.
- Knowledge relationships need to be more intimate than product relationships.
- Knowledge relationships require complex networks. Product relationships were usually established with competitors, whereas knowledge relationships are also established

---

[39] Badaracco (1991).

with universities, consultants, inventors, licencers, educators, customers, suppliers and internally with functional departments.

- Knowledge relationships have a greater potential, as knowledge is more general than a product, which is one single application of knowledge.

Today, products are designed in minute detail and the design is meticulously documented. Despite this, there is tacit knowledge which has not found its place in the documents and is possessed by the master or a professional team. Lowe prefers the terms 'connoisseurship' and 'finesse', which epitomize the more subtle aspects of knowledge.[40] Those properties belong to the master and are difficult to describe; they must be learnt through experience and socialization. Not even computer programmers succeed in documenting all their knowledge about a piece of software, in spite of the thick manuals and the allegedly rational behaviour of computers. Instructions and signs are often hard to interpret, or are based on a logic which is different from the user's logic. In the age of IT we all live with this; we are brought into a jungle of instructions and industry jargon. Assembling furniture from IKEA can be quite an ordeal, but the customer friendliness of the 'follow me' instructions – written in the international language of pictures – has been continually upgraded.

Gustavsson (2001) goes further below the surface by introducing *collective consciousness* as the substance of the organization. This is more than knowledge, it is the shared insights and wisdom which are revealed in the mode of operating, it is the activation of the deeper layers of our consciousness. Knowledge in this sense is more holistic and embraces not only the knowledge itself, but also the process of creating the knowledge and the personality of the bearer of the knowledge. It is common sense in its broadest sense: 'common to all senses'.

Innovation networks can be established between suppliers and customers and other parties. The seller is usually described as the active driving force of the market through continuous change and innovation. According to one study,[41] however, innovations sometimes emerged among suppliers, sometimes among the future users and sometimes in other organizations. Scientific instruments were developed in 77 per cent of the cases by customers, 90 per cent of ploughs were developed by suppliers, and of equipment for cable connections 56 per cent was developed by secondary suppliers, 33 per cent by primary suppliers and 11 per cent by customers.

Intellectual capital, of which knowledge is part, is not visible in the traditional balance sheet. It exists all the same and may be the most crucial resource of the company. Leif Edvinsson was appointed the first Corporate Director of Intellectual Capital, a new position that became a model for companies worldwide. The notion behind his title is

---

[40] According to a lecture by Andy Lowe at Strathclyde University, Glasgow, 1993.
[41] von Hippel (1988).

expressed in the following way:[42]'While most companies appoint directors of finance and operations and focus company valuation on finance and operations, they lack a function to deal with hidden values ... The mission of this function [Director of Intellectual Capital] is to identify and improve the visibility of intangible and non-material items, to capture and package these items for transfer to users, to cultivate and develop these items through training and knowledge networking, and to capitalize and economize on these items through rapid recycling of knowledge and increased commercialization.' The work is performed in teams in order to secure the representation of all types of knowledge: 'Critical for this development is a federated global organization with competencies and alliances built on intellectual capital, information technology, and leadership around core cultural values'.

Finally, in S-D logic 2 of its 8 original fundamental premises (FP) have knowledge in focus: FP1 'the application of specialized skill(s) and knowledge is the fundamental unit of exchange (service is exchanged for service)'; and FP4 'knowledge is the fundamental source of competitive advantage (operant resource, especially know-how, are the essential component of differentiation).'[43] Later FP9 was added: 'Organizations exist to integrate and transform micro-specialized competences into complex services that are demanded in the marketplace'.[44]

To be successful in the future economy, we need network organizations based on knowledge from many contributing sources, and from which tacit and embedded knowledge can be made accessible. With co-creation between suppliers and customers as the foundation (R1, the parent relationship of marketing) we need to supplement it with a whole network of stakeholders, just as many-to-many marketing prescribes.[45]

 ## Mega alliances change the basic conditions for marketing

Among the mega relationships we have so far met social networks, mega marketing, alliances and knowledge. Mega alliances operate above companies, industries and nations. They offer new conditions for business. Mega alliances are established not only through parliaments, governments and referenda, but also through resolutions taken on a supranational level. They give birth to new relationships and network constellations which become part of marketing.

---

[42] The quotations in this paragraph are taken from Buck-Lew and Edvinsson (1993). Intellectual capital will be treated further in Chapter 6.
[43] Vargo and Lusch (2006, p. 44).
[44] Lusch and Vargo (2006b, p. 283).
[45] For a treatise on knowledge as part of a network economy, see Kohlbacher (2007).

Mega alliances have several missions where they may help to speed up the economic development of nations. They can stabilize peace through economic co-operation; by abandoning tariffs and dysfunctional regulations, they facilitate trade; and by supporting economic activity, they reduce poverty. The boundaries between corporate alliances and alliances between nations are partly blurred. Nations have been called 'the cartographic illusion of the interlinked economy'. It is meaningless to proceed to view the world as a set of nations:[46] 'Put simply, in terms of real flows of economic activity, nation states have already lost their role as meaningful units of participation in the global economy of today's borderless world.' So it is not only the borders of organizations that become increasingly fuzzier, but also those between states. This is obvious in mega alliances, where the objection often is that the member states lose their independence.

The increasingly larger global corporations are on their way to take charge over nations. It has been estimated that over half the 100 largest economic units in the world are private companies. IBM, BP and Ford are financially bigger than the most smaller nations. Wal-Mart's revenue is higher than that of states such as Poland, Slovakia, Ukraine and Hungary.[47] The World Trade Organization (WTO) makes decisions behind closed doors and these decisions are enforced on the member states. Its decisions seem to be more and more in confrontation with the decisions of national parliaments and governments, and in favour of the interests of private corporations. For example, the WTO's resolutions about limitations on what we may eat, can in turn mean increased health risks.[48]

Nations form mega alliances around the world. The biggest are EU and NAFTA. Among the others are the Free Trade Area of the Americas (FTAA) which is a so far failed attempt to expand the NAFTA to the rest of Latin America; and in Asia ASEAN Free Trade Area (AFTA) and South Asia Free Trade Agreement (SAFTA).

It is demanding to manage individual firms and alliances between firms, but to manage mega alliances is impossible; they are such complex networks. EU and NAFTA are each approaching half a billion inhabitants. Managing the world's biggest business enterprise, Wal-Mart with a measly 2 million employees, must be a piece of cake compared to managing the mega alliances. Many national governments must come to agreements. Politicians are caught between considerations for national, local and party interests and their own re-election, and international co-operation. One of the dangers with the EU is the growing mammoth-like bureaucracies, another is the abuse of subsidies. Assessments have been made that 5–10 per cent of the EU budget is awarded to fraudulent applications. The many conflicting goals, the bureaucracy and the abuse offset market forces. Again there is the need to balance the forces of competition, collaboration and regulations/institutions

[46] Ohmae (1995, p. 11).
[47] Taken from Hertz (2002).
[48] The Guardian (1999); and Fairness and Accuracy in Reporting (1999).

of the marketing equilibrium. The difficulties may change shape but they won't disappear. Marketers have to adapt their behaviour accordingly, both accept the EU regulations and apply a certain flexible creativity. The economist and outspoken advocate of free markets, Milton Friedman, has argued that the NAFTA has not introduced free trade but 'government managed trade' and installed a new level of national government bureaucracies. Similar critique has been voiced against EU which exhibits elements of a planned economy and the detrimental effects of trying to standardize citizen and consumer behaviour through legislation and punishment.

Building mega alliances is a long-term undertaking. The EU springs from the aftermath of the Second World War, when British Prime Minister Winston Churchill proposed a United States of Europe. In 1947, the defence alliance NATO was formed and the US Marshall Plan brought new capital for the resurrection of Europe. In 1951, the Coal and Steel Union was formed with the purpose of preventing new wars. The Rome Treaty in 1957 established the European Economic Community, known as the Common Market, and it contained the seeds to the future mission of the EU: '... to work for a harmonious development of economic activity, continuous and balanced expansion, increased stability, faster increase of living standards, and closer relationships between the member nations'. In 2007, there were 27 EU member states and a few more were preparing for entry. EU is the largest economy in the world with a gross domestic product of €11.8 (US$16.6) trillion which is 31 percent of the world's total economic output. It is the largest exporter in the world and the second largest importer. One-third of the world's largest corporations are headquartered in the EU.

A major advantage with mega alliances is free trade. Economists claim that there is overwhelming evidence that free trade leads to increased wealth[49] but others are doubtful and claim that it leads to widening gaps between poor and rich. A harsh reality is that more than 40 per cent of the EU budget is subsidies to the agricultural sector. These subsidies are of course not in line with the axioms of a market economy; they upset it. The reason for keeping them so far is the necessity to avoid social disorder, mass unemployment and poverty.

There are also other difficulties as the following case explains.

CASE STUDY | **The four freedoms of the EU**

In 1958, the Treaty of Rome put the four freedoms on the European trade agenda: free movement of goods, services, money and people across member state borders. The least successfully implemented freedom is services. It

---

[49] Norberg (2003).

clashes with national culture, tradition, legislation, political power and local competition and consequently is tough to handle in practice. The service freedom has met with resistance and red tape to hold the 'foreign intruders' at bay. Eventually, on 15 November 2006, the EU Service Directive was agreed. Its aim is to have the stumbling-blocks removed by 2010. Until then, however, we will not know if the goal has been reached. However, the reference to 'services' is vague. The problem concerns certain, specific situations and it would make more sense to specify these than to speak of services in general.

The EU creates mega conditions which determine the rules of the marketplace. Large multinational manufacturing companies, irrespective of national origin, have for decades been gradually adjusting to the new situation by establishing subsidiaries and alliances inside the EU. Domestic companies and smaller companies, particularly in the formerly protected service sector, are less prepared.

EU spawns new networks of relationships in which to interact. Lobbying is such an example. As was shown in R19 on mega marketing, companies and industries try to influence business conditions through lobbying at EU headquarters. The number of EU lobbyists has grown from an estimated 300 in the early 1990s to 15 000 in 2008. It is hard to tell how much the lobbyists can intervene, and how much is just keeping abreast with changes and sending home information for strategic marketing decisions. Close relationships to influential EU politicians and bureaucrats of course mean informal power. There is the misgiving that rich corporations can buy the 'best' professional lobbyists while the less rich will be in a constantly inferior position. But lobbying has both a bright and a dark side.

CASE STUDY | **The bright side and dark side of EU lobbying**

A Brussels law firm, Laffineur, in advertising their service on a website say: 'As a lobbying firm, we defend the interests of our clients through the EU decision-making process.' They further state that 70–75 per cent of laws passed in member nations are adopted from EU legislation. It is then important for individual companies, industries, NGOs and interest groups that want to work in 'a favourable legislative framework' to be proactive at the stage of preparation of legislation. This is of course commendable as political decisions are often based on ideology and on ignorance of facts and practical consequences. As a supplement to political and democratic processes, lobbying has an important task in a democratic society.

There is a bright and a dark side to everything; the discriminating factor is ethics and social responsibility. Within the EU there is demand for transparency of lobbying activities, which the lobbying firm clients are and how much they pay. This has been vehemently resisted by the lobbying sector although the same demand in the United States has been recognized through the Lobbying Disclosure Act. To draw attention to the sides lobbying that are in conflict with public interest, 'The Worst EU Lobby Award' has been established. The 2006 winner was oil giant ExxonMobil for paying climate sceptics to manipulate the EU debate and denying transparence of their funding. An additional prize, 'The Worst Greenwash Award' was added in 2007, meant for those who use advertising to cover up their real environmental impact.

The EU demands adaptation in many details, which has provoked consumers in member countries. Local lifestyles are challenged which offer new marketing opportunities and threats. The favourite cigarette of the French, Gauloise, became thinner, to the great dismay of its fans, and French cheese made with non-pasteurized milk ('lait cru') was threatened with prohibition. The typical French citizen walking from the local 'boulangerie' with a fresh non-packaged 'baguette' under the arm will be history if unpackaged bread, as suggested, is forbidden.

The North American mega alliance between the United States, Canada and Mexico, NAFTA, was signed in 1993. Canada, Japan and Mexico are the largest trade partners for the United States, and two of these are now integrated in the mega alliance. It has eliminated most of the tariffs between the member states and removed the restrictions on motor vehicles, computers, textiles and investment. As with EU, the agricultural sector needs a long-period of adjustments. Most agree that NAFTA has had positive effects, but measurement is difficult. Already during the first quarter of 1994, Mexican trade with the Unites States went up by 17.5 per cent and that with Canada by 30 per cent. Trade increased dramatically during the first 10 years but so did trade between the United States and other countries outside NAFTA. US retailing chains, such as JC Penney and Wal-Mart, could open up stores in Mexico, where large-scale retailing has so far been absent. Wal-Mart has entered an alliance with Mexico's largest retailer, Cifra. Alliances with local businesses are often necessary. Mexican consumers have a low *per capita* income and different lifestyles expecting, for example, more individual service. 'People greeters' wish you welcome to the store and accompany you inside and hand you a trolley; 'the 10-foot rule' states that customer contact must be established within the first 10 feet. For consumers, a visible sign of NAFTA is the increase in trilingual labelling of products – English, Spanish, French – to allow distribution of the same product in all member states.

Through the larger market opened up by NAFTA, the possibilities increase for large-scale mass production and cost reductions. The bigger markets and deregulation also imply tougher competition. Banks, insurance companies and telecommunications are other industries that see new opportunities. Mexico entered the mega alliance with only 8 telephones per 100 inhabitants, while the United States and Canada had over 90. During the first NAFTA year, Detroit's three largest car manufacturers increased sales from 1000 to 60 000 cars.

Mega alliances are permeating business in the United States and Europe changing the marketing conditions and relationships and the same is happening throughout the world. History shows that mega alliances have always been part of politics, defence and economy. The future value of mega alliances is hard to evaluate. It is hard to evaluate even in retrospect, as we do not know what would have happened without them. The outcomes of referenda in many countries – where yes or no has won with small margins – show insecurity and confusion among citizens. It is obvious though that the EU, NAFTA and other mega alliances change the rules of the marketing arena and require new relationships and networks. They need to be treated as an integral part of marketing theory in the light of relationships, networks and interaction.

The mass media relationship

Media report events from corporations, governments and markets. Media have an impact on marketing, but exercise their influence primarily on the mega level; they are part of society rather than of the market. To relate to the media today, specialist are employed or hired as consultants. Their task is referred to as public relations or PR.

According to *The Encyclopedia of Public Relations*,[50] PR '... is a set of management, supervisory, and technical functions that foster an organization's ability to strategically listen to, appreciate, and respond to those persons whose mutually beneficial relationships with the organization are necessary if it is to achieve its missions and values'. PR comprises relationships to stakeholders with the purpose of maximizing image and brand equity of a corporation or industry. The relationships can embrace society at large, a town, a trade union, the investor market and others. Often PR is primarily a marketing tool. Lobbying, which was treated in R19, can also be part of a PR function and the mass media relationship.

The terms public relations and PR are often associated with gimmickry and manoeuvring. Other terms are used to mitigate the negative connotations, such as corporate communications and corporate affairs. Many consultants talk about 'perception management'

---

[50] Heath (2004).

with it origin in the military and warfare. Its purpose is to influence perceptions – knowledge, attitudes, values, feelings – of customers and other stakeholders towards a company, a product, a service, new technology or a person.

The media relationship can be split into three types:

- The relationship between an organization and the media.
- The relationship between the media and their audiences.
- The relationship between an organization and the media audience.

There are also intermediaries such as Reuters and United Press (UP) that select and distribute information. They are the wholesalers of the 'news' distribution networks, with television and radio networks, newspapers and journals as the retailers. Some of the readers, listeners and watchers are customers or prospective customers (the market relationship), some are politicians, legislators or investors who can exercise influence over a company or industry (the mega relationship), and some are employees (the nano relationship). Currently the media landscape is in a flux with all the new digital media available. Above all traditional media have lost in power through websites and bloggs, which are controlled by citizens who can get messages through at little cost without being censored or edited by someone else.

Media relationship are important to companies and customers whether they are willing to interact with media or not. Therefore, it is part of a rational and proactive marketing strategy to pay attention to media relationships. Even if companies and media need each other, there is a goal conflict. Companies want the good news to be published and the bad news to be held back. They want media space as free advertising, with the higher credibility that may be attributed to an editorial text than to a journal advertisement or a television commercial. Media want facts that make news and often preferably news that is sensational and even offer a scandal. The mission of media in democracies is to reflect society and analyse, interpret and report events, and particularly hold misuse of power at bay. Editors and reporters have many incentives, such as passion for the truth, personal integrity, reaching a large audience, fame, esteem among colleagues, vanity and revenge.

Corporations and media nurture a love–hate relationship but they have to stay married for better and for worse. It is essential to strike a balance between the value for both parties, so that both – at least over the longer term – perceive themselves as winners. If the relationship remains asymmetric – one party feeling exploited – the value of the relationship may become continuously negative for both, at the same time as divorce is no solution.

The ability of business leaders to create relationships with media can sometimes be their most important marketing activity, the activity that determines the corporate image. In the 1980s, Lee Iacocca of Chrysler made the headlines worldwide; in the 1990s, Jack Welsh of General Electric became Mr GE; and today Bill Gates of Microsoft and Richard Branson of Virgin have high visibility. The host of dotcom whiz-kids in the late 1990s scored high in the media but were largely forgotten a few years later. The turnaround of SAS from a traditional airline to a customer-centric service company got extensive coverage, not least through the personality of its CEO and his relationship to the media.

CASE STUDY | **Scandinavian Airlines**

As the new and young president of Scandinavian Airlines (SAS) Jan Carlzon became a media pet. Particularly in the beginning he devoted ample time both to the media and to individual communication with employees on all levels. He skilfully used television to address existing and new groups of passengers as well as employees; much of his internal marketing went via the ordinary television networks. He could explain the role of leadership, the necessity of putting the customer in focus, and the advantages of service and quality. He made new market segments try air travel. He did it in a different and charismatic manner. Friendship with the media is not forever though. When SAS failed to form strategic alliances with European and US major carriers – a necessity for marketing and survival – the media turned against Carlzon with headlines such as 'Are you finished now?' His private life was scrutinized. It all gave free publicity, but it is unclear whether it was beneficial to SAS or not. It certainly kept up the public interest in the company name – and the market needs continuous reminders. After leaving SAS and from having been extremely accessible to the media, Carlzon became selective and cautious.

There are all sorts of grades in the media relationship and all sorts of reason for being exposed or not being exposed. Here are some examples of the variety:

- To gain media exposure when novelties are launched is the dream of all companies. In 1948, Victor Hasselblad launched his new camera at a press conference in the United States. He was unknown, but invited 20 reporters from the professional photo press. They hailed the camera as the perfect product. Hasselblad's relationship to this small group of opinion leaders was decisive for the rapid success of the camera. It became the natural choice for the first journey to the moon. When Buzz Aldrin, the first astronaut to walk on the moon came to Gothenburg, Sweden, in 2004 he said that the highlight of his previous visit was a tour of Hasselblad. Sixty years after its introduction, the Hasselblad camera holds its position among professional photographers as the king of cameras; it has a 20 per cent global market share in its niche. It has kept its position as a media pet so there is little need to advertise the new products.

■ Bergene – a leading manufacturer of chocolate bars in Norway – were taken by surprise when an outbreak of salmonella was located in the raw chocolate used in their bars. The management chose to co-operate closely with media and health authorities and to be totally open. An internal task force, including representatives of the authorities, was appointed and no cost was spared to take necessary action. After an initial drop in sales and a bad year financially, Bergene recaptured its market position.

■ It became known that the Ford Explorer, a van equipped with Firestone tyres, had met with unexpected accidents caused by tyre explosions. It began in Venezuela and in 2 years, 174 people were killed and 700 injured. It continued in the United States. Ford and Firestone tried a cover-up strategy. First, they kept silent and did not alert the Explorer owners. When exposed to the events, they rejected all responsibility, blamed the drivers, each other and poor maintenance of the vans. Their efforts to prevent further accidents were half-hearted. The case was being tried in US courts for years, costing fantasy sums and tarnishing the corporate brand. Initially there was little trace of RM values in the behaviour of these two gigantic companies. The bottom line was bad publicity and a tarnished image. It did some good to the consumer because it initiated a public 'auto rollover rating' to guide car buyers and expose potential risks.

■ One of the most publicized and horrid cases is the Union Carbide/Dow Chemical disaster in Bhopal in India. In 1984, an explosion killed 3800 people and numerous others were poisoned and injured. Almost 25 years after the event, compensation to the victims is still not paid out and there is still recurrent mention in the media. Partly parallel to the Bhopal disaster another disaster concerned Dow Corning's breast implants. The producer was sued for having caused ill health among masses of women who wore their implants. Such crises last for decades and can cause companies to go bankrupt. To repair the damage, professional PR consultants are engaged to improve the image of the supplier in the eyes of a number of stakeholders. The detailed instructions from the PR firm, which is an excellent lesson in how opinions can be influenced, is found on the web (www.consumerlawpage.com).

These examples show different situations of the media relationship and different types of interaction. Instant and sustaining success through the media like Hasselblad is the dream of every CEO and marketing director. Bergene was totally unprepared but found a transparent and successful strategy, forming a friendly and open alliance with the media. It is amazing how such giants as the companies in the last two examples, who have the money to engage the best advisors, can fail so completely in their relationship to the market. It raises the problem of transparency, of being honest and quick to warn and inform when a disaster is in the making.[51] Transparency can also have its perils as public

---

[51] Based on Fung, Graham and Weil (2007; quotation from p. 7).

announcements are the outcome of compromise and therefore become incomplete, inaccurate, obsolete, confusing or distorted.

In their 'crisis life-cycle model', Howell and Miller (2006) show that when a crisis arrives it is essential to take action on initial warning stages and be as proactive as possible. Multi-dimensional networks of relationships will be activated during the crisis process: victims, the media, courts and others, and PR professionals are needed. But little research in crisis management has integrated PR with marketing and other management activities.

In today's escalated media noise, publicity may not have long-lasting effect. Memory is short. Who remembers what made the headlines in yesterday's newspaper or what CNN reported during the past week? Essential information drowns in the love affairs of presidents and political scandals; red herrings fill much of the information space. 'A weekday edition of *The New York Times* contains more information than the average person was likely to come across in a lifetime in seventeenth-century England', says Samuel Wurman in his book *Information Anxiety*.[52] Even if there is sometimes no visible response at all, media, including advertising, have a reinforcing role and can activate an interest that is already there. There is no doubt that mass media, not least for establishing and maintaining the parasocial relationship (R13), will remain important even if RM/ CRM advocates individualized approaches to both consumers and organizational customers.

An essential distinction must be made between investigative journalists, who are knowledgeable and apply systematic research techniques in long-term fact-finding missions, and the general reporter who is expected to cover any type of event and have an article or newsflash ready in the next few hours. There are reporters and media specialized in certain industries, such as telecom or cars, which they follow continuously. Once there was even a special group of reporters and consultants around IBM – 'the IBM watchers' – who focused singularly on IBM reporting and interpreting its decisions and activities.

When something of interest to the media comes out, the media will court, even attack, businesses. When business want to reach out, traditionally media can be approached through a variety of means: formal press conferences, informal meetings, press messages, interviews and so on. It is not just a matter of offering news, but also of a personal and trusting relationship. With today's digital media there are also other ways of reaching out. In any case, the media relationship requires proactivity, planning and stamina, just like all types of marketing. The media relationship is part of a total communications process, including internal marketing activities.

---

[52] Wurman (1989, p. 32).

Virtual reality is an IT creation. Photos can already be manipulated with fairly ordinary computers. Characters, including animals and aliens, come to life through software, and in the movie *Forrest Gump* he shook hands with President Kennedy, who died 30 years before the movie was made. Information and entertainment merge into *infotainment*.[53] Another unreal reality has long been around, the *pseudo-event* and the pseudo-news. *A pseudo-event is engineered to be reported, it is not reported because it happened naturally.* Examples are the use of celebrities in the launching of a film, book, restaurant, sports game or an art exhibition. Celebrities add glamour to these events; in fact, the events do not receive media coverage for what they are, but for the celebrities. These events build on the marketing of people: actors, authors, chefs, athletes and artists, and also CEOs, scientists and politicians. Media play a major role, maybe even *the* major role in their marketing. Talk shows with celebrities have become everyday programmes of television channels.

The following lines from a book on 'celebrity marketing' succinctly sum up the importance of the media relationship:[54] 'Because the media make up the most powerful of channels, they are crucial to winning high visibility. Other channels are capable of moving celebrity images out of the warehouse and into the marketplace, but none approaches the cost-effectiveness and audience impact of the mass media.'

QUESTIONS FOR DISCUSSION

1 Social relationships are classified as mega relationships as they occur on a level above the market relationships. Have you ever benefited from your own personal contacts as a business person or consumer? Do you know anyone else who has?

2 Increasingly lobbying and public relations are used by companies and whole industries to pave the way for marketing. It is a way to control the political process and the mechanisms of the free market economy. What do you see as benefits and abuses of these activities from the perspective of (a) a company or an industry; (b) customers; and (c) society and citizens?

3 R20 states that alliances change the market mechanisms. What are the advantages and disadvantages of forming an alliance with another company compared to owning it through a merger or acquisition?

---

[53] See Postman (1987), who treats the confusion between reality and entertainment which above all television has contributed to.

[54] Rein, Kotler and Stoller (1987, p. 255).

4 'Knowledge' has a magic ring. S-D logic sees the transfer and co-creation of knowledge and skills as the core of a value proposition, and 'knowledge management' has become a popular theme for conferences and executive training. Do you have any comments to the role of knowledge in RM?

5 Mega alliances set the stage for nations, industries, individual firms and consumers. What are their advantages and disadvantages?

6 Why is it important for a company to have a good and personal relationships to representatives of the media?

5

Nano relationships

INTRODUCTION

The previous chapter discussed relationships above market relationships. This chapter deals with the opposite, relationships below the market proper, that is, inside an organization. These nano relationships (R24–R30) are found in the suppliers' organizational structure, networks, systems and processes. They provide the antecedents for implementation of marketing activities and success with the market and mega relationships. They also provide a basis for handling mega relationships. The nano relationships show that there exists a market economy inside a company and that the boundaries between a company's external and internal work have become increasingly blurred. Companies have become network organizations.

RELATIONSHIP 24 — Market mechanisms are brought inside the company

Parallel to networks and alliances that curb the free market mechanisms outside the company, there is a long-term trend to install market mechanisms inside the company. The market mechanisms have partly replaced the internal planned economy, and it is not always clear who is the seller, buyer or competitor. The boundaries between 'them' and 'us' become blurred. New marketing strategies are needed to handle the new internal and external market relationships.

In its purest form, a company can be seen as a planned economy where clearly defined activities are co-ordinated toward clearly defined objectives with the help of a business mission, goals, strategies, production systems, organizational structures, budgets and financial control systems. Planned economies, as we know them from communism, have gigantic problems with productivity, quality and growth. They are known for rigidity, lack of initiative, corruption and a general inability to manage their countries. As has already been pointed out, moving from this type of economy to a market economy has proved to be a huge undertaking. In terms of number of employees, but not necessarily in terms of financial resources, corporations are tiny as compared to nations. The EU is approaching half a billion inhabitants and there are EU power people who want to transform it into an increasingly centralized bureaucracy. Even with their limited size companies run into the problems with the internal planned economy and have therefore constructed an internal market economy to enhance initiative and entrepreneurship. This trend has been sustained for decades. It is usually referred to as decentralization, but within the concept of RM, I would prefer to see it as an expression for internal deregulation and re-regulation.[1]

This is pertinent to RM in so far as the relationships inside the organization change in two ways. First, market relationships are brought inside the company, constituting a new base for external market relationships. Second, from having had internal stability (at least in theory) via administrative routines, a market-like relationship is born between the internal supplier and the internal customer.

The introduction of a market economy inside the organization becomes visible in the organizational structure in several ways (Figure 5.1):

- The company is organized in four types of units:
  - Top management and the board.
  - Operational units with production and marketing/sales as the core.
  - Internal service units.
  - Support or staff units.
- The operative units and service units become profit centres: business areas, division, subsidiaries and smaller profit centres within these. The most important units – strategic business units (SBUs) – are given considerable independence.
- Separating staff units from internal service units is often not easy. Support units are an extension of management at different organizational tiers. As such, they are treated as cost centres, even if they support and serve profit centres. With the purpose of utilizing the strength of the free-market forces, the strategy is usually to turn as many units as possible into service units. However, going too far in this direction may cause ineffectiveness through internal avoidance of the units, and a stifling and costly internal accounting system.
- The original idea is that profit centres should enjoy autonomy. This means, for example, that a manufacturing unit can deliver to a marketing and sales unit, but the marketing and sales unit can use an external supplier if it does not find a brother or sister offering the right conditions. An internal service unit can deliver service together with an external provider and the specialists of an operating unit, but could also sell its service to external companies.

The internal business requires an internal pricing system which should be competitive with the prices on the market. There is no marketing theory treating the internal market

---

[1] In an anthology, Halal, Geranmayeh and Pourdehead (1993) have focused on the internal markets and their deregulation. They use an approach from organization theory and to some extent from economics. RM/CRM adds dimensions to this analysis by including service, network approaches and quality management, together with concepts from S-D logic the customer's role, internal marketing, internal and external customers, as well as new accounting theory (intellectual capital, balanced scorecard).

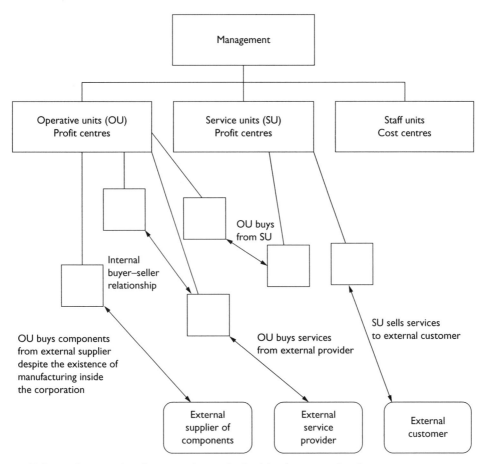

Figure 5.1 Market mechanisms are brought inside the organization

mechanisms, despite the fact that decentralization and internal deregulation have gone on for so long. The notion of internal pricing indicates that the market has been let in, although less on market conditions than on accounting conditions. During the 1980s, even governments began decentralization with profit centres.

Internal pricing may lead to inertia in relationships. If every cent must be accounted for – you can hardly talk to somebody in another profit centre without receiving an invoice – efficiency is arrested. It is possible for management to use regulations and interfere only when the market mechanisms are not adequate, thereby establishing internal marketing equilibrium. Internal pricing is important for core activities, less so for support functions. If a more rational and cost-effective mode of operations has been established with the assistance of internal pricing and competition during a period, continuous internal charging becomes less important. The practice of internal pricing is, however, an attempt to get away from arbitrary cost-plus pricing, which has the character of internal taxation.

According to transaction cost analysis, the rationale for the existence of organizations is the notion that external information is less accessible and internal information is easily accessible.[2] The analysis assumes that internal relationships are well under control, and therefore the internal transactions become more efficient than transactions with external parties. It is consequently easier to operate inside an organization than being dependent on market research techniques and other intelligence for learning about customers, competitors and others, some of them intentionally obstructing access to information. However, the assumptions of transaction cost analysis evaporate if we cannot clearly separate the organization from its environment, if there is interference with the external market mechanisms, and if market mechanisms are introduced inside the organization.

Corporations have been divided into profit centres for decades, but the early efforts created confusion about responsibility and authority. Although relationships between corporate headquarters and divisions are often strained, the ability to manage divisionalized organizations has improved and profit centres are common in all types of organizations.

The internal relationship market may be seen as a triad embracing the supplier and the buyer, each of them a profit centre, and a relationship between each of the profit centres and corporate management.[3] The relationships are characterized by collaboration and competition, affinity and conflict. Corporate management enforces a certain amount of regulation. The three units – supplier, buyer and management – are in turn nested in a larger network within which their relationships are affected. In the relationships between supplier and customer, there is exchange between value propositions, money and information. Certain peripheral service can facilitate the relationships, such as computer-based ordering and invoicing systems within a business and CRM system. The following case serves as an illustration of a triad of internal relationships in a profit centre-based organization.

CASE STUDY   **Electrolux, Husqvarna and Mecatronic**

The members of the triad are Electrolux corporate headquarters (HQ) and its then subsidiaries Husqvarna (selling sewing machines on the external market) and Mecatronic (internally selling components for sewing machines):

In the study of the triad, it is not apparent that the relationship between Husqvarna and Mecatronic was affected by actions from HQ. The two profit centres were left alone. There were no signs that the internal

---

[2] Transaction cost analysis is discussed further in Chapter 7.
[3] This is based on Hultbom (1990, p. 101; case study quotation from pp. 136–137).

interaction between the two was smoother and the transaction costs lower than if they had been totally independent companies and acted on the external market. Both seller and buyer considered price negotiations cumbersome and information on deliveries was not easily available. Mecatronic found cooperation on R&D and manufacturing issues essential, but Husqvarna employees considered themselves on top of technology and claimed product development was best handled by them. There was an apparent risk for sub-optimization from the point of view of the corporation. The hierarchical power of HQ indirectly affected the selling–buying relationship. Husqvarna, being one of the world leaders on sewing machines, felt secure. Mecatronic, on the other hand, had been through a fundamental restructuring process. It had commenced the manufacturing of a new product which developed rapidly (as viewed from an engineering perspective). It gave rise to insecurity and a protective attitude. HQ demanded a quick return on the investment which could disturb the long-term development of Mecatronic. The cumbersome price negotiations were probably caused by HQ's demand for rapid return. The demand and the internal competition created far less satisfactory information flows in the buyer–seller relationship.

By bringing the market into a company, new types of internal networks materialize. Management will still exercise governance through hierarchical power in the network. In an analogy with the external market, management is a government who can introduce regulations that limit free-market mechanisms:

- Management monitors the profit centres through financial reports.
- The acquisition of financial resources is usually centralized, which means there is internal competition for capital. The independence of the operational units in allocating their profits is often limited, for example when new investment and development projects are planned.
- Top management hire and fire the heads of business areas, subsidiaries and divisions.
- Everyone is expected to work in alignment with the corporate business mission, goals and strategies.
- There is informal pressure.
- The internal units may do business with any supplier or customer outside the corporation if they find this more profitable, but in practice, one cannot be certain that corporate management will support such freedom.

Within this framework, the internal units are allowed to act on market conditions in the relationships with one another. Markets exist inside the company and the internal units send invoices to each other. Consequently, the relationships between the employees and functions will be different than in a traditional planned economy hierarchy. The difference between the internal operations of the corporation and the external market becomes less evident.

Internal exchange of information can be smooth or filled with conflict, and the same applies for external markets. As there is a defined hierarchical structure above the profit centre relationships in combination with market mechanisms, the relationships may even become more complex internally. Market mechanisms require that the interests of different parties are constructively confronted so that goal conflicts can be resolved.

The market system involves duplication of work. From an accounting perspective, this is not considered cost-effective and is to be avoided through co-ordination. At the same time, co-ordination of human activity only works to a limited degree and if driven too far will cause inertia, lower productivity and impede flexibility.

Critics also claim that the profit centres are just shovelling money around inside the corporation and not adding value. The fact that companies keep decentralizing could be evidence that there are more advantages than disadvantages in the use of profit centres. The dynamics of the shorter and quicker decision routes and the opportunities for profit centres to develop their own relationships and networks outweigh the disadvantages. Inside the organization as well as in the market there is a trade-off between freedom and regulations.

| INSIGHT | In the same way as we need to strive in the direction of marketing equilibrium externally – in the market and society – we must strive for marketing equilibrium inside the organization. We may never reach equilibrium and it will never remain stable, though. This will be explained further in Chapter 7. |

| RELATIONSHIP 25 | ## Internal customer relationships |

This classic example is taken from Lee Iacocca, who took over as CEO of Chrysler, one of the major car manufacturers in America. He described his first impressions in the following way:[4]

> Nobody at Chrysler seemed to understand that interaction among
> different functions in a company is absolutely critical: People in

---

[4] Iacocca (1984, p. 162); see also the discussion by Reynoso and Moores (1996) on internal relationships.

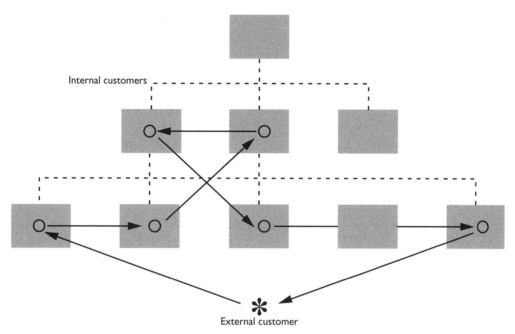

Figure 5.2 Relationships between internal customers, internal suppliers and external customers in a hierarchical structure

> engineering and manufacturing almost have to be sleeping together. These guys were not even flirting … The manufacturing guys would build cars without even checking with the sales guys. They just built them, stuck them in a yard, and then hoped that somebody would take them out of there. We ended up with a huge inventory and a financial nightmare.

Although this happened 25 years ago, relationships and dependency between different functions in a company remain vital issues. It is missing or only mentioned in passing in marketing theory. Here, I will borrow two concepts from quality management: the *internal customer* and *process management*.

In Figure 5.2, each ring represents an internal supplier and internal customer, beginning and ending with an external customer. It is a matter of *interfunctional dependency* and *horizontal interaction*, knocking down walls between specialist functions and organizational silos. It is also a matter of *interhierarchical dependency* and *vertical interaction*, as there are also walls between the tiers of the organizational pyramid.

The relationship between operations management – R&D, engineering design, purchasing, manufacturing – and marketing is particularly important. It will be treated as a special case in R26, the reason being that modern quality management is specifically addressing the gap between engineers and marketers.

Traditionally, there are conflicts between specialized functions and between organizational tiers. They form subcultures and tribes within the company and tribal warfare is common. But organizations could be perceived as bundles of processes rather than piles of boxes. One such process is visible in Figure 5.2. *Process thinking* is dominating the renewal of corporations. According to Harrington:[5] 'Everything we do today can be done better by concentrating on the process. Management has taken away our employees' ability to produce error-free output by saddling them with obsolete, cumbersome, bureaucracy-laden business processes.' Process thinking supported by IT is one way of reinventing a business and increasing efficiency. It has often been accused of being too technical and inconsiderate of the human aspect and the work situation for employees. Here, too, it is a matter of finding a high tech/high touch balance.

The arrows in Figure 5.2 indicate how a process can wriggle its way through a hierarchy. If we mentally erase the hierarchical structure we can visualize the relationships and the process more clearly and surmise a network structure. Principles of process management have been used for many years within manufacturing, but are now also applied to internal service and administration. 'If you're not serving the customer, your job is to serve someone who is.'[6] Expressions like 'white collar work', 'office work' and 'administrative routines' are no longer viable; they obscure more than they enlighten.

During the Second World War, the task force of the military became a new mode of operation. In order to reach an objective – beat the enemy at a defined location – a temporary collaboration between different organizational units was established within the allied forces. This way of organizing was introduced in business and it became common to work in projects. Projects were characterized by being temporary and focused on solving a specific task. They used people from various parts of the extant organization, sometimes supplemented with consultants and other external suppliers. With the task completed, the project organization was dissolved. Inside the project there was a certain hierarchy, usually a management group, a reference group and work groups. Today, projects are common in organizations, for example in product development, where they can include people from design, engineering, manufacturing, purchasing and marketing. It is an organized way of achieving interfunctional co-operation.

The notion of the internal customer brings customer–supplier relationships into the company. It requires employees to see other employees as customers. The give and receive service of components, documents, messages, decisions and so on; it is co-creation. The term internal supplier could be added as a companion to internal customer. Usually, an employee fulfils the role of being both a recipient of something as an internal customer and to deliver something in a value-added state to another internal customer. Only when

---

[5] Harrington (1991, p. x).
[6] Albrecht and Zemke (1985).

the customers are satisfied – and it is satisfied customers that count whether these are external or internal – a job is completed. Ishikawa, one of the fathers of total quality management (TQM), used the slogan 'the next process is your customer' back in the 1950s '… to resolve fierce hostility between workers from different production processes of a steel mill … [and] still uses it today in his lifelong effort to break through the barriers of sectionalism in business organizations'.[7]

If a company does not consider the links between all functions, there will be 'broken chains', which are one of the 'invisible competitors'; these are more obstructing to success than the visible competitors.[8] One of the messages in network approaches to B2B is the interdependency between marketing and all aspects of operations management. This is particularly striking in the manufacture and assembly of complex, customized equipment. In traditional services marketing it has been found that service delivery, production, marketing and service development are largely handled by the same people, thus making interfunctional relationships indispensable.

A process should not be perceived as if there was only one natural sequence of activities. The value chain,[9] which is constantly referred to in business, gives the impression that core functions such as R&D, manufacturing and marketing must be performed in that very order. The *value network* is a better designation as a network, contrary to a chain, is not based on linear processes but offers any kind of required combination with iterations back and forth between functions. Further, the value chain stops when the customer enters and the consumption and user process begins. In line with S-D logic the customer is a co-creator and thus supplier and customer processes must be viewed in conjunction. This is supported by the developments in lean production which has now added lean consumption and in an integrated form talk about lean solution.

Like the external networks, the internal networks can be complex. A web is spun between the many-headed internal suppliers and the many-headed internal customers, establishing both formal and informal links between everyone in the organization. Alliances, therefore, are not established only with external partners; there is also an internal alliance market. Purchasing may be handled by a profit centre on its own or through 'pooled purchasing', meaning that a purchasing department might achieve better conditions if buying larger quantities for several profit centres. Sourcing teams may be used, consisting of members from different functions.

Figure 5.3 shows interaction patterns between different departments in an R&D project. The development took place in an interfunctional project within the spirit of concurrent engineering, but most of the interaction took place within the R&D department. The

---

[7] Quotation from Lu (1985, p. viii).
[8] See also McKenna (1985, pp. 129, 142, 143).
[9] Porter (1985).

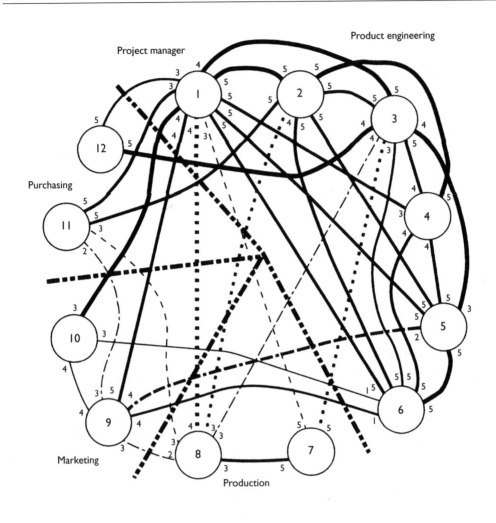

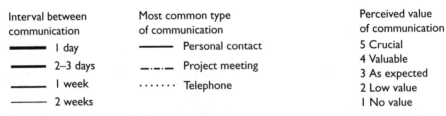

Figure 5.3 The interaction in an interfunctional R&D project. Twelve participants (drawn as circles) are connected through a line and the thickness of the line indicates the frequency of interaction. At the ends of each line, a number shows the participant's evaluation of the interaction (5 is best). The participants include the project leader, and representatives for design, purchasing, manufacturing and marketing. Source: Carlsson and Lundqvist (1992, p. 9). Reproduced with permission

interaction was also evaluated differently. For example, marketing people valued the interaction with designers higher than vice versa. In another case, the designers were highly negative to the marketers, but appreciated contacts with the buyers.

Complaints that boundaries between departments and tiers are a hindrance against efficient processes date long back. Yet these hindrances are maintained. Within quality management it has become obvious that quality and customer satisfaction cannot be achieved as long as processes are not operating smoothly.

Common sense tells us that the outcome to external customers cannot be satisfactory if the internal customer relationships and collaboration are walking with a limp.

> INSIGHT   By introducing the internal customer–internal supplier concepts, the nano
>   view of an organization becomes a natural part of RM. The organization
> becomes a network of relationships, processes and projects.

Quality and customer orientation – the relationship between operations management and marketing

Marketing literature often presents two opposite perspectives, marketing (or customer) orientation and production (or product) orientation. R25 treated interfunctional dependency, and marketing and operations management are two mutually dependent functions. There are reasons to treat their relationship separately. First, they are the core functions of any company, and second, driving them closer together is the most noteworthy contribution of modern quality management.

Quality management is one of the theories that inspired the 30R approach.[10] Modern quality thinking is not only a revolution in quality management, but also a rejuvenation of customer orientation. In marketing, quality was long used in a general and loose sense. It became a cliché, which was routinely appended to advertising copy, which sales people allowed to litter their talk, and which CEOs boasted about at conferences and dinners. Quality became an empty word.

Quality management can be approached externally from the market or internally from the organization. Together, these two approaches constitute TQM. Externally oriented quality management is market-driven, in contrast to internally oriented quality management which is technology- or systems-driven. The drivers in the market are found among

---

[10] For a literature inventory and an empirical study of the synergy between quality management and marketing and value, see Mele (2007).

a supplier's existing customers, those customers who buy from the competition, future customers who have not yet purchased, and existing and potential competitors.

In order to reinforce marketing orientation, changes in values and personal attitudes are necessary. Values change slowly and the new way of approaching the market must find support in business missions, goals, objectives, strategies, organizational structure and management systems. This in turn requires changed leadership style. Much of the literature on quality today is focused on leadership and the development of employees.

Two frequently quoted definitions of quality emphasize the relationship between the market and operations management. Crosby (1984) defined quality as 'conformance to requirements', meaning that companies must be able to produce according to drawings and specifications; deviation from these is 'non-quality'. If the drawings and specifications are correct, ideal conditions for quality exist. This is the core of internal quality management, which can also be expressed as 'Do things right!'

A critical question for the marketer is whose requirements the offering shall conform with and how this generates value for the customer as well as for the supplier. In the second definition, Juran (1992) puts the emphasis on 'fitness for use', which means that the supplier creates value by making certain that the offering is adjusted to customer needs. This is external quality management and its imperative is 'Do the right things!'

Success is not the outcome of an either/or strategy, either production orientation and internal quality management or marketing orientation and external quality management. It is a both/and strategy, a trade-off between the two. We must understand customer needs and be able to design offerings that satisfy needs, and organize for their fulfilment.

Today, the word quality is interpreted as 'customer perceived quality', meaning that it is marketing-centric and oriented towards customer satisfaction. The customer side of quality, however, should not be promoted at the expense of the technology aspect of quality. Prior to the quality revolution during the 1980s, technology aspects were in the driver's seat, and a bias toward customers was called for in order to restore balance. The customer approach to quality management is of course directly pertinent to marketing, although in the long run, I advocate a balanced view.

Systematic approaches to quality management grew out of operations management with manufactured products as its focal point of interest. It had limited or no base in marketing until the 1980s. The contributions to service quality came from marketing.

The quality perspective has successively moved from the shop floor to the management of the whole corporation. This is evident in the now widespread quality awards. The Malcolm Baldrige National Quality Award in the United States, and later its European correspondence EFQM Excellence Award have become role models for international, national and local quality awards.

Baldrige provides a comprehensive list of criteria which an organization must consider to make quality happen. The criteria and the assessment grounds are continuously being improved. Baldrige and similar awards have given rise to the most comprehensive approach to quality that had hitherto seen the light. It could even deserve to be called a meta theory of quality. The perspective is holistic; the theory consists of quality factors as well as a discussion of links between them. The word quality represents so many dimensions of life and the quality systems are so many. Apart from Baldrige we have already talked about ISO certification and lean production with its extension into lean consumption. A currently much used tool is six sigma, originally developed by Motorola.[11]

A brief description of the Baldrige 2007 Criteria for Performance Excellence will give an idea of the structure of quality prizes.[12] Baldrige offers 7 categories of criteria. A total of 1000 points are divided between the following categories (points in brackets):

1 Leadership (120).
2 Strategic Planning (85).
3 Customer and Market Focus (85).
4 Measurement, Analysis and Knowledge Management (90).
5 Workforce Focus (85).
6 Process Management (85).
7 Results (450).

This is nothing less than a list of criteria for a complete company audit! It shows that quality cannot be achieved unless all activities inside a company are directed toward quality; they are *enablers* and constitute just above half of the points. The remaining points concern *results*; it is results we are after really. Although marketing aspects are omnipresent in the criteria – remember the part-time marketer (PTM) from R4 – marketing aspects are specifically addressed in Category 3 'Customer and Market Focus' with 85 points and in Category 7 'Results' with 140 points. On customer driven excellence Baldrige declares that 'Performance and quality are judged by an organization's customers. Thus, your organization must take into account all product and service features and characteristics and all modes of customer access that contribute value to your customers. Such behaviour leads to customer acquisition, satisfaction, preference, referrals, retention, and loyalty and to business expansion.'

Baldrige has gradually learnt from RM/CRM. It acknowledges the multiple relationships to allied partners, shareholders and others; it is a stakeholder or network approach. Its questions on customer relationship building are:

1 HOW do you build relationships to acquire CUSTOMERS, to meet and exceed their expectations, to increase loyalty and repeat business, and to gain positive referrals?

---

[11] See Dahlgaard and Dahlgaard-Park (2006) for a comparison between different quality systems.
[12] The data on Baldrige and the quotations are taken from the 2007 Baldrige Criteria for Performance Excellence and interviews with former Baldrige CEO Curt Reimann.

2 HOW do your KEY access mechanisms enable CUSTOMERS to seek information, conduct business, and make complaints? What are your KEY access mechanisms? HOW do you determine KEY CUSTOMER contact requirements for each mode of CUSTOMER access? HOW do you ensure that these contact requirements are DEPLOYED to all people and PROCESSES involved in the CUSTOMER response chain?

3 HOW do you manage CUSTOMER complaints? HOW do you ensure that complaints are resolved EFFECTIVELY and promptly? HOW do you minimize CUSTOMER dissatisfaction and, as appropriate, loss of repeat business and referrals? HOW are complaints aggregated and analyzed for use in improvement throughout your organization and by your PARTNERS?

4 HOW do you keep your APPROACHES to building relationships and providing CUSTOMER access current with business needs and directions?

Baldrige further points to interfunctional and interhierarchical interaction. This does not mean that the quality concept has taken over all management, only that quality development requires contributions from each and everyone. It would of course be surprising if badly managed internal work would end up in quality excellence.

Only US-based organizations can apply for the Baldrige. It it usually not the whole company that wins, but a specific division. Among recent recipients were in 2006 Premier (a healthcare strategic alliance of not-for-profit hospitals), in 2005 Park Place Lexus (a Texas firm selling and servicing Lexus cars), and in 2002 Motorola Commercial, Government & Industrial Solutions Sector (the leading worldwide supplier of two-way radio communications). The European correspondence, EFQM Excellence Award, has a somewhat different angle but essentially the same purpose. Among its winners were in 2005 BMW Chassis and Driveline Systems Production (Germany); in 2004 TNT Post Group Information Systems (UK); and in 2000, Nokia Mobile Phones, Europe and Africa (Finland).

The most important conclusion from the recent unfolding of the quality concept, and which has vast implications for marketing, is the following: Quality management in its modern form fortifies the relationship between operations management and marketing management.

I consider this a hitherto neglected but dramatic change in the management of a business. In Figure 5.4, characteristic features of the internal and external orientations are listed with quality management as the bridge. The quality concept has succeeded in doing what marketing has strived to do for decades, unite production orientation with marketing orientation.

The external part of quality management starts with customer perceived quality and market needs. The most comprehensive contributions are found in the marketing literature, often expressed in terms of needs, need satisfaction, and satisfied customers. It is even

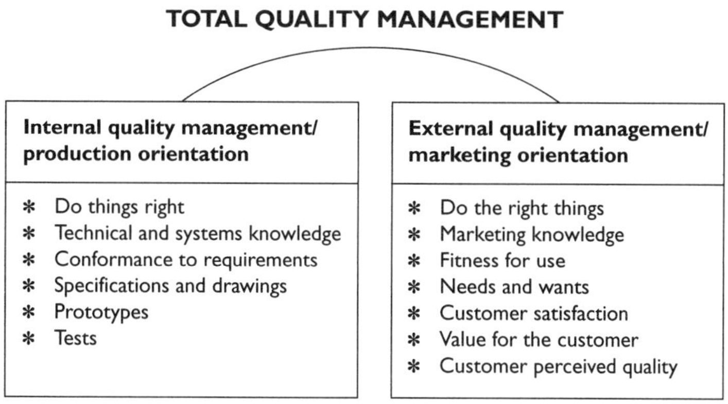

TOTAL QUALITY MANAGEMENT

Internal quality management/ production orientation	External quality management/ marketing orientation
* Do things right * Technical and systems knowledge * Conformance to requirements * Specifications and drawings * Prototypes * Tests	* Do the right things * Marketing knowledge * Fitness for use * Needs and wants * Customer satisfaction * Value for the customer * Customer perceived quality

Figure 5.4 TQM forging a relationship between marketing functions and technical functions

described as creating customer delight and glowing fans sounding like the 'lustomers' in the Duveen case from Chapter 1. Within market research, there is a long tradition of studying consumer satisfaction, consumer behaviour, organizational buying behaviour and customer relationships to brands. The quality concept from service research is above all externally oriented, toward customers and revenue.

Two efforts to design models for facilitating the technology–market link will be mentioned here. The first is quality function deployment (QFD). Its purpose is to unite customer requirements with the properties of goods and service. It is also referred to as 'the quality house' after the house-like form of its matrices. What customers want is found out in detail and linked with how the supplier shall achieve this technically in order to design an offering. The connections between the whats and hows are established and analysed, technical conflicts between properties are listed, and finally a specification is established. It is an ambitious approach which has turned out very demanding to implement but is used extensively by certain companies, not least in Japan.

The second technique is based on process descriptions of service activities, already mentioned together with the service encounter in R5. It concentrates on the interaction between the customer and the provider's front staff, and the interaction between front staff, support staff and management. The vantage point is the 'customer's path', that is, the customer's way of moving from considering to buy a service and to getting the service produced and delivered.[13]

Certain service is performed at the customer's site, for example cleaning services. The cleaning company can focus on the customers' need for clean premises, their need for

---

[13] See also Gummesson (1993, p. 198ff) and the discussion on contextual matrices (pp. 108–110).

cleaning at a specific hours, or on the amount the customer is willing to pay. If the cleaning company can influence the layout of an office before it is built, it can achieve better quality and productivity, which means better value for the customer as well as for the service provider. If a building is difficult to keep clean, efficient techniques and aids can facilitate, but only within the limits of the construction of the building. Improved quality then requires co-operation in an early stage between those who design, construct and maintain the building.

Daily, we interact with deficiently designed and badly manufactured products. Bitner has drawn the following conclusion about the impact of the physical environment on service quality: 'Typically, decisions about employees and the design of physical evidence are not made by marketing managers, but rather by human resource managers, operations managers, and design professionals.'[14] The internal logic then takes over at the expense of the customer logic.

Psychologist Donald Norman has studied the psychopathology of everyday things, their 'mental' shortcomings. Let me end this section with his summary of the designer's dilemma:[15]

> Designing well is not easy. The manufacturer wants something that can be produced economically. The store wants something that will be attractive to its customers. The purchaser has several demands. In the store, the purchaser focuses on price and appearance, and perhaps on prestige value. At home, the same person will pay more attention to functionality and usability. The repair service cares about maintainability: how easy is the device to take apart, diagnose, and service? The needs of those concerned are different and are often in conflict. Nonetheless, the designer may be able to satisfy everyone.

Obviously there are many stakeholders with different needs: designers, suppliers, retail outlets, buyers, users and those who handle the maintenance, plus, eventually, society and the environment. And which of these stakeholders should be considered the customers? For whom should the design be targeted? And how should we build relationships to them and interact with them? We can conclude that unfortunately a customer-centric strategy which includes a balanced view of the interaction between producer and user – balanced centricity – is still not reality.

---

[14] Bitner (1990, p. 79).
[15] Norman (1988, p. 28).

Internal marketing – relationships with the 'employee market'

So far we have encountered at least two phenomena which could be labelled internal marketing: the marketing between units in the same corporation (R24) and the relationships between internal customers (R25). We should then add the special case of internal customer relationships: operations management and marketing unified by quality (R26). However, the current marketing terminology reserves internal marketing for a another phenomenon, defined as follows: Internal marketing is the application of marketing knowledge – which was originally developed for external marketing – on the 'internal market', that is, the employees. The concept appeared in the late 1970s and has since been treated in many ways and increasingly been approached through RM eye-glasses followed by an expansion to the many-to-many eye-glasses with consideration of networks of people and stakeholders.[16]

Figure 5.5 shows that internal marketing is in-bound and directed to the personnel. External marketing can also have an impact on the internal market, which is shown by the arrow to the right. For example, advertisements for a company sometimes attract the employee's attention more than it attracts the consumer's attention, and if the CEO is interviewed on television the employees watch with particular curiosity.

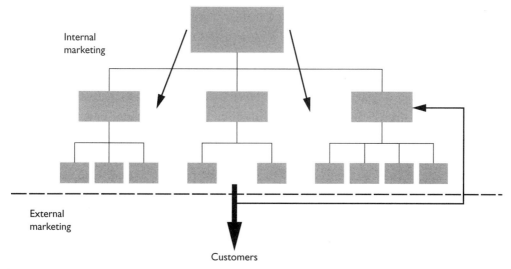

Figure 5.5 The difference between internal and external marketing, and the link between them

---

[16] See Ballantyne (2003) and Grönroos (2007, pp. 383–413). A comprehensive review of internal marketing is found in an anthology edited by Varey and Lewis (2000).

Internal marketing in the network organizations is much more complex than in the simple hierarchy shown in Figure 5.5. Not only must own staff be reached but also other actors in a company's total network. Reasons to apply internal marketing can originate from several sources, and people can belong to several networks. The distinction between internal and external marketing becomes fluid. This stands out clearly as the Internet is usually perceived in marketing as an external relationship builder. It can also be used to establish an intranet which extends to the traditionally internal, the employees, and an extranet for 'specially invited' customers, partners in alliances, own suppliers and others who form a company's network organization. The group of stakeholders with whom you aspire for long-term relationships becomes an 'in-between group', one between the strictly internal and the strictly external. For example, VISA has linked its employees in an intranet which offers a list of the staff, newsletters, lunch menu and more. Its extranet application includes the thousands of allied banks who handle the daily operations of the VISA card. This could also be viewed as an extension of an e-CRM system beyond the mere customer focus.

As with the Internet, the technology itself is only of benefit when put to constructive use. The role of managers as well as the tasks of information departments may change, as much information is interactively available on the Internet. Despite this, and particularly when internal marketing is used in major changes, personal contact is critical. High tech will never make the need for high touch obsolete.

The objective of internal marketing within RM is to create relationships between management and employees and between functions. The personnel can be viewed as an internal market, and this market must be reached efficiently in order to prepare the personnel for external contacts; *efficient internal marketing is an antecedent to efficient external marketing.* Techniques from external marketing can be applied internally, mainly from the areas of promotion and communications. Internal marketing can be based on personal and interactive relationships, as well as on a certain amount of mass marketing. Traditional activities to reach the employees are often routinely performed and build more on bureaucratic principles and wishful thinking than on professional marketing and communications know-how.

To a large extent, internal marketing must be interactive. Traditional ways of internal mass marketing – such as the distribution of formal memos and internal magazines – is insufficient. Social get-togethers are important. My own experience shows that kick-offs have become established as important interactive instruments for management to reach out both with facts and to shape attitudes and foster a corporate culture. One rapidly growing company in Norway with 250 employees (average age 30) orchestrated a weekend kick-off which opened with some serious reprimands from the CEO. It continued with presentations by external consultants, one being the coach for the Norwegian national ski-jumping team, proceeded with entertainment by the number one rock star and popular singer, all introduced by the number one TV personality. It ended with a big banquet with awards for best employee performances and dancing. A Swedish global company hired a theatre group from London. Together with the client they set up a 3-day interactive kick-off in a large film studio, with both mental, social and physical exercises. The theatre group had done similar jobs for McKinsey, Disney and Dell. It shows that such viable external marketing strategies as offering experiences through event marketing and story-telling are equally important inside the organization.

Internal marketing emerged from services marketing. Its purpose was to get the front-line personnel – who have interactive relationships with external customers – to handle the service encounter better and with more independence. It is essential that the contact people are well informed about a company's offerings, but also that they understand the business mission, goals, strategies and organizational processes. It is equally important for support staff to be knowledgeable in order to be able to handle successfully the internal customer relationships.

In two classic articles on 'Mickey Mouse Marketing', the story is told of Disney's successful management of internal marketing (although it was not called so).[17] The staff was either on-stage or off-stage. On-stage, everyone participated in a show whether they were actors in the traditional sense, or sold tickets, served food or picked litter. Consequently, they should know their part and create satisfied customers. In the 'Ten Standards of Excellence' at Disneyland Paris hotels, 'Commandment no. 8' says: 'We're on stage and we know our role in the show. We're entertainers, we know our "script", we know our standards and we never miss a cue. We consistently give a good show – all the time.'

Even if internal marketing as a concept comes out of services marketing, it is applicable to all types of organizations. This conclusion is based on the observation that companies in general have taken the concept to their hearts and use it. This supports the S-D logic which does not distinguish between goods and services but sees them as mutually dependent in all value propositions. The following case from Ericsson components echoes the conclusion.

CASE STUDY   **Ericsson**

Ericsson's business area for components (formerly Rifa) manufactured electronic components of strategic importance to Ericsson's telephone switches. There is a need for a certain amount of in-house manufacturing to protect and develop the core competence, but the company also wanted to exploit its knowledge on the external market. After a long life of internal deliveries without competition, the business area was required to prove its ability to meet the

---

[17] Pope (1979a, b).

competition from other manufacturers, among them the successful Motorola. A transition to a more business-like and market-oriented culture was called for, and internal marketing is one way of contributing to a new corporate culture. After a survey of possible means of reaching out to the personnel, a publication was made to explain the new situation. It was inspired by the SAS publication Carlzon's Little Red, a much hailed effort to inform and motivate employees. It became an unsophisticated pamphlet with short sentences and simple drawings which presented essential facts and strategies. Two pages from Rifa's pamphlet are shown in Figure 5.6.

In internal marketing, as in everything else, management commitment is crucial. It was important for the head of the business area and his divisional managers to show that they stood behind the message. After discussions and tests it was concluded that the best way would be to appear in person, even if that would take time. How do you do this with 2000 people working in three towns far apart? Fifty-six appearances by the head of the business area and his management team were called for.

Most executives would claim they could not spare the time. Groups of 40 employees participated in half-day programmes, which ended with lunch or dinner with management. Considering that many of them worked shifts, several programmes had to be performed at night, ending with coffee and cake. The management team presented ongoing changes and made comments, followed by the participants working in groups around a number of themes with a subsequent plenary discussion. The publication was distributed as documentation when the participants left.[18]

Everytime a RIFA employee meets a customer, a MOMENT OF TRUTH occurs

Negative   or Positive

It is the sum of all moments of truth that determine success or failure

Figure 5.6 From the pamphlet used in Rifa's internal marketing. Drawing by Bengt Mellberg

[18] Gummesson (1987a).

The interaction between employees and external customers can be extensive. This was shown in R5 (the service encounter) and R6 (the many-headed customer and the many-headed supplier). Even if many employees have limited contact with customers, companies are looking – with some desperation – for better ways of preparing employees for changes in business missions, systems and organizational structures. The launching of new value propositions, new technologies and new methods requires participation and motivation. There can be a colossal gap between what management wants (and believes is happening) and what actually happens in the minds of employees and external customers and how this eventually affects financial results. This has come out clearly in problem detection studies (PDS).[19] In a PDS, the researcher makes an inventory of as many problems as possible. Customers are asked about the importance of these problems, and management is asked what they think customers will answer. The match between customer and management responses is invariably low.

At Ericsson the internal marketing was targeted to the traditional, well-defined organization, the nano relationships. In the case of Karlshamns the internal marketing also has a clear effect on market and mega relationships.

CASE STUDY | **Karlshamns**

Karishamns make oil-based food products. At Christmas all employees were given a variant of Trivial Pursuit, one of the world's most loved quiz games. The mission of the factory of only supplying consumer co-operative stores had been broadened to include the sales of its products to all types of retailers. A major organizational audit had been performed and the problems of informing everyone were massive. Of the 2000 questions in Trivial Pursuit, 500 were substituted. The new questions were of a local nature, both of general interest such as 'Which year were the first winter Olympics held?' to direct questions regarding the company, for example 'How many small soap bars for hotel rooms does the subsidiary in Stavanger, Norway, produce in 1 year: 2, 4 or 6 million?' and 'Which are the two most important ingredients in our margarine?'

The game was a hit. Employees played it over Christmas, in their spare time. That was also the idea; it was handed out during the last hours before the Christmas holiday. This way, its messages also reached family members

---

[19] The conclusions from PDS are based on my own participation in several studies and discussions with market researchers and their clients.

and friends. Others who did not work in the factory asked for the game after it made the news in the local paper and radio station. So the internal marketing activity reached beyond the staff and had a positive mega communications effect, particularly in the home town of the factory.

Internal marketing stresses human resources as key to the development and maintenance of a successful operation. Employees are best motivated to demonstrate service spirit and customer orientation if they are well informed; this effect is best achieved through a marketing approach. It requires both active learning and influence on attitudes. Internal marketing can be a way of knocking down walls between departments and the expertise of employees can be combined in novel ways to challenge the internal activities that need to be changed.[20]

Traditionally, all employees work in the same place at the same time. Flexible working hours have changed this, and so has presence in many locations. More people work from home, not least because of the opportunities offered by IT, but also because of the waste of time on suburban transportation. Laptops with wireless broadband connection and mobile phones offer a new type of flexibility bus have in practice extended working hours as people are increasingly expected to be available at all times. Growing globalization requires more employees to be travelling but they can still be in constant touch with their home base. This may lead to a hollow corporate culture, as working in face-to-face contact with colleagues is also a source of inspiration. On the other hand, not all people are happy to work in the same office space all the time. Conflicts are common and incidents of sexual harassment are increasingly being noted. Relationships are upheld via email and the Internet, without those involved ever getting into direct face-to-face contact. The system with lifelong employment supports what the Japanese call 'mimikosuri', the ability to 'massage somebody's ears'. The massage facilitates decision-making, smoothes criticism and prevents employees losing face. Marshall McLuhan, the Canadian media philosopher became known for his claim that 'The medium is the message' rather than the more rational belief that the content is the message. Later he added 'The medium is the massage'. In light of what we experience these days with electronic media both were prophetic statements.[21]

A personal relationship that has been built over decades gives security and support also in the age of the Internet. In contrast, using IT without this personal equity as a foundation can cause problems. Hallowell (1999) points out how increased use of email inside the company can alienate the staff: 'The irony is that this kind of alienation in the work-place

---

[20] Ballantyne (2003) and Grönroos (2007).
[21] McLuhan (1964); McLuhan and Fiore (1967).

derives not from lack of communication but from a surplus of the wrong kind.' High touch is knocked out by high tech when internal e-relationships take over from internal h-relationships, and when a distant relationship takes over from a close relationship.

'Management by email' can supersede 'management by walking around' but the fact that the Internet has the potential of interactivity is not enough. There are delayed reactions, and written text – which is deprived of body language – is perceived differently from face-to-face communication and immediate feedback. However, new generations which grow up with email may accept an email message more readily. Today changes in a company can reach all staff worldwide in 24 hours via the Intranet and quickly be followed by visits from the head office, an effort to combine high tech and high touch.

What do we know about the effects of internal marketing? It is easy to measure changes in attitude and motivation among employees and if knowledge has increased. But in order to see if internal marketing has an effect on everyday behaviour one has to be part of the organization; it can only be sensed through involvement and qualitative assessment. As the head of the Ericsson components business area said to me years later: 'The internal programme we ran made all the difference'. Still internal marketing is an enabler and antecedent but the pertinent outcome only shows in the bottom line: Did we make more money? This can of course be measured but it may still be difficult to objectively claim a cause and effect relationship.

Finally, some practical advice:

- Profit from the techniques of external marketing on the internal market. By applying an inbound perspective we see things other than if we just stick to the outbound marketing perspective. We are reminded that external marketing is dependent on the success of internal marketing.
- Invest in interactive internal relationships, even if internal mass marketing has a role in the value-creating network society.
- Apply internal marketing with a network view. Organizations are networks of relationships within which employees interact. Internal marketing can be restricted to employees but there is an equal need to reach the whole network. The market and mega relationships can also be included in a broadened internal network, as the whole network organization must function.

The two-dimensional matrix relationship

The word hierarchy comes from the Greek 'hieros' (holy) and 'archein' (order or control). A hierarchical organization is based on clear ranking and absolute obedience. We know today that this holy order is not the best way of getting an organization to perform.

The hierarchy offers a one-dimensional relationship, the matrix organization a two-dimensional relationship and the network organization a multi-dimensional network. The matrix organization is an effort to get out of the rigid mould of the hierarchy, and a step toward increased network thinking and improved interfunctional and interhierarchical relationships. The matrix has become commonplace and exists in many variants, often in an organization with product managers. A product manager's job includes these or similar tasks:

- be responsible for product planning and implementation throughout the product lifecycle
- collect and analyse product and customer requirements
- closely co-operate with design, engineering, purchasing, marketing and sales
- ensure that revenue goals are fulfilled
- ensure that customer satisfaction standards are met
- compare own products with competing products
- ensure that the product fits overall corporate mission, goals and strategies.

Viewed in the light of RM, both the hierarchy and the matrix stand out as crude and a bit naive. The former lives on the dream of unity of command, the latter on the acceptance of the somewhat more realistic – but not too realistic – dual command. We are reluctant to endorse complexity and tend to see its existence as a failure, not having been able to get reality properly sorted out. The experience of most companies seems to be that the matrix is awkward to manage at the same time as they cannot live without it. On closer inspection behind the neat facade of the matrix, there is a multi-dimensional, informal, complex and often contradictory network. It is a challenge to find oneself trying to manage such a network characterized by a series of negotiations, unstable balance of power, far-reaching delegation of profits, and a variable structure. It certainly requires co-creation. But reality provides this dynamic complexity whether we approve of it or not. Studying the matrix, however, may have an educational purpose. It helps us to foresee the complexity inherent in the networks of RM and many-to-many marketing.

The matrix concerns relationships of principal interest to RM/CRM. There are many species of matrices:

- *Product/service group versus geographical area*: This is a combination of products on one side and districts, regions, countries or groups of countries on the other. As an example, a global corporation was divided into 6 product-based business areas, while headquarter sales units and local subsidiaries throughout the world were in charge of sales. The biggest business area had divided its geographical market into 5 country groups: Northern Europe, continental Europe and Australia, the United Kingdom, North

America, and finally Asia, Africa and Latin America. The areas reflected the importance of the markets.

■ *Product/service group versus customer segments*: A simple matrix in food production consists of product lines on one side and two segments on the other: the retail market and the restaurant market. Sales can be direct or go via wholesalers. The buying behaviour of the two segments is different, and often so is the design of the products and packaging, and the purchased volume, and price.

■ *Product/service group versus function*: As product manager at a subsidiary of Reader's Digest, the international publishing and direct mail-order operation, I was responsible for special books. This included development of the product line, production of the books, marketing, and profit centre responsibility. There were two more product managers, one for its magazine and one for music albums. I co-operated with a series of internal functions: editorial; the printing of books and promotion material; distribution of direct mail and the books; accounting with budgeting and follow-up of financial results; and some others. I was not in charge of any of these functions and I had to compete for their attention with other product managers. Moreover, in competition with some 20 subsidiaries, I utilized functions at the European headquarters in London and the international headquarters in Pleasantville, New York, for example in market research.

■ *Geographical area versus function*: The geographical representation, for example, of a chain of stores, restaurants or hotels consists of a local unit and its customers. A chain of stores may have a central purchasing department with purchasers for different parts of their product line. The central purchaser of clothing must assess the fashion of the next seasons, prices and expected demand, and the stores are then required to sell the garments.

■ *Key account management (KAM) of strategic customers*: KAM was mentioned in R6 (the many-headed customer and the many-headed supplier), pointing to the fact that this is not a new issue. But it is a special case of RM with increasing significance. It is '... aimed at building a portfolio of loyal key accounts by offering them, on a continuing basis, a product/service package tailored to their individual needs. Success depends partly on the degree of receptivity demonstrated by the customer to a partnership approach ... To co-ordinate day-to-day interaction under the umbrella of a long-term relationship, selling companies typically form dedicated teams headed up by a 'key account manager'.[22]

■ *Temporary projects versus the base organization*: The matrices that have been described so far are part of the fixed structure of the organization. This matrix variant is an *ad hoc* organization with projects on one side and a task force of people from different functions on the other. Projects are common in all types of organizations. As organizations

---

[22] Quoted from McDonald, Millman and Rogers (1997, p. 112).

change at a faster pace, even the 'fixed' structure becomes a project; it could be called the parent project. If an organization is a bundle of projects, it is already on the way to becoming a network organization.

It is obvious that the intersections between two types of responsibility can induce constructive dialogue, but also heads-on confrontation of strong egos. One product manager competes with another for the attention of a functional department. A store manager may feel that central purchasing orders the wrong articles at the wrong prices so that they cannot be sold. At the intersections there are several opinions and wills, but a joint decision is called for. Who shall yield? What happens if both drive ahead at full speed? Can we find a form of collaboration that allows both 'vehicles' to cross the junction in accord? The decisions must build on consensus, or the disputes are moved on to the executive level above the crossroads. The exercise in reaching agreements can be educational, or inertia and insecurity can grow. The internal relationships may take up more time than the external ones; they can be demanding on patience, personal maturity and social skills. Even if the matrix in itself carries difficulties, there is an advantage in being able to address the product and the geographic market in combination.

Before its merger with Brown Boveri and the creation of the ABB, one of the world's leading engineering companies in the use of electrical power, Asea, had an international product/country matrix. An former executive vice president described its intricacies which seem to represent a timeless dilemma:

> The international matrix holds a potential for conflicts. We tell
> division and subsidiary managers that they have profit responsibility
> worldwide, and country managers that they are responsible for
> everything inside their country. These are two completely different
> roles, both necessary in a multi-product/multi-market organization.
> The roles need open-minded managers who can solve a problem
> together. If the matrix managers cannot agree on a solution they
> can come to us for help. If this is repeated time and again, we have
> to replace one or several of them. We need quick decisions in a
> flat organization with frequent interfunctional contacts within an
> overriding philosophy.[23]

Like all other organizational principles, the matrix must be deployed in the right situation. There are those who repudiate matrices as being unmanageable. They claim matrices engender controversies. An alternative interpretation is that they put the spotlight on existing but hidden conflicts.

---

[23] Arne Bennborn, quoted in Brandes and Brege (1990, p. 131).

In summary, the advantages of the matrix organization are:

- The product managers 'own' the product and can work with all aspects of the product line. They can acquire a complete overview of the product, new technology, customers, competitors, volume, market share, profits and other aspects.
- The geographical area managers 'own' their area and its customers. They have local closeness to the customer. But they also enjoy central support with a product line, advertising and sales promotion, through which experience from many local markets is shared and transferred between markets.
- There is less risk that an issue is abandoned and left in a vacuum. It is particularly important that the customers do not leave the supplier because of obsolete products, vanishing segments or dissatisfied customers. Revenue, cost and profits are monitored both from a product and market view.

The disadvantages are:

- Managers must handle a large number of relationships, both externally and internally. Conflicts easily emerge at the matrix crossroads. For example, a product manager wants to replace a current product for long-term profit growth, while an area manager is first assessed by his or her ability to meet the current budget and prefers to bet on existing products.
- Management does not give enough support to the product managers but is still expecting superior performance. The responsibility placed on product managers is frequently not matched by their authority to make decisions and act. At the matrix crossroads, they run into area managers who are often empowered by a considerably larger organization and budget.

Management consultants Booz Allen Hamilton offer the following advice, especially directed to global firms in packaged consumer goods.[24] Multi-dimensional business is a management challenge which is universally failed. The reason is that authority is blurred at the intersections where the most critical decisions are made. Therefore the matrix requires active management at the intersections between brand/category, geography and function. It should take advantage of both scale and local positioning, balancing the trade-offs between global brands, local tastes and scale efficiencies. They stress that the matrix can take many forms. They have further found that two key organizational principles have to be implemented to make the matrix work:

1 Consideration of the 'Organizational DNA'. The crucial genes are decision rights, especially in the intersections; information, to be accessible and not siloed in departments;

---

[24] From Galioto *et al*. (2006).

motivators, to accelerate performance; and, finally, structure as the tangible manifestation of the three others. All genes must be in good shape or the whole will collapse.

2 Where to place the fulcrum. This is the core of planning and co-ordination functions and how goals should be defined, monitored and adjusted through strategic planning, financial analysis, forecasting, marketing strategy, consumer insights and so on.

Constructive dialogue, lack of prestige, recognition of different roles, and a holistic view are required human properties in a matrix. Rapid resolution of problems, flexibility and a willingness to change are needed without ending up in diluted compromises.

 If we cannot manage the simplified two-dimensional network of the matrix, how then can we expect to manage the complex multi-dimensional networks of RM?

 ## The relationship to external providers of marketing service

Several marketing tasks are not performed by employees but by external providers. This was conceptualized in R4, with the introduction of the full-time marketers (FTMs) and the part-time marketers (PTMs). External providers to the marketing function can be viewed as FTMs at the time the buyer pays for them. In these relationships, the providers become part of the customer's marketing and sales organization without belonging to it in the traditional sense. They become part of a network that transcends the organization/market boundaries. The service of the external providers can be split into three groups:

1 Service concerning the physical distribution of goods is offered by haulage firms, wholesalers and retailers. Transportation is one of the major sectors of any economy and has been so for hundreds of years; only now we have more alternatives than before. Physical distribution, logistics and supply network management were discussed in R3.

2 Service primarily concerned with selling and delivering. The service of wholesalers and retailers belong in this group. So do agents and brokers, even if they never physically touch a product. So does telemarketing service. In some countries, including the United States and the United Kingdom, insurance to individuals is sold by brokers; in some countries they are primarily sold by the insurance companies' own sales organizations. These two approaches generate different market relationships. In both cases the insurance company has to keep up its image and the interest of the consumer. In the broker

case, keeping up the spirit of brokers and helping them do good business becomes the number one priority. This can occur through frequent innovations, quality improvements and supportive campaigns.

3 Consulting service such as performed by advertising agencies, market research institutes, Internet consultants and designers of CRM systems. These providers are primarily advisory. They provide specialist expertise but they can also execute much of the craft, such as the printing of brochures, field interviews, the establishment of websites, and the installation and testing of CRM software.

The external providers reinforce and supplement the marketing function; it's integration of resources in S-D logic terms. They offer both strategic outsourcing and outsourcing of repetitive routine service. The providers become a hybrid between external firms and internal departments. If the customer interacts closely and continuously with them, in practice they become part of the customer's organization; they may even have permanent office facilities on the customer's premises. The buyer must ask two pivotal questions: 'What shall we do ourselves and what shall the independent provider do?' and 'Is this an occasional transaction or is it going to be a long-term relationship?'

The first two types of external providers connect with physical distribution and sales. The rest of this section will focus on the third type, primarily advisory consulting service. Today, all companies use consultants in their marketing function, either on a continuous or *ad hoc* basis. The consultants provide expertise which is lacking or is in short supply at a specific moment. Numerous types of consultants are consequential for the success of the marketing function. These will be discussed together with the import of interactive relationships between client and consultant and the ability to obtain satisfactory support to the marketing function.

Consultants in communications

The advertising agency is the oldest, most ostentatious and most common of all consultants to the marketing function. This is most likely so because marketing is still predominantly directed to mass communication to consumers, and consumer advertising has high public visibility. An ad agency is either hired until further notice and works continuously with its client, or the assignments are tied to specific projects. The agency relationship is constantly under scrutiny, sometimes inspired by the size of its latest invoice. With few exceptions, measurement of advertising effects on revenue is obscure, while fees, price of printed material, and media space are easy to measure. And how do you measure the value of creativity? The strengths of ad agencies include visualization, creative design, and the planning and execution of campaigns. Their knowledge on strategy varies considerably. At some agencies, individuals master a broader field than advertising and those can compete with management consultants.

In-house advertising production exists but is supplemented by agencies; complete in-house agencies are not often found any more. There must, however, be a defined flesh-and-blood client with whom the agency can interact, usually a marketing manager, product manager or advertising manager. Many companies use several agencies and each profit centre has the right to make its own choice. Others request that all their units worldwide use the same advertising agency chain. Advertising brings the mind back to mass marketing from traditional marketing management – a subgroup under the third P (promotion) – and not to RM/CRM. Individual and mass marketing will exist in tandem; we live with the 'paradox' of customized mass marketing. Not least because of the need for interactive marketing strategies in the RM spirit, ad agencies have diversified in all kinds of directions but the diversification of marketing strategies has also spawned specialized in public relations (PR), events, sponsoring and RM/CRM. The various ways of communicating with the market and society are overlapping even if consultants are more or less specializing in one area. The diversification is caused by the much more focused use of marketing strategies, treated in Chapter 8 under 'The 4Ps are neither 4 nor Ps any more'. All the specialist providers of service are difficult to classify; they may be both in communications, strategy and research. As among the most common are the following:

- PR and lobbying. Some of the largest international consultants today are found in these areas. That their presence has grown was obvious in mega marketing (R19) and the mass media relationship (R23).
- Branding. The snowballing attention given to brands as a ground for constructing parasocial relationships (R13) has made branding increasingly sophisticated, requiring advanced specialists.
- Telemarketing. These specialists with their origin in telephone sales have added fund-raising, customer surveys and outsourced call centres to their product line.
- Internet and website consultants. They became a rocket that illuminated the sky and dazzled clients but today they have matured and glow with a more realistic light.
- Sponsoring and event marketing. These consultants are dependent on networks and personal networks and they are becoming increasingly important. To add glamour to events such as company anniversaries, theatre and movie premiéres, and the opening of new restaurants, another type of consultant emerged, the one who sets up the event and makes sure that the right celebs and media are present.
- Legal advice. In the United States in particular, lawyers have become key players in the marketing arena (R16).
- Former US Secretary of State Henry Kissinger was mentioned as advisor on political risks in international markets (R18). Futurists help to discern trends in consumption patterns and lifestyles.
- Others. There are specialists in numerous small but critical niches, for example helping firms to design and present bids on major contracts.

Consultants in marketing strategy

Consultants in communications are also advising on strategy but in this section I am thinking of those who represent a broader knowledge of management and specifically work with the marketing aspects. Their strength is the understanding of management and the marketing function, and they work directly under the CEO or marketing director. Their knowledge concerns marketing aspects of areas such as strategy, organization, planning, research, cost reduction and downsizing. Some are specialized in industries, such as retailing or IT. They are found in management consulting companies but also in niched specialist firms. Beginning in the 1980s, quality has become more important to management consultants. Since the current quality concept is strongly customer-centric, the job of the TQM consultant is closely knit to the marketing function. A series of consulting services have followed in the wake of quality awards and ISO certification. In many B2B markets today, companies cannot do business without ISO certification and usually assistance from consultants is needed.

Installing a CRM system is a more strategic issue than many companies have understood. It should connect to the total business system used to support the management of a company. Developing websites, especially if these are used for taking orders and aim to improve and maintain customer retention, is not only a marketing and IT issue. It requires redesign of company structure and processes and attention from top management.

Market research institutes

These are specialists in data generation[25] and the application of certain research techniques. They primarily research consumer attitudes to value propositions such as current and new service and brands, and compare competitors. They do this at regular or *ad hoc* intervals, collectively for industries or as separate customized projects. Apart from proficiency in research techniques, their strength is the management of field interviewers and computer systems for the planning, processing, analysis and reporting of a study. Customer satisfaction surveys, in particular, have had a rapid rise. Email and the Internet now offer online research opportunities and quicker and simpler processing of data.

To some extent they also draw conclusions and recommend strategies and activities. In order to draw conclusions, two types of knowledge are required, but are rarely represented in one individual. One is the technical dexterity to investigate a phenomenon, for example how customers behave and why. The second is institutional knowledge about the industry, the client company, its value propositions, competitive situation, and the

---

[25] I prefer the term *data generation* to the mainstream term *data collection*. Data in social contexts are usually not there to be collected but are generated through an analysis and interpretation process, governed by a preconceived notion of what is essential and what is not, or by total openness and sensitivity to what reality wants to tell the researcher.

more secluded mechanisms that can only be understood by those who live with them continuously: the power game, which decisions are possible to implement and what financial risks are acceptable. The first type of knowledge is best represented by the research institute, the second best by the client. The quality of the research will be the outcome of interaction between the research institute and the client, and their ability to constructively coalesce their competencies. It is a frequent nuisance that the client does not attach enough weight to the contact with the researcher, but delegates the contact to a staff unit on a middle or lower management level. When the results are presented for decisions, the decision-makers lack in-depth understanding of the quality of the data; those who present it know too little about the whole context of the decision and have no power.

Educators, speakers and entertainers

These are found among specialists on training and education, university professors, writers, management consultants, and successful business executives. Some have agents, speaker's bureaus, just like actors. They can embrace anything from formal training programmes on general and special aspects of marketing to speaking at kick-offs, business lunches and conferences. The market for this type of service has grown continuously. There is a need to lift the vision from the daily myopic routine and to be inspired by success stories, enthusiastic crusaders and celebrities. Currently, customer in focus themes, such as closer relationships to customers, measuring customer satisfaction, customer loyalty programmes, customer clubs, KAM, brand equity and brand identity, and everything associated with e-business and e-CRM, captivate the minds of marketing practitioners, which today also includes public sector representatives. Inviting external speakers is equally often a symbolic event, as it is an event to disseminate actual knowledge; sometimes it is mere entertainment, especially if the speaker is a celebrity. Increasingly it seems as celeb status of the speaker is more important than content; actors, TV personalities and sports champions speak about leadership, attitudes, relationships and so on. In this way, the appearance of a speaker is more of a symbolic happening and an emotional kick than an actual learning experience.

Executive search, recruitment and outsourcing of functions and manpower

Executive search and recruitment is handled both by niche firms and management consultants. The recruitment of salespeople is big business. Recruitment of executives and managers in marketing is handled by head-hunters, who search for individual candidates that fit a specification set up together with the client firm. They do not advertise, but approach candidates through personal contacts. Part of what the client is buying is an entry ticket to their network of relationships. They can approach a person without others knowing that a position is open and can guarantee confidentiality. They have experience in assessing a person's suitability for executive work. The cost of hiring the wrong marketing manager is excessively high, not least through lost opportunities and foregone revenue, so the recruitment procedure should be handled cautiously. Another type is management for hire, where a consultant is placed in an executive position for 6 months to 2 years, usually when a company is already in a crisis or to prevent an upcoming crisis, and the outsourcing of manpower, single people or a whole function, such as a sales force.

The relationship between the outside consultant and the client requires interactive service encounters. It means co-creation between client and provider. It is not a matter of giving orders and obeying orders except in certain standardized instances, for example a print order for a brochure. For example, the ad agency should understand the needs of both their customer and their customer's customer (R7). The planning of an assignment must occur in close relationship between consultant and client. It is imperative that the real decision-makers participate. Intermediaries should be avoided; through them the information – which is often complex and subtle – will be filtered and sometimes distorted. Those who are going to implement the assignment need proper briefings, straight from the client's mouth.

The reinforcement to the marketing function is an example of outsourcing. It is not new, but it has become more significant and elaborate in today's complex, fast-changing and network-based economy.

 ## The owner and financier relationship

Not only loyal customers but also loyal owners exert influence on marketing success. A trusting and long-term relationship between owners (and other financiers) and management and the marketing function is a necessary condition for building long-term relationships with customers, suppliers, competitors and others.

The owners' importance for finance is explored in the literature, but its importance for marketing is rarely mentioned. Investors appear in many shapes, with diverse demands on short- and long-term return on capital. They can be active or passive, big or small, known or anonymous. Investors finance the operations of a company at the same time as a company has other financiers, primarily banks and other financial institutions, but also customers, suppliers and governments (through subsidies).

There is an irony that investors have been in the focus of management attention – not customers, not employees – as these have become less and less loyal.[26] However, investor

---

[26] Reichheld (2001a).

relationships vary considerably between countries. Germany and Japan have had stable long-term owner relationships. Compared to the United States, Japanese stockholding is 4 times more stable and 7 times more likely to be reciprocated.[27] Reichheld[28] claims that the loyalty of the American investor has been reduced as online trading has '... accelerated investor annual churn rates toward 100 per cent.' He adds: 'Customer loyalty hinges ... on committed teams of high-caliber employees and suppliers, which in turn require a core of owners committed to building an enduringly successful enterprise'. He strongly warns against 'Wall Street Wisdom', which has led many otherwise successful companies into unfortunate diversification. Examples are Harley-Davidson that was warned by Wall Street for its dependency of one product, the motor-bike, which led to the disastrous acquisition of Holiday Rambler; and the bank which owned the loyalty leader in credit cards, MBNA, was criticized for its dependence on MBNA earnings and diluted its investment into areas with weaker prospects.

These advisors have their own agenda: to earn a percentage of any merger, acquisition or stock exchange introduction. The more deals they can initiate irrespective of future success for the companies involved, the higher their commissions.

The turnover of investors has increased from 14 per cent in 1960 to 52 per cent in 1995.[29] This means that the average investor holds shares for less than 2 years, albeit with a variation of a few minutes to several decades. Maximum short-term return on capital has taken priority over long-term survival, and shares are bought and sold as transaction goods, much like ice-cream on a hot day on the beach. The relationship between a company and its investors has also become increasingly anonymous; it is sometimes even handled by computers programmed to search for the quickest buck of the day or the minute.

A countermove is *corporate governance* that stands for active, supportive and responsible ownership.

Demonstrating success through a high and climbing share price can be the most important input to a favourable public image and brand equity. If the share price is down, customers may feel insecure. This is especially true for cases such as computers and future compatible updates of software, equipment that requires spare parts, and motor vehicles for which the second-hand price is important.

The customers' image of a firm may be affected by the image of its major owner, but most often customers, especially consumers, do not know who owns a company or a brand name. If you stay at the illustrious Beverly Hills Hotel in California, you are a guest of the Sultan of Brunei, one of the richest men in the world. Of the shares of Disneyland Paris 39 per cent are owned by Disney but the next major shareholder is Prince Al Waleed

---

[27] Gerlach (1992, p. xvii).
[28] Reichheld (2001b, quotations from pp. 1–2 and 66–67).
[29] Reichheld (2001a).

of Saudi Arabia, with 24 per cent; the rest is free-floating or publicly held. The Prince arrived as a saviour in a financial crisis, which was basically caused by deficient customer proximity and excessive pricing, resulting in a cultural clash and too few visitors.

The annual report has been directed to tax authorities and other controlling agencies and to the stock market. The monthly and quarterly reports and the requirement that companies as early as possible warn against lowered profits are directed to the stock market. These indicators of the state and progress of a company primarily offer short-term financial information. In order to educate and inform investors, indicators are needed that show the importance of long-term goals. The balanced scorecard offers a framework for a more complete evaluation of a company (see Chapter 6). I am not, however, a believer in the folklore of measuring everything. Investment decisions are taken out of strategic necessity and estimates of profits are not always possible, for example of the change-over from one technology to another or a long-term product development project.

Figure 5.7 puts the marketing function in a financier and management context. Ownership affects marketing, and the relationship between general management, marketing management and major owners (who are often on the board of directors) becomes vital.

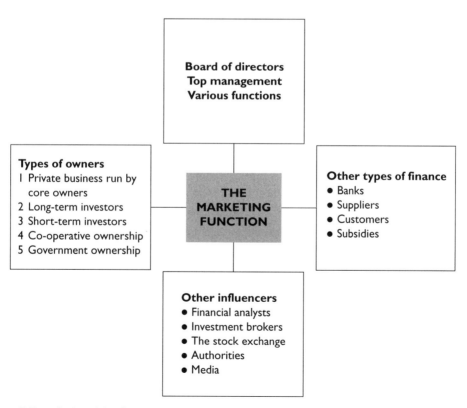

Figure 5.7 Relationships between marketing, ownership/investors and other influencers

Five types of ownership and financier relationships will be explained below. They are not mutually exclusive categories but each is focused on a certain aspect of ownership.

Private businesses run by core owners

The core owners are personally engaged in operating the enterprise; it is part of a lifestyle. This is typical of the small business, like the mom and pop store, the restaurant and the repair shop. The values of the founders and private owners are often strong and consistently applied.

Owner families often continue to run enterprises when they have grown large, and they still know the operations in detail. In retailing there is a series of smashing successes, companies that have expanded through the founder's and owner's vision and perseverance. Examples of strong owner commitment are the Nordstrom department stores in the United States, known for superior service quality; and Feargal Quinn's Superquinn stores in Ireland, focused on customer service and fresh food. Another is IKEA; its founder has three sons, one daughter, his wife and his brother-in-law by his side. In 2007 the retailing operation consisted of 260 furniture stores and some 70 Habitat stores, an upmarket version of IKEA. It is owned by a family-controlled foundation in the Netherlands. Inter IKEA Systems owns the IKEA concept and trademark and has a franchising agreement with every store. The Ikano Group includes banking, real estate, asset management, retail and insurance. The corporate culture emerging from the founder persona is extremely powerful. Strong values are instilled both in personnel and suppliers. It is a highly commercial company but it also has a human and social side to it. The founder talks about 'democratic design' and asks the questions: 'Why must well-designed furniture always be so expensive? Why do the most famous designers always fail to reach the majority of people with their ideas?'[30]

Even if these private companies should go public, core owners and subtle core values can continue to control the operations. The separation between the role of core owner and the role of manager is common in industrialized nations. A closer look at executives in Europe, however, indicated that they are often directly or indirectly linked to a network of owner families.

The reasons for going public are usually a need for cash flow, but often also to reduce total family control. Family ownership has its hazards, especially when new generations take over. There are also cases when the best strategy should be to go from public back to private, provided that this were financially feasible, which it often is not. A viable strategy is actively to recruit investors and establish long-term relationships to those who constructively help build the future.

---

[30] Edvardsson, Enquist and Hay, 2006; quotation from p. 235.

Founders and entrepreneurs are seldom easy to please and an employee who does not comply with their leadership had better try another job. They may also be perceived as ruthless in their pursuit of their business mission and survival. In the green and corporate social responsibility (CSR) relationship (R15) we met the Roddick family, founders and major owners of The Body Shop. They have been accused of driving their franchisees too hard,[31] at the same time as Anita Roddick said: 'I have never been able to separate Body Shop values from my own personal values.'[32] As said earlier, with the sale in 2006 to French cosmetics giant L'Oreal, she has been being accused of abandoning these values.

Single corporations and families can even keep a tight control over total markets and countries. An extreme case is De Beers and its owners, the Oppenheimer family. They are best known for their control over world sales of non-industrial diamonds. Companies and countries long tried to break out of the influence of De Beers, but with no apparent success. So the overriding production and marketing strategies of diamonds are globally determined by one owner family. At long last a change is beginning to take place in the 2000s.

Long-term investors

The owners see their involvement as long term, but are engaged in different types of industries and do not directly take part in daily operations. Despite the fact that their ownership is limited, the Wallenberg family has kept exerting a controlling influence over such diverse global corporations as Atlas-Copco, Electrolux, Ericsson, Saab and SKF. The family has for four generations focused their investment on long-term industrial development, internationalization and stability. There used to be commitment, above all in financial and strategic issues, but the knowledge of the daily operations and industry-specific issues is limited. However, this commitment seems less strong today.

Long-term ownership may put companies together even though they do not belong together for marketing reasons. It may be right at one time, but not at another. The Saab passenger car operation is now controlled by GM, but the Saab aerospace products and Scania, one of the world's largest truck makers, were owned by Saab. They have the same roots but their products have grown apart. In 1996 they were demerged; there was absolutely no marketing synergy. In 2008, Scania was taken over by Volkswagen.

Warren Buffett and his company Berkshire Hathaway has been held up as a model of a long-term and extremely successful investment strategy. Buffett invests in a limited number of select companies, retains the investment and says that short-term stock price is unimportant. This type of owner is the best to make RM become successful. It allows a company to build long-term relationships with customers and others.

---

[31] Entine (1996).
[32] Roddick (1991, p. 123).

Short-term investors

The owners are investors looking for maximum short-term return on investment. Just as customers can be unprofitable even in the long run, investors can be of little support, even be outright parasites. For these investors there is no responsibility, only rights and demands; owning shares is an alternative to gambling in Las Vegas. Institutional investors, such as pension funds, have increased their role on the stock market. They have no sentiments for a specific company, merely for enhancing short-term investor wealth. Investment brokers are paid per transaction, meaning that the more frequently they can encourage big investors to buy and sell, the more they earn. So they are rewarded for transactions and owner promiscuity, not for long-term relationships and loyalty. This, of course, is counter-productive to RM.

It is regrettable when the heart that beats for a product or service – the restaurateur who loves food and ambience, the engineer who enjoys the factory environment, the retailer who understands fresh vegetables and fish – stops beating and is replaced by cash flow analysis, accountants and investment brokers. The publisher who loves books, authors and readers is almost extinct in favour of financial groups who shuffle publishing companies around based on the bottom line and competing investment opportunities in any industry. There is not much 'heart power' left in these ownerships.

For many decades investors are characterized by changing ownership based on short-term speculation. Corporate raiders made hostile takeovers financed by junk bonds (high risk bonds with no collateral). Their strategy was cost reduction, downsizing and asset-stripping; there was no intention of developing the companies over the long term and no emotional attachment to their products and services. No doubt a shake-up of complacent or inefficient management is necessary at times, but then the purpose should be futures-oriented and if possible long-term survival. Some raiders became unbelievably rich, but many also had severe setbacks and were taken to court, even to jail.

Behind this is the eternal dream of becoming rich quickly and preferably without effort. Greed can never be an acceptable business mission; earnings are just a means. Employees often have no clue who owns the company they are working for, nor do customers know. Infiltration from organized crime is a growing problem. As they say in Palermo, Italy, the capital of the mafia, and according to one businessman: 'The mob does not rob banks any more, they own them.'

Four active strategies for more stable ownership have been suggested:[33]

1 Educate current investors.
2 Shift to more stable investors.

---

[33] Reichheld (2001a).

3 Attract the right type of core owners.
4 Go from public to private.

When instability rules, management attention is directed to things other than the core activities of production and marketing. The top executives risk getting fired any day and it is meaningless for them to make a long-term commitment; on average, a new CEO in a public company in the United States lasts only a few years. They are driven to look at short-term results and discard investment in customer loyalty, product development and development of personnel.

The current economy accommodates more rapid change than the industrial era did. It has become acceptable, even fashionable, to be an entrepreneur; it is not an emergency exit for misfits and the less talented. Business administration has turned into innovation and leadership. We have especially seen this happen to fast-growing IT companies. Whereas several have had stable growth both in size and profits, others have just travelled the fast lane of ridiculous stock price increases based on hype from financial analysts and the media. It is made possible because too many are dreaming about sudden fortunes and driven by greed rather than more urgent values based on a desire to contribute to society and showing corporate social responsibility.

We see an increasing number of mega mergers. The stated rationale is better products, better service, higher quality, a broader range of offerings and sometimes reduced prices. Some of this may at times be true, but the real motives behind mega mergers are more likely to be the desire to control consumption and reduce competition.

Co-operative ownership

True co-operative ownership has the special commitment that characterizes the successful family firm, but it goes one step further – the owners and the customers are the same people. The customers own the supplying organizations and they do their purchasing in their own stores. Employees are owners and customers as well, and sometimes co-ops are operated by unpaid volunteers. The relationship between co-op members and the personnel in the store is close. This is all very well as long as the co-op is limited in size or split into small independent units. If it grows and functions become centralized and controlled from a distance, it becomes like any other company. The co-operations become corporations and the owners no more feel they are owners than I feel I own a Ford, having bought a few Ford shares. The members become just customers and the authenticity of the membership is lost; the owner/customer becomes a pseudo-member, as was pointed out in R11. There are retailer co-ops, and producer co-ops are common in the agricultural sector.

Government ownership

In many countries, but to a lesser degree in the United States, the state owns and runs basic service like the post, telecom, railroads and airlines. The health, education and utilities sectors are often owned by governments. These produce infrastructural service and only in part does this service lend itself to the forces of the market. Unfortunately, governments have previously based their management style and values on a bureaucratic–legal paradigm and not on a relationship and service paradigm. It means that governments and their operations have lagged behind, not seeing themselves as service to citizens. They have become kingdoms of their own, closed off from the environment. They have been heavily criticized but learnt to accept that as the natural state of affairs. They have spent more time on 'explaining' why things do not work than on making them work. But they are not without competition. For example, FedEx renewed US postal services as a private alternative, operating with service quality and customer-in-focus strategies.

The wave of deregulation and privatization that started in the 1980s has changed the scenery gradually. In the United Kingdom, former premier Margaret Thatcher's privatization included the Airport Authority, British Telecom and British Rail. Regional and local governments have increasingly become involved in business-like operations. Governments have both a role as authorities and as service providers, and a long tradition of muddling up the two by covering up for bad service with reference to legal authority. There is a risk that they compete successfully by establishing their own companies, beating private companies with lower bids made possible with taxpayers' money. This has been reported in construction and building, transportation, leisure activities and other markets. But there is no doubt that there were unrealistic expectations attached to privatization and deregulation. Some efforts have backfired and been put to a halt.

The ultimate owners of all government organizations are the citizens, that is, the consumers. In modern terms: They have outsourced certain activities to governments to make the production and delivery of them more efficient. Unfortunately, the owners' prospects of exerting influence through the democratic voting process are appallingly meagre. To influence a state-run mail operation, the citizens are supposed to vote for their candidates at the next election and hope that the right party wins, that the right person is appointed postmaster general, that the right people are recruited to perform to the customers' satisfaction, and that the needs and wants of the citizens are transmitted through leadership, business mission, strategies, organization and systems. This chain of intermediaries is far too long; it is a distance relationship to the customer, so distant that it is pre-empted of all muscle. The direct contact with the post – the citizen in the role of customer – is possible but the citizen has little clout; it is an unusually asymmetric relationship. The relationship between the citizen as an owner of the post and eventual responsibility for its bill via taxes – the same citizen as customer – and the state as administrator is not easily handled from a marketing point of view.

Should the sole goal of the company be to maximize shareholder value, counted in euros and dollars? The short-term investors answer this question with a distinct yes. But could wealth also be to uphold a tradition of a certain industry, like retailing, car manufacturing or film-making, or to operate a business in a specific town, region or country, and be a good corporate citizen? For example, several of the film-making giants in Hollywood are neither owned by Americans nor are the owners knowledgeable about film-making. Metro Goldwyn Mayer was sold to an Italian swindler, backed by the French state-owned bank Credit Lyonnais, which was forced to take over the studio. Columbia was sold to Japanese Sony, Universal to Japanese Matsushita and later to Canadian Seagram, and 20th Century Fox to Australians. AOL, America Online, was a pioneer of dial-up Internet access and perhaps the most successful dotcom. In the beginning of 2000, it acquired the world's largest media company Time Warner and became AOL Time Warner encompassing film studios, cable television, CNN, books, newspapers, music and the America On Line portal. Both of the recent mega-movies, *Harry Potter* and *The Lord of the Rings*, were AOL Time Warner releases. In 2002, an alliance with American Express was announced. Since then new ownership constellations have emerged; industry scenery keeps changing continuously. Only two years later and after the acquisition severe conflicts arose and 'AOL' was erased from the name. The deal became a symbol for the hype of 'the new economy' and a return of sound and basic business thinking. The dotcom era stands out as driven by anything but common sense and ethical standards: revolutionary optimism and get rich fast.

If a company is being quoted on a stock exchange, yet other relationships are born. New demands are put on its financial reporting and this is watched by a number of stakeholders: the big institutional investors as well as the little guy, the stock exchange, financial reporters, analysts and public authorities. Managing investor relations (IR) has become a profession in its own right.[34]

Ownership is an alternative to alliances. When the Volvo–Renault alliance was preparing for a merger, the meaning of ownership was assessed in the light of Volvo's future prospects. Renault was a French state-owned company for which privatization had been suggested but had not been decided. There was a warranted fear that Volvo would be controlled by the French government. Even if Renault was privatized, Volvo was likely to become powerless in its relationship to the considerably bigger Renault.

Doubts were raised about the purpose of the merger and then about its conditions. The Volvo president called it 'a new model' but it was uncertain how the model would function

---

[34] Tuominen (1997); Hägg and Preiholt (2004).

in a live test. The president was accused of playing a game in order to secure eternal power and that the merger proposal had no direct link to car manufacturing and car sales. Who would decide about new car designs, distribution networks and other marketing strategies? A financial reporter called it 'a multi-national monster'. In defence of the merger, cost reductions and co-ordination advantages were claimed to follow, and furthermore Renault would place large orders with Volvo. The merger collapsed during the autumn of 1993 after protests from owner groups and executives. In 2000, Volvo took over Renault's truck manufacturing and became number two in the world after Mercedes, with a market share in the United States and Europe of 25 per cent. Renault bought 10 per cent of Volvo. And then Ford bought Volvo passenger cars.

A board of directors represents owners, management and other stakeholders. Criticism is often aired against the choice of board members who know little about the company and provide no functional expertise. It is obvious that support from knowledgeable owners and board members, as well as a trusting relationship between them and the corporate and marketing executives, is imperative in order to build a stable position on the market.

RM/CRM have had an impact on certain industries, especially those involved in business systems. In the following case, new owners claim that a takeover will be beneficial to future developments and to both customers and shareholders.

CASE STUDY   **RM/CRM and business systems**

SAP, the German giant in business and CRM systems is in a race with California headquartered Oracle to dominate the market. When bidding on French Business Object in 2007, SAP gives as the reason that the acquisition will lead to substantial co-ordination gains. A more credible reason is that SAP wants to acquire Business Objects' 44 000 customers thus increasing their control and power over the market for systems. The offer is 4.8 billon euro, another mega deal, which means that each customer is assessed to be worth more than 100 000 euro. Oracle quickly responded by giving an offer to their Californian competitor BEA Systems. Said Oracle President to the media: 'We have made a serious proposal including a substantial premium for BEA … We believe our all cash offer provides the best value for shareholders … We intend to protect the investment customers have made in BEA's systems …' He refers to the long term view taken on the previous acquisition PeopleSoft and Siebel, and further says that customers will benefit from this increase in investment for future generation systems.

We can learn about this and similar transactions every day. Some are real dramas. Even though long-term aspects and value for customers and other stakeholders are claimed to drive the new ownerships we cannot tell until later. There are certainly also short term and personal benefits involved that would not be announced to the media and the public.

It is unfortunate if owners are seen by management as a necessary evil which has to be soothed and cajoled. They should be partners. This requires the selection of the right owners, those who not only enhance their wealth through ownership, but also add value to the companies in which they invest. It then becomes a win–win relationship within the RM spirit.

QUESTIONS FOR DISCUSSION

1 Marketing used to be limited to relationships with external customers found in the marketplace. Today marketing is also considered applicable to the internal processes in a company, thus creating nano relationships. Explain
   (a) what it means that market mechanisms are brought inside the company;
   (b) what is meant by 'internal customer'; and
   (c) what 'internal marketing' is.
2 An especially crucial nano relationship is that between operations management and marketing. The book says that modern 'quality management' has become a unifying concept between the two functions. Explain in what way.
3 According to R28, the hierarchy offers a one-dimensional relationship, the matrix organization a two-dimensional relationship, and the network organization a multi-dimensional network. Explain the problems and opportunities inherent in the matrix solution.
4 Why have companies progressively outsourced many of their functions to external suppliers?
5 Owners and other financiers are treated as part of the nano relationships; in a sense they a internal decision-makers. Why are they important for RM?

Chapter

6

Marketing metrics and return on relationships

INTRODUCTION

Chapter 6 deals with marketing metrics and especially return on relationships (ROR), that is, the impact of RM on revenue, cost, capital employed and eventually profits. It ends with a section on strategies for improved ROR, and an RM-inspired marketing plan and audit, introducing the notion of the relationship portfolio.

Marketing metrics

Someone has said (I think it is Peter Drucker) that 'the language of management is money'. In business life, we want to know the financial impact of our activities; the 'bottom line' is a magic concept. Managers therefore must ask themselves: Do RM and CRM pay? And how do we know it? It is a matter of making a profit, but short-term profit is not the only indicator of success. RM is long term, and related factors are strategic and qualitative, such as planned growth, basic research and development, and the acquisition of resources through networks; all of these are insurance for the future. Businesses continuously measure return on financial capital. Is it also possible to gauge the ROR, networks and interaction?

There have been many efforts to measure marketing costs and the value that is created by marketing in the form of revenue and profit. The best-known effort is *PIMS* (Profit Impact of Market Strategy), a project which started in the early 1960s. It shows that the dream of unambiguous measurement and metrics has a long history. It is not a discovery in the new millennium as it may sometimes stand out to be. The goal of PIMS was to bring law and order to the wild west of marketing by quantifying and defining – objectively – the effect on profit caused by advertising, quality, market share, sales volume and other marketing strategies. In reality, it rather measured co-variation between fuzzy and arbitrarily defined phenomena. Although it sorted out some factors and their links in marketing, it did not create the desired rigour and clarity.

The high claims of *operations research*, *management science* and *MIS* (management or marketing information systems) promoted around 1970 under the slogan 'eventually management is turned into science' became little more than a red herring. Today, *micro-econometricians* are trying similar conjecture with cross-sectional and time-series data about individuals, households and firms, unfortunately based on poor input and unrealistic assumptions. In my view, they offer what US marketing Professor Shelby Hunt has called 'irrelevant elegance'.

The hope that a toilsome wandering through the desert would lead up to the country of milk and honey in the shape of precise metrics and the prophecies has not vanished, but perhaps matured somewhat. *Marketing accountability* is a current term for more general efforts to measure marketing's effect on profitability. In one research programme it is named as 'the new discipline'. It is new compared to previous efforts in the sense that it is addressing an economy where the Internet, globalization with mega-corporations, new rules of competition within the EU, NAFTA, WTO and other mega-alliances, and the growth of new capitalist economies like China, India and Russia offer new realities. The research programme asks questions such as: 'How can value be created by marketing and be defined and measured? How can management processes be aligned, with the aim of driving marketing value creation higher and higher? How can traditional financial and purchasing controls be re-engineered to support marketing value creation? How can employee feedback and learning be improved, to motivate and reward them to maximize marketing value creation? How can IT be applied to measure marketing value and support daily decision-making?'[1] These questions are all of general significance for marketing.

One book offers some 60 marketing metrics which they claim that 'every executive should master'.[2] It works great as an encyclopaedia but how many metrics can a marketing director use in daily practice?

Return on relationships, ROR

The interest in measuring the value of relationships and networks has grown parallel to the rise of RM/CRM. With the above discussion as a general framework, the next section will deal with ongoing efforts to develop marketing metrics and accounting systems to better mirror the realities of the new economy. My stance is that indicators are useful to a degree, but they are supplementary to other types of information. I do not subscribe to the idea that we will eventually discover the universal measurement cure; it is a search for a phantom and will remain science fiction. Attempting to measure quantitatively, one by one, the myriad factors and influences in marketing is a dead end.

What, then, can be expected of marketing metrics on the customer and revenue side? In the Baldrige Quality Award criteria for 2007[3] this is stated in Item *7.2 Customer-Focused Outcomes: What are your customer-focused performance results?* where it ...

> '... examines your organization's customer-focused performance results,
> with the aim of demonstrating how well your organization has been

---

[1] Shaw and McDonald (2000).

[2] Farris *et al.* (2006).

[3] Malcolm Baldrige National Quality Award 2007 *Criteria for Performance Excellence*, p. 49.

satisfying your customers and has developed loyalty, repeat business, and positive referrals, as appropriate.' Its focus is '... on all relevant data to determine and help predict your organization's performance as viewed by your customers. Relevant data and information include customer satisfaction and dissatisfaction; retention, gains, and losses of customers and customer accounts; customer complaints, complaint management, effective complaint resolution, and warranty claims; customer-perceived value based on quality and price; customer assessment of access and awards, ratings, and recognition from customers and independent rating organizations.' It further '... places an emphasis on customer-focused results that go beyond satisfaction measurements, because loyalty, repeat business, and longer-term customer relationships are better indicators and measures of future success in the marketplace and of organizational sustainability.'

I would like to propose the following definition of ROR:

 ROR is the long-term net financial outcome caused by the establishment and maintenance of an organization's network of relationships.[4]

Some statements pertaining to ROR have already been presented, for example that the lifetime value (LTV) of an existing Cadillac customer was $332,000, and that it costs 5 to 10 times as much to get a new customer as it costs to keep an existing customer.

The following sections offer a review of mindsets, indicators and models and suggest approaches and show examples of applications. It is not an effort to be complete and give justice to all the work that is being done and to evaluate different measurement techniques. We have learnt from PIMS and other ambitious projects that the problem is in the first place one of mindset and the actual ability to make a technique operational in a messy marketing reality. The sections treat: customer satisfaction, loyalty, value and ROR; duration, retention and defection; the link between customer interaction and quality, productivity and profitability; intellectual capital and the balanced scorecard; return on the non-measurable and an extension to RON, return on networks.

As was mentioned in Chapter 1, RM and CRM are not fundamentalist religions, even if they offer an improved paradigm of marketing. Sometimes transaction marketing and

---

[4] Related concepts are *return on quality*. Rust, Zahorik and Keiningham (1994); Duncan and Moriarty's (1997) *brand equity*, which covers integrated communications and relationships; and Schultz and Walters (1997) measuring return on investment on brand communications. See also *Journal of the Academy of Marketing Science*, Special Issue (2005).

the zero relationship – the price and convenience extreme on the relationship scale – is the best strategy for the supplier and the best option for the customer. ROR is not pertinent to transaction marketing.

As CRM offers tools to implement RM strategies it is of course consequential how well it succeeds. Payne[5] lists studies from several research institutes which have assessed the effect of CRM:

- 69 per cent of CRM projects have little impact on sales performance.
- Companies think that their CRM projects are significantly less successful than their consultants and suppliers think.
- 70 per cent of CRM initiatives will fail over the next 18 months.
- 60 per cent of CRM projects end in failure.

The conclusion is that the majority of CRM installations fail in one way or the other. It shows how difficult it is to systematically control the complex reality of relationships. It is thus necessary to combine whatever can be systematized with our experience, commons sense and intuition.

Satisfaction, loyalty, value and ROR

A common assumption is that an improvement in customer-perceived quality will increase customer satisfaction, loyalty and profitability. Thus the value for both parties goes up which is what win–win is about. *The customer relationship life cycle* is based on the belief that the ability of the provider to satisfy needs and fulfil promises determines the chances of retaining the customer. According to *the service profit chain*, the following happens:

> good internal quality → satisfied employees → employees stay →
> good external quality → satisfied customers → customers stay → high
> profitability.[6]

A corollary to these approaches is that vicious circles and failure chains have to be broken.

This logic seems indisputable; when everybody is happy we will do well. But the general validity can be questioned as the market logic sometimes follows other patterns.

---

[5] Payne (2006, p. 20). The sources of the results are (in order) Insight Technology Group, The CRM Institute, Giga and Gartner.

[6] Heskett, Sasser and Schlesinger (1997); and Grönroos (2007).

Doyle[7] has expressed his concern about the role of marketing and the limited power of marketers in the boardroom and on the executive floor. One reason can be lack of credibility as 'Marketers can no longer afford to rely on the untested assumption that increases in customer satisfaction … will automatically translate into higher financial performance.'

Although certain studies indicate that customer satisfaction is a predictor of future profits,[8] it is not enough to ascertain that 73 or 86 or even 94 per cent of the customers are satisfied. Volvo, who started a long-term comprehensive RM programme, had previously considered satisfied customers to be loyal. There was considerable leakage though. In the Volvo RM programme, the next step has been taken actively to provide incentives for satisfied customers to remain loyal.

Most of those who leave a supplier say that they are satisfied but they switch for a variety of reasons, such as another supplier's marketing, being persuaded by friends, the desire to test something new or mere coincidence. According to the exit-voice-loyalty choice from R9, many dissatisfied customers remain despite the fact that a supplier is charging more or offers lower quality than the competition. They do not switch for lack of time or knowledge or they remain loyal, for example, for nationalistic or ideological reasons. The switching cost can be considerable in the short run. However, retention coupled with dissatisfaction is a ticking bomb.

Some studies reveal that there is a sizeable difference in retention rate between those who say (in a questionnaire) that they are *very satisfied* and those who are just *satisfied*. Pitney Bowes, manufacturers of postage machines, found that 78.2 per cent of very satisfied customers said that they would remain customers in the future, whereas only 20.9 per cent of satisfied customers said they would remain. For Xerox the corresponding figures were 80 and 14 per cent.[9]

A further analysis is found in the *loyalty accounting matrix* (Figure 6.1). The matrix combines the *attractiveness* of a supplier ('brain appeal') and the *strength of the relationship*

	Strength of relationship	
Risk	Loyal	Ambassador
Searching	Risk	Loyal
Lost	Searching	Risk

Figure 6.1 Loyalty accounting matrix. Source: Johansen and Monthelie (1996, p. 23). Used with permission

---

[7] Doyle (2000, p. 310).
[8] Fornell (1992); Johnson and Gustafsson (2000).
[9] Quoted from Johansen and Monthelie (1996, p. 17).

('heart appeal'). The most satisfied customers are called ambassadors. They find the supplier highly attractive, have a strong relationship to the supplier and recommend him or her to others. The next groups consist of loyal customers who are less enthusiastic than ambassadors, but have top scores on either attractiveness or relationship strength. The diagonal represents risk customers who are easy prey for competitors. The last two groups are those who are actively searching for a new supplier and those who are already lost customers.

A study of one company showed the following pattern: ambassadors 32 per cent, loyal 30 per cent, risk 25 per cent, searching 9 per cent and lost 4 per cent. Ambassadors and loyal customers constituted almost two-thirds of the customers, a result that might or might not be satisfactory, depending on the type of business.

It was less comforting to learn that ROR was not well correlated to loyalty. The ambassadors did not make the most profitable customers; those were found among the least loyal groups. There is a paradox that states that the less profitable customers are, the more satisfied they are, while the more profitable customers are, the less satisfied they are. This can be illustrated with the price of the return air fare from New York to continental Europe. An economy ticket might cost US$500, a full first or business class ticket US$5,000. The business traveller is highly profitable and highly demanding. The economy traveller contributes marginally to profits but is grateful for the low price and not as demanding. Value for the business traveller is primarily punctuality, comfort, the opportunity to work or rest. For the economy traveller, value is primarily low price. The likelihood is high that the business traveller is less satisfied than the economy traveller, although in objective terms the business traveller is offered a much better service.

One ROR model further expands the links between satisfaction and profits. Figure 6.2 shows how stages and properties of the relationships between suppliers and customers

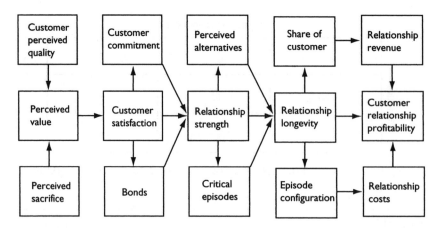

Figure 6.2 A 'relationship profitability model'. Source: Storbacka, Strandvik and Grönroos (1994, p. 23). Reproduced with permission. © MCB University Press

are linked together.[10] Starting from the left, *perceived value* is defined as the outcome of customer-perceived quality and the customer's sacrifice (cost in a wide sense). The perceived value is an antecedent to *customer satisfaction*, which in turn influences customer commitment, bonds to the supplier and *relationship strength*. The higher the relationship strength and the customer's feeling of loyalty towards the supplier, the fewer the perceived alternatives; when there is a monopoly, however, the customer is a prisoner. The number of alternative suppliers and their attractiveness impact on *relationship longevity*, which is also influenced by the positive, negative or indifferent interaction with the supplier (critical episodes). A long and beneficial relationship may lead to increased concentration of the purchases from a single supplier and share of customer goes up. A single-sourcing strategy pursued by the customer gives the supplier a 100 per cent share and maximum revenue. The length and strength of the relationship also affects the types of interactions that form the relationships (episode configuration), which in turn determines costs. Finally, relationship revenue minus relationship cost establishes the *customer relationship profitability* or ROR. Today we could add the S-D logic and stress the co-creation of value and the customer's work to actualize the service proposition.

Companies may dry out because business has become constant firefighting and eventually there is no water left to throw on the fire. RM promotes long-term thinking, but sometimes today's business has to be saved before the long-term aspects can be addressed. Certain decisions must be taken out of strategic necessity; they are market investments and cannot be financially assessed with simple indicators. They do not belong in the short-term profit and loss statement. You either do it, and stand a chance to survive, or you don't and you risk to disappear from the market. Declining customer loyalty often builds up in small steps which may not be discernible until it is too late to reverse the vicious circle. The tipping point appears as a surprise.

Duration, retention and defection

Loyalty and ROR can be tied to several key indicators. Among them are: the *duration* of a relationship, how long the customers remain customers; the *retention rate*, which is the percentage of customers who remain after 1 year, 2 years, etc.; and the *defection rate*, which is the percentage of customers who leave a supplier.

A central question in RM is how much should be spent on retaining existing customers and increasing the duration of the relationship, and how much should be spent on getting new customers. A study in the United Kingdom showed that 80 per cent of the managers

---

[10] Storbacka, Strandvik and Grönroos (1994).

of service operations felt that they spent excessive resources on attracting new customers and 10 per cent that existing customers occupied too much of their resources. Only 10 per cent were happy with the balance between resources spent on new and existing customers.[11]

It is also a matter of adjusting the RM strategy to the buyers' needs and wants. One supplier may badly want a relationship with certain customers, but the customers do not respond simply because they are unwilling or unable to make the commitment. Conversely, suppliers may pursue a transaction marketing strategy without being empathic to the customers' desires to establish a long-term relationship.[12]

A frequently cited study[13] shows that 68 per cent of customers who defected from a supplier did so because the supplier seemed indifferent and 14 per cent because of unsatisfactory complaints handling. These two failed relationships accounted for 82 per cent of the defection. Only 5 per cent were lost through competitor initiatives and 9 per cent because of lower prices elsewhere.

Complaint management is an important part of retention. Stauss and Seidel[14] go as far as to say that complaints are the heart of CRM. Instead of marginalizing or dodging complaints, the authors recommend the CRM system to encourage them. In the same spirit as S-D logic, the customer is given a chance to co-create value with the supplier. The outcome of complaint management can be measured. According to their research, customers primarily evaluate complaint handling on four central quality dimensions: accessibility, quality of interaction, promptness of reaction, and adequacy/fairness of the solution.

In an article on 'zero defection', the authors draw the conclusion that a supplier could double net profit if the defection rate is reduced by as little as 5 per cent.[15] They advise companies to make defection analyses. These include interviews with lost customers but should also address the weak signals of a customer entering the risk zone.

Direct Tire Sales specializes in tyres and brakes, and makes three quarters of their sales with regular customers.[16] These customers spend twice as much as the first-time customers who come through advertising ($173 against $90). First-time customers who come through the recommendation of a regular customer spend as much as $224 at the first visit. Credit Card company MBNA America did a defection analysis and learned from it.[17] The defection rate went down from 10 to 5 per cent, which was half the industry average, and profitability was dramatically improved. An average cardholder who stays

---

[11] Payne and Rickard (1994).
[12] Jackson (1985a).
[13] Research from the 1980s by Miller Business Systems.
[14] Stauss and Seidel (2004); about measurement and quality dimensions, see pp. 146–154.
[15] Reichheld and Sasser (1990, p. 105).
[16] Johnson (1992, p. 85).
[17] This and the following examples are based on Reichheld and Sasser (1990).

1 year causes a loss of $51, one who stays for 5 years a profit of $55, and one who stays for 20 years a profit of $525. For industry laundry, the profit for Year 1 was $144 and for Year 5 was $256; for auto repair, $25 for Year 1 and $88 for Year 5. If defection rates go down from 20 to 10 per cent per annum and then to 5 per cent, the duration will increase from 5 to 10 to 20 years with a consequent increase in profits. If a customer is lost, the whole of the future profit potential goes down the drain. In a comparison between 9 industries in which the defection rate was reduced by 5 per cent – among them insurance brokers, computer software and auto repair – profits grew by 25–85 per cent.

Reichheld (2001a) presents an elaborate, yet practical, system for assessing ROR. His research has shown that customer loyalty cannot be earned in isolation. It is closely dependent on the loyalty of two other stakeholders: employees and investors as was stressed in some of the nano relationships. Those who stimulate loyal relationships with customers, employees and investors are amply rewarded. For example, the advertising agency Leo Burnett loses only 2 per cent of its customers per year and its productivity is 15–20 per cent higher than that of its principal competitors. Chick-fil-A, a chain of 600 quick service restaurants, has a turnover of store operators of 4–6 per cent per year, while the industry average is 40–50 per cent. Moreover, its store operators earn 50 per cent more than those of competing restaurant chains. As compared to the industry average, State Farm Insurance agents stay twice as long, have 40 per cent higher productivity and a 95 per cent customer retention rate. Lexus, Toyota's luxury car, has the highest repurchase rate among premium cars. It once was 2 per cent of Toyota sales but 33 per cent of its profits. This may have changed now but Toyota remains both a growing and profitable car maker.

Market share is a traditional indicator in marketing management, showing the percentage of a total market or market segment that a supplier serves. Fewer and more select customers, each buying more during a longer period, could be a superior way to profits as compared to more customers with a small volume and shorter relationships.[18] *Share of customer* (also called *share of wallet*) is recommended as an alternative ratio to market share. Milliken Company, a leader in textiles and winner of the Baldrige Quality Award, monitors share of customers. A bank can estimate what share of a customer's financial assets and transactions is handled by the bank. Taco Bell is a successful and rapidly growing fast-food chain with Mexican cuisine. The company does not measure market share but 'share of stomach', thereby establishing how much of the customer's intake is delivered by Taco Bell.

The old concept of LTV has been revived by CRM. It usually refers to the net value of an individual consumer's purchases over his or her lifetime, sometimes widened to the whole family, even to both private and professional consumption. LTV may stand

---

[18] Johnson (1992, p. 79).

out as fairly clear-cut for consumers, although one has to consider that certain offerings, such as nappies and baby food, are only of interest during a limited (but highly varying) period in a family's lifetime. LTV in B2B is somewhat more ambiguous: What is the life cycle and lifetime of a company? Rust *et al.*[19] define *customer equity* as 'the total of the discounted LTVs of all its customers'. Customer equity is the combined outcome of *value equity* (defined as relatively cognitive, objective and rational customer perceptions of quality, price and convenience), *brand equity* (perceptions of a supplier that are relatively emotional, subjective and irrational) and *retention equity* (repeat purchases). According to the authors: 'Customer Equity is the key to the long-term profitability of any firm, and analysing the key drivers of Customer Equity provides an overall framework for effectively focusing strategic resources.'

Triplets and tribes

The vantage point of this section is condensed in the statement that: 'Quality, productivity and profits are triplets; separating one from the other creates an unhappy family.'[20]

Are the quality awards – which are as much about productivity and financial results as about quality – drivers of future success, for example showing in stock price and growth? This is has not been obvious in the short term.[21] At the same time we must remember the difficulties to make accurate measurements. There are so many other factors that can exert influence and we don't know what the situation would be if the quality improvements had not been made.

The triplets are all concerned with the same issue: 'How well is the company doing?' But the focus between the three is different and represented by different tribes within the organization. We have the *marketing tribe* and the *accounting tribe*, the *quality tribe* and the *productivity tribe*. They embrace different traditions, vocations and cultures; each tribe's awareness of the total welfare of the company is limited.

Quality tribe members are devoted to revenue issues, they think of customers and revenue, and are closest to the marketing tribe. Members of the productivity tribe are obsessed by costs; in practice, a productivity increase usually means cost reduction and downsizing. The accounting tribe must produce periodic reports with balance sheets and profit and loss statements. Its behaviour is largely controlled by legislation and investor relations. The tribes do not mingle well, although they play in the same orchestra and

---

[19] Rust, Zeithaml and Lemon (2000; quotations from pp. 4–8 and 12).

[20] Gummesson (1998a).

[21] See the effort by Balasubramanian, Mathur and Thakur (2005) to compare two quality awards and measure their impact on performance.

should be playing the same symphony. They all contribute valuable expertise, but in order to get the best from each, top management must be conductors and lead them in the right direction.

A misleading but recurrent statement claims that service productivity is lagging behind goods and manufacturing productivity. The statement is based on lack of understanding for service productivity, trying to manage and measure it on the terms of manufacturing. There is also a political and ideological debate on the productivity of the government sector as compared with the private service sector.

The interconnection between productivity, quality and profitability – the *triplets at play* – is graphically shown in Figure 6.3. At the top of the figure is quality, defined as: (1) producing a defect-free product or service right from the beginning and (2) producing a value proposition that customers need and want. If quality improves in these senses, it can have a positive impact on *revenue* (left section of the figure), *cost* (middle section) and *capital employed* (right section). When function and reliability improve, they boost the image in the market, customer retention and share of customer (i.e. the percentage of a customer's purchase of a certain product which is made from a specific supplier). These changes stimulate sales volume growth, differentiate a supplier from the competition and make the supplier less dependent on price competition. When sales and share of customer go up, the supplier can profit from scale economics (up to a certain level) and production costs per unit go down. This affects both productivity and profitability. Further, service costs for machinery go down, and so do the costs of inspection, testing, rework, scrap, complaints and warranties. The capital employed is reduced as less inventory needs

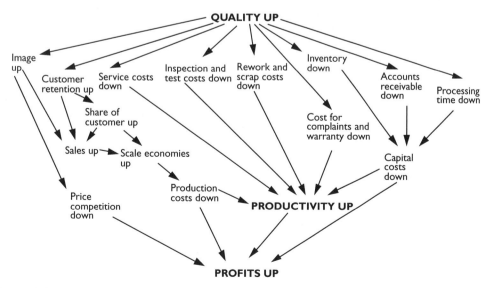

Figure 6.3 The triplets at play. Gummesson (1998a, p. 6). Reproduced with permission

to be kept; accounts receivable go down because payment comes earlier; less payment is delayed because of complaints; and reduction of processing time frees resources. As the cash flow becomes quicker, the money can be used elsewhere and capital costs are reduced. Improved productivity becomes an antecedent to profitability.

The figure is conceptual and its interpretation goes as far as to conclude that something may go up or down. ROR can be enhanced by changing the balance between revenue, cost and capital employed. Cost and capital employed can be increased in order to increase revenue even more. A revenue reduction – for example, eliminating unprofitable customers – can reduce cost and increase net profits. By myopic concentration on cost, the attractiveness of a company is reduced and customer relationships are jeopardized.

There is always a desire and need to measure, preferably precisely, the financial consequences of marketing strategies. This has been tried for at least 50 years without any remarkable progress. Currently fresh efforts are being made.[22]

With time, the old and accepted ways of accounting become senile but live on despite the fact that organizations become networks and RM has devised a new ground for marketing. A particularly critical question is: How shall the role of the customer as co-creator of value and thus productivity and quality be assessed? Both customers and suppliers have relationship costs. If the customer is a consumer, costs are incurred in the consumer's spare time and are not part of the GDP. Grönroos[23] examines relationship costs and profitability in service operations and their connection to inferior quality. He makes a distinction between three types of costs that hit both consumer and companies. A consumer pays a certain price for a service (short- and long-term customer sacrifice), but in addition there are costs to correct mistakes caused by the consumer (direct relationship costs), costs caused by the provider (indirect relationship costs) and mental and social discomfort caused by the correction procedure (psychological costs). If the relationship between the customer and provider is perfect, these costs disappear. In conclusion, relationship costs and quality go in opposite directions – high service quality causes low relationship costs and low service quality causes high relationship costs.

Our research has brought to the fore that quality and productivity emerge from five sources:

- the supplier as independent actor;
- the customer as independent actor;
- the interaction between the supplier and the customer;

---

[22] See Ambler (2000); Rust, Lemon and Zeithaml (2004); and Farris et al. (2006).
[23] Grönroos (2007, pp. 147–148); see also the elaboration of the financial dimensions of relationship quality, based on both service management and a network approach in Holmlund (1997); and the analysis of service productivity concepts in Ojasalo (1999) and Grönroos and Ojasalo (2004).

- the interaction between customers, C2C, and sometimes others in a broader network and
- a supportive infrastructure.

Traditionally, quality and productivity are treated as the sole outcome of the first, the provider's independent work. Neither customer input nor the contribution from the provider–customer interactions are taken into account. Service research has shown that the customer–supplier relationship may be a prime source of quality and productivity. Service production is interactive, as was pointed out in R5, and the inputs from provider personnel and customers are partly substitutes. Furthermore, C2C interaction contributes both to quality and productivity. As an independent actor, the customer has several value-adding roles:

- As *consumer*: This is the traditional way of seeing the customer and is the only role that is generally treated in theory.
- As *producer*: Here both conventional services marketing, B2B and the S-D logic have made it evident that the customer is a co-producer.
- As *marketer*: R4 covered the role of the customer as part-time marketer (PTM).
- As *manager*: Often the customer both in B2C/C2B and B2B works as the coordinator of production, delivery and sales. This is necessary, especially if the supplier is weak and is not able to keep the whole process together.
- As *supplier of knowledge*: The customer contributes with specifications, statements of needs and other input which the supplier lacks.

In a network approach of B2B, relationship costs have been classified as the sum of *activity costs* (activities in a network) and *structural costs* (network investment and maintenance costs).[24] Furthermore, cost in a relationship is a matter of both static utilization of extant resources and dynamic development of the potential of new combinations that the resources of the network hold.[25] Changes in business networks occur every day. The network organization is an expression of this dynamic aspect, the continuous resourcing in an enhanced 'opportunity space'.

We have already referred to the well-known value chain.[26] It is composed of nine elementary internal activities. Primary activities are in-bound logistics (incoming raw material), operations, outbound logistics (distribution of finished products), marketing and

---

[24] Eriksson and Åsberg (1994).
[25] Håkansson and Snehota (1995).
[26] Porter (1985, pp. 36–43).

sales and service. Support activities are procurement, technology development (both technical and systems development), human resource management and firm infrastructure (organization and systems). The value chain attempts to isolate individual activities and see their added value and costs. The chain is essentially sequential and each function is well delimited. To some extent it deals with inter-functional interaction, parallel activities and alliances, which means that there is a slight affinity to RM. But even if value for the customer is given as a goal, the customer remains a lost soul and a passive recipient of the provider's output.

The traditional value chain is a supplier chain; it is supplier centric. We have also mentioned the customer value chain, the further developments of the successful application of lean production and the extension to lean consumption. My interpretation is that this offers a hands-on strategy for improving customer centricity. The concerted outcome of lean production and lean consumption into lean solution approaches balanced centricity where many stakeholders are considered. Lean consumption is being tried on retailing and health care among others. Tesco is becoming the lean consumption exemplar as Toyota once was for lean production. The new knowledge has emerged out of inductive empirical research and a trial and error process. From that the following principles have been derived:[27]

1 Solve the customer's problem completely by ensuring that all the goods and services work, and work together.
2 Don't waste the customer's time.
3 Provide exactly *what* the customer wants.
4 Provide what's wanted exactly *where* it's wanted.
5 Provide what's wanted where it's wanted exactly *when* it's wanted.
6 Continually aggregate solutions to reduce the customer's time and hassle.

This is probably as far as we can go in considering the customer's situation, the ultimate in customer centricity. The effects of the principles can be measured to an extent but are of course also exposed to ambiguity and practical considerations.

Many of the ideas of S-D logic and lean consumption can be traced in the service management literature (which is also recognized in S-D logic). The *value constellation* (or *value star*)[28] is such a contribution. If both the customer and the supplier are part of the same value-creating process, among other things the role of price is altered: 'This means that both profits and losses ... should be shared between supplier and customer. Instead of price setting, it becomes a question of remuneration for participation in the creation of

---

[27] Womack and Jones (2005a, p. 61, and 2005b)
[28] Normann and Ramirez (1993).

value. This kind of remuneration must be discussed in very open-minded negotiations between the two parties.'[29]

Intellectual capital and the balanced scorecard

As numbers from accounting exert a significant influence on decisions and practices, supportive accounting is an antecedent to sound RM/CRM applications. Marketers all too often find accounting rigid, traditional and bound by legal restrictions, seldom giving support to essential marketing strategies.

Employees represent different specialities. We have already met the accounting tribe that does not mingle so well with the marketing tribe, there is even the risk of civil war. New accounting theories and practices, most notably the *balanced scorecard*, register indicators of other types of capital than financial capital. Among them are indicators concerning the customer base and retention. The original balanced scorecard contains indicators in four groups of capital:[30] *financial, customer, internal business process* and *learning and growth*.

It has long been popular for executives to say that 'people are our most valuable resource'. The statement alludes to employees, not customers, investors or vendors, even if most of these are human too and provide resources. In the spirit of RM, each and everyone who has an impact on the success of a company should be included, meaning each party in a network of relationships, not least the customers who constitute the *customer capital*.

Traditionally, the balance sheet consists of tangible, hard assets, above all money, inventory, machines and buildings. In this format human beings are worthless, while the chair on which they sit represents value only to be slowly depreciated according to some accounting principle. The customer represents no official value. However, when a company is sold or its stock is traded on an exchange, buyers pay for intangible assets like goodwill, brands and expected future earnings.

Accounting systems do not catch the value of customer relationships, although building relationships is an investment in marketing. The accounting tribe has often been suspicious of intangible, soft values and sometimes for good reasons. When profits are down, it is tempting for management to misuse soft values, and claim that book values are not telling the whole truth and that the situation is not all that precarious. These values have therefore acquired a bad reputation. Although it is a slow process, the interest in human

---

[29] Wikström and Normann (1994, p. 62).
[30] Kaplan and Norton (1996).

resource accounting, social audits and the financial aspects of personnel is on the increase. More often these days we encounter such concepts as customer capital, relationship capital, human capital, knowledge capital and social capital.

The traditional balance sheet is not particularly informative about service and knowledge-intensive companies. Efforts have been made to find procedures for presenting a more realistic value of these companies. As today all companies, according to S-D logic, are in service, driven by knowledge and skills the issue is of general concern.

In new and broader accounting systems, the concept of *intellectual capital* is challenging the supremacy of short-term *financial capital*.[31] Financial capital must of course exist in every organization, and in the balanced scorecard financial capital is assessed together with intellectual capital. When capital is defined as 'something of value' – a resource – we realize that money and other hard assets are not the only capital.

Intellectual capital can be defined as the total value of a company – the price of its shares – minus its book value. It means all assets except those in the balance sheet.

A company's survival and growth are eventually determined by its financial outcome. The issue is to recognize the long-term importance of intellectual capital for the generation of financial capital, and to gradually convert intellectual capital into financial capital.

Intellectual capital can be divided into two major types: *human* (or *individual*) *capital* and *structural capital*.

Human capital consists of employees and their qualities. It includes the individual's knowledge, behaviour and motivation, and also the individual's network of relationships. This network consists of personal relationships which have been cultivated over a long period, and the trust and confidence that an employee has established among customers and others. The power and prestige of individual capital is evident for an advertising agency or a partnership of lawyers who thrive on their personal interaction with clients. But it is also important for a retail store, a bank branch office, a car repair shop or a manufacturing operation. This was pointed out in the service encounter (R5) and the many-headed customer and supplier relationship (R6).

There is also capital built into an employee who can quickly gain a customer's confidence, a quality which is particularly essential in a salesperson. In R1, the story was told about the top performing Electrolux door-to-door salesman. He said that knocking on doors gives him 20 seconds to gain the confidence of the consumer.

If an employee leaves a company, the individual capital vanishes. You cannot own human beings, that would be slavery. The company borrows them 'from 9 to 5', a concept made classic by Dolly Parton in a movie and a song.

In the knowledge relationship (R21), knowledge was presented as a prime reason for alliances. Two types of knowledge were discussed: migratory knowledge, which is

---

[31] Edvinsson and Malone (1997); Sveiby (1997); and Stewart (1997).

portable; and embedded knowledge, which is inseparable from its environment. Embedded knowledge is part of the *structural capital*. It does not disappear if an employee leaves; it is owned by the company. In an RM sense, structural capital consists of relationships which have been established with a company as such, and are tied to culture, systems, contracts, image and the network to which a company belongs. The more successfully a company ties relationships to its structure, the less dependent it is on individual employees.

CRM is a means to convert human capital into structural capital. eCRM is primarily structural capital. The customer information which was previously stored in the heads of one or a few people can now be stored in data warehouses and be exposed to data mining. The information stays even if the employee leaves. However, keeping the data warehouse in shape is the overshadowing challenge which the computer cannot manage on its own; it is primarily an hCRM task.

As all companies and marketing situations are unique in at least some aspects, applications must be adapted to each specific situation. ABB has changed to more focus on soft investment: software and service have in part replaced locomotives and nuclear plants. This requires new accounting approaches. Electrolux and SKF are companies that test new ways of measuring performance.[32]

A case which shows the application of the balanced scorecard and intellectual capital and their significance for RM will be presented below.

CASE STUDY **Banks**

The Banks case will illustrate the critique that Johnson and Kaplan (1987) have pronounced against the lost relevance of accounting. It essentially concerns arbitrary distribution of cost. The way costs are distributed on products, services and departments is reminiscent of Russian roulette; the lucky one survives but you cannot influence the outcome. In a later book, Johnson (1992) revised and further developed the critique by blaming the problem on top-down management and remote control via ratios. Ratios offer simplistic and delayed information. They do not heed quality, neither the degree of customer satisfaction, nor the degree of employee motivation. They disregard the living processes of a company.

Activity-based costing (ABC) offers certain new opportunities to assess cost. It is focused on activities and processes. This is particularly important for service, which consist of activities, co-created with customers. Like most cost and

---

[32] Olve *et al.* (2003).

revenue assessments, however, ABC has indulged more in cost and less in revenue, and consequently not paid attention to the contributions of marketing. Despite its strengths, there is criticism claiming that ABC preserves industrial society features: mass manufacturing, top-down management, remote control and preoccupation with cost. ABC needs to be expanded into D and E, 'demand' and 'effectiveness'.[33] In RM jargon it means that customers and quality need to get a place in the accounts.

Cooper and Kaplan (1991) consider ABC to give rise to better assessments than Pareto optimality or the 20/80 rule (stating that 20 per cent of customers or products account for 80 per cent of profits). They introduced the 20/225 rule, which claims that 20 per cent account for 225 per cent; consequently, the majority of customers or products are unprofitable!

Storbacka's comparison between banks underscores this conclusion.[34] His 'Stobachoff curve' shows the distribution of profits from different customers. According to his bank study, profits can be a maximum of 100 per cent, which was reached with the help of 10 per cent of the most profitable customers. Twenty per cent of customers contributed 140 per cent of profits, but 60–80 per cent of profits were erased by the remaining and unprofitable customers.

In making such assessments, one problem is the hidden links between the service offered by banks. These links imply that seemingly unprofitable service may be necessary requisites for cash cows and customer retention. Furthermore, the unprofitable service/customers carry allocated overheads. By abolishing these service/customers, the base for the overheads is narrowed and currently profitable service/customers will become unprofitable.

Profit estimates have traditionally been tied to organizational units or products. Data are arranged to calculate the profits on a single transaction and are thus counterproductive to RM; in fact, the accounting system does not allow an RM strategy. Data on ROR of customers as consumers, family members, or a combination of consumers and small business owners, are currently not retrievable from bank databases, and LTV needs to be part of their CRM systems.

Automated teller machines (ATMs), which handle bank transactions, are considered cost-effective. Studies claim that it costs three to four times as much to deliver the service via a person than via an ATM. It is, however, necessary to know how these estimates have been made and if all costs are included. Since

---

[33] Frenckner (1993).
[34] These data and the treatment of the banks case are based on Storbacka (1994).

ATMs were introduced, the number of transactions have increased, therefore the estimates may be deficient. The increase in transactions is probably mainly caused by an increase in consumption; it is not a consequence of ATMs. But it is evident that customer relationships are affected. Relationships to bank managers or clerks are personal and, especially in small branch offices, customers and staff know each other; it is a moderately high touch relationship. Relationships to ATMs and Internet banking are electronic, mechanical and impersonal; they are high tech. How this transition in relationships will affect customer loyalty and retention, we do not know.

Return on the non-measurable

Particularly in the United States we hear: 'What gets measured, gets done'. There is a truth in this, but also a danger. Indicators are often selected because of tradition and because they are easy to grasp, not because they are useful. For example, it is easier to quantify short-term profits than the long-term profits lost because of mismanaged relationships.

It may come as a shock to some, but the word 'measurement' is derived from the Sanskrit word '*maya*', which means *illusion* or *witchcraft*. It sounds like it came out of Hogwarth's School of Witchcraft and Wizardry where Harry Potter got his education. It can also mean *image*. Measurements should be images of reality, whereas in practice they are often illusions or witchcraft.

Obsession with measurement means handing over the future of a company to the accounting tribe, abolishing vision and leadership. Many 'leaders' never become leaders, just grossly overpaid accountants. The blue ocean strategy and its approach to competition was discussed in R2. It's a focus on the big picture, the vision of the innovator and leader, and the way to visualize the strategy – without focus on numbers.[35]

There are marketers who suffer from measurement fright. They can neither count nor analyse numbers. But there are also measurement fetishists and security seeking CEOs, accountants and marketers. They cherish the illusions of measurement. Their fetishes[36] are the bottom line and short-term profit ratios, which are often devastating to long-term stable development. When indicators are used to pinpoint certain phenomena with

---

[35] Kim and Mauborgne (2005); see also Simon, Bilstein and Luby (2006).

[36] Fetishes are objects – strangely shaped stones, animal teeth, claws, feathers – which are reputed to bring strength and success to their owners, who are usually medicine men, magicians and shamans.

reasonable accuracy and validity, there is no problem. When indicators pinpoint the wrong things, employees will go for the indicators that promote their careers and not go for the real thing. Measurement becomes self-deception even if the tables and graphs look impressive. Let's see what we can learn from the case of Feargal Quinn.

CASE STUDY   **Feargal Quinn**

Certain things must be measured in terms of money, others should never be associated with numbers. Feargal Quinn will serve as an example of the importance of the non-measurable. He is founder and president of Superquinn, a prosperous Irish chain of supermarkets. Quinn expresses his philosophy in the following way:[37] 'Most businesses focus on maximizing the profit from current sales. Of course they are 'interested' in repeat business – who isn't? – but often they see it as a bonus rather than the main pay-off. And so they tend to concentrate on what they see as the main pay-off, with the lesser part of the energy devoted to creating a bonus.'

According to Quinn, we should do it the other way around: 'If you look after getting the repeat business, the profit now will largely look after itself.' This is completely in line with RM; short-term profits are an outcome of long-term investment in relationships and consequently one should prioritize the long term.

Quinn found it difficult to prove long-term profit effects to his accounting tribe; confidence in his own judgement and gut feeling was necessary. He says that leadership is not making all decisions based on numbers, but instead to make qualitative evaluations. Leadership is risk-taking, action and vision; it is consciousness about the situation, common sense and intuition. Numbers and accounting can be of assistance within leadership, but they cannot replace leadership. Johnson (1992) says very distinctly in his assessment of ABC that it can improve accounting, but it is no substitute for marketing decisions. Quinn offers the following examples.

■ Example 1 – Superquinn stores introduced playrooms for children so that the mothers would be free to do purchasing. If the children enjoy the playroom, mothers were likely to stay longer, buy more and return. But it is not possible to measure the profitability of this investment in hard short-term figures.

[37] This section is based on a book and an article by Quinn (1990, 1994); the quotations are from the article.

- Example 2 – Sweets at the cash registers stimulate impulse buying, which gives easily measurable short-term income. While waiting to pay, children are tempted by the sweets and their parents get under fire. Irritation occurs, parents feel uneasy and may prefer to patronize another outlet. This effect cannot be figured out in accounting terms; it must be observed and the decision must feel right.

- Example 3 – When the Irish Post was restructured, it wanted the public to notice the change. The idea was suggested that the old postage cost from the last century, one penny for a letter, should apply during the day of celebration. It was agreed that this would be a costly campaign. To their great astonishment, the campaign paid off in a couple of weeks. People who used to write letters took the opportunity to write more and the number of letters increased dramatically during the cheap day. But return on investment came by return of mail, as the recipients of letters replied and then at full postage. It was the ideal campaign; the payback was instant and the Irish Post reached the public with its message.

In all these examples, the activities are chosen to enhance revenue more than cost, and to achieve long-term and sustainable effects. Correct short-term costs are easy to forecast, whereas long-term revenue can only be assessed strategically and qualitatively.

If the supplier is handling relationships well, the customer comes back. Quinn sums up his philosophy in the *boomerang principle*: 'One of the beauties with the boomerang principle ... is that you and the customer end up on the same side ... So the relationship with your customer is not an adversarial one, it is a partnership.' Sounds like S-D logic and the idea of ONE.

Feargal Quinn is a prominent spokesman for common sense and so is Stew Leonard, a renowned retailer in Connecticut. Rod, a manager at one of Stew Leonard's fresh food stores, expressed this very distinctly to us in explaining the three origins of success: 'The first is attitude! The second is attitude! And the third is ATTITUDE!' The attitudes, perceptions and paradigms – our way of facing reality and identifying problems and opportunities – are more essential than IT and sophisticated measurement techniques. Zohar and Marshall express it in this way: 'For the physicist, *measurement* is a way of looking at the situation ... *Attitude*... is the human equivalent of measurement.'[38] Surely both Quinn and Leonard use metrics, but they are not the only input in their decision-making.

---

[38] Zohar and Marshall (1993, p. 100).

ROR and some day even RON

The review of the 30Rs showed that RM is not only about customer–supplier relationships, although they are the focal point for CRM. Even if we primarily think of the relationship to our immediate buyer, customer–supplier relationships also include intermediaries, our own suppliers and others. Furthermore, market relationships include relationships to competitors and their many faces, being first and foremost rivals, but often being customers, suppliers and partners as well.

Return on non-market relationships – the mega and nano relationships – is not as obvious, especially in the short term. They are antecedents to successful market relationships. Mega relationships are often strategic and structural necessities; without them the supplier will be out of business. Nano relationships offer internal and necessary conditions for external relationships.

Håkansson and Snehota[39] summarize three levels of cost and revenue effects in B2B networks. First, business relationships generate revenue from customers and the costs are incurred by suppliers; these revenues and costs are traceable. Second, other costs and benefits of relationships are less obvious and less measurable. These are the costs/ revenues of maintaining networks and the quality/productivity emerging from operating in networks. Third, there are the costs and revenue effects that will only become apparent in the future. Although the current outcome of a network is essential, the potential benefits of harvesting, securing survival and growing may be even more important.

The authors stress the network dependency: '... every business enterprise is a product of its context as much as a force shaping the context.' And they proceed: 'What makes the economy of relationships so special is indeed that a relationship has functions (has economic consequences) for several actors and thus that the outcomes of different relationships are interdependent ... Thus it is not enough for any actor to be concerned just about itself in order to be successful, as is suggested in all recommendations based on market theory.' We can't just ask 'What's in it for me and my company?' We also have to ask 'What's in it for the other members of the network?' and 'How can we help to improve the competitiveness of the network as a whole?'

'Tomorrow's company will understand and measure the value from all its relationships,' says a British report by an organization with the impressive name of *The Royal Society for the Encouragement of Arts, Manufacture & Commerce* (1994). We are not there yet, if we will ever be. I still like to introduce *RON*, which considers all stakeholders in a network:[40]

---

[39] Håkansson and Snehota (1995, pp. 382–97); the following quotations are from pp. 396 and 284–285.
[40] Based on Gummesson (2008a)

RON is the long-term effect on profitability caused by the establishment and maintenance of an organization's network of relationships.

Like ROR it is an umbrella concept that can harbour many approaches – but it is a bigger umbrella. In the same spirit as RON, Simons and Dávila (1998) suggest *ROM, Return on Management*. They consider management and its energy as the scarcest resource. It has to be taken care of better: focus on the essentials, set clear goals and rules for the organization, and make sure that all members of management have these in front of their eyes all the time. It reminds me of two criteria which an English boss I once had often referred to. One was 'management bother', meaning something that took up management time but was not really worth dealing with. One example was a company who bought real estate hoping it would be a good investment. When later real estate went down in value, they had to put in all their time in saving their money despite the fact that they were not knowledgeable about real estate and did not want to be engaged in it. The other concerned hassle; commit to core activities and do not get stuck in activities that do not add value: 'Do the obvious well'.

ROM is defined as 'the productive energy in an organization which is let loose' divided by 'the time and attention that management devotes to the organization.' ROM is a qualitative measure – it is assessed as high, medium or low – even if it can hold quantitative elements.

The complexity that is added when you go beyond the two-party relationship and get dependent on networks is reflected in the case of frequent flyer clubs. The case also epitomizes that metrics can be and should be used whenever they can deliver, but not for their own sake. The measurable is always embedded in the non-measurable whether we approve or not. Returning to the customer-related criteria in the Baldrige case in the beginning of the chapter, we can ask: Do the frequent flyer programmes fulfil their demands; would they win the award?

CASE STUDY | **The metrics and non-measurable effects of frequent flyer programmes**

One example of ROR measurement necessitated by an RM strategy concerns the revenue, cost and profit attributable to customer clubs. As was shown in R11 (the customer as 'member') frequent flyer loyalty programmes are the most intricate of such clubs. Some of its effects can be measured in quantitative terms, others are non-measurable and require qualitative assessments.

When competing airlines have clubs, staying out may mean driving yourself out of business. Your hands may even be tied if you are a member of one of the airline alliances – yet another RM club-type concept spelled out under mega relationships (R20–22) – and have to conform with the other allies and their bonus programmes. Low-price airlines don't have bonus programmes but the option, which may not fit, is to clone yourself on them: cut air fare, limited service, use smaller airports, no frills. These airlines, such as Ryanair, operate with another logic basing their marketing on low and continuous supply–demand adapted pricing and the Internet, tailoring a lean organization from the start to fit just that. The established airlines had probably hoped that these aggressive upstarts would collapse. That forecast was not a bad one looking back in history, but in 2007 Ryanair passed British Airways in size. Ryanair has partly worked with a blue ocean strategy by attracting new customers who were not used to travel by air or could not afford ordinary airlines, but partly they have entered the red ocean attracting, for example, business travellers.

The cost of operating loyalty clubs includes administrative staff and IT; the work of interacting with customers and promoting the club; and the extras such as upgrades, priority treatment and lounges. Then there is the cost when a traveller uses his or her points to get a free ticket. It can be divided in three parts: (1) extra costs for handling the passenger and his or her luggage, boarding card, meals, fuel and so on; (2) lost revenue when a non-paying passenger occupies a seat which would otherwise be occupied by a paying passenger; and 3. lost revenue when a customer uses an award instead of buying the ticket. The first cost is always there and the last two may or may not be there. If a member uses the points on an allied airline the hosting airline has to buy the ticket. Thus there is a market consisting of allied airlines.

This should be seen in the light of total marketing costs. A club becomes part of a CRM system in which the airline can store and process customer data and stimulate loyalty and retention. The alternative ways of promoting air travel are judged to be more expensive and less effective. In fact, frequent flyer programmes are considered so effective that they have spawned a second market. Being extensions of air travel, hotels and car rentals became partners when American Airlines first introduced frequent flyer programmes and its AAdvantage. The partnerships now embrace lots of others, even small shops who give 'milage' when customers buy. They pay a small amount to the airline but they don't need to invest in their own loyalty programme. It is co-creation of value in a B2B setting; the partners benefit from the halo effect of the airline brand and the airline can boost many partners, some of them reinforcing the brand of the host. In a B2C/C2B context, customers get an incentive to retain suppliers who give milage points. So it is a set of win–win relationships.

> If you decide to have a loyalty programme you have to do your metrics but the rest is leadership and vision: we believe clubs are good!
>
> What is the bottom line of these calculations? Adding it all up – measurable cost, measurable volume of passengers and measurable revenue – we are mixing hard and soft data. Even doing your metrics carefully, you have to put them in a context of qualitative considerations and the final decision is a judgment call. And today the loyalty club is perceived by travellers as an integral part of the value proposition of a full-service airline. The only way to pull out is if everybody else does. So you are left to keep up the quality and productivity of your programme.

Strategies for improved ROR

A series of approaches to ROR have been presented. They help us understand aspects of RM, but none of them offers the complete and ultimate solution.

The following paragraphs will summarize consequences and strategies that are essential for improving ROR.

Customer–supplier relationships

- Marketing costs go down when retention goes up; you do not have to recruit as many new customers as before. New customers often have to be acquired with special offers and discounts that make them initially unprofitable. Such campaigns are often successful, but they also attract 'junk customers' with little profit potential. Customers frequently have several suppliers and especially new customers may be low users. If the relationships work out well, they are likely to favour fewer sources and the share of customers increases. Suppliers and customers become better partners, co-producers and even co-developers if they interact more frequently. As a consequence, quality, productivity and profitability improve. Good relationships mean less hassle, for example, if delays occur and faulty goods or services are delivered. It is easier to sort out problems between 'friends' who trust each other. Suppliers get to know their customers better. They can build more useful CRM systems to make them more sensitive to customer needs and wants, and to target their offerings better. The parties should find a balance between their roles as customer and supplier, what each should do independently and what they should do in interaction.
- Satisfied customers are not necessarily profitable. Watch out for unprofitable customers who hide among the profitable ones. When customers are unprofitable it could be that they are and will remain just that. It could also be that the supplier has not been able to

appreciate the actual needs of the buyer and is offering the wrong product at the wrong price. It could further be that senile accounting systems and indicators, which are geared to the mass manufacturing of the industrial era, are used. They are not suitable maps in the value and network society. Therefore, develop sound indicators that consider the impact of relationships on profit. Consider the customer's profitability over a lifetime, LTV, and the profitability links between different products, services and customers.

■ Measure what impacts ROR – if it is measurable. Do not fall into the trap of thinking the non-measurable – such as culture, leadership, vision and long-term network building – is unimportant just because it can't be replicated in numbers. Numbers must be linked to common sense, sound judgement, wisdom, vision and endurance.

■ Whenever possible, make sure that relationships become part of the structural capital, as the human capital is transient and less controllable. However, caring for the human capital is also imperative. To a degree computers can take over the buying and selling process within B2B and also actively search for information. M-to-M gives rise to a new type of RM which we know too little about.

■ Appointing relationship managers, CRM managers and key account managers can be successful organizational solutions for supporting the transfer to an RM-oriented approach. RM values and strategies, however, must permeate the whole organization and become part of the corporate culture and daily operations.

■ Good relationships make customers better PTMs, who add marketing muscle without burdening marketing and sales budgets. The PTMs spread positive word of mouth, give referrals, and nourish your image and brand.

■ Loyal customers become less price sensitive – within limits – as they also value trust, commitment, convenience, easy access, and social and parasocial relationships. Remember though that customers have to be continuously encouraged to remain loyal.

■ Satisfaction indicators must be interpreted; 'satisfied' in a survey can be far away from 'very satisfied'. 'Satisfied customers' may just be 'happy slaves' who think this is the way it must be. A competitor may change all this. Sometimes the customer finds no option, which gives the supplier a real or a perceived monopoly, but the customer may feel imprisoned.

■ Dissatisfied customers do not necessarily defect. They do not often complain openly and even if they do the supplier may not be ready to listen and understand.

Competitor relationships

■ Competitors have a tougher time when retention and loyalty increase; they are not served new customers on a plate.

■ Relationships between competitors are multidimensional. Competitors are often also customers and partners. By collaborating with competitors in certain areas, both suppliers and customers gain advantages through, for example, cost reduction and joint development of products and services.

- Through associations competitors can help each other improve conditions for an industry as a whole and enhance its image, a task where lobbying, public relations and media contacts are frequently used.
- In the network society, individual companies are rarely competing with individual companies – as the conventional wisdom from economics claims – but networks compete with networks.

Non-market relationships

- Return on mega relationships is obvious when, for example, a lobbying campaign is successful or an alliance brings valuable knowledge to a product development project. Nano relationships are partly internal market relationships, such as the supplier–customer relationship between profit centres. ROR can then be measured in the same way as external market relationships. Other nano relationships are sometimes more difficult to assess, such as the value of cooperation between operations management and marketing through quality.
- Analyse the roles of the parties in a network, such as the supplier role and the customer role. Who should do what and what should be done in interaction?

An RM-inspired marketing plan and audit

If we ask companies today how they practise RM, they are most likely referring to the installation of eCRM systems, loyalty and satisfaction indicators, and efforts to increase the interactive skills of their staff. Other bits and pieces of RM are embedded in their marketing, but they are not clearly discernible and they are called something else. In fact, companies are doing a lot of RM, but for lack of concepts, models, a common language, and marketing planning and auditing tradition, the relationship activities are often not openly acknowledged and put to use in a systematic and conscious manner.

It is particularly important to take a fresh look at the planning and evaluation of marketing efforts as RM/CRM offer new conditions. This should be done in two areas of marketing, the marketing plan and the marketing audit.

The RM plan and the relationship portfolio

To carry weight, RM/CRM aspects must be introduced in the marketing planning process. Marketing in the light of relationships, networks and interaction becomes *marketing-oriented management*, and therefore the marketing plan must be an integral part of the *company's overall business plan*.

There is little research available on marketing planning in networks of relationships. One of the exceptions is Benndorf (1987), who studied relationships and networks in B2B and their meaning for the marketing planning process. He concluded that companies in a network become dependent on each other's plans. Their resources and activities should ideally be co-planned with regard to network dependencies. Such co-planning is not easy in practice, though.

We know too little about how RM should best be integrated into the planning of a company. The only ways to find out are through trial and error in our companies and through research. For lack of experience of RM planning, it seems reasonable to start by adding RM/CRM dimensions to the marketing plan in use, retaining its basic format.[41] A marketing plan which is focused on the opportunities offered by RM can include the relationships and networks that need to be built, maintained or abandoned.

Activity planning is a normal part of a marketing plan, and activities and interactions in relationships should also be the object of planning. Traditional goals of the marketing plan, such as sales volume and market share, must in part be substituted or supplemented by ROR goals, such as customer retention and share of customer, in the spirit of intellectual capital and the balanced scorecard.

Activities in marketing are usually described as a marketing mix – the four or more Ps – including price, sales calls, physical distribution, and other activities and strategies. These are not replaced by the 30Rs, but the way RM has been presented here, the relationships are the vantage point – what we see through the relationship eyeglasses – and the Ps and other activities can be supportive to the relationships (see further Chapter 8). The relationships broaden the interplay between marketing and other functions, such as production and internal service.

Instead of starting with mixing Ps, a company needs to define and review its *relationship portfolio*. I have chosen the word portfolio rather than mix to accentuate a novel perspective and novel values, a paradigm shift. A portfolio is a collection of components and their total benefits should be greater than the sum of the parts; there should be synergy effects. The term financial portfolio is used for a combination of investments that fulfil chosen goals such as balanced risk, maximum short-term yield or maximum long-term growth. In strategic management, portfolio is used for the choice of products to offer on the market (product portfolio) and the choice of customers to target (customer portfolio). The relationship portfolio is a combination of RM activities to be performed during the planning period.

---

[41] For a review of systematic marketing planning procedures in use, see McDonald (1995).

In summary, the following tasks should be integrated with the RM/CRM-oriented marketing plan:

1 *Select a relationship portfolio!* Analyse the currently interesting relationships and networks, and assess your ability to interact in these. Do this as an active part of the marketing planning and business planning processes. Use the 30Rs as a checklist. Each relationship must be defined to fit a specific company and its specific situation. Select relationships of particular importance which are currently not handled well enough but are gauged to have development potential. Acknowledge that sometimes the zero relationships, transaction marketing, is the best strategy.

2 *Set goals, measure results and monitor implementation!* Goals are an important part of the marketing plan, not only quantitative and short-term goals, but also qualitative, long-term and strategic goals. The implementation processes must be monitored and the outcome compared to the goals. Make certain that implementation is systematic and committed. I have previously claimed that '... the ability and strength to execute a decision is more crucial for success than the underlying analysis'.[42]

3 *Assess RM consequences for organization, processes, systems and procedures!* RM/CRM put new demands on the organization and its processes, methods and procedures. This is particularly essential to consider in a company's overall business plan. RM/CRM cannot be isolated to marketing and sales departments and the marketing plan. In the next chapter, the importance of organizational structure and processes for RM/CRM are discussed further.

The RM audit

Marketing is reviewed continuously during the working day and it is reviewed as part of the marketing planning process at least once a year. Marketing is also reviewed in management and board meetings; in meetings with others in a company's network; in special projects for new products, services and marketing channels, and for assessing changes in the marketplace; in troubleshooting missions by task forces; and at kick-offs and marketing and sales conferences. It may be reviewed by our partners in networks. It may even be reviewed by the media. So what is really the use of a marketing audit?

The following definition of marketing audit has been suggested:[43] 'A marketing audit is a comprehensive, systematic, independent and periodic examination of a company's – or business unit's – marketing environment, objectives, strategies, and activities with a view

---

[42] Gummesson (1998b, p. 242).
[43] Kotler, Gregor and Rodgers (1989).

to determining problem areas and opportunities and recommending a plan of action to improve the company's marketing performance.'

A marketing audit is closely connected to marketing and business plans and reporting systems. The corporate business planning and marketing planning processes are recurrent events, but they primarily produce documents to guide the next planning period. Usually they do not include a systematic evaluation challenging fundamental strategic issues. According to McDonald:[44]

> Often the need for an audit does not manifest itself until things start
> to go wrong for a company, such as declining sales, falling margins,
> lost market share, underutilized production capacity, and so on.
> At times like these, management often attempts to treat the wrong
> symptoms ... introducing new products or dropping products,
> reorganizing the sales force, reducing prices, and cutting costs ...
> But such measures are unlikely to be effective if there are more
> fundamental problems which have not been identified.

This is where the marketing audit enters. It goes a step further than the marketing plan to analyse fundamental marketing issues. In contrast to the aforementioned review activities, the audit must also fulfil the four criteria of the definition. The audit should be:

1 *Comprehensive*, thus covering all marketing aspects.
2 *Systematic*, by using an orderly method.
3 *Independent*, by being conducted by a person or team who do not have a stake in the company's marketing.
4 *Periodic*, that is, be conducted regularly and not just on an ad hoc basis.

RM adds an extra and revolutionary dimension to marketing planning and the marketing audit. In viewing marketing as part of the interaction and events in a network of relationships, we have to broaden the marketing function beyond marketing and sales departments and company boundaries.

Companies and consultants have developed various formats for marketing audits. Even if a company starts out with a general marketing audit checklist, it should adjust it to its specific needs as experience is gained with its application.[45] Although the checklists may cover certain aspects of RM/CRM, they are not based on observations made through the relationship eyeglasses. We are not yet ready to suggest a general RM checklist; the

---

[44] McDonald (1995, pp. 28–29).
[45] See marketing audit checklists in McDonald (1995, pp. 30–2); and Kotler and Keller (2006, pp. 719–723).

empirical base is too thin. In order to be practical, I will settle for suggesting RM additions to existing audit checklists. Therefore, look at each of the 30Rs and their parts and answer the following questions:

- Is the composition of our relationship portfolio satisfactory?
- How well are we handling specific relationships and their parts?
- Are specific relationships or parts of them crucial for success?
- Could specific relationships add to our performance if we improve them?
- Should certain relationships be terminated?
- Do we measure and assess ROR in the best possible way?

IN BRIEF

Quantitative measures and qualitative assessments are supplementary. Like yin and yang, they are both needed. ROR is an attempt to put the light on the necessity to make systematic assessment of RM/CRM and their value to our business.

QUESTIONS FOR DISCUSSION

1 What is marketing metrics, marketing accountability, ROR and RON?
2 List and explain some of the efforts that have been made to measure effects of marketing in general and RM/CRM in particular.
3 What is meant by tribes and triplets in the context of RM?
4 Discuss the pros and cons of the traditional value chain and the customer value chain, and lean production and lean consumption.
5 What is intellectual capital and the balanced scorecard?
6 It is often claimed that 'what gets measured, gets done' and 'what can't be measured does not exist'. Can or should everything be measured in numbers?
7 What is a 'relationship portfolio'?

Chapter

7

RM and the network organization

INTRODUCTION

The network organization and its connection with RM/CRM has been examined throughout the text. This chapter deals with this intriguing issue at more length both from the perspective of the corporation and the market economy.

Organizing: creating networks of relationships

In working with RM, marketing and organization began to stand out as two expressions of the same thing. My conclusion became that *RM is a marketing perspective on the network organization and the network society*. RM requires organizations to change and not least the experiences from installing CRM systems show that changes in both organizational structure and culture are inevitable.

The reason for treating organization separately and more at length is to give the marketer a better understanding of its significance in the new economy and the network society. RM lives in three environments: *the market, society* and *the organization*, reflected in the market, mega and nano relationships. The RM approach means that these three are woven together into a network. The nano relationships show the importance of the internal environment. The notion of network organizations has been used in the book as an umbrella for new organizational thinking. I find that the network structure and its tie to RM and CRM with interaction inside the network constitutes the core of contemporary organizations. But it stretches beyond that to a whole network society, as was pointed out in Chapter 1 with reference to Castells' (1996) comprehensive work. The term virtual organization is also frequently used. According to one definition, the virtual (also called 'imaginary') organization[1] is 'a system in which assets, processes, and actors critical to the 'focal' enterprise exist and function both inside and outside the limits of the enterprise's conventional 'landscape' formed by its legal structure, its accounting, its organigrams, and the language otherwise used to describe the enterprise'. The idea behind this type of organization is to make the invisible visible and to acquire new frames of reference, to 'imaginize'. The organization is looked at through new lenses, and a new business logic for entrepreneurship and renovation of existing companies emerges. The organization consists of: an own base, which in turn consists of a leader company and an 'imaginator'

---

[1] Hedberg *et al.* (2000).

(the leader, the entrepreneur) and their strategic map; a customer base which is tied to the leader company through systems for production, delivery, market communications and payment; and partnering companies and others that contribute resources.[2]

The network organization is larger than it seems from the organizational chart. Its most important resource – apart from financial capital – is intellectual capital, which is not found in the conventional balance sheet. Customers are involved in co-production and thus joint value creation and become part of the network. There is a business mission that mentally keeps the network of internal and external relationships together and the organization develops its own unique culture.

The Internet supports the construction of network organizations. By exploiting the Internet infrastructure, the core of the organization can be small but still the company can operate globally, grow quickly and be a market leader in its niche. Amazon.com is not one of the large retailers in conventional terms – its workforce is just one per cent of that of Wal-Mart – but has become the world's largest global bookstore. Even if Amazon still primarily sells books (a choice, by the way, that was accidental), the company is not first and foremost product-based but network-based. Its capital is its network of relationships, not only the customer base, but also the relationship to publishers, distributors, authors, and not least investors and the media. It went for growth and not initially for profitability with the idea that a critical mass of customers is required to be able to sell a diverse range of products. Its value on the stock exchange has had little to do with its assets and profits; it is a matter of expectations and the ability to cash in on the network.

Organizational and network properties have emerged in the 30Rs. My guess is that network organizations, just like RM, have been there a long time, perhaps always. Our way of approaching marketing and organization in textbooks and education leads us astray. Even though RM and other developments have shown that we have entered a different economy, the textbooks that influence new generations of marketers too often are closer to industrial era nostalgia than to contemporary and future vision. We have come to a point where the new – or rather the old but newly uncovered – is starting to be visible and is developing with more zest. It is the outcome of a new type of economy, which I classify as a value-creating network society, accentuating that customers buy and co-create value and the resources and structures that contribute are networks.

In the next sections, my personal interpretation of network organizations will be unfolded in the light of RM/CRM.

---

[2] New organizational thinking offers a rich fauna of concepts and terms and some will be referenced in the text but other will not. For additional references, see for example Handy (1990); Mills (1991); Quinn (1992); Tjosvold (1993); and Czarniawska and Hernes (2005). They all have affinity to the network organization.

Have you ever seen a corporation?

The heading may seem absurd, but when we talk about a corporation we refer to something abstract, although it has certain tangible features. When the CEO is interviewed on TV or when the new model of a car is shown, we catch a glimpse of the being of the corporation. We cannot take a photo of a business but we can photograph a product, a building, a group of employees, an organizational chart, or a logotype, but these are surrogates and only represent aspects of the corporation. We see the tracks of the elusive animal in the snow, we surmise its presence, and we may even catch a quick glimpse before it slips away.

Morgan (1997) approaches the organization with a series of metaphors. The organization is looked upon as if it were a machine, biological organism, brain, culture, political system, psychic prison, flow and change, and finally a tool to dominate society. Metaphors draw our attention to certain qualities of an organism, but they only provide fragments, not the whole. They should not be stretched too far; if they do, they lose their value.

'Objectification' happens when we compare an organization to something tangible, and 'reification' when we mistake the phenomenon for its tangible representation.[3] This may lead to myopia and imprisonment in existing concepts and definitions. Our perceptions about organizations take over, and we become their slaves instead of making them our servants. Inferior quality, disinterest in the customer, erroneous decisions and inertia are blamed on the organization and the system: 'I'm sorry, I can't do anything about it.' This has been called 'learnt helplessness'. Such a state of mind makes lousy marketing and lousy customer relationships. It can be found among companies and those government organizations which have become a 'reality' separated from us – the impersonal system, the authority, the computer, the state, society, public opinion – and which we ultimately cannot or dare not affect. The map takes over and the landscape gets lost. The renowned painting of a smoking pipe by Belgian artist Magritte, with the inscription *'Ceci n'est pas une pipe'* (This is not a pipe), is named *'La trahison des images'* (The treachery of images). The artist makes us understand how easily we can mistake an image of an object for the object itself.

According to Weick,[4] organizations are relationships and interaction:

> Most 'things' in organizations are actually relationships, variables tied together in a systematic fashion. Events, therefore, depend on the strength of these ties, the direction of influence, the time it takes for information in the form of differences to move around circuits. The word organization is a noun, and it is also a myth. If you look

---

[3] Gustavsson (1992, 2001).
[4] Weick (1979, p. 88).

for an organization you won't find it. What you will find is that there are events, linked together, that transpire within concrete walls and these sequences, their pathways, and their timing are the forms we erroneously make a substance when we talk about an organization.

Whereas Weick's interest is directed to nano relationships, Badaracco[5] describes the transition from the closed and well-defined firm, the citadel, to a market and mega network: 'Firms were ... islands of managerial coordination in a sea of market relationships. But this is an outdated view. Companies are now breaking down barriers which, like the Berlin Wall, have endured for decades. Their managers are now working in a world that consists not simply of markets and firms, but of complex relationships with a variety of other organizations.'

Consequently, management cannot take for granted that the boundaries of their corporation are clear. They are expected to defend a moving fortress which continuously changes character and has different boundaries depending on whose vantage point is prevalent, that of the owners, the customers, the authorities, production or whatever.

Catching the soul of a corporation through relationships, networks and interaction is not meant to become another limiting reification. The relationship eye-glasses offer a language to help us understand what is happening. But modern network theory as part of the family of complexity theory sees networks as more than a metaphor; it is perhaps even capturing the essence of life.

The company and the market: same thing – but different

It has already been said that company boundaries are fuzzy, which the next case will show.

CASE STUDY   **Volvo and Procordia**

When a deal between Volvo and Procordia was announced, there was reason to ask what the corporations and the market really were. Volvo already owned 43.5 per cent of Procordia stock. Procordia was going to buy Volvo, but the new corporation was going to be called Volvo. Procordia produced tobacco, lozenges and hamburgers, Volvo passenger cars, trucks, buses and aircraft engines. There was no product synergy in sight. The smoker could not care less if the plants were owned by Volvo and some 100 000 anonymous stockholders who change

[5] Badaracco (1991; quotation from p. ix).

from day to day. The relationship existed between the consumer, the brand and the store where the cigarettes were bought. Moreover, the two companies owned stock in other companies. There was partial ownership between Volvo and Renault, although Volvo was primarily owned by private investors and Renault primarily by the State of France. A large number of subcontractors were tied to their customer Volvo, and from an operations viewpoint they were part of the Volvo empire. Where actually are the boundaries between these two companies, their markets and society? And later Volvo sold its passenger car division to Ford. How do we handle the boundaries to competitors who are part of our company?

The dilemma will be further explained in this section by means of neoclassical economics, transaction cost analysis, systems theory – all with the aspiration of establishing boundaries – and finally network theory which sees organizations as scale-free and boundaryless.

Neoclassical economics

In economics, the market and the company are treated as two clearly delimited entities. The market is governed by *supply* and *demand*, with the help of *price* and *competition*. The corporation is an anonymous black box to the economist, who studies aggregates of companies in industries, regions and nations, unfortunately often based on poor statistics. In a basic book on management from the 1950s, the following definition was found: 'a company is a unit within which a planned economy rules', the ideal model being all employees marching like tin soldiers in good order towards a clearly set destination. In R24 – market mechanisms are brought inside the company – it was shown that this model is false and furthermore that the external deregulation of markets has its internal consequences. Decentralization and the split-up of companies into subsidiaries, business areas and other profit centres have expedited the dissolution of the internal planned economy.

Transaction costs

Transaction cost analysis[6] claims to be able to guide the establishment of boundaries between a company and its market. The analysis has received extensive exposure as a synthesis between economics, organizational theory and contract theory from law.

---

[6] Transaction cost analysis is treated by Coase (1937, 1991); and Williamson (1985, 1990). In Johanson and Mattsson (1987), there is a comparison between transaction cost analysis and the network approach to B2B.

Unfortunately, the analysis is based on simplified assumptions about the industrial society and manufacturing, and does not pay attention to the service-based economy. It is limited to the 'pure' company and does not treat hybrids such as franchising and alliances. General marketing management has not been included, nor services marketing and the ideas of RM. The assumptions, therefore, seem obsolete and simplistic.

Its basic tenets, however, embrace some elements that can shed light on the differences between RM and the traditional perceptions of organizations and marketing. In neoclassical economic theory there are no transaction costs, so transaction cost analysis, in spite of its shortcomings, adds a new element of realism. The analysis sets the business deal – the transaction – in focus, and postulates that companies strive to minimize transaction costs. These concern the costs of performing business transactions, meaning in practice marketing and purchasing costs. It is cost effective to perform certain activities inside the own organization, and to handle others via the supply–demand mechanism of the market economy by purchasing from external suppliers. According to transaction cost analysis, the cost comparison between own production and purchasing explains the boundaries of the company.

Transaction cost analysis is based on three assumptions about the emergence of a company:

- By organizing a company under the same owner and management, they can plan the work so that dual tasks and suboptimization are avoided.
- As an organization consists of a number of co-ordinated units under one management, it is easier to solve problems and disputes than it is in a market with a number of independent actors.
- Inside their own organization, access to information is better.

These, however, are a theoretical conjecture and are not based on real world data.

So there are two possibilities to handle transaction costs: inside the organization if that is the more cost effective (Figure 7.1a) or in the market if that is cheaper (Figure 7.1b). RM, however, offers a third option which is a combination of the first two, namely to handle transaction costs through a deeper relationship with an outside supplier (Figure 7.1c).

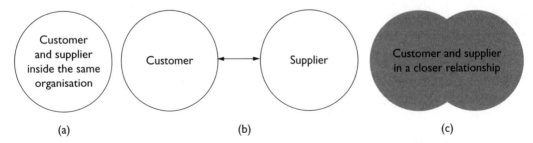

Figure 7.1 Three cases of transaction costs. Cases (a) and (b) are treated by transaction cost analysis. Case (c) is becoming more frequent, and is characteristic of RM and imaginary organizations

In this way, a company can reduce its transaction costs without increasing its size or ownership.

According to transaction cost analysis it is difficult to analyse and measure relationship aspects, and therefore they are disregarded. The analysis does acknowledge two hazards, though: the *bounded rationality* of human beings, and *opportunistic behaviour*. To put it more simply: stupidity, selfishness, greed and dishonesty are such important components of human nature that they affect the applicability of transaction costs analysis.

Every company must have both a strategic core and supporting, ancillary activities. The core is the remainder of the citadel. Transaction cost analysis talks about *asset specificity*, the specific resources which constitute the core. Part of the core must be kept intact to preserve the unique competence of the firm. In the industrial era this was usually manufacturing. In today's economy it may equally well be finance or the maintenance of a brand. Other activities can be handled through outsourcing and partnering, the reason being that external resources can be better equipped to add value, provided transaction costs are not prohibitive.

According to Quinn,[7] ancillary activities are not the only objects of outsourcing, which is often claimed, but so are certain core activities. He recommends that own production be focused on a very select number of internal resources based on knowledge and services where the company has muscle to maintain a sustaining competitive edge. The company must, however, protect its core competency by building moats around the remainders of the citadel. This is argued by the proponents of hypercompetition, who claim that the core competency must be continuously remodelled; you do not survive and prosper by protecting the extant regime, you do it by continuous disruptions of the status quo.

Systems theory

Applied to the company and the market, systems theory assumes that the system (the organization) can be delimited from the *environment* (the market and society), and that it comprises *subsystems* and *components* (the inner functions of the organization). This approach helps to recognize the whole and its parts. In a network, however, boundaries are many and ever-changing. The difference between the company and its market, as well as its functions, is a matter of grade, transitions and difference in species. If decisions are the outcome of negotiations, consensus or power through interaction in a network, clear systems boundaries cannot be upheld. The traditional image of the atomistic market, populated by a large number of independent companies who act against relatively passive buyers, is still promoted in the textbooks, however.

---

[7] Quinn (1992, pp. 47 and 53).

The dichotomy of *open* and *closed* systems from systems theory is eluded by the properties of the network organization. A network is a more open system than the corporation in its classic 'citadel' sense. Networks, however, can also be closed, with openness inside the network, but closeness towards those who do not belong to the network.

The company as an open system means that it interacts with the environment. Today, it may be more appropriate to describe the company *as both interacting with the environment and being integrated with it*. The customer also becomes part of the company, which has stood out most clearly in services marketing. One example of both interaction and integration is Ernst & Young, one of the world's largest firms of accountants. Their office in Chicago was transformed into a 'virtual office' for 500 of its 1360 employees. The accountants work in the clients' offices and conference rooms, in hotel rooms, at airports and in airplanes, in their cars and at home. If they plan to work in their office they call in and book a room the day before ('hotelling') and a room is prepared for them with their telephone connection. From a daily, operative view, the boundaries between the accounting firm and the client do not stand out as particularly important.

Network theory

Although the three approaches explained above highlight important aspects of organizations they are pre-occupied with boundaries. This puts emphasis on restrictions and does not open up for the holistic and dynamic view of organizations and markets.

I have found network theory to be the most advanced and helpful way of addressing the issue of organizing. Network theory has roots both in the social and natural sciences. Its current development seems to be faster and more creative in the natural sciences.[8] It is supported by today's IT which makes it possible to treat data and make graphics that are difficult or impossible to make otherwise. But we do not have to go as far as that. The basis of network theory is the concepts of nodes, links and hubs. A node can be a person who knows another person (link) and several people may be attracted to a specific node, a hub. The hub may be a person who is popular for some reason or transferred to RM, a company (hub) has many customers (nodes) who buy from it. The RM idea is than to keep this network and develop it further.

Network theory is closely related to systems theory but I have found it to be more comprehensive and offering more opportunities for analysis and creativity. The case study of Amazon will illustrate.

---

[8] See Granovetter (1973); Barabási (2002); Capra (2002); and Buchanan (2003).

CASE STUDY   **Amazon: more than customer relationships[9]**

Amazon.com is best known as the largest global Internet bookstore even if they sell other products, both B2C/C2B and B2B. They also offer opportunities for C2C interaction.

Amazon does not only have a one-to-one relationship to its book buyers. Through the many-to-many eyeglasses we can quickly see that success is dependent on networks. Prominent actors are, besides the book-buyers, publishers, authors, distributors, investors, financial analysts, and the media (Figure 7.2). The company must be able to deal with all the members of its network. In the center of the figure are the US and the UK websites; they are the door to the company. An author tells a critical incidence:

I discovered that the presentation of my two books which are sold through the Amazon contained several mistakes. For example, the new revised version of one of my books was not there. Instead the buyer was offered my ten year old first edition. Furthermore, they offered only the hard cover version which was three times as expensive as the paperback version. I rang both publishers, one in the USA in and the other one in England, and told them about it. They promised to do something. When I checked after several months nothing

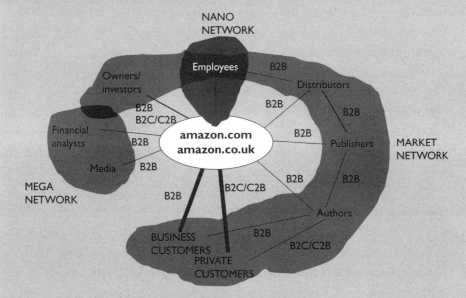

Figure 7.2 Parties and links in Amazon's network

[9] Based on Gummesson (2008a). Used with permission.

had happened. I called again, somewhat irritated over the inability of the publishers to interact with the author. The editors of both publishers said roughly the same thing: 'It has no purpose. Amazon won't listen.' One even wrote an e-mail to me and said: 'We don't own Amazon, we can't influence them'. I then tried to get into the Amazon website and find the e-mail address for authors. I succeeded, but it took a while. I sent e-mails both to America and England and pointed out the mistakes and suggested a new text. Within twenty minutes Amazon.co.uk had corrected the mistake. But they had entered a new mistake by a spelling my name wrongly. This took me several hours and then I had to dash off so I never had the time to follow up the American site.

The incidence shows the importance of good relationships between authors, publishers, distributors, and Amazon employees in order to create conditions for maximum book sales. One of the cornerstones of Amazon's marketing strategy is quick delivery which requires smooth cooperation between Amazon, publishers and distributors. The market network grows to include not only customers but also lots of others.

Most websites have the problem of getting known, especially if they come from a new company. So was the case when Amazon started in 1995 (in a garage, where else?). Traditional advertising can be used to make a brand known, but it is costly and the result is difficult to forecast. Amazon got enormous free support by the news media and its CEO Jeff Bezos became an international celebrity.

It got even more publicity when it was introduced on the stock exchange in the midst of the dotcom boom. Reports from Wall Street analysts and reactions from investors filled the financial press. In a short time the price of Amazon shares skyrocketed and Bezos became 'Businessman of the Year' with his portrait on the cover of *Time*. When dotcom shares lost their attraction in the beginning of 2000 the publicity turned the opposite direction. The company had expanded without control. Growth was the number one goal, the idea being that a giant customer base and a unique global network should be built. Profitability would follow. This took time however, but Amazon became one of the survivors.

As long as the brand Amazon is pumped into the minds of people via the media, customers know that the company exists and look for its website. Today Amazon is established as a general designation of an Internet bookstore, in the same way as all paper copies are called Xerox copies.

Amazon built its success on high tech, but high touch is just as important using high tech as an arena. The Internet offers the prospect of swift communication, easy ordering, the possibility to learn about customers and to interact with customers and authors. Amazon facilitates C2B; customers are encouraged to ask questions, grade books and write book reviews.

It is obvious that all stakeholders are important. The media and investors belong to the mega network, which is perhaps the most important one to communicate the message of Amazon, provided that the website develops and the physical trade with books and the other products works. Traditional marketing becomes less important.

Network theory, which is both a theory of life and a methodology to explore life, can accommodate more dimensions of reality than any other scientific approach. Its runner-up is case study research, but network theory is more systematic and rigorous and offers more techniques.[10] Above all it can accommodate so many more realistic dimensions than other methods can do. These dimensions are:

- *Complexity*: Marketing deals with complex issues. Simplifying them too far, which is done by current research techniques and models, deprives them of life and maybe of their most crucial aspects.
- *Context*: Everything happens in a context; in B2B companies buy and sell within networks and are influenced by their network belonging; in B2C/C2B consumers belong to families, sports clubs, neighbourhoods and so on and consumption takes place in this environment. Current research methods and models usually exclude or disregard context.
- *Change*: Stability is not the natural state of a company or market, change is going on continuously or intermittently, but it is forever around.
- *Non-linearity*: A linear equation is favoured by social scientists and researchers in marketing, but reality is non-linear, that is, it is not sequential but iterative and contains phenomena which cannot be easily ordered and predicted. Non-linear equations are difficult but network theory accepts non-linearity.
- *Both parts and the whole*: If we could take a completely holistic view on everything it would be great. But we can't and therefore we make up boundaries and delimit our approaches and view to a simplified picture. The solution is to swing between the whole and the part, which networks theory allows us to do.

---

[10] For an overview of network theory and a comparison with case study research, see Gummesson (2007b).

- *Both structure and process*: Networks are often perceived as just structures; perhaps network graphs convey that impression. But increasingly network theory also deals with processes, what is going on in the nodes and links and the network changes shape.
- *Both tech and human aspects*: The importance of a high tech/high touch balance in marketing has been stressed. Networks incorporate both machines and people.

All these dimensions can be grouped into *complexity theory* which embraces many other theories and methods such as chaos theory, self-organizing systems (autopeisis) and fractal geometry.

If may still be practical to talk about boundaries but we chose them subjectively for special purposes. A company thus becomes many different organizations. The desire to draw generally valid boundaries is not possible to fulfil if we require the boundaries to be sharp; generally, companies are fuzzy sets. Several boundaries co-exist:

- Law based, for a specific corporate format, taxes and annual reporting.
- Financial, concerning the procurement of money.
- Operative, concerning the daily work with partners, customers, suppliers and others.
- Strategic, such as a joint development project with competitors, research institutes and consultants.
- External/internal, customers are found both outside and inside the organization, depending on how the boundaries are drawn.

Looking at business as relationships, networks and interaction makes it difficult to pinpoint the beginning and the end of a company. We need new concepts and models in order to obtain mental access to reality. Figure 7.3a shows the traditional terminology, the company as a clearly defined, hierarchical structure and the market consisting of distinctly identifiable customers, both other organizations and consumers. In Figure 7.3b, we see a network of relationships which contains all types of actors. In this network, we can more or less distinctly delimit clusters of relationships and call them organizations for a specific purpose. The black dots represent core competencies.

We move from the *exclusive* organizational structure – one that excludes and delimits – to the *inclusive* structure – one that includes and unites.

Paradoxes that are not

A paradox is a seemingly absurd or contradictory statement but it need not be absurd or contradictory if you dive under the surface; it may just be that we call it paradox when we don't understand it. Naisbitt (1994) has defined a number of global paradoxes. One

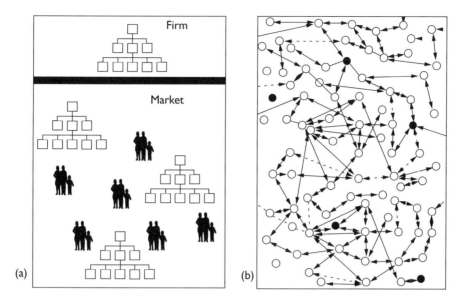

Figure 7.3 The traditional image of the firm and the market in systems theory, transaction cost analysis and economics (a) versus the complex network reality (b)

of these claims that the more integrated the world economy becomes, the more important become the small actors. In other words, the larger the global corporations, the more important the small local firms. If this paradox is valid, the atomistic division of companies in either/or – either large, small or medium – becomes meaningless. The division may be acceptable in colloquial language, but does not apply in financial assessments and statistical classifications, or in forecasts.[11] In light of network theory where a more holistic view is taken, seeming contradictions exist, and are not seen as contradictory but as complementary. Again, this is both/and instead of either/or. Or yin and yang, if you wish.

Companies today strive to unify things that we have learnt to be contradictions. They try to be both *local* and *global*, both *small* and *big*, both *centralized* and *decentralized*, both *stable* and *dynamic*. They want to *become bigger without growing*. They want to *serve the customer with standardized mass manufacturing, customized mass manufacturing, and individually designed value propositions simultaneously*. These are oxymorons in the mechanically and sequentially formatted brains of Western civilization, but within the logic of RM and the network organization they provide realism.

You can have local presence and be a global player, you can be 'glocal'. It does not mean that you can necessarily sell the same product or run a company with standardized

---

[11] For a discussion on the increasingly more inadequate division of companies into small, medium-sized and large, see Gummesson (2002); see also Hult et al. (2000) and their discussion about the 'solo company'.

Organisation	Body	Brain
Dinosaur organisation	Big	Small
The network organisation	Small	Big

Figure 7.4 The 'dino organization' versus the network organization

techniques throughout the world. In some cases it seems feasible – American TV shows and movies are the same everywhere, except that they are dubbed or have subtitles in the local language – while in other cases it does not work as well. It did not work so well for Disneyland Paris in the beginning. IKEA sticks to its core concept but makes local adjustments. Sensitivity is needed to exploit the same offering, and sensitivity is needed to make amendments. Standardization and customization unite. According to an executive at General Electric, employees must have '... networking skills, and be able to work in a boundaryless organization'.[12] The desire is to unite the best of the big corporation with the best of the small firm.

The giants of the business world have acquired their muscle from size and they have also become bigger through mergers and acquisition. In the same way as the dinosaurs, extinct 65 million years ago, they risk becoming too clumsy to proact, act and react swiftly and efficiently. The planned economy of the totally integrated company is replaced by a modular company, which preserves a few core competencies inside and buy the rest in the market.

The new network organization could be contrasted against an old dinosaur organization (Figure 7.4). The 'dino organization' has a big body but a small brain, the network organization has a small body but a big brain. The dino organization is a reflection of the industrial society when a company was composed of a few skilled and powerful people who ruled over hordes of blue and white collar workers.

Internal and external 'employees'

In the network organization it is not so evident who is employed and who is otherwise engaged. The network organization can be described with the human resource ratio, the

---

[12] Quotations from interviews in *International Management* (Lester, 1992).

I/E ratio.[13] It stresses the fact that more human resources (people involved, I) are available for the company than the people employed (E).

'The shamrock organization' has been proposed as a metaphor for the different roles in a company.[14] A shamrock normally has three leaves. These symbolize three types of human resources. The first leaf is the employees, those who work with the core activities of the company. The second leaf is the suppliers who supplement the corporation with resources. The third leaf is the part-time employees and temporary workers.

But a special shamrock may have four leaves; better known as the four leaf clover bringing luck to its finder. The fourth leaf could be customers. In the service management tradition, customers have long been treated as part-time employees during the service encounter and the production, delivery and marketing process. Customers are professional representatives of needs of a value proposition and those who actualize the value; they are co-creators. Without customer, there are no employees and suppliers. The customer base is also increasingly accepted as the most crucial resource of a company.

Although suppliers are not employees, the boundary between suppliers and own employees is fuzzy. 'Cottage industries' in manufacturing have a long history, particularly in textile production. The workers provide flexibility, add resources when sales peak, but cost nothing when sales go down. The 'knowledge industry' employs intellectuals who need to be organized, but is strategically dependent on free intellectuals such as poets, authors and reviewers. The former are officially part of the organization, the latter are part of the external network. The search for the organization of the knowledge-based company partly concerns the form of affiliation for those who generate revenue: employment, full- or part-time work, ownership or shared ownership, and legal design. Financial and tax considerations may influence the structure of the organization. Self-employed freelance workers are common in, for example, journalism and the performing arts. A one-man firm can grow of course from hiring employees but the more common way is through partnering. This is typical for most consultants and craftsmen. The employment service industry is one of the fastest growing industries providing both temporary and permanent staff on many levels. One reason for their growth is increased outsourcing of internal service. Computer consulting firms have often earned the major share of their revenue from renting programmers on long-term contracts. When visiting a corporation today, we may be met at the reception desk by personnel provided by a security company. Building projects have always been network organizations, set up for a specific job and limited in time. Some projects are small, others are huge and last for decades, such as the construction of the Eurotunnel under the English Channel and the bridge between Denmark and Sweden.

---

[13] Hedberg et al. (2000).
[14] Handy (1990, p. 87ff).

Finally, an interesting observation and paradox is that while relationships between suppliers and customers are becoming closer, relationships between employers and employees are becoming looser and more flexible. This is further evidence of the network properties of an organization, and that the distinction between the company and the market is being blurred.

From fenced structures to boundaryless processes

Hierarchy means 'holy management', a designation that may fit the egos of many executives. Its next of kin is *bureaucracy*, which means 'management from the desk', totally impersonal. The dawn of the dissolution of hierarchy is found in the establishment of profit centres and the introduction of market mechanisms inside the company (R24). *Heterarchy* (multi-dimensional management) and *adhocracy* (management to fit a temporary state of affairs) are better designations for today's organization and management.

Bureaucracy and adhocracy are two extremes; the demand for rule-based governance is confronted with the demands for flexibility and adaptability to individual situations. The *project organization* – which was dealt with in R25, in connection with the internal customer and interfunctional and interhierarchical dependency – used to be a temporary supplement to a relatively fixed hierarchical base organization. Today, the base organization is increasingly dynamic and becomes more of a parent project for a series of subsidiary projects. Compare the dichotomy parent company–subsidiary which applies to stable base organizations related to each other through formal and legally obliging decisions. The network organization can be characterized as a sophisticated and timely version of the project organization.

The variability of adhocracy is also part of culture and lifestyle. Adhocracy is characterized by sensitivity for the unexpected, quick action, high degree of freedom, support from management and colleagues, generosity, accepted and necessary messiness, and only the sky is the limit. Bureaucracy stands for the planned and repressive, where the rule and ritual are given priority to the actual issue and the outcome. Bureaucracy in the government sector, industrial companies and consulting firms has a proven record of suffocating adhocratic tendencies.

Further, in bureaucracies the rule is the rule; common sense and results are overruled by ritual. But it sounds like a contradiction that it is not uncommon in corporate and government bureaucracies alike that formal organization is merely a front. Behind it, management and employees play a different and flexible game where those who are best at dodging the rules become the most powerful. I doubt that this is a good strategy as an internal mess and insecurity will taint the way the company relates to customers and other stakeholders.

In its extreme application adhocracy leads to chaos. Again, paradoxically, a great deal of discipline is required to make adhocracy work. The knowledge-based organization therefore needs a dash of bureaucracy. In the language of Tao, *yin* is the adhocratic property and *yang* the bureaucratic. The dynamism is in the tension and oscillation between yin and yang. If yang is given too much rope, the organization is petrified. If yin takes over, chaos and destruction follow. The extremes are companions, not adversaries. The combined outcome is *dynamic stability*.

Chaos and ambiguity are central concepts in Peters and Watermans' classic book *In Search of Excellence* (1982), and later in Peters' books *Thriving on Chaos* (1985) and *Liberation Management* (1992). Ehrlemark (1978) said that 'to consciously keep the firm unmanaged and unmanageable to such an extent that its stability and development is created out of disturbances and disorder is perhaps the true skill in management'. Stacey (2007), in *Strategic Management and Organisational Dynamics*, takes chaos research from physics as his vantage point. The concept *dissipative structures* was used by Nobel laureate and chaos scientist Ilya Prigogene. Dissipative structures are spawned in volatile processes in systems which are in disequilibrium:[15] '… most of reality, instead of being orderly, stable and equilibrial, is seething and bubbling with change, disorder, and process'. Disorder and order coexist and become conditions for each other. Chaos theory in its popular form has become known for the 'butterfly effect': 'When a butterfly flaps its wings in Beijing it affects the weather in New York'. Teeny-weeny episodes have an impact in the spirit of the adage 'the straw that broke the camel's back'. When networks become complex and interactions are countless, a small episode can propagate in the network with an unpredictable and significant impact. The tipping point has been reached.

The staff of a knowledge-based organization consists largely of intellectuals and professionals. Independence and opportunities to develop are conditional for their performance. Managing intellectuals is 'institutionalized anarchy', it is managing the unmanageable: 'Managing them is a craft or trade, maybe even an art. It is definitely not a science'. [16] Or in Drucker's terms:[17] 'As the business organization is restructuring itself around knowledge and information, it will increasingly come to resemble nonbusiness – the hospital, the university, or the opera – rather than the manufacturing company of 1920, in which there were a few generalists called 'managers' and a great many unskilled and unknowing 'hands' doing as they were told.'

The mechanical mode of operation from manufacturing which contaminated – and still contaminates – life in many organizations is obsolete even for its original application. But hospitals, universities and operas also face gargantuan hardships and are searching for

---

[15] Prigogine and Stengers (1985).
[16] Donovan (1989).
[17] Drucker (1988b, p. 3).

new structures. Health care in most countries is in a state of flux and transition, and university bureaucracies are notorious.

Even 20 years ago, Zuboff (1988) called hierarchies obsolete and dysfunctional in an era when real power is IT-based knowledge. But there are also proponents for hierarchies, and hierarchies are common in practice. Jaques claims that '... 35 years of research have convinced me that managerial hierarchy is the most efficient, the hardiest, and in fact the most natural structure ever devised for large organizations'.[18]

Entrepreneurship is in vogue. It is associated with innovation but it has got more to do with an ability to implement rather than innovate. Seldom is the inventor of a product or method the best person to market the product. Most of those who we think of as entrpreneurs took an existing concept and exploited it systematically and ferociously. Add to that luck; the right timing is hard to figure out intellectually. Nokia is an example of a declining company which had never really made a good profit and whose stock was worth very little. It was a conglomerate of rubber boots, toilet paper and TV sets – and a little division in telecom. Ericsson was offered Nokia but did not want it. Around 1990, the tide turned. The current CEO had been fired and an unusually bright and committed person who worked at Nokia, Jorma Ollila, was appointed CEO after the chairman of the board had committed suicide. Everything seemed to be ripe, every little piece fell in place. They decided to sell out the diverse products lines and focus on mobile phones. The mobile technology was mature, a phone could be sold at a low price, and there was a dedicated leader. The rest is history. Nokia is a world leader, innovator and entrepreneur and marketer.

Peters and Waterman (1982) provided an expressive epithet for an informal phenomenon: skunk works. In R&D and engineering, skunk works are guerrilla operations; they are the outlaws of the formal organization. The skunks are passionate technicians and hackers obsessed with an idea. They hide their work from management who may be too remote from the pulse of the market and new technology. Some of the most successful innovations were skunk products in a period of their development. Among them are the Saab Turbo, the first commercially successful application of the turbo engine on a passenger car, and Losec, an ulcer medication, which has made Astra-Zeneca one of the world's richest pharmaceutical companies. We do not know how many excellent ideas have been systematic victims of abortion. One should not forget, however, that many of the skunk products fail in the market even if the technology is supreme.

Skunks are illegitimate adhocrats. They can be punished and rejected. They can be tacitly tolerated, thus giving innovative minds and entrepreneurs opportunities to realize ideas with support of company resources, without being burdened by internal red tape; they become 'intrapreneurs'. A passive skunk tolerance seems to be quite common. The

---

[18] Jaques (1990, p. 127).

global corporation 3M – best known to consumers for Scotch tape – allows its R&D people to set aside 15 per cent of their time for own projects. There are also 'extrapreneurs' who leave as employees but continue to collaborate with the 'parent' or take over some of its customers.[19]

The network organization has affinity to the 'transcendent organization.' It is an organizational format which exists deep in the consciousness of the members of the organization; and it is the base for collective consciousness. In simple terminology it means 'gang mentality'. We have probably all noticed that individuals can behave in one way when you are alone with them, while they become something else – better or worse – when the are together in a group. It goes deeper than the observable signs and activities of a corporate culture, its formal and informal structures and dos and don'ts. It is manifested in our intuitive and spontaneous reactions.[20] Zohar and Marshall, who talk about the quantum society, an approach inspired by the quantum theory of physics, say:[21] 'Persons are not quite the same as solitary individuals, nor are they a crowd. Persons are living networks of biology and emotions and memories and relationships. Each is unique, but none can flourish alone. Each in some way contains others, and is contained by others, without his or her personal truth ever being wholly isolated or exhausted.' This is a fitting description of the Russian relationship doll, which was used to demonstrate the existence of intertwined market, mega and nano relationships in Chapter 1.

A daring metaphor is provided by quantum physics in approaching reality as either particles or waves. 'The wave aspect is associated with our unstructured potential, with our spreading out across the boundaries of space, time, choice and identity. The particle aspect gives us our structured reality, our boundaries, our clearly defined selves, our ordered thoughts, our social roles and conventions, our rules and patterns,' says Zohar and Marshall. They say that atomism rejects relationships and gives rise to confrontation, whereas we need 'relational holism'. This holistic view of society is akin to both RM and network organizations, and the statement from Chapter 1 that society is a network of relationships. We can let the particles be the well defined, the individual, the formal organization, the buildings, the equipment, that is, everything visible and tangible. The waves then represent the relationships, the collective consciousness and the organizational culture, the coherent processes and the dynamics.

In conclusion, dynamic processes receive a progressively larger role and fixed hierarchies play a diminishing role. This does not mean that well-structured hierarchies become meaningless, rather that processes are given the lead part, as is shown in Figure 7.5. The understanding of processes expands, which was pointed out in R25. The whole company

---

[19] Johnsson and Hägg (1987, pp. 64–74).
[20] See Harung (1999); Gustavsson (2001).
[21] Zohar and Marshall (1993; quotation from p. 64; subsequent quotations from pp. 82, 6 and 85).

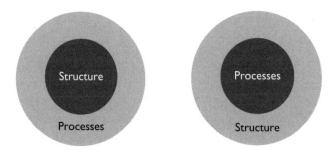

Figure 7.5 Shifting from structure in focus supported by processes, to processes in focus supported by structure

can be regarded as a coherent business process and not as insulated activities which occur in functional compartments and hierarchical tiers. The processes extend beyond the corporation and unite it with the market. The network is boundaryless and inside the network there is interaction. The sequential has lost in importance and the simultaneous has gained, as has been shown in concurrent engineering and the value constellation.

Our need for security

In Chapter 1, the rationale for RM was defined as:

- Enhanced retention and duration in order to improve financial performance;
- A way of creating better conditions for efficient marketing and management.

In the most militant of cases – hypercompetition – competitors turn into lethal adversaries and marketing warfare breaks loose. In the most benevolent case, competitors turn into colleagues and buddies. Or maybe they try to be a bit of both: 'Businessmen and industrialists who on the one hand fight for radical freedom of the *laissez-faire* market none the less find themselves clubbing into lobbies and cartels.'[22] History also shows that relationships and collaboration have always been in the centre of business activity. Why is this so? Let me venture an explanation.

Both consumers and companies need a basic level of security. Security is associated with words such as promises, honesty, trust, reliability, predictability, stability, fear of being swindled or let down, and reduction of uncertainty and risk.

Promise is a core concept in all relationships.[23] Only in exceptional cases are promises, legal promises – contracts, which can be forcibly honoured with the help of courts. Most

---

[22] Zohar and Marshall (1993, pp. 73–74).

[23] The promise concept is little treated in marketing literature: see Levitt (1983); and Calonius (2006).

promises are made without written contracts, they are moral and ethical promises to perform a service, deliver goods or collaborate in a development project. The qualities of certain suppliers and their offerings are easy to assess in advance (search qualities), whereas others must be tried (experience qualities). For customers it may often be difficult to assess what they got even after the purchase; they are left to trust the promises of the supplier (credence qualities).[24] Such is the case with, for example, management consulting services or a visit to the doctor.

The market – customers, suppliers, intermediaries, competitors – as well as society in general offer so much insecurity and risk that only what is by nature unpredictable should be left pending. What can be planned should be planned. What cannot be planned can best be handled through constructive acceptance of the unexpected. Companies must make certain that promises are fulfilled, both in their role of suppliers and customers. The supplier must be reliable and deliver the right thing at the right time to the right place; JIT (just-in-time) is the most advanced manifestation of those requirements. The customer should be reliable and not cancel an order or dodge payment. Companies need predictability so that, for example, production can be planned and performed with high productivity and quality.

If society offers a weak infrastructure, companies cannot work efficiently. Frequent electricity failures, unreliable airlines and airports, and a corrupt and unpredictable government sector make it difficult to compete with more reliable societies. When US Mail could not promise delivery, a market was opened for FedEx, DHL and others, who took responsibility for delivery promises. Also, the internal market must be reliable and predictable. There is the story about a New York company that sent internal letters and parcels, addressed to people in the very same building, via Federal Express. The mail first went to the Federal Express hub in Memphis, Tennessee, and then back to the building in New York. Delivery within 24 hours was guaranteed, whereas the internal mail needed a couple of days and offered no guarantee. Having experienced the internal mail of large corporations, this anecdote could very well be true. Companies can obtain security through several sources:

- *Relationships* can create security. People trust each other and feel committed to make future business with each other. The relationships open up for a plus sum game, for win–win. This is what the whole book is about; it is the soul of RM.
- Security may also be created through *laws and other formal regulations as well as institutions* that secure compliance. Its unique properties and consequences were discussed in R16 and R17, the law-based relationship and the criminal network. But law is no

---

[24] 'Search qualities' and 'experience qualities' are terms borrowed from Nelson (1970), and 'credence qualities' from Darby and Karni (1973).

automatic source of security: 'Formal contracts are often ineffective in taking care of the uncertainties, conflicts and crises that a business relationship is bound to go through over time.'[25]

- *Knowledge* as a relationship driver was treated in R21. If the customers' knowledge is high, they can rest securely in their knowledge. For most consumers it is a problem to buy medical services or a used car; consumers rarely possess the expertise to assess their quality. The used car trade seems to remain an industry where customer ignorance is a natural part of its business mission. In today's society – which is frequently referred to as the knowledge-based society – knowledge is fragmented. We are dependent on value propositions which we only understand to a limited degree. We may be able to use them, but we do not know what is underneath the surface. We become dependent on intermediaries – brokers in knowledge and insecurity[26] – to help us, especially if something goes wrong. Even if we gain more knowledge in absolute terms, the need for knowledge grows faster and we become increasingly ignorant in relative terms. We are left to base our decisions on symbols such as corporate identities and brand names, and what we believe they represent. The image and the parasocial relationships from R13 become important substitutes for knowledge.

- *Business culture and ethics* – the informal regulations/institutions – can also contribute to security. The culture can be very distinct, with clear rules and a clear ethical code telling us what is right and wrong. It can work like the parlour game where the rules are not negotiable; if the dice shows five dots, you move five steps. The culture can comprise clear rewards and punishments, and those who misbehave are excluded from the business community. If it is a commercial predatory culture as in Russia and many other immature market economies today, insecurity rules. As is emphasized by transaction cost analysis, the rational behaviour of organizations is impeded by human opportunism.

These ways of achieving security are not mutually exclusive. Even strong relationships and excellent knowledge may need a dash of formal law. A strong business culture includes social relationships and personal proximity. The United States is an example of a culture with legal dominance and weaker relationships with Japan as its opposite. Inside a country there are also differences in cultures between industries and places. Global competition and mass markets create anonymity and insecurity about the rules of the game, which can explain a growing need for trust. Con artists are successful in business life through their ability to instil trust and confidence.

---

[25] Håkansson and Snehota (1995, p. 8).
[26] Giarini and Stahel (1998).

The ratio between the importance of the four sources can vary. If you are highly knowledgeable in one field, this may be enough to instil security. If the business culture is strong and no one breaks the rules and the law, security also becomes high.

| INSIGHT | *My conclusion is that long-term and close relationships best satisfy the need for security, albeit with some support from the other sources.* |

Synthesis 1: from exclusive hierarchies to inclusive networks and processes

The theme for this chapter has been RM and the network organization as reflections of one another. With a certain amount of graphic playfulness, the treatment of this theme can be summarized in five images of the corporation (Figure 7.6). The first image (a) is the fortress, the *clearly delimited hierarchical structure*. The second (b) is the *matrix organization* that was treated in R28 as an expansion of the hierarchy and a rudimentary network. Both are traditional images, even if the matrix signals the dissolution of the strict hierarchy. The third image (c) shows *a multi-dimensional network*. Its core, the unique competency which empowers the organization, is marked in black. We recognize the characteristic features of RM, the network of relationships within which the parties interact. We surmise the network organization in which actors other than employees are let in, among them customers. The fourth image (d) accentuates the *boundaryless and amorphous amoeba* features of the network organization, the corporation as a fuzzy set. The last image (e) takes a full step toward the *process organization*, a series of harmonious waves and completely concerted processes.

The new is often presented as an extreme alternative, an opposite to the old. The network organization as the completely flexible organization with low transaction costs and rapid adjustment to new conditions is an idealized and absurdly simplistic image. The same can be said for RM, which may seem too benign and harmonious to gain credibility in a greedy and imperfect business environment where hypercompetition is lurking around the corner. The new images may appear as mirages in the wilderness; perhaps they can even erect a new mental prison. We may be conned into 'seeing' something in the same way as we 'see' the magician sawing someone in half. RM and the network organization are rather directions and intentions, emphasizing properties in marketing and organization which have been neglected and must now be given more prominence.

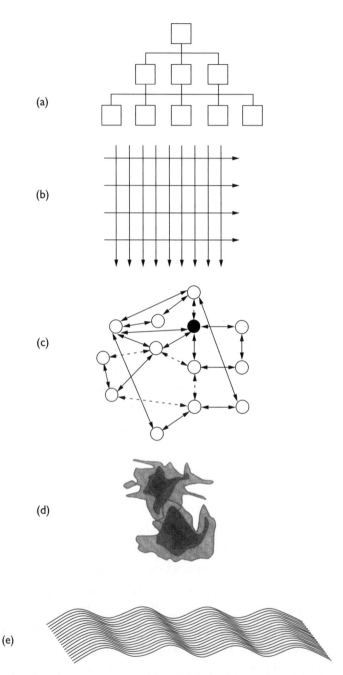

Figure 7.6 Organizational structure transitions: (a) the hierarchy with clear boundaries; (b) the matrix, the two-dimensional network; (c) the imaginary organization first reproduced as a network; (d) then as an amoeba with fuzzy boundaries which dissolve from a core competency; and (e) finally, the process organization, the corporation as a series or processes of waves

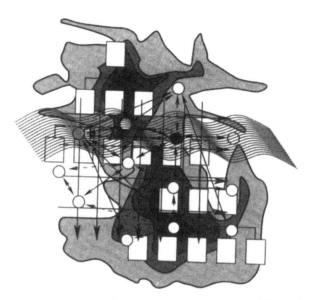

Figure 7.7 The corporation as many images at the same time: hierarchy, matrix, network, amoeba and processes

In Figure 7.7, the hierarchy, the matrix, the network, the amoeba and the processes have been superimposed on each other into one single image, but without merging their structures. All these structures coexist in various proportions. But the proportions are being re-examined; the role of the hierarchy is reduced in favour of dynamic changes and processes. As the figure shows, it is hard to visualize all of this at the same time; we risk seeing nothing at all, or we just see a mess.

In summary, these are the characteristics of the link between RM and network organizations:

- RM lives in the market, society and organization. The network organization adds dimensions, which enhance our understanding for the evolution and functions of RM.
- An organization exists, but not in a physical and tangible body. Its most important resources – its intellectual capital and core competency – do not show in the balance sheet; they show in the network. This in turn leads to a conclusion which has been stated in previous chapters: companies do not compete with companies but networks compete with networks.
- The network organization is an inclusive organization as compared to the exclusive hierarchy that puts up boundaries. The boundaries between the company and its markets are fuzzy and people engaged are not the same as people employed. A large part of those engaged, sometimes the larger part, are found outside the formal organization. The customer is integrated with the organization and the customer base is a central

resource, sometimes the most important resource. In this way, the roles of supplier and customer become less obvious; value is co-created through their interaction.

■ Increasingly ubiquitous, mobile and flexible IT offers new opportunities for RM and the network organization to develop. The e-relationship must, however, be balanced against social and human relationships. High tech needs high touch; eCRM needs hCRM.

■ The company becomes a parent project and what is traditionally known as a project becomes a subsidiary project. The organization becomes a series of dynamic and coherent processes rather than a stable, compartmentalized hierarchy.

Synthesis 2: from partial to complete marketing equilibrium

A conclusion from R2 (the customer–supplier–competitor relationship) was that the market is governed by competition, collaboration and regulations/institutions. Together, these three forces strive in the direction of a marketing equilibrium – without ever reaching this heavenly state though. It is important to remind ourselves what we said earlier about dissipative structures and the tensions that create a dynamic state as long as no single force becomes excessively dominant.

This conclusion will be carried further in this section by integrating it with the network organization. Marketing equilibrium concerns the state of the external market, whereas the same notion can also be applied to the internal market of a company. Each of these two instances will subsequently be referred to as a partial equilibrium.

The circle that showed the three forces of partial marketing equilibrium in Figure 2.1 is equally needed as a balancing force inside an organization. The corporation is regulated by its control systems, both hard and soft ones. Among the hard ones are the financial control system, production planning and marketing planning; among the soft ones are business missions, values and collective consciousness. These control systems correspond to regulations/institutions. Competition and the price mechanism have been brought inside the company according to R24, and many of the other Rs support that notion.

The market and the company are thus governed by the same three mechanisms: competition, collaboration and regulations/institutions (Figure 7.8). The proportions between the forces as well as their content can vary between companies and markets. Each specific marketing situation – both inside and outside the company – struggles to reach its own specific marketing equilibrium.

Figure 7.9 combines *partial marketing equilibrium* from R2 (Figure 2.1) with the image of the complex network reality from Figure 7.3, where the clear boundary between the company and the environment has been dissolved. We can then speak about *complete marketing equilibrium*.

	Competition	Collaboration	Regulations and Institutions
Traditional perception of a firm's internal operations	No	Yes	Yes
Traditional perception of the operations of the market	Yes	No	No
New perception of the firm and the market	Yes	Yes	Yes

Figure 7.8 Today, the company and the market are controlled by the same forces

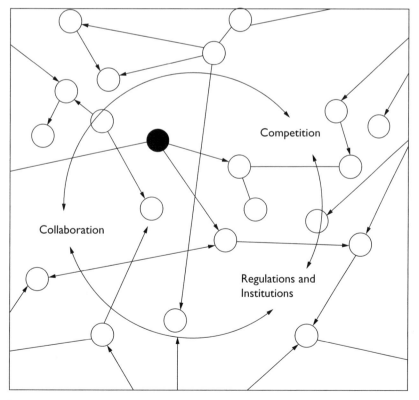

Figure 7.9 Complete marketing equilibrium in the network, both 'outside' and 'inside' the organization

---

IN BRIEF

This chapter has dealt with the consequences of RM/CRM for organizational structures, and also its effect on society. The organizational consequences of RM and the RM consequences for network organizations have been analysed. The emphasis that RM puts on security through relationships, with collaboration as one of the three forces that make the market economy work, and attempts to reach complete marketing equilibrium have been explained. This is a tentative synthesis of several trends in today's management, made visible through the mental images provided by RM and the network organization.

QUESTIONS FOR DISCUSSION

1 How do (a) neoclassical economics; (b) transaction cost theory; (c) systems theory; and (d) network theory relate to RM?

2 What is characteristic of network theory and why is it claimed that network theory is superior to other theories in developing marketing thinking?

3 We try to achieve stability and security in companies at the same time as we may want change and development to take place, also knowing that change will occur irrespective of what we do. How can RM help to create security?

4 What is meant by the expressions 'exclusive hierarchies' and 'inclusive networks'?

5 What is meant by 'partial marketing equilibrium' and 'complete marketing equilibrium'?

Chapter

8

RM/CRM – drivers of a paradigm shift in marketing

INTRODUCTION

This chapter is about the evolution of RM/CRM, and its theoretical and practical foundation. The chapter sums up the message of the book. It claims that RM/CRM – fuelled by S-D logic, lean consumption and the many-to-many network approach – provide a paradigm shift, a new way of approaching marketing. In a sense we have come to the end; in another sense we are only starting out on an adventurous expedition into the consequences of a new marketing paradigm.

Summing up theoretical and practical contributions to RM/CRM

The word *theory* comes from Greek and has the same roots as *theatre*. Both theory and theatre present mental images or scenes, which can show something of interest to an audience. It is an old truth that nothing is so practical as a good theory. In an applied discipline like marketing, good theory should be grounded in the real world – but often is so only superficially. A map is a theoretical representation of geography. It is obvious that it must be well drawn and currently valid to provide guidance and not lead us in the wrong direction, lure us into morasses or make us drive straight into a rock.

I have also stressed the need to utilize tacit knowledge, the knowledge we have but cannot communicate in words, numbers or graphs, just through action and results. Tacit knowledge holds elements of integration between scientific knowledge and a host of other influences: experience, intuition, common sense, instinct, insights, wisdom, sound judgement. They may be frowned upon in science but they don't care; they are there anyway. Just pretending they are not counterproductive; they contribute to theory and practice alike. Theory and science are always dependent on the personality of both the individual and the groups to which they belong.

The quality pioneer W. Edwards Deming has said that 'experience tells nothing unless it is related to theory'[1] and Robert Pirsig, in his philosophical novel *Lila*, says that 'Data without generalization is just gossip.'[2] These statements imply that data are of no value unless they can be structured and organized in a category, concept or theory, which can later be applied in more than a single case. Theory is a tool to derive meaning out of interviews, observations, statistics, advice, ideas and experiences thus helping to generate usable knowledge. The most burdensome task is not to collect – or rather generate – more data, but to analyse, interpret and combine what is already there and make some sense out of it. Theory provides a context, a map that offers guidance.

---

[1] As quoted at the Ninth World Productivity Congress, Istanbul, June 1995.
[2] Pirsig (1992, p. 70).

Table 8.1 Contributions to the shaping of RM/CRM

Marketing management	Relational approaches	Non-marketing influences	Practitioner contributions
Consumer goods	Services marketing	Quality management	Cases
Marketing mix	B2B	Accounting	Memoirs
4Ps	RM	Organization theory	Media reports
More Ps	CRM, one-to-one	IT	My own experience in
Sales management and negotiations	Lean consumption		business and as consumer
	S-D logic		
	Many-to-many marketing		

If the marketing that is presented in textbooks and seminars built only on the fragmented contributions from scholarly research, it would be lightweight. It is necessary to fill the gaps with the best available knowledge, namely the knowledge from 'those who were there when it happened'. It is not evident what should be counted as theoretical contributions and what are contributions from practitioners. In scholarly research, theory is accompanied by empirical data. Empirical comes from the Greek *empeiria*, meaning *experience*. In the language of science, empirical refers to real world data generated with certain methods and techniques. Note that the language of many business schools has been impoverished by limiting the term empirical to quantitative data and statistical processing.[3] It is therefore imperative to add the knowledge and experience of *the reflective human*. Going back to Chapter 1, this guy appeared in many shapes: *the reflective practitioner, the reflective customer* and *the reflective researcher*.

It was mentioned in Chapter 1 that RM is inspired by many sources. They are summed up in Table 8.1. The imprints of these sources are found in the description of the 30Rs.

The 4Ps are neither Ps nor 4 any more

We will first take a look at the characteristics of traditional marketing management, marketing mix and 4P approaches; then proceed to look at its role today, today's marketing mix and its 'Ps' where P stands as a symbol for a marketing activity or strategy and finally relate them to RM/CRM.

---

[3] For a discourse on the limitations of methodology in research in marketing, see Gummesson (2001b).

Textbooks and teaching in marketing management are primarily structured around marketing mix theory.[4] The core of this theory is the use of various means to influence the market. The best-known variant is based on four parameters which all start with a P: product, price, promotion, place. It is popularly known as the 4Ps.

In Chapter 1, the 2004 definition of marketing by the *American Marketing Association* (*AMA*) was scrutinized and amended to fit relational developments in marketing. The previous definition from 1985 represented marketing management and mix thinking: 'Marketing is the process of planning and executing the conception, pricing, promotion, and distribution of ideas, goods, and services to create exchanges that satisfy individual and organizational objectives.'

In the world of marketing management, marketing mix and the 4Ps, suppliers are perceived as independent units in the market. Using various means, the supplier exercises an impact on the market. This may occur under conditions which are more or less uncontrollable by a single firm, such as consumer tastes, the general economic situation and legislation. How much of these conditions the supplier can influence depends on its size, power, creativity, persistence and not least coincidence. Even if there is a desire to keep one's customers, marketing management theory and education are mainly about transaction marketing.

The thinking behind the marketing mix is that a supplier who feels capable of satisfying a need must go for it and make sure that the consumer buys. In practice the 4P approach has led to a manipulative attitude to people.[5] If we just select the right measures in the right combination and with the right intensity, the consumer will buy; it is a matter of putting pressure on the consumer. The consumer is often a locked black box, maybe with a tiny peephole. We often know little of what is in the mind of consumers, how they think and feel and what their motives are. It is more of a stimulus–response model, similar to the fisherman's relationship to fish. If we improve the bait, the fish will bite and it is hooked. How the fish feels about it has been less considered. The supplier and its salespeople are the active party. Sometimes the consumer is pigheaded and rejects an offering. Conclusion: we used the wrong bait. To face such a challenge – 'Never take no for an answer!' – and turning it to our advantage is part and parcel of an aggressive sales culture. The Duveen legacy from Chapter 1 illustrates this in its extreme. It requires a lot of tacit knowledge, intuition and experience and theoretical models may help – and so could a bit of luck.

---

[4] Those who wish to study marketing management and mix theory can turn to any book with 'marketing management' in the title. See also the critical discussions in Brownlie and Saren (1992); Grönroos (1997); and Gummesson (2002), and the anthology edited by Saren *et al.* (2007).

[5] Anthony Cunningham, Ireland's first marketing professor, has pointed out to me that consumer manipulation was not the intent when marketing thinkers began to teach need orientation and the 4Ps. In practice, however, it may have turned out otherwise.

Instead of being customer oriented, marketing management in practice is *supplier oriented*. There is ample experience behind the use of the marketing mix and it is often functional as seen from the supplier's perspective. The marketing mix contains problems, however. One is how to mix the activities. What will be the effect of a certain mix and what happens to the other measures if the value of one of them is altered? What will happen if we reduce the price by 10 per cent? If we invest more in advertising? If we launch a new product for a new segment?

The marketer tries to find an *optimal mix* – or more realistically a *satisfying mix* – which gets a superior response on the market and at the same time, creates profits. Because of the complexity in the interaction between different factors and the uncertainty in a competitive market, the mix will be the outcome of the availability of data, analytic rationality, experience, opinions, emotions, intuition and visions.

In Chapter 6, we mentioned the preference for clear guidelines about the rights and the wrongs in marketing and their effect on return on relationships (ROR). We would prefer strict, scientifically proven links between what we do and the outcome. Failure to establish such desired links was mentioned.

The marketing mix theory is founded on studies of the marketing of consumer goods, not of services, not of B2B. The literature usually zooms in on the narrower concept of consumer and shows less interest in the generic concept of customer. However, a large share of the studies concern distribution channels, thereby including a part of both service and B2B, namely wholesalers and retailers. The channel companies are service producers, but they are treated from a goods perspective.

Marketing mix concerns mass marketing and standardized consumer goods. Such goods are usually packaged and piled on shelves in self-service stores. The interaction between the personnel of the store and the consumer is minimal and left to brief encounters at the cash register. The stores are 'service factories' and the service consists of convenient location and opening hours; goods available on the shelves; packaging and signs that display information about product and price; several checkout points; and aids such as trolleys, baskets and bags. Consumer goods also include capital goods such as freezers and DVD players. The sales through independent small stores and stores with manual service are frugally treated in the literature. They rely more heavily on personal interaction, whereas supermarkets represent an impersonal mass marketing approach.

The 4Ps have been widely exposed after their introduction in a textbook by McCarthy, first published in 1960. The 4P structure is a role model for globally circulated textbooks, all with very similar content. The Ps have also been expanded into more Ps in order to cover the marketing domain more completely. An inventory of marketing mixes shows that there is a rich variety and little coherence.[6]

---

[6] Constantinides (2006)

Table 8.2 4Ps and more Ps

McCarthy, 4P	Judd, 5P	Booms and Bitner, 7P	Baumgartner, 15P
Product	Product	Product	Product
Price	Price	Price	Price
Promotion	Promotion	Promotion	Promotion
Place	Place	Place	Place
	People	People	People
		Physical evidence	Politics
		Process	Public relations
			Probe
			Partition
			Prioritize
			Position
			Profit
			Plan
			Performance
			Positive implementations

The 4P logic is straightforward. A supplier needs products, needs to price them, to promote them and distribute them to the place where the customer can buy them. The Ps have been extended into 5Ps by adding *people* (Judd 1987), and Booms and Bitner (1981) suggested the 7Ps for services marketing, the original ones plus *people, physical evidence* and *process*. The three new service Ps stress that the customer is a participant in production together with the supplier and through this is exposed to marketing, that goods influence services marketing, and that services are a series of activities and not static objects. In the last column is Baumgratners (1991) attempt to be complete, having found 15 Ps (Table 8.2).

There is a lot of truth in the 4Ps and other mixes, and they are a good start. But the pedagogical beauty of the P format may curb more visionary attempts to develop marketing theory. The major problem is that they are supplier-centric first, and only secondarily consider customer needs.

Even if the 4Ps form the hard core of the marketing mix theory, they are incomplete and therefore many other areas have been added in marketing management textbooks. These include marketing strategy and its link to business mission, goals, objectives and corporate strategies; market segmentation; market research techniques; marketing planning procedures and the design of the marketing and sales organization. At the same time, the marketing mix theory excludes or treats marginally such things as complaints handling, invoicing, design and production. The 4Ps approach is narrowly limited to functions and it is not an integral part of a business and CRM system. It is marketing management, but not marketing-oriented management.

The marketing mix theory is a child of the standardized mass production of the industrial society and its dissociation from the individual consumer. The contemporary value-creating network society clamours for another type of production. Even if mass production and mass marketing will always play a significant role in economic life, it should not be the reigning godfather. Instead, the centre of attention should be customization of value propositions and a more individualized marketing, often in a combination expressed by the paradoxical concept of *customized mass marketing*.

Marketing management and marketing mix theory particularly treat four phenomena connected to relationships, networks and interaction:

- The zero relationship (R0): The main focus on transactions has influenced the definition of the zero relationship. Price, being one of the 4Ps and the core variable in economics to explain the functioning of the market economy, is part of the zero relationship together with convenience.
- The relationship between the supplier and the customer (R1): In the marketing mix theory, this is 'personal selling', a subcategory to the third P, promotion. It deals with the face-to-face encounters between a salesperson and a customer with the purpose of persuading the customer to buy.
- The treatment of competition, which is comprehensive in both marketing management and specific competition literature and economics. Here it is defined as the relationship between the buyer, the current supplier and the competitors (R2). It attempts to find marketing equilibrium – not just the market equilibrium between supply and demand – where competition, collaboration and institutions/regulations strive towards balance.
- Physical distribution of goods is found under the fourth P, place, presented as networks of distribution channels far beyond the physical goods (R3).

Within the marketing mix theory, image and brands are treated, but not with a relationship angle. I still do not consider it a classic area for marketing, especially as the knowledge on brand management – with brand equity, brand identity, brand architecture and the far-reaching suggestion that brands are the core business rather than the product – are children of recent attention and theory. They have contributed to the parasocial relationships (R13).

If RM/CRM take the place of traditional marketing management and marketing mix theory as an overriding structure for marketing thinking, the question comes up: Are the 4Ps (5Ps, 6Ps, etc.) dead? The answer is – No! Product, price, promotion, place and the other Ps will always be important – and they have their role in RM/CRM – but their role changes. In short, I see it this way.

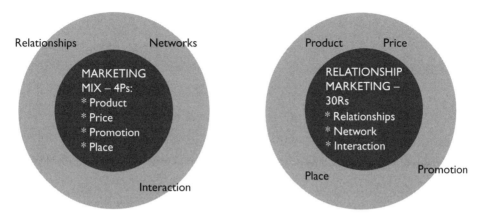

Figure 8.1 A shift in hegemony: from the 4Ps to relationships, networks and interaction

I would like to dissolve the 4Ps and just talk about Ps as symbols for supplier-controlled activities for managing customers and persuading them to buy. A certain element of persuasion and manipulation will always be needed in marketing. But the role of the Ps should be on level 2 instead of a level 1; a focus shift should take place (Figure 8.1). In practice, the Ps became too manipulative – even if this was not the original intention – and this has damaged the credibility and functionality of the marketing discipline. The Ps are also directed to mass marketing, which is becoming less dominant, but will always be part of marketing.

Let us see what the marketing mix includes today. Every strategy is a large topic in itself and here I can only touch on some aspects. Pricing service is such an intricate and not well-researched area, and so is the distribution of service (place). They deserve future attention. I will expand on the two Ps that I have studied more in depth, product and promotion. They are not so easy to tell apart and they require relationships, networks and interaction.

Originally 'product' was *goods* and later *services* were added. Marketing makes many efforts to find a deeper meaning behind what we are buying and consuming. *Value proposition* has been advanced here, supported by S-D logic. We are also known to seek *experiences*, *kicks* and *dreams* through motorcycles, parties, diving in the Barrier Reef or visiting the Vatican Museum to marvel at Michelangelo's paintings. The product can also be an international *event* like the European Song Contest or a local exhibition of roses. The product is also defined through *storytelling*; we buy a story rather than the product itself. For example, all stories about the love lives of celebrities help build fame and sell tickets to theatres. The product today is also *information* where websites and search engines such as Google have opened up a new marketplace.

'Promotion' once consisted of *advertising, personal selling* and *sales promotion (SP)*. Today the forms for promotion have become more sophisticated. Advertising pops into our homes through television, radio and computers. It enters music through music videos and movies through product placement. What car James Bond will drive in his next film and what mobile phone he will use to call his girlfriends depend on which manufacturer pays the most.

Advertising through the mass media and direct mail is supplemented by *public relations, PR*, with the aim to create a positive image of a company in the market and society, preferably through editorial text and documentaries to make it stand out as more credible. A lot is about *branding* and loading offerings with perceptions about the supplier and their products. In a Formula 1 race the cars are covered by logotypes and World Cup skiers are advertising pillars. Events are increasingly dependent on such *sponsorship*. A cultural or sports event gives the sponsoring companies an opportunity to expose themselves to the market and even get in personal contact with customers. They become associated with the event and the glory of the winner of an Olympic gold medal is reflected on them.

On a mega strategic level *politics, lobbying* and *public opinion formation* come in. These means are used in both honest and dishonest ways. Public opinion sometimes acts with common sense, sometimes not. For example, lobbyists can educate ignorant politicians but they can also corrupt them for selfish reasons and circumvent the democratic process.

Scientific research and *education* have also received growing attention by companies. The most obvious example is the pharmaceutical industry and their influence over medical research. Scientists are dependent on their sponsorship and pharmaceutical companies need the knowledge produced in research hospitals, but also to bask in the prestige of science, thus adding to their credibility in the public eye.

IT has given rise to *call centres* which companies themselves run as customer contact and help desks or outsource to specialized call centre companies. *Telemarketing* has entered into a new phase. Both these operations require plenty of staff and add employment opportunities, but are equally dependent on IT. *Email* and *websites, mobile phones* and *text messaging* have redesigned the marketing landscape. The dissolution of the boundaries between telephones, TV and computers is spawning a new world for marketers and customers. IT also causes problems. The Internet architecture is not built to protect against dishonesty and today 30 per cent of the cost of a computer and its software goes to patching unsafe systems and continuously developing new security programmes to curb abuse. Spam and pop-up windows are annoying elements, but even worse is the financial fraud that customers get exposed to.

Figure 8.2 shows these strategies on a network background. Why? Because these strategies, with a large number of sub-strategies, are all interrelated and appear in numerous combinations, all depending on the specific marketing situation.

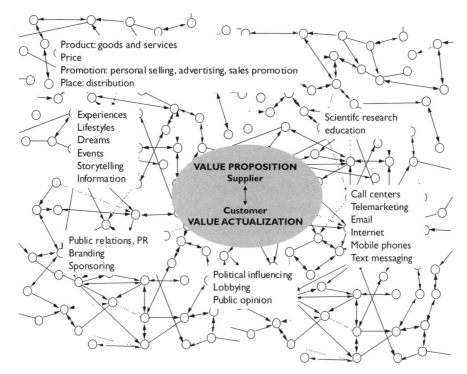

Figure 8.2 Today's 'Ps' are more than 4 (Copyright E. Gummesson 2008)

RM/CRM literature – a comparison with the 30R approach

Throughout the book, ample references have been made to those who have furnished inspiration and illustrations. To review everything being presented on RM/CRM in the expanding number of publications and websites is simply not feasible, not even if we limit ourselves to the English language. It is especially difficult to separate the chaff from the wheat when we are exposed to CRM in consultants, survey results presented in academic journals and conferences, company success stories and the news media.

RM/CRM are given different meanings by different authors. The influx and vitality of the current research and debate about relational issues, although mostly fragmented and addressing special issues in terms of traditional marketing management, has become an extra impetus to the evolution of my approach. These sources have modified and broadened my understanding. The 30R approach has received both praise and criticism. It has not been seriously challenged, although some show indifference and some have expressed a negative opinion, unfortunately without any tangible ideas on how to advance the field or make improvements. My conviction to stick to the path laid out by the 30R approach has been reinforced 'as time goes by'.

This section first points to the distinction between the *term* relationship marketing and the relationship marketing *phenomenon*, a greatly misunderstood issue. It proceeds to compare a selection of RM/CRM definitions and multi-relationship approaches.

The term and the phenomenon

There is an unfortunate mix-up between the *term* RM and the understanding of the actual *phenomenon*, a mix-up that should be ducked by scholars in particular but unfortunately is not. A *term* is only a label of the *phenomenon*, it is not the *phenomenon* as such (recall the discussion on objectification, reification and Magritte's pipe in Chapter 7). In order to avoid an intellectual Titanic disaster, scholars must consider the whole iceberg (*the phenomenon*), not just its visible tip (*the term*). *RM/CRM are new terms, but represent an old phenomenon.*

The *phenomenon* of RM is as old as trade itself – recall the case of the Chinese rice merchant in Chapter 1 – but it has gone unnoticed by most marketing professors, economists, marketing textbook writers and business school educators. Since the 1970s, many *terms* have been used to catch the *phenomenon*, among them the network approach; the interaction approach; long-term interactive relationships; a new concept of marketing; customer loyalty; interactive marketing; database marketing; direct marketing, niche marketing; one-to-one marketing; wrap-around marketing; dialogue marketing; customized marketing and client management.

The *term* relationship marketing was used by Barbara Bund Jackson in her project on B2B in the early 1980s, and published in a seminal book and a *Harvard Business Review* article, both in 1985. She used the *term* as an opposite to transaction marketing. The *term* was used by Len Berry in a conference paper in 1983, but exclusively for services. In other words, the *term* appeared simultaneously in B2B and services marketing. During the 1990s, the *term* became a general marketing term – accompanied by CRM – although most of the seminal writings on the *phenomenon* before that had used other terms. Considering its long history in the practice of marketing, and the diversity of *terms* used to pinpoint the *phenomenon* in theory and literature, it is pointless to ascribe the 'discovery' of the *phenomenon* of RM to a specific date or individual. The *phenomenon* was part of indigenous knowledge in business cultures around the world. It is beyond my comprehension that marketing and management as disciplines did not conceptualize this phenomenon until recently, and that the discipline of economics still has not made even a note of it.

Many have contributed to make the phenomenon of RM visible. In books and articles researchers and consultants have developed their own approaches.

RM/CRM books have been published in many languages in many countries. Most likely, the phenomenon of RM has also been treated in now forgotten texts. An upsurge in RM/CRM articles and conference papers present different approaches to RM. Some of these references have been used in this book. Others are found in overviews, which show that different roads lead to RM.[7]

Definitions

The majority of books and articles on RM/CRM do not offer definitions, which makes it difficult for the reader. Short definitions are never complete or unambiguous, but they hint at the core of a phenomenon and thus provide initial guidance. A selection of RM definitions is listed in Table 8.3 and later CRM definitions are listed in Table 8.4.

Table 8.3 Selected definitions which emphasize different aspects of RM

Source	Definition
Gummesson (see Chapter 1)	'Relationship marketing is interaction in networks of relationships.'
Berry (1983, p. 25)	'Relationship marketing is attracting, maintaining and – in multi-service organizations – enhancing customer relationships.'
Jackson (1985a, p. 165)	'Relationship marketing is marketing to win, build and maintain strong lasting relationships with industrial customers.'
Morgan and Hunt (1994, p. 22)	'Relationship marketing refers to all marketing activities directed to establishing, developing, and maintaining successful relational exchanges.'
Grönroos (2007, p. 29)	(The purpose of) … marketing is to identify and establish, maintain and enhance, and when necessary terminate relationships with customers (and other parties) so that the objectives regarding economic and other variables of all parties are met. This is achieved through a mutual exchange and fulfilment of promises.'
Ballantyne (1994, p. 3)	'An emergent disciplinary framework for creating, developing and sustaining exchanges of value, between the parties involved, whereby exchange relationships evolve to provide continuous and stable links in the supply chain'.
Porter (1993, p. 14)	'Relationship marketing is the process whereby both parties – the buyer and provider – establish an effective, efficient, enjoyable, enthusiastic and ethical relationship: one that is personally, professionally and profitably rewarding to both parties.'
Lusch and Vargo (2006a, pp. xvii–xviii)	'Marketing is the process in society and organizations that facilitates voluntary exchange through collaborative relationships that create reciprocal value through the application of complementary resources'.

---

[7] Webster (1992); Morgan and Hunt (1994); and Sheth and Parvatiyar (2000) with a US perspective; Gummesson, Lehtinen and Grönroos (1997); Grönroos (2000, 2006); and Gummesson (2006) with a Nordic School perspective.

Table 8.3 shows that the definitions vary in scope and emphasis. My own definition is founded on three core variables – relationships, networks, interaction – that have emerged out of research. The variables are general to marketing and form the vantage point to the 30R approach. Whereas the other definitions list activities or properties, my definition provides variables as vehicles for thought and action. They offer a relational perspective, hence the notion of the relationship eyeglasses.

Berry's definition is developed within services marketing. He explains his concern to be customer retention and the allocation of resources to keep customers and strengthen relationships, and not just attract new customers. Jackson's definition involves B2B customers and individual accounts as compared to mass markets and segments. Her concern is to make the B2B supplier choose whichever is the best strategy for each individual customer in each specific situation, either RM or transaction marketing. The messages of the two definitions are similar, even though they are grounded in different types of marketing realities; services marketing and B2B.

The message from Morgan and Hunt's definition is also similar but it is intended as a general RM definition. Grönroos goes one step further in seeing his RM definition as general to all marketing. It proposes that RM is more adequate as a general marketing theory than traditional marketing management, marketing mix and the 4Ps. He has gradually broadened the definition to encompass relationships to many stakeholders and not exclude not-for-profit government and voluntary sector NGOs. He also points to the need to divest in relationships and that the outcome is achieved through mutual exchange and fulfillment of promises.

Ballantyne claims that RM is an emerging school of thought. This stills rings true with reference to the *term* and to its academic treatment, but not with reference to the *phenomenon* and practice. Relationships not only go far back in the history of business practice, but they are in the core of both services marketing and the B2B network approaches, even when other terms than RM are used.

Porter[8] adds important social elements. Relationships should not only be efficient and effective, but also enjoyable, enthusiastic, ethical and personally and professionally rewarding. Marketing theory seems to forget the importance of social interaction and personality dimensions in a commercial relationship: business is fun! Furthermore, ethical aspects are at the core of RM, which is reflected in the importance that many authors place in trust, for example Morgan and Hunt.

Morgan and Hunt as well as Grönroos and Ballantyne offer broad definitions. Grönroos, Porter and Ballantyne stress win–win aspects (fulfilment of promises, rewarding both parties, value exchange) and, in alignment with Jackson, include the long-term aspect (continuous and stable, lasting).

---

[8] Clive Porter, who is an Australian consultant.

Table 8.4 Selected definitions which emphasize different aspects of CRM

Source	Definition
Gummesson (see Chapter 1)	'CRM is the values and strategies of RM – with special emphasis on the relationship between a customer and a supplier – turned into practical application and dependent on both human action and information technology.'
Payne and Frow (2005, p. 168)	'CRM is a strategic approach that is concerned with creating improved shareholder value through the development of appropriate relationships with key customers and customer segments. CRM unites the potential of relationship marketing strategies and IT to create profitable, long-term relationships with customers and other key stakeholders. CRM provides enhanced opportunities to use data and information to both understand customers and co-create value with them. This requires a cross-functional integration of processes, people, operations, and marketing capabilities that is enabled through information, technology and applications.'
Eggert and Fassot (2001, p. 5)	'eCRM embraces the analysis, planning and management of customer relationships with the aid of electronic media, especially the Internet, with the goal of the enterprise to focus on select customers.'

All of these RM definitions except mine use terms such as creating, establishing or maintaining relationships. On the other hand my definition is the only one that includes the concepts of networks and interaction.

Finally I have included Lusch and Vargo's marketing definition based on S-D logic. By underscoring three essential elements it is fully in line with RM thinking: '(1) marketing is not only an organizational process but also a societal process; (2) marketing emphasizes voluntary exchange and collaborative relationships and (3) parties obtain value by the application of complementary resources'.

Table 8.4 lists three CRM definitions. My definition puts emphasis on CRM as a way to implement RM philosophy and strategy. So does the definition suggested by Payne and Frow too, but it is more detailed. Eggert and Fassot define eCRM, where IT with the Internet has the lead role. They also stress the conscious selection and targeting of individual customers, which data warehousing and data mining should make possible.

Multi-relationship and network approaches

Most RM/CRM definitions limit themselves to the supplier–customer dyad, while some include several parties or stakeholders. In Table 8.5, the 30R approach is compared to

Table 8.5 Comparison between categories in multi-relationship approaches (the number of relationships included in each subcategory is shown in parentheses)

Source	Categories	Subcategories
Christopher, Payne and Ballantyne (2002)	6 markets	Customer markets (1)
		Supporting markets (5)
Kotler (1992)	10 players	Immediate environment (4)
		Macro-environment (6)
Morgan and Hunt (1994)	10 partnerships	Buyer partnerships (2)
		Supplier partnerships (2)
		Lateral partnerships (3)
		Internal partnerships (3)
Gummesson (1994; see Chaper 1)	30 relationships	Market relationships:
		■ Classic (3)
		■ Special (14)
		Non-market relationships:
		■ Mega-relationships (6)
		■ Nano-relationships (7)

three other approaches which go beyond suppliers and customers and see marketing relationships as embedded in a network of multi-relationships.

Christopher, Payne and Ballantyne propose a 'six markets' model, which 'the Cranfield School' has kept in later publications.[9] The six markets consist of: *customer markets* (existing and prospective customers) surrounded by *supporting markets* which are *referral markets* (satisfied customers who recommend the supplier to others); *supplier markets* (to be a partner rather than an adversary to their suppliers); *employee markets* (making certain that the right employees are recruited and promoted); *influence markets* (such as financial analysts, journalists and governments) and *internal markets* (the organization and its staff).

Kotler has been hesitant to accept that a paradigm shift is taking place based on service and RM. In his concept 'total marketing', however, he comes closer to a relationship and network view, albeit as a supplement to traditional marketing management: '... there are at least 10 critical players in a company's environment, of which the immediate customer and the ultimate customer are only two'. He makes a distinction between four players in the *immediate environment* of the firm – *suppliers, distributors, end-users* and *employees* – and

---

[9] The 'Cranfield School' is used here as a designation for researchers from the Cranfield School of Management, a leading business school in the United Kingdom, where research on RM/CRM is active; see Peck *et al.* (1999).

six in the firm's *macro-environment – financial firms, governments, media, allies, competitors* and *the general public.*

Morgan and Hunt suggest 10 relationship exchanges with four partnership groups: *buyer partnerships* (ultimate customers, intermediate customers); *supplier partnerships* (goods suppliers, service providers); *lateral partnerships* (competitors, non-profit organizations, governments) and *internal partnerships* (functional departments, employees, business units).

The fourth classification, the 30Rs, has been presented in this book. It goes further than the others and involves not only parties, but also certain properties of relationships. In that respect it is less consistent than the other classifications, but it is more comprehensive. Generic relationship properties that were listed in Chapter 1 are inherent in the relationships, and other properties have been added to form their own Rs. Some are based on content, such as the green relationship, the law-based relationship and the criminal relationship; others on form, such as alliances; and yet others on conduit, such as the electronic relationship.

In a comparative analysis it became evident that the relationships of all four approaches can be classified as market or non-market relationships and can further be subgrouped into both mega and nano relationships. There is a good match between the approaches, although the emphasis and scope vary. There are no obvious contradictions or conflicts.[10]

Contemporary Marketing Practices

Another classification deserves mentioning because it is based on extensive empirical data from practitioners. It has led up to a scheme called *Contemporary Marketing Practices,* positioning relational approaches in a context of different dimensions of current marketing.[11] The first is *transaction marketing,* the traditional approach in marketing management. It is a zero relationship situation which is focused on making each single transaction profitable in the first place and with no planned effort to create long-term loyalty. The second is *database marketing.* It is a more elaborate version of the mailing list and the salesperson's box of cards with notes on each customer, now charged with IT; it represents the most common type of CRM. The third step on the relationship scale is *interaction marketing* which involves face-to-face interaction as is common in the service encounter and in B2B cooperation between buyers and sellers. Fourth, there is *network marketing,* addressing the

---

[10] There are also other efforts to consider the integrated aspect of dealing with all stakeholders, instil consistent behaviour in the organization, and communicate a consistent image of a brand or company. One such tradition pertinent to RM is using communication as the key variable. See Duncan and Moriarty (1998, p. 9); Gronstedt (2000); and Schultz and Kitchen (2000).

[11] Coviello, Brodie and Munro (1997); and Coviello, Milley and Marcolin (2001).

complexity of multiple relationships between many stakeholders, and which I call many-to-many marketing.[12] Finally, *e-marketing* has been added embracing interactive technologies that allow a dialogue between suppliers and their customers.

Concluding comment

This presentation of a selection of RM/CRM definitions shows that there is a rich literature searching for an identity for these concepts. The growth rate is currently exponential. The approaches have varied in emphasis and scope, all the way from market relationships based on a consumer–seller dyad to a series of supportive, non-market relationships. Some limit RM/CRM to specific applications, such as services marketing or a technique such as the use of databases and the Internet. The 30R approach is the broadest, also aiming to reach a high degree of generality.

A paradigm shift in marketing

A paradigm shift implies that a science or discipline is given a new foundation, with new values, new assumptions or new methods. The accepted and established must be set aside. It either disappears completely, merges with the new, or takes the role of one of several coexisting paradigms. An established paradigm can be a springboard, but it can also be a mental prison.

The American automotive industry is a case in point. When the small car came from Europe and Japan it was not taken seriously by US manufacturers, but it was taken seriously by the consumers. Morgan offers an explanation: 'American auto industry in the early 1970s was a prisoner of its early success. And numerous firms in other industries have shared a similar experience, declining and decaying as a result of policies that made them world leaders in earlier stages of development.'[13] It echoes Levitt's (1960) article on 'Marketing Myopia' where he uses the American Railroads as an example of an industry who thought they were in the railroad business, not in travelling; and Hollywood thought it was in movies and not in entertainment.

Organizations get caught in mental traps, 'knowing' how everything is and erecting monuments over their prejudices. 'Group think' is hubris linked with the security in the power group, such as a corporate or marketing management group. No one dares openly challenge the conditions for decisions and action. Snug in 'The Yesmen Choir', the singers

---

[12] The reason for my preference for many-to-many is that the network marketing is sometimes used to denote direct selling or multilevel marketing, that is marketing door-to-door or at home parties.
[13] Morgan (1997, p. 201).

are sheltered by the perceptions that might have once reflected reality realistic, but in a changed market are nothing but shared illusions.[14]

Some claim that RM/CRM are just marginal add-ons to established marketing management. With such a view, they are brutally forced into the old and will never be allowed to display its qualities. Paradigm shifts break existing patterns. A small car is not a shrunk limousine; a tanker is not a blown-up rowing boat. They are based on different concepts and obey different laws. In the same spirit, I see RM/CRM as a paradigm shift in marketing.

The book has shown that RM/CRM in many ways offer a fresh view on marketing. This was so 15 years ago when the 30Rs approach was first presented but later developments, not least S-D logic and many-to-many marketing, have shown it to be sustainable. Table 8.6 sums up RM/CRM and their contribution to a paradigm shift and the beginnings of a new theory of marketing.

The paradigm shift has partially taken place in the real world of marketing, but the shift is not properly echoed in theories, textbooks and education. Students bring theoretical knowledge – marketing maps – to their current and future jobs. This knowledge must be usable knowledge, representing the terrain. This year's marketing reality cannot be tackled with previous years' theories.

New thinking requires new concepts – reconceptualization – so that the new will be allowed to live on its own terms. Several new concepts have been introduced in this book or they are developments of concepts I have used before. I believe I have innovated some of them or used them with a novel touch. If I am mistaken I would appreciate being corrected; it's easy to mistake the ego-centric 'brilliance' of oneself with ideas that are in the air and maybe have been aired by others and unobrusively have sneaked into one's mind. As has been pointed out before, it is vital to make a distinction between a phenomenon and the term used to catch the phenomenon. I have not invented any of the phenomena, I have conceptualized some of them and given them names.

Among these concepts are: the relationship eyeglasses; mega and nano relationships; faceless relationships; alliance markets; decision markets; service collision; horizontal and vertical interaction; power company and power industry; the pseudo-personal relationship and pseudo-membership; the value-creating network society; the bureaucratic–legal paradigm; ROR; relationship portfolio and marketing equilibrium. Recent additions to this third edition of the book are many-to-many marketing, RON and balanced centricity.

Several of the relationships are under-represented in current 'general' marketing literature, such as: the full-time and part-time marketers, the FTMs and PTMs (R4); the many-headed customer and the many-headed supplier (R6); the customer or supplier as prisoner (R10); the e-relationship (R12); the parasocial relationships (R13); the green relationship and

---

[14] For a discussion on the yesman, see Ortmark (2000).

Table 8.6 The characteristics of my RM/CRM concept and its contribution to a paradigm shift in marketing

Definitions	*RM* is interaction in networks of relationships. *CRM* is the values and strategies of RM – with particular emphasis on customer relationships – turned into practical application. Many-to-*many marketing* further stresses the network and the stakeholder.
Making RM real	Specification of 30 relationships, the 30Rs, both operational market relationships, and mega and nano non-market relationships.
Relationship portfolio	Selection of the relationships that a company should focus on in its marketing.
Values	Collaboration is in focus; the parties in a network are co-creators of value; more win–win and less win–lose; more equal parties; all parties carry responsibility; long-term relationships; and each customer is an individual or a member of a community of like-minded people.
Theoretical and practical foundation	Built on a synthesis of marketing and management strands from both theory and practice.
S-D logic emphasis	The conceptualization offered by S-D logic has merged with RM, leaving the goods/services product centric paradigm for 'service', further putting weight on co-creation of value and the customer as an operant resource. In its wake lean production and the supplier value chain are extended into lean consumption and the customer value network.
Balanced centricity	The broadening of the marketing concept of customer centricity to balanced centricity where the needs and wants of multiple stakeholders are provided for.
B2B, B2C/C2B and C2C	Considering both the differences and similarities between B2B and B2C and their interdependence; balancing the initiative of supplier and consumer as both operant resources into replacing B2C with B2C/C2B; acknowledging the pivotal role of C2C interaction in marketing.
High tech/high touch balance	Recognition of IT and automation, high tech, as a driver of changing marketing, but balancing this against the need for human activities, high touch.
Links to management	RM/CRM represent marketing-oriented management – an aspect of the total management of the firm – and are not limited to marketing or sales departments; the marketing plan becomes part of the business plan; the CRM system part of the whole business system.
Links to accounting	The balanced scorecard provides a tool for measuring ROR.
Links to organization	RM is the marketing manifestation of the network organization.
Advantages to the firm	Increased customer retention and duration; increased marketing productivity and thus increased profitability; and increased stability and certainty.
Advantages of the marketing equilibrium	RM adds collaboration to competition and regulations/institutions; the symbiosis of these three contributes to a dynamic marketing equilibrium.
Advantages to society, citizens and customers	RM is the marketing of the value-creating network society with increased focus on customized production and marketing to the individual, and reduced focus on standardized mass production and mass marketing.
Validity	By focusing on relationships, networks and interaction, RM offers a more realistic approach to marketing in the contemporary economy than is currently prevailing in marketing education. In practice, marketing works through a network of relationships.
Generalizability	RM/CRM can be applied to all types of organizations and offerings, but the relationship portfolio and the application are always specific to a given situation.

corporate social responsibility (R15); the law-based relationship (R16); the criminal network (R17); the knowledge relationship (R21); mega alliances (R22); quality management linking marketing and technology (R26); and the owner and financier relationship (R30).

Other concepts and terms are other people's innovations, such as mega marketing, internal marketing, internal customer, the service encounter, network organizations, the knowledge-based organization, migratory and embedded knowledge. S-D logic and lean consumption. But the concepts have been given a more central role here than in other general marketing presentations and they have been looked at through the relationship eyeglasses.

The new language of RM/CRM accommodates a dilemma. One purpose is to show that the boundaries in a network of relationships – both from a marketing and an organization perspective – are blurred. The boundaries change depending on what they are used for; they are always fuzzy and changeable. At the same time I feel forced to use terms such as internal/external and company/market for want of better. Close friends and colleagues can communicate without words and do so through action and body language. Reading Marlo Morgan's book (2004) on a walkabout with Australian aborigines through the outback made me envious. These 'primitive' people had a collective consciousness that allowed tacit communication and understanding with an effectiveness that was almost instantly validated in action and results.

The value-creating network society, modernism and post-modernism

Concepts such as the post-industrial society, the service economy, the knowledge era or the information age try to spot key changes in the economy. As has been said already, I advocate the use of two dimensions. One is the *value society* that epitomizes value creation as the desired outcome of economic activity; the other is the *network society*, which describes the structure of organizations and society. I have used a merger of the two in this book: the value-creating network society. It is a natural step for S-D logic to advance further and include networks, and this is also endorsed by the S-D logic originators.[15]

Two additional concepts – modernism and post-modernism – keep intriguing me. Even if they are nebulous, they tease our brains. They attempt to uncover essentials in a long-term passage from certain governing values and behaviour to others. Modernism

---

[15] Lusch and Vargo (2006, p. 285).

coincides with the logic of the industrial society, post-modernism with the value-creating network society.[16]

These represent mega paradigms, a term that may cause cardiac arrest for those who are already at war with the terms of paradigm and post-modernism.

Modernism is characterized by a belief in progress and unbounded trust in science, the rational approach to life represented by the expert; by our ability to take charge over nature and social behaviour; by finding universal laws and absolute truths. Everything is measurable, and if it is not, it does not exist. Common sense and experience are degraded to superstition, subjective opinion and anecdotal evidence to be progressively replaced by facts and objective knowledge. Society will become neatly ordered by means of social engineering, and social equality is infused through planning, regulations and institutions. If we only have enough data we can control and predict society. A current case is orthodox western medicine which has launched the notion of 'evidence-based medicine'. It thrives in the spirit of total control of illness and health – although it is based on arbitrary assumptions and limited research techniques, intersubjectively 'approved' by an autocratic elite of peers.

Post-modernism turns these tenets upside down. We live in an age of uncertainty.[17] The expert becomes 'a broker of uncertainty', not the sage and assured expert who knows 'how it is' with reference to 'scientific evidence'. The volatility of stock exchanges does not represent real value but perceived, manipulated and unknown future value; it is neurosis over cold analysis. There is no way of forecasting the price of shares even for a short period. We have seen that the organization, the supplier, the customer, the competitor and other phenomena are ambiguous. Companies can be suppliers, customers and competitors, and they can own one another. The supplier and the customer are recognized as co-creators of service. The physical marketplace is challenged by the marketspace of Internet technology. Personal and organizational relationships, which contain both technical rationality and emotions, are central to marketing. It is accepted that we deal with fuzzy phenomena with a unique core but with blurred boundaries, perspectives that are multiple and overlapping, and knowledge that is incomplete and variable.

The network organization is post-modern, it flows and changes. Complexity, ambiguity and change are natural, not inconvenient and nerve-racking. Chaos is part of everyday marketing, but even if chaos cannot be managed we can learn to manage in chaos. There is lack of equilibrium, but there is an aspiration to reach a balance which will never be reached. Trends are not continuous and many trends appear simultaneously and move in different directions; they carry the hallmark of the paradox but not of the oxymoron.

---

[16] The discussion on post-modernism is primarily inspired by Brown (1995, 1998); and Firat, Dahlokia and Venkatesh (1995).

[17] Giarini and Stahel (1998).

The profound transformation – the discontinuity, the quantum leap, the paradigm shift – can be released suddenly, like the oil crisis in the 1970s; the Soviet perestroika and the fall of the Berlin Wall in the 1980s; the Internet carnival in the 1990s; and in the first years of the new millennium with dotcom collapse and the attacks against the World Trade Centre and the Pentagon, symbols of the capitalist market economy and power. Technical innovations such as the Internet, the mobile phone and gene manipulation, and social innovations such as deregulation and privatization, shake society.

To a large extent, successful marketing has always been post-modern. Joseph Duveen and his ability to play tricks, and their contemporary applications by Apple, H&M and Harry Potter are more post-modern than modern. Innovation and entrepreneurship are always unpredictable and create commotion. The issue is not being either post-modern or modern, but where to place the emphasis. RM is an attitude and CRM is a tool; neither represents a fundamentalist religion. RM does not exclude transaction marketing or anonymous mass marketing when those are justified. RM does not throw the 4Ps overboard, just changes their scope and position.

A future-oriented note on methodology and theory generation

Peter Drucker has said that '... we are prone, both in academia and in management, to ... mistake the surface gloss of brilliance for the essence of performance. But it is so easy to fall for sophistry – to mistake clever techniques for understanding, footnotes for scholarship and fashions for truth ...'[18] This needs to be observed both by those who appear as attorneys for the defence of the established and those who advocate the new.

Heeding current issues is not the same as being faddish. The phenomena of RM and later CRM, S-D logic and the network-based many-to-many marketing caught my interest because I believe they are here to stay. When my attention was first drawn to relationships back in 1968, I had no idea what I was getting into. I had opened the lid to a deep well – and 40 years later I still cannot see its bottom. RM was a step in the direction of a black-hole theory and like black holes in outer space it still seems endless. Although stars are glistening here and there, a lot is darkness.

It is all about contributing to a more realistic understanding of marketing through the generation of a new and more general theory, grand theory if your wish. Or rather grand theories, as a single unified theory is too far ahead and may never emerge. Natural scientists are much bolder in addressing 'complexity theory' and 'a theory of everything'.

---

[18] Drucker (1988b).

Although the old physics paradigm was modern, from the theory of relativity and quantum theory and onwards, physics feels post-modern as well.

In a more modest search of a theory for marketing, relationships, networks and interaction have qualified as the foundation. These concepts have stood the test over many decades now and their generality has been underscored by the developments in IT, S-D logic and the emerging network view represented by many-to-many marketing.

My most important criterion in selecting and defining the 30Rs has been the pinpointing of phenomena which are of prime importance to practitioners and scholars alike. Observations of current issues in companies and markets, and the study of literature and research, together with interpretations of these sources, have given birth to RM. But 'current' can be deceptive; it can easily be a trap of ephemeral fashion and hype which we are fed with 24/7 by the media. The issues that have been included here are those that I believe have a future. This is based on judgement calls, however, as no one has but a subjective understanding of what is to come.

As the Rs emerged – without my having a clue how many there would be – I tried to find a unifying logic. The failure to find that logic felt embarrassing until I realized I was misguided. It is unfair to demand that the relationships in some rationalistic and modernist mode should yield to established patterns. Eventually, the Rs formed a pattern of classic and special market relationships, and mega and nano non-market relationships.

The definitions and content are controlled by current practical and theoretical relevance as I have interpreted it. Behind the 30Rs is a strong influence of *grounded theory* as developed by sociologists Barney Glaser and Anselm Strauss but I am anxious to point out that my research is in no way a fully fledged grounded theory study. But the openness and sensitivity required by the inductive approach to science stressed by grounded theory has been a source of inspiration and revelation; when you think of it, really it is just common sense. As long as you keep searching for a type of phenomenon – in this case RM – persistent and systematic search will make patterns, categories and systems emerge. Glaser says: 'The researcher must have patience and not force the data out of anxiety and impatience … *He must trust that emergence will occur and it does* [italics added].'[19]

That the relationships became 30 is an outcome of emergence. It does not mean that the Rs need to be 30. Anyone who can motivate more or different categories or condense them into fewer is welcome to do so. Further, successful theory construction goes beyond mere description. It offers conceptualization so that the essence of a marketing phenomenon can be better understood. It strives to reach a higher degree of generalization, thus facilitating for marketers to making their work more effective and manageable.

---

[19] Glaser (1992, p. 4) and Glaser (2001).

This book is a synthesis of data from own research, research by others, practical experience, and other management disciplines than marketing. There is also opinion and advocacy. How do we get it all together, subjective thinking being biased and research methodology being incomplete and lacking robustness?

Glaser[20] warns against 'immaculate conceptions' that '… draw on some data even though conjectured. There exist … theories based on lots of experience, but not systematically researched.' As an example he takes lawyers and medical doctors; they are 'walking surveys' grounding their claims in first-hand and second-hand experiences and knowledge. He quotes Robert Stake who calls them 'naturalistic generalizations which develop within a person as a product of experience. They derive from the tacit knowledge of how things are … they seldom take the form of predictions, but lead regularly to expectations. They guide action'.

Lowe and Glaser (1995) have advocated the relevance of grounded theory for developing RM and claim that it would hasten its development. I agree. Christiansen[21] who found 'opportunizing' to be the core variable in business is more detailed in his critique: 'Opportunizing explains how companies create, identify, seize and exploit situations in order to sustain their survival or growth. Essentially, opportunizing is what the business people, who were the focus of this study, did all the time. The model of opportunizing explains the main concern and its recurrent solution of these business managers – that is the most important and the most problematic for these managers – and it explains most of the variation in the recorded behaviour. Mapping of business *networks* among companies may reveal much. It may also reveal the importance of the concept of *networking*. Part of generating a grounded theory is also the conceptualization and grounding of theoretical codes that explain how the substantive concepts relate in the resolving of the main concern'.

With this background he proceeds: 'Gummesson mostly provides conceptual descriptions, but not conceptual explanations of how the substantive concepts are related by theoretical codes. Thus, while *relationship marketing*, *customer relationship management*, *networking* and the *30 marketing relationships* undoubtedly may be very important concepts in business, these concepts do not conceptually explain with parsimony and scope how they do 'relationship marketing' or 'customer relationship management' '… Hence, it is suggested that Gummesson will find a solution in the theory of *opportunizing*. He will in particular find solutions in the concepts of *perpetual opportunizing* (*conditional befriending and prospecting*). Of course, coding of new data for emergent fit with these pregrounded

---

[20] Glaser (2007, pp. 2–3).
[21] Christiansen (2006, pp.179–180).

concepts may become necessary, and the required precautions against preconception traps will be necessary in such a coding'.

Referring to RM, Glaser says that 'Network is not a core category. It is a theoretical code, which models substantive theory ... Its relevance must be earned, not forced ... Otherwise you produce vague out data since you are lost between description (descriptive capture) and conceptualization. Make a choice. Do a grounded theory study. You'll love it.'[22]

I may very well do just that. If I were to start over again, say, three decades back, I would centre my research and writing around grounded theory, network theory and case study research. I have needed time to scurry about in all three of them until I gradually realized that they are the most comprehensive and useful scientific approaches for generating theory. Grounded theory is the outcome of a defined research procedure; its approach is even a lifestyle. Network theory is common to both natural and social sciences; it is both a theory of life and a set of techniques. Case study research where I have most experience, allows us – in a verbal discourse – to get beyond the limitations of statistical research. As both grounded theory and network theory can work with cases they are supplements although I am not sure how grounded theory and network theory are related to each other.[23]

Whenever I am writing I recurrently find myself thriving on a process of tacit knowing. The outcome, tacit knowledge, can only be communicated and understood through first-hand experience and intuition. I have tried hard to find words and structures and offer something more coherent and elegant, even new theory. Our explicit knowledge is not adequate and the tacit touch is needed to make the marketing bumblebee fly.

Approaching the end of the book – or the beginning?

Although this book has come to an end, it is meant to be a springboard for something better. I possess boxes of material which I have not yet been able to benefit from and which have not been given a fair chance in this text. Some of this material – if it stays in the archives for a year or two – will have lost its significance; hypes loose their flair and changes occur rapidly. Better RM/CRM approaches will hopefully advance our understanding of marketing. Personal and scholarly reflections, and a constructive dialogue around RM/CRM and the 30Rs – and I consider reflection and dialogue the most viable scientific principles – are respectfully invited.

---

[22] Email from Glaser, August 2007.
[23] For a comparison between case study research and network theory, see Gummesson (2007b).

I like to close the book with a non-academic reference, one that may make some professors feel uncomfortable. I'm referring to Paulo Coelho's philosophical novel, *The Alchemist* (1995). It was rejected by literary critics as second rate; one even wrote that it was for uneducated people. If they had been marketers and acknowledged customer centricity they would have considered its sales: over 30 million copies. It illustrates a dilemma about quality: Is the customer stupid or smarter than the critic who is insensitive and arrogant? Or is the critic right? Marketing people are alchemists; they want to turn everything into gold. In Coelho's book a shepherd sets out on a strenuous journey to find a true master alchemist with solid knowledge. But he learnt that the real gold of life was not the metal as such; gold represented value. The answer lay on his doorstep, but he needed the many aggravating experiences from the journey to see the obvious. And above all he had learnt that you must listen to your heart, read the signs, and follow your dreams. Perhaps we need all the detours of marketing models to find the genome of marketing. We have not arrived yet but if we listen to our hearts, read the signs and follow our dreams rather than get stuck on received theories and methodological rituals, we may succeed to advance marketing.

IN BRIEF

This last chapter has summed up and discussed the theoretical and practical contributions to RM/CRM and the contributions of RM/CRM to marketing. It has shown my idea about how marketing management and the 4Ps relate to RM/CRM, but also that the 4Ps are neither Ps nor 4 any more; that the current 'Ps' have a relational content; and that they have a major role on a level below the overriding concepts of relationships, networks and interaction. I claimed in previous editions of the book that there is a paradigm shift going on, and fuelled by S-D logic, many-to-many marketing and other contributions this is more evident than ever. I am hoping for the tipping point to show any time now. In the RM spirit we live in a value-creating network society with both modern and post-modern elements. Anyone remember Doris Day from the Alfred Hitchcock movie *The Man Who Knew Too Much* singing 'Que sera, sera', 'Whatever will be, will be'? However mundane and non-scientific this may sound it pretty much sums up the modernist dilemma that we cannot predict and control the future. Even if we see changes coming we do not readily accept what we see; we start by rejecting them. A current example is the 'green' aspects. It took the former US Vice president Al Gore and a huge global campaign to convince people that the greenhouse effect and melting ices are realities. In science we should apply productive methodology and duck rites and ritualism. To refer to myself: If I had started out as a researcher now I would have been grounded theory-centric, network theory-centric and case study-centric. But it is not too late!

QUESTIONS FOR DISCUSSION

1 How do the marketing mix and the 4Ps fit into RM/CRM, and which are the 'Ps' today?
2 What is the difference between the *term* RM and the *phenomenon* RM?
3 There is a plethora of definitions of RM and CRM and a selection is listed and discussed in the chapter. Which is your favourite and why? You can also add other definitions if you wish to.
4 How does Gummesson's RM/CRM concept with the 30Rs contribute to a paradigm shift in marketing?
5 Why could our current economy be referred to as 'the value-creating network society'?

References

Achrol, R. S. and Kotler, P. (2006), 'The Service Dominant Logic for Marketing: A Critique'. In Lusch R. F. and Vargo S. L. (eds.), *Toward a Service-Dominant Logic of Marketing: Dialog, Debate, and Directions*. New York: M.E. Sharpe, pp. 320–333.

Albinsson-Bruhner, G. (1993), 'Den rationella välfärdsstatens kollaps'. *Svenska Dagbladet*, 4 September.

Albrecht, K. and Zemke, R. (1985), *Service America!*. Homewood, IL: Dow Jones-Irwin.

Alderson, W. (1965), *Dynamic Marketing Behavior*. Homewood, IL: Irwin.

Ambler, T. (2000), *Marketing and the Bottom Line*. London: Financial Times/Prentice Hall.

Anderson, J. C. and Narus, J. A. (1991), 'Partnering as a Focused Market Strategy'. *California Management Review*, 33(Spring), 95–113.

Andreassen, T. W. (1997), *Dissatisfaction with Services*. Stockholm: Stockholm University School of Business.

Apéria, T., Brönn, P. S. and Schultz, M. (2004), 'A Reputation Analysis of the Most Visible Companies in Scandinavian Countries'. *Corporate Reputation Review*, 7(3), 218–230.

Arndt, J. (1979), 'Toward a Concept of Domesticated Markets'. *Journal of Marketing*, 43(Fall), 69–75.

Arndt, J. (1983), 'The Political Economy Paradigm: Foundation for Theory Building in Marketing'. *Journal of Marketing*, 47(Fall), 44–54.

Badaracco, J. L. Jr. (1991), *The Knowledge Link: How Firms Compete through Strategic Alliances*. Boston, MA: Harvard Business School Press.

Bagelius, N. (2003), *Svenska företag åter i Österled*. Stockholm: Stockholm University School of Business.

Baker, M. J. (1976), 'Evolution of the Marketing Concept'. In Baker M. J. (ed.), *Marketing: Theory and Practice*. London: Macmillan.

Baker, M. J. (1999a), 'Marketing – Philosophy or Function?' In Baker M. J. (ed.), *The IEBM Encyclopedia of Marketing*. London: Thomson.

Baker, M. J. (1999b), 'The Future of Marketing'. In Baker M. J. (ed.), *The IEBM Encyclopedia of Marketing*. London: Thomson.

Baker, M. J. (2006), 'Editorial'. *Journal of Customer Behaviour*, 5(3), 197–200.

Balasubramanian, S. K., Mathur, I. and Thakur, R. (2005), 'The Impact of High-Quality Firm Achievements on Shareholder Value: Focus on Malcolm Baldrige and J. D. Power and Associates Award'. *Journal of the Academy of Marketing Science*, 33(4), 413–422.

Ballantyne, D. (1994), 'Marketing at the Crossroads'. *Asia-Australia Marketing Journal*, 2(1), 1–7. Editorial

Ballantyne, D. (2003), 'A Relationship-Mediated Theory of Internal Marketing'. *European Journal of Marketing*, 37(9), 1242–1260.

Barabási, A.-L. (2002), *Linked: The New Science of Networks*. Cambridge, MA: Perseus.

Baumgartner, J. (1991), 'Nonmarketing Professionals Need More Than 4Ps'. *Marketing News*, 22 July, 28.

Benndorf, H. (1987), *Marknadsföringsplanering och samordning mellan företag i industriella system*. Stockholm: MTC/EFI.

Berry, L. L. (1983), 'Relationship Marketing'. In Berry L. L., Shostack G. L. and Upah G. D. (eds.), *Emerging Perspectives in Services Marketing*. Chicago: AMA.

Berry, L. L. (1989), 'The Service Quality Agenda for the 1990s'. *Distinguished Papers*, no. DP 89F-2. New York: St John's University, December.

Berry, L. L. and Parasuraman, A. (1991), *Marketing Services*. New York: The Free Press.

Bitner, M. J. (1990), 'Evaluating Service Encounters: The Effect of Physical Surroundings on Customers and Employees'. *Journal of Marketing*, April, 69–82.

Bitner, M. J. (1992), 'Servicescapes: The Impact of Physical Surroundings and Employee Responses'. *Journal of Marketing*, April, 57–71.

Björkman, I. and Kock, S. (1997), 'Social Relationships and Business Networks: The Case of Western Companies in China'. *International Business Review*, 4(4), 519–535.

Bliemel, F. W. and Eggert, A. (eds.) (1997), *Relationship Marketing under Fire*. Kaiserslauten, Germany: University of Kaiserslauten, Schriftenreihe Marketing. Heft 4/97

Blois, K. (1996), 'Relationship Marketing in Organizational Markets: When is it Appropriate?' *Journal of Marketing Management*, 12, 161–173.

Blumberg, P. (1989), *The Predatory Society*. New York: Oxford University Press.

Boissevein, J. (1976), *Friends of Friends*. Oxford: Basil Blackwell.

Booms, B. H. and Bitner, M. J. (1981), 'Marketing Strategies and Organization Structures for Service Firms'. In Donnelly J. and George W. R. (eds.), *Marketing of Services*. Chicago: American Marketing Association, pp. 47–51.

Bradford, H. (1991), 'A New Framework for Museum Marketing'. In Kavanagh G. (ed.), *The Museums Profession: Internal and External Relations*. Leicester, UK: Leicester University Press.

Brandenburger, A. M. and Nalebuff, B. J. (1996), *Co-opetition*. Boston, MA: Harvard Business School Press.

Brandes, O. and Brege, S. (1990), *Marknadsledarskap*. Malmö: Liber.

Brodie, R. J., Glynn, M. S. and Little, V. (2006), 'The service brand and the service-dominant logic: missing fundamental premise or the need for stronger theory?' *Marketing Theory*, 6(3), 363–379.

Brown, S. (1995), *Postmodern Marketing*. London: Routledge.

Brown, S. (1998), *Postmodern Marketing Two*. London: Thomson.

Brown, S. (2000), 'The Three Rs of Relationship Marketing: Retroactive, Retrospective, Retrogressive'. In Hennig-Thurau T. and Hansen U. (eds.), *Relationship Marketing*. Berlin: Springer-Verlag, pp. 393–413.

Brown, S. (2007), 'Turning customers into lustomers: the Duveen proposition'. *Journal of Customer Behaviour*, 6(Summer), 143–153.

Brownlie, D. and Saren, M. (1992), 'The Four Ps of the Marketing Concept: Prescriptive, Polemical, Permanent and Problematical'. *European Journal of Marketing*, 26(4), 34–47.

Bruhn, M. (2003), *Relationship Marketing*. Harlow: Financial Times/Prentice Hall.

Buchanan, M. (2003), *Small World*. London: Phoenix.

Buck-Lew, M. and Edvinsson, L. (1993), *Intellectual Capital at Skandia*. Stockholm: Skandia.

Business Week (2007), 'Little Green Lies'. October 29, 44–52.

Buttle, F. (2006), *Customer Relationship Management*. Oxford: Butterworth-Heinemann.

Calonius, H. (2006), 'The Promise Concept'. *Marketing Theory*, 6(4), 419–428.

Cang, Stephen (1976), 'Organisational Change and the Doctor–Patient Relationship as the Model for Client–Consultant Relationships'. Paper presented at *The Seminar on Client–Consultant Relationships*. Groningen: University of Groningen, The Netherlands, November.

Capra, F. (2002), *The Hidden Connections*. London: HarperCollins.

Carlsson, M. and Lundqvist, M. (1992), *Work with and Implementation of New Concepts for Management of Product Development – Some Emperical Findings*. Gothenburg: Chalmers.

Carnegie, D. (1936/2007), *How to Win Friends and Influence People*. London: Vermilion. OH: Vermilion

Castells, M. (1996), *The Rise of the Network Society*. Oxford: Blackwell.

Christiansen, Ó. (2006), *Opportunizing: How Companies Create, Identify, Seize and Exploit Situations to Sustain their Survival or Growth – An Orthodox Grounded Theory Approach*. Tórshavn, Faroe Islands: Faroe Islands University.

Christopher, M. (2004), *Logistics and Supply Chain Management: Creating Value – Adding Networks*. London: Financial Times/Prentice Hall.

Christopher, M., Payne, A. and Ballantyne, D. (2002), *Relationship Marketing*. Oxford: Butterworth-Heinemann.

Cialdini, R. B. (2006), *Influence*. New York: Collins.

Clark, M. S. (1983), 'Reactions to Aid in Communal and Exchange Relationships'. In , *New Directions in Helping*, Vol. 1, Chapter 11. New York: Academic Press, pp. 281–304.

Coase, R. H. (1937), 'The Nature of the Firm'. *Economica*, 387–405.

Coase, Ronald H. (1991), 'The Institutional Structure of Production'. Stockholm: The Nobel Foundation, *Prize Lecture in Economic Science in Memory of Alfred Nobel*, 9 December.

Coelho, P. (1995), *The Alchemist*. London: Harper/Collins.

Constantinides, E. (2006), 'The Marketing Mix Revisited: Towards the 21st Century Marketing'. *Journal of Marketing Management*, 22(3–4), 407–438.

Cooper, R. and Kaplan, R. S. (1991), 'Profit Priorities from Activity-Based Costing'. *Harvard Business Review*, May–June, 130–135.

Cova, B. (1997), 'Relationship Marketing: A View from the South'. In Meenaghan, T. (ed.), *New and Evolving Paradigms: The Emerging Future of Marketing, Conference Proceedings*. Chicago, IL: American Marketing Association and University College, Dublin, pp. 657–672.

Coviello, N., Brodie, R. J. and Munroe, H. J. (1997), 'Understanding Contemporary Marketing Practices: Development of a Classification Scheme'. *Journal of Marketing Management*, 13(6), 501–522.

Coviello, N., Milley, R. and Marcolin, B. (2001), 'Understanding IT-enabled Interactivity in Contemporary Marketing'. *Journal of Interactive Marketing*, 15(4), 18–33.

Cowles, Deborah L. (1994), 'Relationship Marketing for Transaction Marketing Firms: Viable Strategy via Command Performance'. In Sheth, J. N. and Parvatiyar, A. (eds.), *Relationship Marketing: Theory, Methods and Applications. 1994 Research Conference Proceedings*. Atlanta, GA: Center for Relationship Marketing, Emory University.

Creamer, M. (2007), 'Ad Age Agency of the Year: The Consumer'. *Advertising Age*, January 8.

Crosby, L., Evans, K. and Cowles, D. (1990), 'Relationship Quality in Services Selling: An Interpersonal Influence Perspective'. *Journal of Marketing*, 54, 68–81.

Crosby, P. (1984), *Quality Is Free*. New York: McGraw-Hill.

Czarniawska, B. and Hernes, T. (eds.) (2005), *Actor-Network Theory and Organizing*. Malmö: Liber and Copenhagen Business School Press.

Czepiel, J. A. (1990), 'Managing Relationships with Customers: A Differentiating Philosophy of Marketing'. In Bowen D., Chase R. and Cummings T. (eds.), *Service Management Effectiveness*. San Francisco: Jossey-Bass, pp. 299–323.

Dahlgaard, J. J. and Dahlgaard-Park, S. M. (2006), 'Lean Production, Six Sigma Quality, TQM and Company Culture'. *The TQM Magazine*, 18(3), 263–281.

Darby, M. R. and Karni, E. (1973), 'Free Competition and the Optimal Amount of Fraud'. *Journal of Law and Economics*, April, 67–86.

D'Aveni, R. A. (1994), *Hypercompetition*. New York: The Free Press.

Davenport, T. H. (1997), *Information Ecology: Mastering the Information and Knowledge Environment*. New York: Oxford University Press.

Davis, S. M. (1987), *Future Perfect*. Reading, MA: Addison-Wesley.

DeBono, E. (1992), *Sur/Petition: Going Beyond Monopolies*. London: Fontana.

Delaryd, B. (1989), *I Japan är kunden kung*. Stockholm: Svenska Dagbladet.

Deming, W.E. (1986), *Out of the Crisis*. Cambridge, MA: MIT.

Donaldson, B. and O'Toole, T. (2007), *Strategic Market Relationships: From Strategy to Implementation*. Chichester, UK: Wiley.

Donovan, H. (1989), 'Managing Your Intellectuals'. *Fortune*, 23 October, 103–106.

Doyle, P. (2000), 'Value-Based Marketing'. *Journal of Strategic Marketing*, 8(4), 299–311.

Doz, Y. L. and Hamel, G. (1998), *Alliance Advantage*. Boston, MA: Harvard Business School Press.

Drucker, P. F. (1954), *The Practice of Management*. New York: Harper & Row.

Drucker, P. F. (1988a), 'The Coming of the New Organization'. *Harvard Business Review*, January–February, 45–53.

Drucker, P. F. (1988b), 'Teaching the Work of Management'. *New Management Magazine*, 6(2 Fall).

Drucker, P. F. (1989), *The New Realities*. Oxford: Heinemann.

Drucker, P. F. (1990), *Managing the Nonprofit Organization*. New York: HarperCollins.

Duncan, T. and Moriarty, S. E. (1998), 'A Communication-Based Marketing Model for Managing Relationships'. *Journal of Marketing*, 62, 1–13.

Dwyer, F. R., Shurr, P. H. and Oh, S. (1987), 'Developing Buyer and Seller Relationships'. *Journal of Marketing*, 51, 11–27.

Edfeldt, Å. W. (1992), *Påverkan*. Stockholm: Proprius.

Edvardsson, B., Enquist, B. and Hay, M. (2006), 'Value-Based Service Brands: Narratives from IKEA'. *Managing Service Quality*, 16(3), 230–246.

Edvardsson, B., Gustafsson, A., Kristensson, P., Magnusson, P. and Matthing, J. (2006), *Involving Customers in New Service Development*. London: Imperial College Press.

Edvinsson, L. and Malone, M. S. (1997), *Intellectual Capital*. New York: Harper Collins.

Egan, J. (2004), *Relationship Marketing*. Harlow, UK: Financial Times/Prentice Hall.

Eggert, A. and Fassot, G. (2001), 'Begriffsabgrenzung und Anspruchspektrum des eCRM'. In Eggert A. and Fassot G. (eds.), *eCRM: Electronic Customer Relationship Management*. Stuttgart: Schäffer-Poeschel Verlag.

Ehrlemark, G. (1978), *OTOM Paper*, 7 November (as quoted in *The ForeSight Entrepreneur*, 1989, no. 3).

Engeseth, S. (2006), *ONE*. London: Cyan/Marshall Cavendish Business.

Enquist, B., Edvardsson, B. and Petros Sebathu, S. (2007), 'Value-Based Service Quality for Sustainable Business'. *Managing Service Quality*, 17(4), 385–403.

Entine, J. (1996), 'Let Them Eat Brazil Nuts'. *Dollar and Sense*, March–April, 30–35.

Eriksson, A.-K. and Åsberg, M. (1994), *Kostnadseffekter av affärsrelationer*. Uppsala: Uppsala University, Department of Business Studies.

Fairness and Accuracy in Reporting (FAIR) (1999), 'Media Advisory: Initial Reports from Seattle Gloss Over WTO Issues'. 1 December.

Falcone, G. and Padovani, M. (1992), *Men of Honour: Truth About the Mafia*. New York: HarperCollins.

Faltermayer, E. (1992), 'Does Japan Play Fair?' *Fortune*, 7 September, 22–29.

Fang, T. (1999), *Chinese Business Negotiating Style*. Thousand Oaks, CA: Sage.

Farris, P. W., Bendle, N. T., Pfeifer, P. E. and Reibstein, D. J. (2006), *Marketing Metrics*. Upper Saddle River, NJ: Wharton School Publishing/Pearson Education.

Feurst, O. (1991), *Kost och hälsa i marknadsföringen*. Stockholm: Stockholm University, School of Business.

Fiorentini, G. and Peltzman, S. (eds.) (1995), *The Economics of Organized Crime*. Cambridge, UK: Cambridge University Press.

Firat, F. A., Dahlakia, N. and Venkatesh, A. (1995), 'Marketing in a Post-Modern World'. *European Journal of Marketing*, 29(1), 40–56.

Fornell, C. (1992), 'A National Customer Satisfaction Barometer: The Swedish Experience'. *Journal of Marketing*, 56, 6–21.

Fornell, C. and Wernerfelt, B. (1988), 'Model for Customer Complaint Management'. *Marketing Science*, 7(Summer), 271–286.

Fornell, C. and Westbrook, R. A. (1984), 'The Vicious Circle of Consumer Complaints'. *Journal of Marketing*, 48(Summer), 68–78.

Forrester, J. W. (1993), 'A New Corporate Design'. In Halal W. E., Geranmayeh A. and Pourdehead J. (eds.), *Internal Markets*. New York: Wiley.

Fortune (2007), 'Go Green. Get Rich'. European Edition, no. 4, March.

Fournier, S., Dobscha, S. and Mick, D. G. (1998), 'Preventing the Mature Death of Relationship Marketing'. *Harvard Business Review*, January–February.

Frankelius, P. (1997), *Kirurgisk Marknadsföring*. Malmö: Liber.

Frenckner, P. (1993), 'ABC-kalkylen: vad behövs mer?'. *Ekonomi & Styrning*, 2, 26–29.

Fukuyama, F. (1995), *Trust*. New York: The Free Press.

Fung, A., Graham, M. and Weil, D. (2007), *Full Disclosure*. Cambridge: Cambridge University Press.

Galioto, F., Kerins, J., Lauster, S. and Mitchell, D. (2006), *The Matrix Reloaded*. Chicago, IL: Booz Allen Hamilton.

Gatarski, R. (2001), *Artificial Market Actors: Explorations of Automated Business Interactions*. Stockholm: Stockholm University.

Gatarski, R. and Lundkvist, A. (1998), 'Interactive Media Face Artificial Consumers and Must Re-Think'. *Journal of Marketing Communications*, 4, 45–59.

Gerlach, M. L. (1992), *Alliance Capitalism: The Social Organization of Japanese Business*. Berkeley, CA: University of California Press.

Giarini, O. and Stahel, W. R. (1998), *The Limits of Certainty*. Dordrecht: Kluwer.

Glaser, B. G. (1992), *Basics of Grounded Theory Analysis*. Mill Valley, CA: Sociology Press.

Glaser, B. G. (2001), *The Grounded Theory Perspective: Conceptualization Contrasted with Description*. Mill Valley, CA: Sociology Press.

Glaser, B. G. (2007), *Doing Formal Grounded Theory: A Proposal*. Mill Valley, CA: Sociology Press.

Godin, S. (1999), *Permission Marketing*. New York: Simon & Schuster.

Goldman, H. (1958/1985), *How to Win Customers*. London: Pan Books.

Goleman, D. (2006), *Emotional Intelligence*. New York: Bantam Books.

Goodwin, Cathy (1994), 'Private Roles in Public Encounter: Communal Relationships in Service Exchanges'. In *Proceedings from the 3rd International Research Seminar in Service Management*. Aix-en-Provence: Institut d'Administration des Entreprises, Université d'Aix-Marseille, pp. 312–332.

Granovetter, M. (1973), 'The Strength of Weak Ties. A Network Theory Revisited'. *American Journal of Sociology*, 78(3), 3–30.

Granovetter, M. (1985), 'Economic Action and Social Structure. The Problem of Embeddedness'. *American Journal of Sociology*, 91(3), 481–510.

Gray, B. (1989), *Collaborating*. San Francisco, CA: Jossey-Bass.

Grönroos, C. (1991), 'The marketing strategy continuum: a marketing concept for the 1990s'. *Management Decision*, 29(1), 7–13.

Grönroos, C. (1997), 'From Marketing Mix to Relationship Marketing: Towards a Paradigm Shift in Marketing'. *Management Decision*, 35(4), 322–339.

Grönroos, C. (2000), 'Relationship Marketing: The Nordic School Perspective'. In Sheth J. N. and Parvatiyar A. (eds.), *Handbook of Relationship Marketing*. Thousand Oaks, CA: Sage, pp. 95–117.

Grönroos, C. (2006), 'Adopting a Service Logic for Marketing'. *Marketing Theory*, 6(3), 317–333.

Grönroos, C. (2007), *Service Management and Marketing*, 3rd edn. Chichester, UK: Wiley.

Grönroos, C. and Gummesson, E. (eds.) (1985), *Service Marketing – Nordic School Perspectives*. Stockholm: Stockholm University School of Business, Research Report R, 1985:2.

Grönroos, C. and Ojasalo, K. (2004), 'Service Productivity: Towards a Conceptualization of the Transformation of Inputs into Economic Results in Services'. *Journal of Business Research*, 57(4), 414–423.

Gronstedt, A. (2000), *The Customer Century*. New York: Routledge.

Gruen, T. W. (2000), 'Membership Customers and Relationship Marketing'. In Sheth J. N. and Parvatiyar A. (eds.), *Handbook of Relationship Marketing*. Thousand Oaks, CA: Sage, pp. 355–380.

The Guardian (1999), 'Feeding Mammon – World Trade Organization: Special Report'. 30 November.

Gummesson, E. (1983), 'A New Concept of Marketing'. *Proceedings from the European Marketing Academy (EMAC) Annual Conference*, Institut d'Etudes Commerciales de Grenoble, France, April.

Gummesson, E. (1987a), 'Using Internal Marketing to Develop a New Corporate Culture: The Case of Ericsson Quality'. *Journal of Business and Industrial Marketing*, 2(Fall).

Gummesson, E. (1987b), *Quality – The Ericsson Approach*. Stockholm: Ericsson.

Gummesson, E. (1987c), 'The New Marketing: Developing Long-term Interactive Relationships'. *Long Range Planning*, 20(4), 10–20.

Gummesson, E. (1993), *Quality Management in Service Organizations*. New York: ISQA.

Gummesson, E. (1994), 'Making Relationship Marketing Operational'. *Service Industry Management*, 5(5), 5–20.

Gummesson, E. (1998a), 'Productivity, Quality and Relationship Marketing in Service Operations'. *International Journal of Contemporary Hospitality Management*, 10(1), 4–15.

Gummesson, E. (1998b), 'Implementation Requires a Relationship Marketing Paradigm'. *Journal of the Academy of Marketing Science*, 26(3), 242–249.

Gummesson, E. (2000), *Qualitative Methods in Management Research*, 2nd edn. Newbury Park: Sage.

Gummesson, E. (2001a), 'eCRM and hCRM: Martial Rivalry or Marital Bliss'. In Eggert A. and Fassot G. (eds.), *eCRM: Electronic Customer Relationship Management*. Stuttgart: Schäffer-Poeschel.

Gummesson, E. (2001b), 'Are Research Approaches in Marketing Leading Us Astray?'. *Marketing Theory*, 1(1).

Gummesson, E. (2002), 'Practical Value of Adequate Marketing Management Theory'. *European Journal of Marketing*, 36(3), 325–349.

Gummesson, E. (2004), 'Service Provision Calls for Partners Instead of Parties'. *Journal of Marketing*, 68(1), 20–21.

Gummesson, E. (2006), 'Many-to-Many Marketing as Grand Theory: A Nordic School Contribution'. In Lusch R. F. and Vargo S. L. (eds.), *Toward a Service-Dominant Logic of Marketing: Dialog, Debate, and Directions*. New York: M.E. Sharpe, pp. 339–353.

Gummesson, E. (2007a), 'Exit Services Marketing – Enter Service Marketing'. *Journal of Customer Behaviour*, 6(Summer), 113–141.

Gummesson, E. (2007b), 'Case Study Research and Network Theory: Birds of a Feather'. *Qualitative Research in Organization and Management*, 2(3), 226–248.

Gummesson, E. (2008a), Marketing As Networks: The Birth of Many-to-Many Marketing (forthcoming).

Gummesson, E. (2008b), 'Extending the Service-Dominant Logic: From Customer Centricity to Balanced Centricity'. *Journal of the Academy of Marketing Science*, 36(1).

Gummesson, E., Lehtinen, U. and Grönroos, C. (1997), 'Comment on Nordic Perspectives on Relationship Marketing'. *European Journal of Marketing*, 31(1–2), 10–16.

Gustavsson, B. (1992), *The Transcendent Organization*. Stockholm: Stockholm University.

Gustavsson, B. (2001), 'Towards a Transcendent Epistemology of Organizations'. *Journal of Organizational Change Management*, 13(4).

Hägg, C. and Preiholt, H. (2004), 'Investor Relations, Financial Marketing, and Target Groups'. *Marketing Management Journal*, 14, 128–132.

Håkansson, H. and Snehota, I. (1995), *Developing Relationships in Business Marketing*. London: Routledge.

Halal, W. E., Geranmayeh, A. and Pourdehead, J. (eds.) (1993), *Internal Markets*. New York: Wiley.

Halinen, A. (1997), *Relationship Marketing in Professional Services*. London: Routledge.

Hallén, L. and Widersheim-Paul, F. (1979), 'Psychic Distance and Buyer–Seller Interaction'. *Organisation, Marked og Samfunn*, 16(5), 308–324.

Hallén, L., Johanson, J. and Seyed-Mohamed, N. (1993), 'Dyadic Business Relationships and Customer Technologies'. *Journal of Business-to-Business Marketing*, 1(4), 63–90.

Hallowell, E. M. (1999), 'The Human Moment at Work'. *Harvard Business Review*, January–February.

Hamel, G. and Prahalad, C. K. (1994), *Competing for the Future*. Boston, MA: Harvard Business School Press.

Handy, C. (1990), *The Age of Unreason*. Boston, MA: Harvard Business School Press.

Harper, R. (1993), 'Hunt for the Holy Grail of Dispute Mediation'. *Scottish Gazette*, 20 October, 10.

Harrington, J. H. (1991), *Business Process Improvement*. New York: McGraw-Hill.

Hartelius, J. (ed.) (2007), *Systemhotande brottslighet*. Stockholm: Förlaget Langenskiöld.

Harung, H. S. (1999), *Invincible Leadership: Building Peak Performance Organizations by Harnessing the Unlimited Power of Consciousness*. Fairfield, IA: MUM Press.

Heath, R. L. (ed.) (2004), *Encyclopedia of Public Relations*. Thousand Oaks, CA: Sage.

Hedberg, B., Dahlgren, G., Hansson, J. and Olve, N.-G. (2000), *Virtual Organizations and Beyond: Discover Imaginary Systems*. London: Wiley.

Heidenry, J. (1993), *Theirs Was the Kingdom*. New York: W. W. Norton.

Hertz, N. (2002), *The Silent Takeover*. London: Arrow Books.

Heskett, J. L., Sasser, W. E. and Hart, C. W. L. (1990), *Service Breakthroughs*. New York: The Free Press.

Heskett, J. L., Sasser, W. E. Jr. and Schlesinger, L. A. (1997), *The Service Profit Chain*. New York: The Free Press.

Hirschman, A. O. (1970), *Exit, Voice and Loyalty* Cambridge, MA: Harvard University Press.

Holmlund, M. (1997), *Perceived Quality in Business Relationships*. Helsinki: Swedish School of Economics and Business Administration.

Howard, P. (1994), *The Death of Common Sense: How Law is Suffocating America*. New York: Random House.

Howell, G. and Miller, R. (2006), 'How the Relationship Between the Crisis Life Cycle and Mass Media Content can Better Inform Crisis Communication'. *PRism*, 4(1).

Hult, E.-B., Liljeberg, U., Lundström, A. and Ramström, D. (2000), *Soloföretag*. Örebro: Forum för småföretagsforskning.

Hultbom, C. (1990), *Intern handel: köpar/säljarrelationer inom stora företag*. Uppsala: Uppsala University, Department of Business.

Hunt, S. D. and Morgan, R. M. (1995), 'The Comparative Advantage Theory of Competition'. *Journal of Marketing*, 59, 1–15.

Hunt, S. D. and Madhavaram, S. (2006), 'The Service-Dominat Logic of Marketing: Theoretical Foundations, Pedagogy, and Resource-Advantage Theory'. In Lusch R. F. and Vargo S. L. (eds.), *Toward a Service-Dominant Logic of Marketing: Dialog, Debate, and Directions*. New York: M.E. Sharpe, pp. 67–84.

Iacocca, L. (with Novak, W.) (1984), *Iacocca*. USA: Bantam Books.

Jackson, B. B. (1985a), *Winning and Keeping Industrial Customers*. Lexington, MA: Lexington Books.

Jackson, B. B. (1985b), 'Build Customer Relationships That Last'. *Harvard Business Review*, November–December, 120–128.

Jaques, E. (1990), 'In Praise of Hierarchy'. *Harvard Business Review*, 1.

Johansen, J. I. and Monthelie, C. (1996), *Lojalitetsredovisning*. Gothenburg: InfoNet Scandinavia.

Johanson, J. and Mattsson, L.-G. (1987), 'Interorganizational Relations in Industrial Systems: A Network Approach Compared with the Transaction Cost Approach'. *International Studies of Management and Organization*, XVII(1 Spring), 34–48.

Johnson, M. D. and Gustafsson, A. (2000), *Improving Customer Satisfaction, Loyalty, and Profit*. San Francisco, CA: Jossey-Bass.

Johnson, T. H. (1992), *Relevance Regained*. New York: The Free Press.

Johnson, T. H. and Kaplan, R. S. (1987), *Relevance Lost: The Rise and Fall of Management Accounting*. Boston, MA: Harvard Business School Press.

Johnsson, T. and Hägg, I. (1987), 'Extrapreneurs – Between Markets and Hierarchies'. *International Studies of Management and Organisation*, XVII(1), 64–74.

Journal of the Academy of Marketing Science (2005), 'Special Issue: The Marketing/Finance Interface'. (33)4 (Fall).

Journal of the Academy of Marketing Science (2008), 'Special Issue on Service-Dominant Logic'. (36)1 (Winter).

Judd, V. C. (1987), 'Differentiate with the 5th P: People'. *Industrial Marketing Management*, November.

Juran, J. M. (1992), *Juran on Quality by Design*. New York: The Free Press.

Kahn, S. and Yoshihara, H. (1994), *Strategy and Performance of Foreign Companies in Japan*. Westport, CT: Quorom Books.

Kanter, R. M. (1989), *When Giants Learn to Dance*. New York: Simon & Schuster.

Kaplan, R. S. and Norton, D. P. (1996), *The Balanced Scorecard*. Boston, MA: Harvard Business School Press.

Karpesjö, A. (1992), *Miljöprofilering*. Malmö: Liber.

Keefe, L. M. (2004), "What is the meaning of 'marketing'?", *Marketing News*, September 15, 17–18.

Keller, K. L. (2007), *Strategic Brand Management*. Upper Saddle River, NJ: Pearson/Prentice Hall.

Keller, K. L., Aperia, T. and Georgson, M. (2008), *Strategic Brand Management: European Edition*. London: Pearson Prentice Hall.

Kim, W. C. and Mauborgne, R. (2005), *Blue Ocean Strategy*. Boston, MA: Harvard Business School Press.

Kingman-Brundage, J., George, W. R. and Bowen, D. E. (1995), 'Service Logic: Achieving Service System Integration'. *International Journal of Service Industry Management*, 6(4), 20–39.

Klein, N. (2000), *No Logo*. London: Flamingo.

Kohlbacher, F. (2007), *International Marketing in the Network Economy*. New York: Palgrave/Macmillan.

Korkman, O. (2006), *Customer Value Formation in Practice*. Helsinki: Swedish School of Economics and Business Administration.

Kotkin, J. (1993), *Tribes*. New York: Random House.

Kotler, P. (1986), 'Megamarketing'. *Harvard Business Review*, March–April, 117–124.

Kotler, P. (1992), 'Total Marketing'. *Business Week Advance*, 2. Executive Brief

Kotler, P. and Keller, K. L. (2006), *Marketing Management*, 12th edn. Upper Saddle River, NJ: Pearson Prentice Hall.

Kotler, P., Gregor, W. and Rodgers, W. (1989), 'The Marketing Audit Comes of Age'. *Sloan Management Review*, Winter, 49–62.

Lappalainen, T. (1993), *Maffian*. Stockholm: Forum.

Lappalainen, T. (2007), *Camorra: en bok om maffian i Neapel*. Stockholm: Bokförlaget Tomas Fischer.

Lee, C. and Fujimoto, T. (2003), 'The Chinese Automobile Industry and the Strategic Alliances of China, Japan and US Firms'. *Discussion Paper for International Motor Vehicle Program*, Boston, MA: MIT.

Lehtinen, J. R. (1985), 'Improving Service Quality by Analysing the Service Production Process'. In Grönroos, C. and Gummesson, E. (eds.), *Service Marketing – Nordic School Perspectives*. Stockholm: Stockholm University, School of Business, Research Report R 1985:2, pp. 110–119.

Lehtinen, U., Hankimaa, A. and Mittilä, T. (1994), 'On Measuring the Intensity in Relationship Marketing'. In Sheth, J. N. and Parvatiyar, A. (eds.), *Relationship Marketing: Theory, Methods and Applications, Research Conference Proceedings*. Atlanta, GA: Center for Relationship Marketing, Emory University.

Lennstrand, B. (1998), 'Diffusion of Information and Communication Technology to Households: How Come it Goes so Slowly when it Goes Fast'. Paper presented at the *Twelfth Biennial ITS Conference*, Stockholm. Also in Lennstrand, B. (2001), *Hype IT*. Stockholm: Stockholm University.

Lester, T. (1992), 'The Rise of the Network'. *International Management*, June, 72–73.

Levitt, T. (1960), 'Marketing Myopia'. *Harvard Business Review*, July–August.

Levitt, T. (1983), *The Marketing Imagination*. New York: The Free Press.

Liljander, V. and Strandvik, T. (1995), 'The Nature of Customer Relationships in Services'. In Swartz T. A., Bowen D. E. and Brown S. W. (eds.), *Advances in Services Marketing and Management*, Vol. 4. Greenwich, CT: JAI Press.

Liljegren, G. (1988), *Interdependens och dynamik i långsiktiga relationer*. Stockholm: MTC/EFI.

Lilley, P. (2000), *Dirty Dealing: The Untold Truth About Dirty Money Laundering*. London: Kogan Page.

Lindqvist, J. (2006), *Outlaw Marketing: En brutal odyssé genom den österbottniska slätten*. Vasa, Finland: The Swedish School of Economics and Business Administration.

Linn, C. E. (1985), *Metaprodukten och marknaden*. Malmö, Sweden: Liber.

Little, E. and Marandi, E. (2003), *Relationship Marketing Management*. London: Thomson.

Lorange, P. and Roos, J. (1993), *Strategic Alliances*. Oxford, UK: Blackwell.

Lovelock, C. H. (1983), 'Classifying Services to Gain Strategic Advantage'. *Journal of Marketing*, 47(Summer), 9–20.

Lovelock, C. and Gummesson, E. (2004), 'Whither Services Marketing? In Search of a Paradigm and Fresh Perspectives'. *Journal of Service Research*, 7(1), 20–41.

Lovelock, C. and Wirtz, J. (2007), *Services Marketing*, 6th edn. Upper Saddle River, NJ: Pearson Prentice Hall.

Lowe, A. (1988), 'Small Hotel Survival: An Inductive Approach'. *The International Journal of Hospitality Management*, 7(3), 197–223.

Lowe, A. (1998), 'Managing the Post-Merger Aftermath by Default Remodelling'. *Management Decision*, 36(3), 102–110.

Lowe, A. and Glaser, B. G. (1995), 'The Potential of Grounded Theory for the Development of Relationship Marketing Theory'. In Glaser B. G. (ed.), *Grounded Theory 1984–1994*, Vol. 2. Mill Valley, CA: Sociology Press, pp. 671–685.

Lu, D. J. (1985), 'Translator's Introduction'. In Ishikawa K. (ed.), *What Is Total Quality Control? The Japanese Way*. Englewood Cliffs, NJ: Prentice-Hall.

Lunn, T. (1990), 'Customer Service: The Joshua Tetley Experience'. Dublin: *Third National Conference of the NSAI*.

Lusch, R. F. and Vargo, S. L. (eds.) (2006a), *Toward a Service-Dominant Logic of Marketing: Dialog, Debate, and Directions*. New York: M.E. Sharpe.

Lusch, R. F. and Vargo, S. L. (2006b), 'Service-Dominant Logic: Reactions, Reflections and Refinements'. *Marketing Theory*, 6(3), 281–288.

Macneil, I. R. (1983), 'Relational Contract: What We Do and Do Not Know'. *Northwestern University Law Review*, 78, 340–418.

Macneil, I. R. (1985), 'Values in Contract'. *Winsconsin Law Review*, 483–525.

Malcolm Baldrige National Quality Award (2007), *Criteria for Performance Excellence*. Gaithersburg, MD: United States Department of Commerce.

Marketing Theory (2006), 'Special Issue on the Service-Dominant Logic of Marketing: Insights from the Otago Forum'. (6)3 (September).

Mattsson, L. G. and Lundgren, A. (1992–1993), 'En paradox – konkurrens I industriella nätverk'. *MTC-kontakten*, 22, 8–9.

Mattsson, J. and den Haring, M. J. (1999), 'Communication Dynamics in Therapy: A Linguistic Study from a Nursing Home for Elderly'. *International Journal of Social Welfare*, 8, 120–130.

McDonald, M. (1995), *Marketing Plans*. Oxford, UK: Butterworth-Heinemann.

McDonald, M., Millman, T. and Rogers, B. (1997), 'Key Account Management: Theory, Practice and Challenges'. *Journal of Marketing Management*, 13, 737–757.

McKenna, R. (1985), *The Regis Touch*. USA: Addison-Wesley.

McLuhan, M. (1964), *Understanding Media: The Extension of Man*. New York: McGraw Hill. reissued 2003 by Ginko Press

McLuhan, M. and Fiore, Q. (1967), *The Medium is the Massage*. New York: Random House. reissued 2001 by Ginko Press

Mele, C. (2007), 'The Synergetic Relationship between TQM and Marketing in Creating Customer Value'. *Managing Service Quality*, 17(3), 240–258.

Mills, D. Q. (1991), *Rebirth of the Corporation*. New York: Wiley.

Möller, K. and Halinen, A. (2000), 'Relationship Marketing Theory: Its Roots and Direction'. *Journal of Marketing Management*, 16(1–3), 29–54.

Moore, J. F. (1996), *The Death of Competition*. Chichester, UK: Wiley.

Morgan, G. (1997), *Images of Organization*. Thousand Oaks, CA: Sage.

Morgan, M. (2004), *Mutant Message Down Under*. New York: HarperCollins.

Morgan, R. M. and Hunt, S. D. (1994), 'The Commitment-Trust Theory of Relationship Marketing'. *Journal of Marketing*, 58, 20–38.

MSI, Marketing Science Institute (2001), *Conference Announcement on B2B e-Commerce*. Cambridge, MA.

Nader, R. (1965), *Unsafe at Any Speed*. New York: Grossman.

Naisbitt, J. (1982), *Megatrends*. New York: Warner Books.

Naisbitt, J. (1994), *Global Paradox*. New York: William Morrow.

Naisbitt, J. (1999), *High Tech/High Touch*. London: Nicholas Brealey.

Nakane, C. (1981), *Japanese Society*. New York: Penguin.

Nelson, P. (1970), 'Advertising as Information'. *Journal of Political Economy*, July–August, 729–754.

Newell, F. (2000), *loyalty.com*. New York: McGraw-Hill.

Newsweek (1990), 'The Kissinger Clique'. 27 March 1990, pp. 34–35.

Nicholls, R. (2005), *Interactions between Service Customers*. Poznan, Poland: The Poznan University of Economics.

Nilsson, J. P. (1993), 'Disney à go-go'. *Nobis Nyheter*, 3, 25–28. 40

Nonaka, I. and Takeuchi, H. (1995), *The Knowledge-Creating Company*. New York: Oxford University Press.

Norberg, J. (2003), *In Defense of Global Capitalism*. Washington, DC: Cato Institute.

Norman, D. A. (1988), *The Psychology of Everyday Things*. New York: Basic Books.

Normann, R. and Ramírez, R. (1993), 'From Value Chain to Value Constellation'. *Harvard Business Review*, July–August, 65–77.

North, Douglass C. (1993), 'Economic Performance Through Time'. Stockholm: The Nobel Foundation, *Prize Lecture in Economic Science in Memory of Alfred Nobel*, Stockholm, 9 December.

Ohlson, J. (1994), 'Interview with Ove Sjögren'. *Upp&Ner*, 6, 6–9.

Ohmae, K. (1985), *Triad Power – The Coming Shape of Global Competition*. New York: The Free Press.

Ohmae, K. (1995), *The End of the Nation State*. New York: The Free Press.

Olsen, M. (1992), *Kvalitet i banktjänster*. Stockholm: Stockholm University/CTF.

Olve, N-G., Petri, C. J., Roy, J. and Roy, S. (2003), *Making Scorecards Actionable: Balancing Strategy and Control*. Chichester: Wiley.

Ortmark, Å. (2000), *Ja-sägarna*. Stockholm: Wahlström & Widstrand.

Orwell, G. (1945), *Animal Farm*. London: Secker and Warburg.

Ottman, J. A. (1992), *Green Marketing*. Lincolnwood, IL: NTC Business Books.

Palmer, A. and Bejou, D. (1995), 'The Effects on Gender on the Development of Relationships between Clients and Financial Advisers'. *Bank Marketing*, 13(3).

Parlour, R. (1993), 'Europe's Fight Against Dirty Money'. *European Business Report*, 3rd Quarter, 63–66.

Patton, M. Q. (2001), *Qualitative Evaluation and Research Methods*. Thousand Oaks, CA: Sage.

Paulin, M., Perrien, J. and Ferguson, R. (1997), 'Relational Contract Norms and the Effectiveness of Commercial Banking Relationships'. *Service Industry Management*, 8(5), 435–452.

Payne, A. (2006), *Handbook of CRM*. Oxford: Butterwoth-Heinemann.

Payne, A. and Frow, P. (2005), 'A Strategic Framework for Customer Relationship Management'. *Journal of Marketing*, 69, 167–176.

Payne, A. and Rickard, J. (1994), *Relationship Marketing, Customer Retention and Service Firm Profitability*. Cranfield: Cranfield School of Management.

Peck, H., Payne, A., Christopher, M. and Clark, M. (1999), *Relationship Marketing: Strategy and Implementation*. Oxford: Butterworth-Heinemann.

Peppers, D. and Rogers, M. (1993), *The One to One Future*. New York: Currency/Doubleday.

Peters, T. (1985), *Thriving on Chaos*. New York: Macmillan.

Peters, T. (1992), *Liberation Management*. New York: Alfred A. Knopf.

Peters, T. and Waterman, R. J. Jr. (1982), *In Search of Excellence*. New York: Harper & Row.

Pirsig, R. M. (1982), *Lila: An Inquiry Into Morals*. London: Corgi Books.

Polanyi, M. (1962), *Personal Knowledge*. London: Routledge & Kegan Paul.

Pope, N. W. (1979a), 'Mickey Mouse Marketing'. *American Banker*, 25 July.

Pope, N. W. (1979b), 'More Mickey Mouse Marketing'. *American Banker*, 12 September.

Porter, C. (1993), *The Marketing Strategy Letter*, May, 14.

Porter, M. E. (1980), *Competitive Strategy*. New York: The Free Press.

Porter, M. E. (1985), *Competitive Advantage*. New York: The Free Press.

Porter, M. E. (1990), *The Competitive Advantage of Nations*. New York: Macmillan.

Postman, N. (1987), *Amusing Ourselves to Death*. New York: Penguin Books.

Price, L., Arnould, E. and Tierney, P. (1996), 'The Wilderness Servicescape'. In *Proceedings of the 4th International Research Seminar in Service Management*. La Londe, France: Université Aix-Marseille.

Prigogine, I. and Stengers, I. (1985), *Order out of Chaos*. London: Fontana/Flamingo.

Quinn, B. (2000), *How Wal-Mart Is Destroying America (and the World)*. Berkeley, CA: The Speed Press. (revised edition)

Quinn, F. (1990), *Crowning the Customer*. Dublin: O'Brien Press.

Quinn, F. (1994), 'The Boomerang Principle'. *European Business Report*, Spring, 36–39.

Quinn, J. B. (1992), *The Intelligent Enterprise*. New York: The Free Press.

Ramsey, R. D. (1991), 'It's Absurd: Swedish Managers' Views of America's Litigious Society'. *Scandinavian Journal of Management*, 6(1), 31–44.

Rapp, S. and Collins, T. (1995), *The New MaxiMarketing*. New York: McGraw-Hill.

Reichheld, F. F. (2001a), *The Loyalty Effect*. Boston, MA: Harvard Business School Press.

Reichheld, F. F. (2001b), *Loyalty Rules!* Boston, MA: Harvard Business School Press.

Reichheld, F. F. and Sasser, W. E. Jr. (1990), 'Zero Defections: Quality Comes to Services'. *Harvard Business Review*, September–October.

Rein, I. J., Kotler, P. and Stoller, M. R. (1987), *High Visibility*. London: Heinemann.

Reynoso, J. F. and Moores, B. (1996), 'Internal Relationships'. In Buttle F. (ed.), *Relationship Marketing: Theory and Practice*. London: Paul Chapman.

Robèrt, K.-H. (1992), *Det nödvändiga steget*. Stockholm: Affärsförlaget Mediautveckling.

Roddick, A. (1991), *Body and Soul*. New York: Crown.

Rogers, M. (2000), 'Foreword' to Newell, Frederick, *loyalty.com*. New York: McGraw-Hill, pp. xii–xv.

Rossander, O. (1992), *Japanskt ledarskap*. Stockholm: Svenska Dagbladet/Affärsvärlden.

The Royal Society for the Encouragement of Arts, Manufacture & Commerce (1994), *Tomorrow's Company: The Role of Business in a Changing World*. London.

Russell, B. (1948/1912), *The Problems of Philosophy*. London: Oxford University Press.

Rust, R. T., Zahorik, A. J. and Keiningham, T. L. (1994), *Return on Quality*. Chicago, IL: Probus.

Rust, R. T., Zeithaml, V. A. and Lemon, K. N. (2000), *Driving Customer Equity*. New York: The Free Press.

Rust, R. T., Lemon, K. N. and Zeithaml, V. A. (2004), 'Return on Marketing: Using Customer Equity to Focus Marketing Strategy'. *Journal of Marketing*, 68, 109–127.

Saren, M., Maclaran, P., Goulding, C., Elliott, R., Shankar, A. and Catterall, R. (eds.) (2007), *Critical Marketing*. Oxford: Butterworth-Heinemann.

Saviano, R. (2008), *Gomorrah: Italy's Other Mafia*. London: Macmillan.

Schlossberg, H. (1992), 'Frequent Mileage Club Sends Consumers Running to Shoe Stores'. *Marketing News*, 3 August, 12.

Schön, D. A. (1983), *The Reflective Practitioner – How Professionals Think in Action*. New York: Basic Books.

Schultz, D. E. and Kitchen, P. J. (2000), *Communicating Globally*. Lincolnwood, IL: NTC Business Books.

Schultz, D. E. and Walters, J. S. (1997), *Measuring Brand Communication ROI*. New York: Association of National Advertisers.

Scott, J. (1991), *Social Network Analysis*. London: Sage.

Sheth, J.N. and Mittal,B. (2004), *Customer Behavior*. Mason, OH: Thomson/South Western (second edition).

Senge, P. M. (1990), *The Fifth Discipline*. New York: Currency/Doubleday.

Sewell, C. (1990), *Customers for Life*. New York: Doubleday.

Shah, D., Rust, R. T., Parasuraman, A., Staelin, R. and Day, G. S. (2006), 'The Path to Customer Centricity'. *Journal of Service Research*, 9(2), 113–124.

Shamir, B. (1984), 'Between Gratitude and Gratuity'. *Annals of Tourism Research*, 11, 59–78.

Shaw, R. and McDonald, M. (2000), *Marketing Accountability: The New Discipline*. Cranfield, UK: Cranfield School of Management.

Shembri, S. (2006), 'Rationalizing service logic, or understanding services as an experience'. *Marketing Theory*, 6(4), 395–418.

Sheth, J. N. and Parvatiyar, A. (eds.) (2000), *Handbook of Relationship Marketing*. Thousand Oaks, CA: Sage.

Shostack, G. L. (1981), 'How to Design a Service'. In Donnelly J. H. and George W. R. (eds.), *Marketing of Services*. Chicago, IL: American Marketing Association.

Simmons, O. E. (1993), 'The Milkman and His Customer: A Cultivated Relationship'. In Glaser B. G. (ed.), *Examples of Grounded Theory: A Reader*. Mill Valley, CA: Sociology Press, pp. 4–31.

Simon, H., Bilstein, F. F. and Luby, F. (2006), *Manage for Profit, Not for Market Share*. Boston, MA: Harvard Business School Press.

Simons, R. and Dávila, A. (1998), 'How High Is Your Return on Management'. *Harvard Business Review*, January–February, 71–80.

Skjott-Larsen, T., Schary, P. B., Mikkola, J. H. and Kotzab, H. (2007), *Managing the Global Supply Chain*. Copenhagen: Copenhagen Business School Press/Liber.

Smith, C. (1994), 'The New Corporate Philanthropy'. *Harvard Business Review*, May–June, 105–116.

Smith, P. G. and Laage-Hellman, J. (1992), 'Small Group Analysis of Industrial Networks'. In Axelsson B. and Easton G. (eds.), *Industrial Networks*. London: Routledge.

Snehota, I. and Söderlund, M. (1998), 'Relationship Marketing – What Does It Promise and What Does It Deliver?' In Andersson, P. (ed.), *Proceedings from the 27th EMAC Conference, Track 1, Market Relationships*. Stockholm: EMAC, May.

Solomon, R. C. (1992), *Ethics and Excellence*. Oxford: Oxford University Press.

Stacey, R. D. (2007), *Strategic Management and Organisational Dynamics*. London: Financial Times/Prentice Hall.

Stauss, B. (2005), 'A Phyrrhic Victory: The Implications of an Unlimited Broadening of the Concept of Services'. *Managing Service Quality*, 15(3), 219–229.

Stauss, B. and Seidel, W. (2004), *Complaint Management: The Heart of CRM*. Mason, Ohio: Thomson/American Marketing Association.

Stenbacka, C. (1998), *Brand Visibility*. Helsinki: Swedish School of Economics and Business Administration.

Stern, L. W. and Reve, T. (1980), 'Distribution Channels as Political Economies: A Framework for Comparative Analysis'. *Journal of Marketing*, 44(Summer), 52–64.

Stewart, T. A. (1997), *Intellectual Capital*. New York: Currency/Doubleday.

Storbacka, K. (1994), *The Nature of Customer Relationship Profitability*. Helsinki: Swedish School of Economics and Business Administration.

Storbacka, K. and Lehtinen, J. (2001), *Customer Relationship Management*. New York: McGraw-Hill.

Storbacka, K., Strandvik, T. and Grönroos, C. (1994), 'Managing Customer Relationships for Profit: The Dynamics of Relationship Quality'. *Service Industry Management*, 5(5), 21–38.

Strandvik, T. and Törnroos, J.-Å. (1997), 'Discovering Relationscapes – Extending the Horizon of Relationship Strategies in Marketing'. In Meenaghan, T. (ed.), *New and Evolving Paradigms: The Emerging Future of Marketing, Conference Proceedings*. Chicago, IL: American Marketing Association and University College Dublin.

Sveiby, K. E. (1997), *The New Organizational Wealth*. San Francisco, CA: Berret-Koehler.

Taira, K. and Wada, T. (1987), 'Business–Government Relations in Modern Japan: A Todai-Yakkai-Zaikai complex?'. In Mizruchi M. S. and Schwartz M. (eds.), *Intercorporate Relations*. Cambridge: Cambridge University Press.

TARP (1986), *Consumer Complaint Handling in America: An Update Study*. Part II, assigned by US Office of Consumer Affairs, 1 April, p. 50.

Thorelli, H. B. (1986), 'Networks: Between Markets and Hierarchies'. *Strategic Management Journal*, 7, 37–51.

Time (1993), 'Corruption 101'. 10 May, p. 16.

Tjosvold, D. (1993), *Teamwork for Customers*. San Francisco, CA: Jossey-Bass.

Törnqvist, G. (1990), 'Det upplösta rummet – begrepp och teoretiska ansatser inom geografin'. In Karlqvist A. (ed.), *Nätverk*. Stockholm: Gidlunds/Institutet för framtidsstudier.

Tse, E. C. and West, J. (1992), 'Development Strategies for International Hospitality Markets'. In Teare R. and Olsen M. (eds.), *International Hospitality Management*. London: Pitman.

Tuominen, P. (1997), 'Investor Relations: A Nordic School Approach'. *Corporate Communications: An International Journal*, 1, 46–55.

Vandermerwe, S. (1993), *From Tin Soldiers to Russian Dolls: Creating Added Value Through Services*. Oxford: Butterworth-Heinemann.

Varey, R. J. and Lewis, B. R. (eds.) (2000), *Internal Marketing*. London: Routledge.

Vargo, S. L. and Lusch, R. F. (2004a), 'The Four Service Marketing Myths: Remnants of a Goods-Based, Manufacturing Model'. *Journal of Service Research*, 6(6), 324–335.

Vargo, S. L. and Lusch, R. F. (2004b), 'Evolving to a New Dominant Logic for Marketing'. *Journal of Marketing*, 68(1), 1–17.

Vargo, S. L. and Lusch, R. F. (2006), 'Service-Dominant Logic: What It Is, What It Is Not, What It Might Be'. In Lusch R. F. and Vargo S. L. (eds.), *Toward a Service-Dominant Logic of Marketing: Dialog, Debate, and Directions*. New York: M.E. Sharpe.

von Friedrichs Grängsjö, Y. (2001), *Destinationsmarknadsföring*. Stockholm: Stockholm University School of Business.

von Friedrichs Grängsjö, Y. and Gummesson, E. (2006), 'Hotel Networks and Social Capital in Destination Marketing'. *Service Industry Management*, 17(1), 58–75.

von Hippel, E. (1988), *The Sources of Innovation*. Oxford: Oxford University Press.

Ward, T., Frew, E. and Caldow, D. (1997), 'An Extended List of the Dimensions of 'Relationship' in Consumer Service Product Marketing: A Pilot Study'. In Meenaghan, T. (ed.), *New and Evolving Paradigms: The Emerging Future of Marketing, Conference Proceedings*. Chicago, IL: American Marketing Association and University College, Dublin.

Webster, F. E. (1992), 'The Changing Role of Marketing in the Corporation'. *Journal of Marketing*, 56, 1–17.

Weick, K. E. (1979), *The Social Psychology of Organizing*. Reading, MA: Addison-Wesley.

Whiting, R. (1998), 'Dangerous Liaisons'. *Software Magazine*, 18, 20–26.

Wiedenbaum, M. and Hughes, S. (1996), *The Bamboo Network*. New York: The Free Press.

Wikström, S. and Normann, R. (1994), *Knowledge and Value*. London: Routledge.

Wilkinson, I. F. and Young, L. C. (1994), 'Business Dancing – Understanding and Managing Interfirm Relations'. *Asia-Australia Marketing Journal*, 2(1), 67–79.

Williamson, O. E. (1981), 'The Economics of Organization: The Transaction Cost Approach'. *American Journal of Sociology*, 87(3), 548–577.

Williamson, O. E. (1985), *The Economic Institutions of Capitalism*. New York: The Free Press.

Williamson, O. E. (1990), 'The Firm as a Nexus of Treaties: an Introduction'. In Aoki M., Gustafsson B. and Williamson O. E. (eds.), *The Firm as a Nexus of Treaties*. London: Sage.

Winai, P. (1989), *Gränsorganisationer*. Malmö: Liber.

Womack, J. P. and Jones, D. T. (2005a), 'Lean Consumption'. *Harvard Business Review*, March, 58–68.

Womack, J. P. and Jones, D. T. (2005b), *Lean Solutions*. London: Simon & Schuster.

Womack, J. P., Jones, D. T. and Roos, D. (1990), *The Machine that Changed the World*. New York: Macmillan.

Worthington, S. and Horne, S. (1993), 'Charity Affinity Credit Cards – Marketing Synergy for Both Issuers and Charities?'. *Journal of Marketing Management*, 9, 301–313.

Wright, R. W. and Pauli, G. A. (1987), *The Second Wave*. London: Waterlow.

Wurman, R. S. (1989), *Information Anxiety*. New York: Doubleday.

Wyckham, R. G., Fitzroy, P. T. and Mandry, G. D. (1975), 'Marketing of Services'. *European Journal of Marketing*, 9(1), 59–67.

Zohar, D. and Marshall, I. (1993), *The Quantum Society*. London: Bloomsbury.

Zuboff, S. (1988), *In the Age of the Smart Machine*. New York: Basic Books.

Index